PRAISE FOR

Then Everything Changed

"Thanks to Mr. Greenfield's own familiarity with American politics and a lot of energetic research, he turns these twists of fate into accelerating historical snowballs that rumble through our recent history, altering the social landscape in ways both small and large. In doing so he's produced three slyly observed novellas that . . . have the verisimilitude of real life."

—*The New York Times*

"You expect intelligence and a devilish sense of humor and a profound knowledge of political history from Jeff Greenfield. *Then Everything Changed* certainly delivers on all three. But there is a deeper, haunting quality to this book as well. By adding a simple twist of fate, Greenfield brings fresh—often exhilarating—insights to the history of our times. Because Jeff knew the players so well, the scenarios that unfurl are entirely plausible and utterly compelling, as if we've been privileged to peek at a secret diary, written joyously and filled with constant *aha!* moments."

—Joe Klein, columnist, *Time* magazine

"Jeff Greenfield is a wonderful storyteller and a keen student of politics. A powerful book that seems painfully, tantalizingly real."

—Evan Thomas, author of *The War Lovers* and *Sea of Thunder*

"Filled with fresh revelations and brilliant speculation, Jeff Greenfield's alternative history is so detailed and persuasive—and the behavior of its protagonists so utterly believable—that it feels like reality itself. This is a remarkable feat of insight, imagination, and storytelling."

—Richard North Patterson, author of *The Devil's Light*

"These insightful and deeply imagined alternative histories are firmly grounded in the plausible, which makes the eye-opening speculation that much more enjoyable."

—Peggy Noonan

continued . . .

"A brilliant and fresh look at three seminal moments in twentieth-century American history. Rendered as a narrative composite of facts, insight, interviews, invention, and Greenfield's first-rate reporting, it is addictive and illuminating."
—Anne Lamott

"Who hasn't asked the question 'What could have been?' By examining perhaps America's most turbulent political period, Jeff Greenfield tackles that question in fascinating detail, with the kind of political insight and imagination only he possesses."
—David Gregory, moderator, *Meet the Press*

PRAISE FOR

Oh, Waiter! One Order of Crow!

"A valuable political commentary wrapped in a wonderfully entertaining package. Breezy, witty, urbane, sophisticated, and erudite all describe Greenfield's 'You are there'–style chronicle. He flawlessly matches laugh-out-loud humor with genuine insight."
—*Publishers Weekly*

"For my money, Jeff Greenfield has long been one of the nation's most astute political commentators. So it came as no surprise that his book-length account of the unforgettable 2000 presidential race was a joy to behold, full of insight and Greenfield's trademark witticisms."
—*St. Paul Pioneer Press*

"Telling the tale freshly, and leaving out the boring parts, Greenfield combines insight and humor to show how it really was just as weird as we all thought."
—*Time* magazine

"Of all the books I've reviewed [on the race], I found none more enjoyable and informative than Greenfield's *Oh, Waiter! One Order of Crow!*"
—John W. Dean, former Presidential counsel, *Salon*

THEN EVERYTHING CHANGED

STUNNING ALTERNATE HISTORIES

OF AMERICAN POLITICS:

JFK, RFK, Carter, Ford, Reagan

— ★ ★ ★ —

JEFF GREENFIELD

BERKLEY BOOKS, NEW YORK

THE BERKLEY PUBLISHING GROUP
Published by the Penguin Group
Penguin Group (USA) Inc.
375 Hudson Street, New York, New York 10014, USA
Penguin Group (Canada), 90 Eglinton Avenue East, Suite 700, Toronto, Ontario M4P 2Y3, Canada
(a division of Pearson Penguin Canada Inc.)
Penguin Books Ltd., 80 Strand, London WC2R 0RL, England
Penguin Group Ireland, 25 St. Stephen's Green, Dublin 2, Ireland (a division of Penguin Books Ltd.)
Penguin Group (Australia), 250 Camberwell Road, Camberwell, Victoria 3124, Australia
(a division of Pearson Australia Group Pty. Ltd.)
Penguin Books India Pvt. Ltd., 11 Community Centre, Panchsheel Park, New Delhi—110 017, India
Penguin Group (NZ), 67 Apollo Drive, Rosedale, Auckland 0632, New Zealand
(a division of Pearson New Zealand Ltd.)
Penguin Books (South Africa) (Pty.) Ltd., 24 Sturdee Avenue, Rosebank, Johannesburg 2196,
South Africa

Penguin Books Ltd., Registered Offices: 80 Strand, London WC2R 0RL, England

The publisher does not have any control over and does not assume any responsibility for author or third-party websites or their content.

PRINTING HISTORY
G. P. Putnam's Sons hardcover edition / March 2011
Berkley trade paperback edition / February 2012

Berkley trade paperback ISBN: 978-0-425-24533-0

The Library of Congress has cataloged the Putnam hardcover edition as follows:

Greenfield, Jeff.
    Then everything changed : stunning alternate histories of American politics : JFK, RFK, Carter, Ford, Reagan / Jeff Greenfield.
        p.   cm.
    ISBN 978-0-399-15706-6
    1. United States—Politics and government—1945–1989.   2. United States—Politics and government—1989–.   3. United States—History—1945–.   4. Politicians—United States— Biography.   5. Imaginary histories.   I. Title.
    E839.5.G748   2011   2010037039
    973.92—dc22

PRINTED IN THE UNITED STATES OF AMERICA

10 9 8 7 6 5 4 3 2 1

To my children, Casey and Dave

Contents

Preface

A SIMPLE TWIST OF FATE

On February 13, 1933, a man with a loaded pistol set out for Miami Beach's Bayfront Park, where a public event was in progress. Because he arrived a few minutes later than he had planned, he found his access to the event blocked by a crowd of people. So he climbed on a chair and pulled out his weapon, catching the attention of a spectator, who jostled him as he prepared to fire. So Giuseppe Zangara did not kill President-elect Franklin D. Roosevelt, who went on to lead the United States through the Great Depression and World War II.

What would have happened if FDR had not been able to steer his country through some of its most dangerous times? The United States would have been led by John Nance Garner, a Texas conservative whose political inclinations make the idea of a New Deal all but impossible to imagine. Would Garner, and the President who would have followed him, have shared Roosevelt's ardent internationalism, his determination to enlist the industrial might of the United States against Germany?

While we cannot know the way this near miss would have played out, we do know—from this and countless other examples—that history is as much a product of chance as of the broader forces at play. Geography, topography, ethnicity, ideology, climate, natural resources, the search for wealth, mass migrations, all set the framework; but the random roll of the dice is as potent a force as any. A missed meeting, a shift in the weather, a slightly different choice of words open up a literally limitless series of possibilities.

I have spent most of my working life in American politics, as a journalist, commentator, and analyst, and before that, a speechwriter, aide, and consultant, and I know that in my field, the near misses have happened with extraordinary frequency, and with extraordinary consequences. Just in recent times, for instance, four Presidential elections between 1960 and 2000 have come down to a relative handful of votes. A statistically insignificant shift would have given us Richard Nixon in 1960, Hubert Humphrey in 1968, Gerald Ford in 1976, and Al Gore in 2000. (John Kennedy bluntly noted this fact early in his Presidency when he saw a *Time* magazine piece that called one of his aides "coruscatingly brilliant." Said Kennedy: "Fifty thousand votes the other way and we'd all be coruscatingly stupid.")

So . . . what would have happened if small twists of fate had given us different leaders, with different beliefs, strengths, and weaknesses? I've tried here to answer that question by exploring, in dramatic narrative form, complete with characters, thoughts, and dialogue, a trio of contemporary alternate American histories, all flowing from events that came a mere hairsbreadth away from actually happening.

While these "histories" take us down radically different paths, I have tried to ground them in plausibility. The beliefs, actions, impulses, and core character traits of the major players are largely drawn from their own words, and from the judgments of the men and women who knew them well, as set down in memoirs, historical accounts, and oral histories. I have also conducted extensive new interviews with many key players and observers, including such distinguished men and women as Brent Scowcroft, Doris Kearns Goodwin, Richard Goodwin, Norman Ornstein, Joe Klein, top LBJ aide Harry McPherson, and many others. They are, of course, in no way responsible for the alternate histories recounted here.

We begin with a fact that has gone almost completely forgotten. On December 11, 1960, a seventy-three-year-old would-be suicide bomber named Richard Pavlick was parked outside the Palm Beach, Florida, home of President-elect John F. Kennedy, holding in his hand a switch connected to seven sticks of dynamite, enough to level a small mountain. His presence ignored by the Secret Service, Pavlick was, in the words of the agency's chief, "seconds away" from murdering the incoming President of the United States. Only Pavlick's reluctance to kill Kennedy in front of his wife and child, who had come to the door to see him off to church, stayed his hand. (He was arrested four days later in Florida by authorities after he sent threatening notes to the postmaster back home in Belmont, New Hampshire.) If Jacqueline Kennedy had slept in that Sunday morning, or was at breakfast, or was tending to Caroline or her infant son John Jr., Kennedy would have been killed before ever becoming President.

And then . . . ?

The second "history" puts Robert Kennedy at the center, but now it is June 4, 1968, the night of the California primary. A series of insignificant, random decisions sent Robert Kennedy unprotected into the kitchen of the Ambassador Hotel. A change in any one of those decisions would have put Kennedy out of harm's way—or would have put a protective barrier between Kennedy and Sirhan Sirhan's pistol. For more than forty years, historians, political journalists, and still-grieving admirers have asked, "Would he have won if he had lived, and what might have been different?"

Here's an answer.

The third narrative illustrates the fact that many twists of fate do not involve matters of life and death. In 1976, President Gerald Ford was rapidly closing the gap between himself and Governor Jimmy Carter, when in the middle of the second Presidential debate, a critical gaffe suddenly swung momentum the other way. If Ford had taken advantage of a panelist's offer to rephrase his clumsy answer, he would have avoided a week's worth of battering by the press, and would have also avoided antagonizing a large voting bloc that was very much up for grabs. How crucial would that have been? It would have taken a shift of only 12,000 votes in two states to keep Gerald Ford in the White House after 1976. And then . . . ? The history of this country might have been dramatically, and surprisingly, different.

These alternate histories I've designed are, of course, only possibilities. Someone else may offer up perfectly plausible scenarios in which the same accidents of fate I chronicle change everything in wholly different ways.

And that's the point. History doesn't turn on a dime; it turns on a plugged nickel. If I'm accused of playing with history, I plead guilty with an explanation. When we consider how our country, our fortunes, our lives might have been different . . .

If it had rained in Dallas on November 22, 1963, so that John Kennedy's car was covered by a bubble top . . .

If security guard Frank Willis hadn't found the tape on an office door at the Watergate complex on June 17, 1972 . . .

If John Hinckley's gun had been aimed an inch or two to Ronald Reagan's right on March 31, 1981 . . .

If Bill Clinton had ordered an aide to banish from the White House that intern who was flashing her underwear at him . . .

If the Democrats in Duval County, Florida, had not inadvertently instructed first-time voters to mark their ballots in a way that invalidated thousands of votes for Al Gore . . .

. . . then playing with history is a small bit of payback for the way history has played with us.

PALM BEACH, FLORIDA

— ★ ★ ★ —

DECEMBER 11, 1960, 9:45 A.M.

He stepped out of the doorway of the house, nodded to the men guarding the entrance, offered a slight wave to the photographers across the street, and began walking to the black sedan parked on North Ocean Boulevard that would take him to St. Edward's Church. He was not the most observant of Catholics, but a visit to church on Sunday, chronicled by the press, came with the territory. He put a hand into the side pocket of his lightweight tropical worsted suit, ran his other hand through his hair, and glanced up at the blue sky with an appreciative nod. A good day for a round of golf, a few hours by the pool working on the speech—Sorensen had sent a draft, a good one, but it was too long and a bit florid; he wanted this to be short, tough, with simple elegance—and later in the evening, some . . . diversion.

If he thought himself among the luckiest of men, he could be forgiven his presumption. He'd been born into wealth; his father had cashed out just before the Crash of '29, leaving Joe Sr. flush enough for comforts like the eleven-bedroom Spanish revival home he'd bought at the depths of the Depression. As a young officer in World War II, he'd emerged a hero after his boat was sunk, and that heroism had helped him win a Congressional seat before his thirtieth birthday. He'd survived illnesses grave enough to have received the last rites of his church, and he'd managed to conceal the severity of his medical condition with the help of complaisant physicians and an incurious press. That incurious press had also kept his private life just that. That same good fortune had sustained him throughout his improbable political journey. Four years ago, he had sought his party's Vice

Presidential nomination after Stevenson had thrown the choice open to the
convention, fought for it through two ballots on the convention floor. (His
father had gone further earlier that year, offering Lyndon Johnson a huge
sum of money if he'd run for the Presidency against Ike and agree to take
Jack as his running mate; Lyndon declined.) He was within a hairsbreadth
of the nomination when the convention chair, House Speaker Sam Rayburn, recognized states that threw their votes to Estes Kefauver, starting a
stampede (Sam had no tolerance for the idea of a Catholic anywhere near
the White House). And had he won that nomination, how many skeptical
Democrats would have pointed to Adlai's landslide loss and said, "See what
happens when you put a Catholic on the ticket?"

When the 1960 campaign began, he and his political team wanted a
big win in the Wisconsin primary—the first real test—big enough to force
Senator Hubert Humphrey out of the race. But the victory there was not
big enough for that, which meant they would compete again—this time in
West Virginia, a state with almost no Catholics, where fears of the Pope of
Rome ran strong. That was where he'd found his voice, assailing the government's meager help to the impoverished, pleading for religious tolerance with words that spoke almost as eloquently as the avalanche of money
that rained down on local sheriffs and court clerks. Without Humphrey
in the race, there was no way his win in West Virginia would have persuaded the Richard Daleys and Bill Greens and Ed Flynns, the men who
controlled the delegations of Illinois and Pennsylvania and New York, to
stand with him.

And then there was Lyndon—my God, what a stroke of luck! The
majority leader presided over the Senate like a puppet master; he had a
preternatural ability to know every member's strengths, weaknesses, vices,
vulnerabilities, ambitions. He had ties to the South and West; enough links
to oil and the financial world to have matched Jack's father dollar for dollar.
Yet Lyndon had dithered so long about even running—was it fear of failure, as some of his closest aides had thought?—that by the time he'd finally
entered the race formally, just days before the convention, it was too late;
the princes of the party whose support he might have won were no longer
in play. Jack had heard from a mutual friend that one of Lyndon's aides,
George Reedy, had said, "In the morning he'd be for a campaign, and then

by noon it would have worn off, and by the evening he would be against it but would have made so many commitments he couldn't back out. It was a strange situation."

But if Johnson's fecklessness was a stroke of luck, then Lyndon's place on the ticket was the winning of the Irish sweepstakes. He'd offered Lyndon the Vice Presidency because he had to, because a Southern or border state Democrat in second place had been a fixture of party tickets for decades. It was a way of mollifying a region that was all but barred from the Presidential slot by virtue of a long-ago civil war and the region's noxious racial policies. More than that, though, it was a geographically and politically attractive pairing: bring together the two strongest rivals for the nomination, unite liberal and conservative Democrats, add the electoral votes of the South to the Northeast and Middle Atlantic states. But what about the downside, the reaction from liberals and labor leaders, who bore the scars of past battles with Johnson? He remembered that in the first hours after winning the nomination in Los Angeles, he'd realized that he and his team had never really thought this through. So he went down two floors to Johnson's suite in the Biltmore to feel him out—and Lyndon had said yes before he was really offered the nomination! ("I didn't really offer him the nomination," he'd told a newspaper friend later. "I just held it out to here"—two or three inches from his pocket—and Johnson had taken it.)

Then came the chaos: furious denunciations from his own aides, from Pierre Salinger and Kenny O'Donnell, labor leaders and liberals threatening a floor fight, and finally, the disastrous decision to send Bobby down to Lyndon's suite to try to talk him out of it, offering him the party's national chair and the patronage that went with it—at the same time Jack was on the phone to Lyndon's closest advisor telling him, yes, he *did* want LBJ on the ticket!

But for all the ill feeling—Lyndon and Bobby had cordially despised each other before this muck-up and God knows what it would be like between those two now—there was one inescapable fact: without Lyndon on the ticket, there was no way he'd be here in Palm Beach preparing for his Inaugural. Lyndon had had his moments on the campaign—the stories about the drinking and the violent outbursts hadn't reached the press, but they'd made it back to the Kennedy campaign—but that didn't change the fact that Johnson and his wife whistle-stopped 3,500 miles across eight Southern states, at a time when the "Solid South" had ceased being so solid for Democrats. They'd barely won South Carolina, held Georgia, and won Texas by 46,000 votes; without Texas, his electoral majority would have come down to those 8,000 suspect votes in Illinois, which might have given his electors in the South some ideas about withholding their votes in return for backing off on civil rights. And Texas was in real doubt until Lyndon and Lady Bird had been confronted by that violent, hysterical crowd in Dallas; it was almost as if Johnson and his wife had shamed the state into voting Democratic (and how could a mob of men and women behave that way, spitting on the wife of a senator? Maybe there was something in the water down in Dallas . . .).

So now the Presidency was his, albeit by the narrowest of margins. There was no mandate, but he was by nature a cautious, prudent political animal, with no burning hunger for radical change. The Cabinet he was putting together would reflect that. Rusk at State was a paper-pusher, but that was fine, he'd run his own foreign policy (he'd put Adlai at the UN; Stevenson would be unhappy, but it was more than he deserved after his temporizing at the convention). Dillon at Treasury was the Wall Street WASP the markets always trusted, and McNamara at Defense was a Republican. There was only one real pick sure to raise eyebrows: in a few days, he was going to name Bobby as Attorney General. Neither of the brothers was especially keen on the idea; Bobby had spent the last three years going after labor racketeers, and was tired, he'd said, of chasing bad men. But Dad was insisting on it. When he'd asked Clark Clifford, the ultimate Washington insider, to try to argue Joe out of it, his dad had said, "It's the only thing I'm asking for and I want it." So he'd name Bobby when he got back to Washington in a few days. Meanwhile, there was a new baby in the house, along with his wife and daughter. In fact, he thought they might be coming to the door to see him off to church. He began to turn back to the house. The last thing he would have noticed was an old Buick parked down the street. The last thing . . .

RICHARD PAVLICK sat behind the wheel, waiting for Kennedy to climb into his car. Pavlick was seventy-three years old, with unkempt silver-gray hair and clothes that had seen better days. He had come a long way to this moment, and not just the thousands of miles he had journeyed, leaving Belmont, New Hampshire, to follow his target to campaign stops in St. Louis and San Diego and who knows how many other towns, up to the compound in Hyannis Port, where he'd gotten within ten feet of him, but lacked the tools to do the job, and now to Palm Beach, where he'd checked out the laughingly weak security, and where he was seconds away from saving the country he loved. For years, for decades, he had been a voice in the wilderness, a prophet without honor, earning for his labors indifference or ridicule. The signs were everywhere, why couldn't they see it? The flag itself was a portent; look at how negligently it was displayed at the school, the town hall, the post office (he'd spent his working years as a postman and it was the same story everywhere he worked).

He'd tried his best. At every Belmont town meeting he'd spoken out, he'd warned the town it was committing sacrilege every single day. And they'd groaned and motioned for him to sit down and let them get on with the budget or the plans for the Fourth of July festivities. They'd even sent a supervisor from the water company to his house to harass him about a water bill. He'd exercised his Second Amendment rights, and met the supervisor with a gun. But it was more, so much more: the dollar itself was a false instrument, Woodrow Wilson had done that when he created the Federal Reserve in 1913, and Roosevelt—Rosenfeld was his real name, of course—had finished the job when he'd taken us off the gold standard. And now, with the election of Kennedy, America was on the brink. The Church of Rome had seized the levers of power. Oh, yes, Jack Kennedy talked a good game, separation of church and state, but Pavlick knew better. When had the church ever kept itself from taking every scrap of power it could? For God's sake, hadn't they tapped every dollar of Old Joe Kennedy's money to steal the election? Young Jack even admitted as much, right in front of the Church's most powerful leaders, at the Al Smith dinner in New York. He'd joked that he'd gotten a telegram from his father that read: "Don't spend one dime more than is necessary—I'll be damned if I'll pay for a landslide." They all laughed, the cardinals and bishops in their robes and jewels, the rich Papists in their white ties and tails, but it was no joke; and Pavlick was going to make sure they wouldn't be laughing much longer.

He'd turned over his house—okay, it was not much more than a shack on the edge of town—to a local youth group, packed up what little he owned into his 1950 Buick, and left town. But America had to know what he was doing—and why. That's why he'd been sending postcards back home to Tom Murphy, the young postmaster, telling him to let the townsfolk know they'd soon be hearing from him "in a big way." And that's why, on his way to Palm Beach, he'd bought ten sticks of dynamite. Seven of those sticks were wired to a switch that he held in his right hand, as he watched the President-elect begin to walk to his car. He knew Americans—real Americans, at least—would understand and sanction what he was about to do; he'd written a note to the people of the United States, telling them exactly why he was doing this: "If death and destruction and injury to persons has resulted from my vicious action then I am truly sorry, but it won't help any. It is hoped that by my actions that a better country and a more attentive citizenry has resulted and corrected any abuses or ambitious moneyed persons or groups, then it will not have been in vain . . ."

As he watched Kennedy head toward his car—when he climbed inside, Pavlick would count to three and go—he saw Kennedy hesitate, turn back to the door. Was he being joined by his wife and children? If Jackie and Caroline and John Jr. were coming with him—even if they were at the door to wave good-bye—he'd have to abort the mission, wait for a better time. He was a patriot, not a remorseless killer; he just couldn't do it in front of the family. So he waited—and held his breath.

LYNDON JOHNSON put his head in his hands and groaned. He had drunk himself to sleep again last night, and he was paying the price this Sunday morning. He'd promised himself and Lady Bird it would stop, but the liquor that had been his constant companion on the campaign trail was still with him in the days after the election. And who could blame him? More and more these days, he was trying to come to grips with the fact that he had made the biggest mistake of his political life. He could have had the Presidential nomination, at least made a hell of a fight for it, but he'd held back, paralyzed by fear of losing, and by doubts about just how much he even wanted it. The last year he'd been discontent with everything—his work, his marriage—and thought more than once about throwing in his hand, going for a very different life. By the time he'd reached for the prize everyone else knew he hungered for, it was too late: the foe he'd derided as "Sonny Boy . . . a scrawny kid with rickets" had wrapped up the nomination on the first ballot. Worse, he had an effortless grace, whose appeal to the public utterly eluded Johnson.

"It was the goddamnedest thing," Johnson told a confidant as he saw the Presidency slipping away. "Here was a whippersnapper, malaria-ridden and yellah, sickly, sickly. He never said a word of importance in the Senate and he never did a thing. But somehow . . . he managed to create the image of himself as a shining intellectual, a youthful leader who would change the face of the country." Just after he'd lost the nomination, he'd gathered his closest advisors around him in his Biltmore Hotel suite in Los Angeles: Speaker Sam Rayburn, *Washington Post* publisher Phil Graham, John Connally, Jim Rowe. Amid the bitterness—Joe's money had been the difference, buying everything from great press to longtime Johnson allies; Kennedy and his doctors had lied through their teeth about Addison's disease, everyone knew that—there was this stark political reality to consider: what if Jack offered him the second spot on the ticket?

Speaker Sam had told him no, that he wouldn't trust Joe Kennedy, wouldn't walk across the street to say hello. But by the next morning, Rayburn had changed his mind; the idea of Richard Nixon as President bothered him a helluva lot more than a Catholic in the White House. Connally warned him he'd be burning a lot of bridges in Texas; Graham had told him to take it, that he'd already pressed the case with Kennedy. In the end, it was his own political instincts that told him to go for it. His grip on the Senate was weakening; a new class of senators had come in '58, more liberal, impatient, unwilling to let him control every piece of Senate business. And the older liberals, men he'd worked with just fine in the past, Paul Douglas of Illinois, Bill Proxmire of Wisconsin, Joe Clark of Pennsylvania, were starting to push back, to say "no" to his wishes. If he stayed on as majority leader, he'd be battling members of his own party every day. And if Kennedy got elected President, what would he be then as Senate leader? Not much more than a water-carrier for the White House.

As Vice President, he could be Jack's go-to man on the Hill. He knew the Congress far better than Kennedy did; Jack would be a fool not to use him to get his program—their program—through. Anyway, he had a Texas-sized insurance policy: He'd simply get the Texas legislature to change the law so he could run for Vice President and his Senate seat at the same time. If Nixon won, he'd still be majority leader, and the most powerful Democrat in the country, with a national profile for '64 or '68. If Kennedy won, he'd be right at Kennedy's side, and in four or eight years, he'd be next in line. And there was more: For years, Johnson had been caught between his own political instincts and the political demands of Texas. FDR was his hero, ever since his days as a Congressional aide in the 30s. His impulses, going back to his days as the twenty-six-year-old director of FDR's National Youth Administration, were all about helping the poor, and the hell with color. Back in '35, he'd been called in to see the Governor, Jimmy Allred, and Jimmy had warned him about sending money to colored schools like Prairie View A & M. And he'd listened, and sarcastically thanked the Governor for showing him how "a fine Christian man" thought, and then told the Governor he was going to double the money for Prairie View A & M, and sent the money out that very afternoon. He even admired Huey Long, the populist demagogue from Louisiana. Huey may have been a world-class crook, but he was a champion for people who badly needed a defender. He got free textbooks for schoolchildren, farm-to-market roads, a better break for widows and orphans.

But those instincts ran right up against cold hard reality. Texas Democrats were conservative, even reactionary, worshipping at the altar of big oil and big capital, more than comfortable with white supremacy as a way of political life. He'd been one of the only Southerners in Congress not to sign the "Southern Manifesto" after the Supreme Court outlawed school segregation in '54, but he'd resisted federal laws against the poll tax and lynching, pushed back on the fire-breathers like Hubert Humphrey, and when he guided that civil rights bill through in '57—he had to have a liberal credential if he was going to run for President in '60—he'd had to tell Southerners like Dick Russell that it was because "the nigras were getting uppity," and the bill had enough loopholes to drive a truck through. No, the only way to become a national Democrat was to free himself from the demands of Texas, and there was no better way to do that than by running on a national ticket. So when Jack came to his suite that Thursday morning, he'd said yes, even if it wasn't absolutely, undeniably clear that he'd been offered the job for sure.

And then it all went south. It wasn't Jack's fault; he was sure it was that runt Bobby, that punk who'd had it in for Johnson for years. He'd probably never forgiven Johnson for that time when Bobby visited the ranch and Johnson took him out to hunt, put a shotgun in Bobby's hands—okay, maybe he'd known it would be a little much for the punk to handle—then watched as the recoil from the gun knocked Bobby to the ground. "Son, you've got to learn to shoot like a man," he'd said to him, and he knew, oh how he knew, how that must have cut with the runt of his family's litter. He knew it was Bobby who was spreading the rumor that he'd suffered another heart attack—it wasn't the same as the stories Johnson's friends were feeding the press about Jack's Addison's disease; those stories were true—and so when Bobby came back down to the suite a few hours later to say that Jack was rethinking the idea, that it would be a tough sell for labor and the liberals, that maybe Lyndon would like to be chairman of the party instead, he knew it was Bobby messing with Jack's head. He'd actually had to sit there with tears in his eyes, telling Bobby how proud he'd be to run, how if Jack really wanted him he'd take it. Meanwhile, his team was burning up the phone lines to Jack's suite upstairs, demanding to know what the hell was going on, until Jack had said, yes, of course he wanted Lyndon, Bobby just didn't know what was going on.

So he'd stood there with Jack at the LA Coliseum, waving and smiling, but already there was that nagging feeling in the pit of his stomach that he'd taken a horribly wrong turn. And as the campaign wore on, that nagging little pebble had become a stone. He'd felt it up at Hyannis Port, caught the sidelong glances, the smirks, heard the snickers, the mockery of his accent. He'd taken his hurt and his rage with him on the campaign, drinking more than he ever had in his life. God, he could still remember a night in El Paso when he'd roamed the hotel corridors, hitting on damn near everything in a skirt, screaming at a poor advance man for typos on a press release that weren't even there. He still had the letter sent him by Jim Rowe, as loyal a friend and aide as you could want, telling him, "Someone ought to tell you the truth occasionally—and there is no one around who does . . . [old friends] find it impossible to work for you . . . And most of the time you, LBJ, are wrong, and they are right." And Jim wasn't working with him anymore. But he soldiered on, riding that whistle-stop all through the South—"The Cornpone Special," he'd heard the Kennedy folks dub it—and when that reactionary Republican Congressman Bruce Alger showed up with a mob of lunatics four days before election at that hotel lobby, screaming, hitting at him and Lady Bird, spitting on them, he'd known just what to do. He told the police to get back, telling them, "If the time has come when I can't walk through the lobby of a hotel in Dallas with my lady without a police escort, I want to know about it." That might have been worth that 46,000-vote margin in Texas all by itself. But somehow he knew it would turn sour; even on Election Night, an old friend had written him, "The night you were elected Vice President, I don't think I ever saw a more unhappy man. . . . There was no jubilation. You looked as if you'd lost your last friend on earth, and later you were rude to me, very rude, and I tried to remind myself that you were very unhappy."

And then . . . sure enough, the walls began to close in around him. He'd gone to Mike Mansfield, who would succeed him as majority leader, with a terrific idea: the Vice President was the President of the Senate, so why not let him preside over the party caucus, just as he had when he was leader? That way he could quarterback Kennedy's program right there at the Capitol. Fine, Mansfield said—and then the Democratic senators, the very people whose roads and dams he'd gotten built, whose colleges he'd funded, whose friends he'd found jobs for, told him, *You're not a senator anymore, Lyndon, we run our own shop here. Don't you remember separation of powers?* And it wasn't just the fire-breathers, it was the loyalists: Olin Johnson and Mike Monroney and Willis Robertson. Oh sure, the caucus had voted to let him preside after Mansfield threatened to quit, but with twenty-seven votes against him, there was no way he hadn't gotten the message. He couldn't show his face in the caucus, much less preside (even his chauffeur refused at first to stay with him—"when I drive the Majority Leader," he'd said, "I'm driving a man with power, but the Vice President doesn't have any power at all").

And then there was Kennedy's silence. Hell, he'd gone out of his way to extend a hand, take some of the burden off that young man's shoulders.

Johnson had had an aide draft an executive order, giving Johnson control over NASA and the Defense Department, making sure he was given all significant documents from every Cabinet member. That was ten days ago, and he hadn't heard a word back from Jack.

As he headed for the bathroom and a fistful of aspirin, he wondered again what had possessed him to take the job. And then he remembered what he'd told Clare Boothe Luce at a Washington dinner party: "Clare, I looked it up. One out of every four Presidents has died in office. I'm a gamblin' man, darling, and this is the only chance I got."

As John Kennedy took a step back to the front door, Richard Pavlick saw that it wasn't Jackie and the kids at the door, but a housekeeper.

"Mrs. Kennedy told me to say she's in bed with the baby," the housekeeper said through the screen. "She says she will see you after church."

"Fine," he said, and turned back to the car where a Secret Service man was waiting to open the rear door. Kennedy would read through a stack of papers on his way to church, then work on his Inaugural—and his tan—when he got back. Down the street, Richard Pavlick saw that Kennedy was alone. He gripped the switch tighter in his right hand, gunned the motor, and sped toward the sedan. An instant before the collision, a Secret Service agent tried to scream out a warning. It was drowned out by an explosion big enough to level a small mountain.

Eight hours later, at six p.m. on Sunday evening, eight men gathered in a twenty-by-twelve-foot room hidden beneath the main floor of the Capitol Rotunda. A high, ornately decorated ceiling reflected the room's original purpose as a meeting room for the House Committee on Territories. For a half century, it had been given to the House Speaker. Under Sam Rayburn, it had long been known as "the Board of Education," where Rayburn and a few favored intimates would gather for drinks and informal conversations. It was a modestly appointed room by Washington standards—a worn Oriental carpet, furniture from the Capitol storeroom, a long leather couch and leather chairs grouped around a long mahogany desk packed with bottles of scotch and bourbon behind which Speaker

Rayburn would preside—but it was the epicenter of political power. It was here on an April day in 1945 that Vice President Truman had heard the news that Franklin Roosevelt had died, but FDR had been seriously ill for a year or more; that death was the passing of a patriarch. What had happened in Palm Beach earlier that day was as if a meteor had come hurtling out of a clear blue sky and smashed headlong into the Capitol.

It had taken a few moments for the news to break. The explosion had killed or maimed the clutch of reporters and photographers gathered outside the Kennedy home, and on this sleepy December Sunday, the skeleton staffs at local news outlets who were tuned to police scanners believed at first they were hearing reports of a gas main explosion. But within a half hour, the first fragmentary reports of what had happened were interrupting the religious services that were a staple of Sunday morning broadcasts, and throwing the Sunday morning political interview programs into utter disarray. On CBS's *Face the Nation*, moderator Howard K. Smith, his voice breaking, was holding a telephone to his ear as he talked with local reporters who were shuttling between the perimeter of the explosion and a pay phone. On NBC, *Meet the Press* host Ned Brooks was displaying wire service still photographs, which—blessedly—showed little of the details. The National Football League canceled its schedule, but not soon enough to prevent a few thousand fans from arriving at Washington's District of Columbia Stadium to watch the Redskins play the New York Giants.

By eleven a.m., the dimensions of the disaster were apparent, and the return of the nation's political leadership to Washington had begun—a process that was as much a logistical nightmare as a political and emotional one. A freak snowstorm had dumped more than a foot of snow on the Washington-Baltimore area, paralyzing air and road traffic. So throughout the day, government jets had ferried the men from Boston, Peoria, San Antonio, Helena, to outlying military airports, then choppered them into the Capitol; convoys of Secret Service men had taken them to their Washington homes, staged vigils as they hastily made their way to the Capitol. There was no way to know with certainty whether the killing of John Kennedy was part of an attempt to decapitate the leadership of the United States, but President Eisenhower was taking no chances.

("Get the Secret Service out there now with every man in the leadership!"

he'd snapped. "We'll worry about the legalities later. If the chief wants to argue about it, he can do it when he goes on trial for criminal negligence. For Christ's sake, that lunatic was stalking Kennedy for weeks!")

They were among the most powerful of political figures, and they were as shell-shocked by what had happened as everyone else. "How could this have happened?" they had asked when they heard the news—a question that grew louder, angrier, when they learned that Pavlick had made no secret of his intentions. Indeed, the Belmont, New Hampshire, postmaster, Thomas Murphy, had warned the Secret Service about Pavlick. Yet somehow, even armed with the license plate of his car, they'd failed to spot him parked on the street near the Kennedy home. The nation was spared the most graphic of images, largely because the blast had killed all of the photographers and cameramen encamped outside Kennedy's Palm Beach home, and because the Secret Service and Palm Beach police had thrown a protective cordon around the blast site. (Later a local police officer was caught trying to sell photos he'd surreptitiously snapped. He and a *National Enquirer* reporter were briefly jailed, and were released a day later with a variety of injuries to their face and ribs.) Still, the country had awakened on Sunday morning with a rock-solid set of assumptions about the way their world worked; a few hours later, Pavlick's car bomb had blown those assumptions apart.

All of which, for the eight men gathered in the Capitol this Sunday evening, was decidedly beside the point. They had not rushed back to Washington to mourn. They were confronting a Constitutional crisis of the first order.

"Bryce," Speaker Sam Rayburn said to the short, courtly man to his left, "before we jump into this thicket, do you have anything for us on arrangements, logistics?"

Bryce Harlow looked at a page of handwritten notes. As President Eisenhower's liaison to the Congress, and as the President's closest aide, he'd forged a close partnership with Rayburn and Senate Leader Johnson.

"The family's in Palm Beach. Bobby flew down this afternoon . . . they've all been moved to a private home. The house took a pretty big hit. Mrs. Kennedy and the baby are okay physically. She's in a state of shock. Caroline was out by the pool with her nanny and got cut up by some flying glass. She's taken a number of stitches, but she'll be okay. As for the funeral . . ." He paused for a moment.

"Nothing left to bury, is there?" Rayburn said. Harlow shook his head.

"Jesus Christ, how the hell could this have happened?" The House Majority Leader John McCormick, a gaunt, sepulchral figure who was in normal times a barely measurable presence in the Congress, pounded a gnarled fist on the table. "My office in Boston is already hearing stories that a postmaster up in Bellmore—no, Belmont, whatever that New Hampshire town is—had warned the Secret Service about that nut—gave them the guy's license plate number, for Christ's sake—and they let the guy park his car down the street?"

"Yes, and there'll be a full investigation, and a lot of heads are going to roll," Harlow said. "Anyway, I think the family is leaning toward a mass in Boston in three days or so."

"We'll have a memorial here, a Joint Session," Rayburn said. "And then, Lyndon"—he looked down the table to the tall figure, slouched low in his seat, heavily lidded eyes half closed—"I think a speech to the Congress— which is why we have to sort this mess out."

Kennedy had been killed on December 11, five days before the Presidential electors were to meet in their state capitals to formalize Kennedy's election. Only when those votes were counted and certified by Congress in early January would Kennedy be officially entitled to take the reins of the Presidency. None of this had ever mattered, at least not since the Hayes–Tilden election of 1876; it was all kind of a ceremonial pageantry from another century. But now, suddenly, it did matter. Could the electors vote for a dead man? Could the Congress legally count the votes of a dead candidate? The Congress had faced that question back in 1872 when Democrat Horace Greeley had died after the election, but he'd lost to Ulysses Grant in a landslide; now they were talking about the candidate who'd won.

"And if you don't count them," the House parliamentarian had told the Speaker in an early afternoon phone call—even as they were counting the bodies in Palm Beach, the forty-five-year career civil servant who seemed to live in the catacombs of the Capitol was researching mold-covered books and monographs—"then you don't have an electoral majority, and the House picks the President—one state, one vote."

"So there's no problem," Rayburn had said. "Democrats control, what is it, thirty-two state delegations? When it gets thrown into the House, they'll just vote for Lyndon."

"The problem," sighed the parliamentarian, "is that the House has to choose from among the top three finishers. Right now, that would leave the choice between Nixon and Harry Byrd—that's who Mississippi and half of Alabama went for. There obviously weren't any electoral votes for Lyndon for President—just for Vice President."

"So what we have to do," Rayburn was saying now to the seven other men in the Capitol, "is to get some of the Kennedy electors to vote for Lyndon on Friday."

"Why not all of them?" McCormick asked. "That way we don't have to drag it out."

"Well," the Speaker began, "it's very complicated. Legally, some of them are free agents; some of them are bound by law. And—"

"I'll tell you why," Lyndon Johnson said. His voice was a low-pitched rumble, barely audible down the length of the table. "Some of those folks wouldn't vote for me if Khrushchev were on the other side. Hell, some of 'em probably would jump at the chance to vote for him. They see me, they listen when I open my mouth, and they think 'Where's the white robe? The burning cross . . . where's the hood?' And there's another thing," he said, his voice rising, the way it would when he'd start to hammer a senator for a vote, when his body and his voice would bend the man backward until his head was barely higher than his waist. "The Kennedys are gonna want that vote—it's their due. I don't think they'd stand for it if that vote on Friday as much as said he never even existed." He took a deep drink from a glass of the Cutty Sark he kept stashed at the Speaker's hideaway.

"If I might say a word here . . ."

Vice President Richard Nixon leaned forward, elbows on the table, thumbs propped under his chin. Without the glare of television lights, the shadow of a beard was less visible, the jowls and furrows under his eyes less pronounced. But his gestures and voice bespoke of solemnity, gravitas, age. *Can he really be only four years older than Jack was?* one of them thought. *I'll bet when he was nine he wanted a briefcase for Christmas.*

"I believe we can all agree that there are two issues before us," Nixon said, holding two fingers aloft. "First," he said, gesturing with his forefinger, "is reassurance. The public must know that their government is strong and functioning. Second," he said, holding up two fingers, "is the issue of legitimacy. The people must believe that the process is fair, that they can fully trust that their will has been followed."

The shuffling of papers, tapping of fingers, flicking of cigarettes stopped.

"And your point is?" the Speaker asked.

"You know damn well what his point is," Senator Everett Dirksen said. The Republican leader's voice, a deep basso profundo, rumbled through the room. "Dick's too polite to say it"—a snicker came from across the table—"but I've said it publicly and I'll say it again. This election was stolen. I don't know where that forty-six thousand vote plurality came from in Texas, but it's mighty curious when Fannin County, with five thousand registered voters, casts more than six thousand votes. And as for that eight thousand vote spread in Chicago . . ." He turned to Nixon, who was vigorously shaking his head.

"I know, Dick, I know," said Dirksen. "You said you wouldn't contest the Illinois vote, you got the *Herald-Trib* to kill Earl Mazo's series on vote fraud. But now we're talking about putting a man in the White House that nobody voted for, who ran on a ticket that may not even have been legitimately elected. Maybe the courts will have something to say about this."

Half a dozen voices were raised at once, and then Bryce Harlow got to his feet and held out a cautionary hand.

"Ev—Dick—this is not a road we're going down. The President has made it absolutely clear to me and everyone else in the White House that he would regard any attempt to turn this into a political conflict as something very close to treason—literally—giving aid and comfort to the enemy. And he would say so loudly, publicly, and repeatedly. Ev, I have no doubt there were some votes stolen in Chicago. Although," he added with a faint smile, "I've heard some stories about Republican vote-counting in Peoria that may raise an eyebrow. But we're talking about what this country looks like today to the rest of the world. What do you think the Russians are telling the Africans and the Asians about us? We've just had the next President of the United States blown to hell and gone by a lunatic. We're not going to paralyze ourselves with a political fight. And as far as the courts are concerned, let's be serious: there's no way on earth the public would ever stand for a court deciding who is going to be the President.

"Mr. Speaker," Harlow said, "Lyndon—Mr. President, I guess I should say—the President wants you and your colleagues to resolve this as you wish. He will be completely and publicly supportive; and he's prepared to fight any attempt by anyone of any party to obstruct you. And by the way, Ev, you might want to sharpen those vote-counting skills of yours. Sam and Lyndon have enough Democrats to count those electoral votes any way they choose; you'd do yourself and the party a lot of good if there weren't a trace of partisanship here. I believe—and the President believes—that anything else would be political suicide."

And Ike will make damn sure of that, Nixon thought. *Son of a bitch didn't lift a finger for me, knew exactly what he was doing when he told that press conference it'd take him a week to think about any decision I'd helped him make.*

"Ev," Nixon said, arranging his face into its Civic Moment expression, "Bryce is right. In fact, Mr. Speaker, I'm going to reach out to our Republican electors. If you need them to give Kennedy a majority, fine. If you need some of them to vote for Lyndon so he can be eligible for a vote in the House, fine."

"That's very commendable, Dick," said Mike Mansfield. The others turned to him with looks that varied between surprise and amazement. Next to the famously taciturn Montana senator, Calvin Coolidge was a loudmouth. "But this still leaves us with a problem: Who's going to be Vice President? If the electors vote for Kennedy and Johnson, and the Congress counts those votes, then there's a vacancy on January 20th and you fill it," he said, pointing to Johnson. "But that means we go without a Vice President for four years. If Kennedy's electors switch their votes for President to you—so you're in the running if the House has to choose—then there's no electoral majority for Vice President. That would leave it up to the Senate to choose between Strom Thurmond and Barry Goldwater—an elector from Oklahoma voted for him." No one said anything for a long moment.

"I remember they were talking about this when I got to the Senate in '49," Johnson said. "Harry Truman had just gone through damn near a whole term with no V.P.—and if anything'd happened to him, you"—he pointed to House Minority Leader Joe Martin—"would have been President—from a different party. But Harry got himself elected and Alben Barkley was the veep and the whole thing just went away." Johnson took another drink from a glass of the Cutty Sark, then took a long drag on his cigarette.

"One thing," he said. "I don't think the country would sleep very well going four years with a President who damn near died of a heart attack five years ago, and still can't give these damn things up and no one next in line, but—" He looked up at Speaker Rayburn. "I mean no offense, Mr. Sam," Johnson said. "You'd make a damn fine President."

"I'd quit first," Rayburn said. "A seventy-nine-year-old President with—how old is Hayden?"—referring to the Senate President pro tempore. "Eighty-two? Eighty-three—next in line? That'd reassure the country, wouldn't it?"

"There is another alternative," Harlow said. "Lyndon, I'd say you have about twenty-four hours to make the first decision of your Presidency."

IF THERE WAS ANY saving grace to the catastrophe, it was that the identity and motive of the killer were never in doubt. Pavlick had posted his suicide note to Tom Murphy, and within a day, under the direct order of Eisenhower, the letter and his earlier threats had been publicly revealed. At a time when historians were still arguing over who was in on the plot to kill Lincoln a century earlier, there was no mystery, no suspicions beyond a tiny fringe. Kennedy had been killed outside his home by a lunatic whose intentions were as blatant as they were deranged. ("Imagine if he'd been killed in Texas," Lyndon Johnson said to a confidant. "I'd be suspect number one.") The appalling failure of the Secret Service was a case not of malicious indifference but classic bureaucratic sclerosis, somehow failing to take seriously enough the warnings of Postmaster Thomas Murphy that a local resident was making threats against the President's life. "Three, four more days and we would have had him," the now-suspended chief of the Service said. Had the identity of the killer been less clear, had there been unanswered questions about the manner of Kennedy's death, it is entirely possible that a whole culture of conspiracy would have flourished in the years that followed.

That was at best cold comfort. It is impossible to measure the impact of what did not happen, but there is no uncertainty about what did happen. The impending ascension of the youngest elected President, with an impossibly glamorous wife (thirty-one years old!) and two very young children, was testament to the country's confidence in its future. It was of a piece with a broader sense that the country was living a life that had made the years of privation and sacrifice worth it. After a decade-long Depression and nearly four years of wartime sacrifice, America had become for most a land of plenty, where security and abundance were the natural order of things. There were twenty-eight million more Americans than there had been a decade earlier, and two-thirds of that growth had come in the suburbs, where for $65 down and $65 a month a family could own a patch of the American dream—and, thanks to tens of thousands of miles of federally funded highways, a man could go from home to work and back again in the privacy of his own automobile. And when he came home to his family, there were more and more possessions for him and his family to enjoy: 21-inch television sets, high-fidelity record players, home-movie cameras, barbecue grills, refrigerator-freezers, washer-dryers, dishwashers. Regular working-class, middle-class Americans could afford these things; the United States was the world's one clear economic superpower; the economy was growing year by year, inflation was nonexistent, and the bank accounts and Christmas Club savings just kept growing, as steadily, as assuredly, as sunrises in the East. Another once-unattainable goal for most Americans—a college education—had now become real for millions of men who'd been pressed into military service: The GI Bill of Rights put eight million of them on college campuses in the years after World War II.

But it was more than just material prosperity. America in 1960 was a country where restraint and boundaries were the natural conditions in all arenas. People married younger and stayed married; even with those added twenty-eight million, there were fewer divorces in 1960 than there had been a decade earlier. People did not have children unless they were married—only 2.5 percent of children were born out of wedlock, though the number in black households was disturbingly high—some 20 percent. People did not have sex unless they were married, at least as far as the entertainment and news they read and heard and watched were concerned. Violent crime was lower than it had been twenty years earlier, despite the hand-wringing over juvenile delinquency. And while politicians pointed with alarm at the violence in comic books and on television, the fact is that when people were killed, they died bloodlessly; carnage, like graphic sex, was confined to the pages of pulp magazines sold furtively in stores at the edge of respectability. And America was not a country whose leaders were killed in broad daylight—it had not happened since William McKinley was shot at the very beginning of the twentieth century—much less blown up in so violent a manner. No wonder one prominent commentator of his time wrote that in the days and weeks after the murder, America "was on the verge of a national nervous breakdown."

In those first days and weeks, Lyndon Johnson's instincts were flawless, nowhere more so than in those first hours. The Capitol meeting was ending, the participants preparing to drive to Andrews Air Force Base to meet the plane bearing what remained of Kennedy to Washington. Lyndon, the others urged him, you need to go on television from the airport, the country needs to hear from you. He said, *No, I'm not the President, I'm not the President-elect—I'm not anything, at least for a few days, and if I'm on television tonight, then I'm the usurper. The only one who should speak tonight is Ike. Mr. Sam and Ev and Joe and me can stand behind him, that'd probably be a good thing for the country to see.*

So late on the night of December 11, Johnson and his colleagues were grouped behind President Eisenhower as a Boeing 707 VC-137, designated SAM 972—"Air Force One" when the President was on board—touched down at Andrews with the casket bearing the remains of John Kennedy, or so the nation and the world was told. In fact, a team of Secret Service agents had scoured the scene of the suicide bombing, retrieving what shards of flesh and bone they could find. They were placed in a casket along with enough ballast to give the coffin weight. The images of an honor guard straining with effort while bearing the casket from an ambulance to the 707 jet reinforced the impression that a human body was being transported. None of the solemn voices narrating the event on television and radio even contemplated raising the unsettling question of just how an intact human body could possibly have been retrieved from so massive an explosion.

When the plane landed at Andrews late that Sunday night, the President and the other high officials of the government were there to meet it—and so was Robert Kennedy. Again, Johnson's instincts were perfectly tuned. Stay here, he motioned his colleagues. *This is Bobby's grief.* No one watching the coverage—and that included just about everyone with access to a television set—would ever forget those black-and-white images of Robert Kennedy standing alone on the tarmac beneath the tail of the 707, watching as the casket was lowered by forklift to a waiting hearse, then helplessly resting his right hand on the casket as President Eisenhower, ramrod-straight, his face torn between sympathy and rage, put his hand on Robert Kennedy's shoulder.

When the hearse drove away, taking the casket to the Capitol Rotunda, Eisenhower strode to a bank of microphones and spoke as the Congressional leaders and Vice President Nixon stood behind him.

"This is a dark night for our country," he said. "A gallant young man who inspired millions has been struck down by a madman. We pray for John Kennedy's soul; we pray for his family. And we resolve that his spirit and energy will give us strength in the days ahead. John Kennedy is dead, but the country he loved and served with bravery and grace will endure." The President and the leaders walked off into the darkness; fortunately, they were beyond the range of the microphones when one of them muttered, "Now what the hell do we do?"

It was Lyndon Johnson who provided the answer.

The men gathered again in Speaker Rayburn's hideaway Monday at six a.m. The room was strewn with newspapers, their front pages all splashed with huge black-bordered banner headlines (no television news penetrated the hideaway; Speaker Rayburn hated the medium, had banned TV coverage even of Congressional hearings; the members didn't like that, thought the TV cameras in Senate hearings made that body even more prominent, but there was no arguing with the Speaker). The men wolfed down the breakfasts brought up from the House dining room—scrambled eggs, sausages, country ham, grits, biscuits, coffee by the gallon—and set down to deal with two urgent questions: first, how to memorialize the fallen John Kennedy; second, how to navigate the treacherous Constitutional waters of succession and leadership.

"Where's Lyndon?" Ev Dirksen asked.

"Said he'd be along in a bit," Speaker Rayburn said with studied offhandedness. "Said to start without him."

There was quick agreement on the pageantry. Kennedy's body was lying in state in the Capitol Rotunda—even in the immediate aftermath of the murder, Jacqueline and Robert Kennedy had agreed to that—and the crowds had begun lining up all night long, waiting to pay their respects. The queue now stretched more than a mile down Pennsylvania Avenue. At noon the next day, Tuesday, a small memorial service would be held in the Rotunda. The formal funeral would be held on Wednesday, in Washington's National Cathedral; that would give leaders from around the world time to attend. The protocol was a mare's nest; John Kennedy was not the head of state, was not even formally the President-elect. But French President Charles de Gaulle had already signaled his intention to pay his respects—"He is a fallen soldier, and deserves the ultimate tribute of my presence," the General had said—and others were bound to follow suit ("After all," British Prime Minister Harold MacMillan said to one of his aides, "his father was ambassador here—even if he did want to sell us out to Hitler"). While the final decision had yet to be made, the Kennedy family was leaning toward a burial at Arlington National Cemetery. Kennedy's service in World War II had earned him that honor, although a quiet debate was underway about the size and nature of the burial plot.

But what then? On Friday, less than forty-eight hours after the burial, the Electoral College would convene; more precisely, the electors from fifty states would gather in the fifty state legislatures to cast their votes. The dilemma posed by Speaker Rayburn the night before was even more pressing: How could Lyndon Johnson legitimately claim the Presidency? And how to legitimately "elect" a Vice President?

The House Parliamentarian had just begun a mind-numbing rehash of the Constitutional maze when the door to the hideaway was flung open. And Lyndon Johnson, trailed by Senators Richard Russell and Hubert Humphrey, nodded to the others, took a seat on one of the overstuffed chairs, leaned his six-foot four-inch frame over, put his elbows on his knees and his chin in his hands, and told them what he had decided to do.

WHEN IT CAME RIGHT down to it, there was only one logical choice for Vice President. One or two of the more zealous members of Kennedy's political family suggested that Bobby should have the post (one even urged Jack's electors to vote for Bobby for *President*); but the whole idea was absurd. Never mind that Bobby was barely eligible—he'd only turned thirty-five two weeks before Jack's murder—he had no credentials. However impressive he'd been as a Congressional staff counsel and campaign manager, he'd held no elective office, no significant executive job, never mind that he and Lyndon couldn't stand each other ("Have you ever seen two dogs walk into a room from opposite sides and all of a sudden there's a low growl and the hair starts going up on the back of the neck?" one of Johnson's closest aides said. "That's how those two reacted").

He'd called Bobby in the first hours after the assassination, telling him there were a hundred million aching hearts around the country, that they would honor Jack however the family wished.

"And when the time is right, you come and see me and we'll talk about how we can work for what Jack wanted," he'd added. "As far as I'm concerned, whatever's happened in the past is over, done with, gone. I know how much Jack needed you, but Bobby, I need you more than he did. You have so much to give to this country. . . ."

Robert Kennedy mumbled a few words of gratitude, and the call ended (when he put the phone down, Bobby turned to a Kennedy campaign worker and said, "You have one job left—make sure I never have to speak on the phone with him again—or at least as little as I can get away with").

Johnson had thought seriously about going beyond the Democratic Party. That new governor of New York, Nelson Rockefeller, impressed him mightily: Rocky thought big, the way Johnson did. Rockefeller was already pushing for a huge expansion of the state university system, for roads and housing all across the state. And he played politics like a contact sport; he'd humbled Richard Nixon last summer by threatening him with a nomination fight, then forcing Nixon to come to Rockefeller's palatial Fifth Avenue apartment to sign off on big changes in the Republican platform, with a huge boost in defense spending—the big contractors in Texas loved that idea. Like Johnson, Rockefeller was a Cold War internationalist: You had to face down the Russians all over the world, with missiles and bombers, yes, but with schools and roads and dams, to give the folks in those poor countries something to hope for, just like Roosevelt had given the

poor in the Pedernales down in Texas something to hope for almost thirty
years ago. Rocky knew that, too—and besides, wasn't a reach across party
lines the best way to show that America was not going to let some lunatic
rip us apart?

But it couldn't work, Johnson realized. The politics of it were just too
daunting. He and his colleagues who'd gathered in Rayburn's office were
about to set out on some very treacherous waters. It was going to be hard
enough to work out the Constitutional arithmetic with the electors, allo-
cating enough votes for President and Vice President to deal with any
potential challenge; asking lifelong Democrats to cast a vote for a sitting
Republican just might be asking too much. Besides, could you really be
honoring the people's will if you put a man who'd flirted with running
for the Republican nomination a suspect-heartbeat away from the Oval
Office? Putting Republicans in the Cabinet, yes; he thought Jack had done
well in picking Doug Dillon for Treasury—C. Douglas Dillon, that first
initial should warm the hearts of the Wall Street boys—and he'd been
mightily impressed by the fellow with the Sta-Comb in his hair, the man
from Ford, Bob McNamara. And maybe down the line, he'd see if he could
persuade Rockefeller to come to Washington, although when a man has
the Presidency in mind, it's a tough thought to set aside. But the Vice
President? No, he knew what he had to do: Stay with a Democrat, and
reach North and Left. And that meant . . . Hubert.

He and Humphrey had both come to the Senate in '49: Humphrey was
the fire-breathing Minneapolis mayor who'd helped trigger a walkout of
Southern delegates at the '48 convention with a fiery speech that called on
the party to move "out of the shadows of states rights, into the bright sunlight of human rights." Johnson was the newly minted segregationist who'd
boasted of his votes in the House against anti-lynching bills and anti–poll
tax bills and fair employment laws. But they seemed to see something of
themselves in the other: both from small towns, both knowing very hard
times in the Depression, both climbing the greasy pole of politics by working longer, harder than anybody else. When Johnson had reached for the
post of Senate Democratic leader, there'd been resistance from the liberals,
but Hubert had said, *No, he's the right man for the job.* When Humphrey
would lead another charge for a civil rights bill, doomed to defeat by the

arcane rules of the Senate, Johnson would tell his fellow Southerners to go easy on Humphrey: "He's my link to the bomb-throwers." And more and more he'd brought Humphrey into his inner circle, managing bills, rounding up votes from liberal colleagues.

For his part, Humphrey had told more than one supporter that if he couldn't have the nomination, he'd want it to go to Lyndon. And in the first hours after the suicide bombing, when some of his longtime allies were speculating about denying Johnson the Presidency—*those electors are free agents, Hubert, they don't have to vote for Lyndon, hell, most of them probably hate the idea of Lyndon in the White House*—he'd been as adamant in private as he'd been in public. *This is the man John Kennedy chose to stand a heartbeat from the Presidency; to do anything else dishonors his legacy and our system of government.*

And now Lyndon Johnson looked around the room, and pointed to Senator Humphrey, and said simply, "I need him—I want him." And Humphrey simply nodded, and welled up, and said, "I'd be proud to stand with you," and then Johnson was gesturing to Richard Russell, the man to whom he'd once said, "I haven't got any daddy, and you're it," the man Humphrey had been fighting on civil rights from the day he walked into the Senate almost twelve years ago.

"Dick and I have talked this through," said Johnson. "He and I and every other Southerner know I could never have become President on my own. The way we talk, and the whole nigra issue, means all any of us could aspire to is to be another John Nance Garner. Dick, you found that out in '52 when you tried to run. Now I have the chance to end this once and for all—if I can be a halfway success, it means a Southern boy can dream of growing up to be President, too. But that means I have to show the rest of the country I'm not some Texas oilman that wants to keep the colored man down. I didn't win this election, Jack Kennedy did—at least as far as the country's concerned. So I have to do the right thing and honor his memory and that means doing things and picking people you might not like. But it's the only chance we have to stop being second-class Americans."

"I don't think you could make a better move," Russell said. "Hubert, I'll be fighting you six days a week on civil rights, but Lyndon, I'll probably be fighting you six days a week on civil rights sooner or later, no matter who your Vice President is. And I can't even imagine who'd be better protection for you when the *New York Times* and the NAACP start complaining that you're not moving fast enough. Hubert, you know I may have to say something tough about you . . ."

"You just call him up first to let him know it's coming," Johnson said. It was the first time any of them had laughed in almost twenty-four hours.

"If you remember back, I'm pretty sure I'm the one who taught you about keeping the waters calm," Russell said, "although I sometimes think you learned this in the womb. Anyway, I'll do what I can to see if I can keep some of the fire-breathers around here from throwing a fit. Lyndon, I don't know any man who's ever come into office with the burdens you're carrying. I'm damned if I'm going to add to them."

It was in the hours that followed that Johnson's powers of persuasion were on full display, as he worked the phones, an instrument that he had long ago mastered as thoroughly as had Rubenstein the piano or Heifetz the violin. His first call was to Martin Luther King, Jr.—Johnson mentioned that fact no less than three times—and he spoke for almost a half hour, a stream-of-consciousness monologue about his days teaching poor Mexican-Americans, about his hunger to be free from the racial prison of Southern politics, his pride in not signing the "Southern Manifesto" that committed virtually every Southern member of Congress to segregation, his shame in opposing anti-lynching and other civil rights bills.

"I mean no disrespect," he said to King, "and I know how much those calls to you and your wife from Jack meant—they may have saved your life, may have won the election for us—but I frankly thought Jack was a bit . . . conservative.

"Those Harvards," he said, "think that a politician from Texas doesn't care about Negroes. In the Senate, I did the best I could. But I had to be careful. I couldn't get too far ahead of my Texas voters. Now I represent the whole country, and I have the power. I always vowed that if I ever had the power I'd make sure every Negro had the same chance as every white man. Now, because of this awful tragedy, I will have it. And I'm going to use it." As soon as was decent—after the memorial service for Jack, after the electoral confusion had been cleared away—he would meet with King and other Negro leaders.

"And, Reverend," he added. "Keep your eyes on the prize: I understand the sit-ins, and the bus boycott—it's a damn disgrace that a Negro can't sit in the front of the bus or get a hamburger at a lunch counter—but it's the vote, the vote, the vote. You said that back in April of '59 at that youth march for integrated schools—when the Negro in the South gets the vote, you're gonna be amazed at how many friends the Negro will find with sheriffs and county clerks and everyone else that needs votes to keep his job."

Then came the calls to the Jews who'd been among his strongest, if least likely, allies and supporters. When he'd first run for the Congress in '37, an all-out supporter of FDR, he'd attracted money from Democrats in New York who were eager to help a young New Dealer running in such hostile territory (one of them had slipped $5,000 to Franklin Jr. for a forged note from FDR implying that Johnson had his support). Jews like Bobby Lehman and Ed Weisl were never that sold on Jack Kennedy; they had too many memories of Old Joe Kennedy's defeatism in the years before World War II, and the old man's ingrained anti-Semitism was an open secret. When he was running for the nomination, Johnson had said, "I was never an umbrella man," meaning Neville Chamberlain, the British Prime Minister who'd come back from Munich waving an umbrella and promising "peace in our time" after selling out the Czechs to Hitler. The message was simple: *You let your liberal friends in New York and Chicago and California know that I mean to finish what Roosevelt started. It'll take time. The country's in shock and we've got a first-class mess to fix before we can give the public a clear idea even of who the President's going to be or how. But you have my word on this. And if you don't think you can trust me on this, ask yourself why I picked Hubert to take over if my heart isn't up to it.*

When those calls ended, he was on the phone to his fellow Southerners in the Senate: to Florida's George Smathers, one of Jack Kennedy's closest friends and a fellow hell-raiser; to Alabama's Lister Hill and John Sparkman; to Willis Robertson of Virginia, whose son Pat had gone into preaching, just started some kind of Christian broadcasting operation in Virginia Beach. It was the same message he had given to Dick Russell, who was burning up the telephone lines as well: *We have a chance to end a hundred years of bigotry against everyone who speaks the way we do, who comes from where we come from. I don't expect you to vote with me on the race question, but*

I need you to understand that the country can't stand to be torn up on black and white, or on North and South. You know that Khrushchev and Mao are over there licking their chops, and if we start falling to pieces, why, we could deteriorate pretty quick.

In those first days, Johnson was as effective in public as he was in private. He had remained in the background during Tuesday's ceremony at the Capitol, and at Wednesday's service at the National Cathedral. He had walked with de Gaulle and the other heads of state from the Cathedral to Arlington—the Secret Service had furiously objected, but de Gaulle had simply shrugged and said, "If they wish to arrest me, so be it," and that was that—but he had deliberately walked a row behind the Kennedy family and the heads of state. It wasn't until Thursday at noon, in an address to a Joint Session of Congress, that Johnson emerged from his self-imposed shadow. He'd understood instinctively that the speech was a tightrope walk between a eulogy to a fallen leader-to-be and a pre-Inaugural address. He'd turned to Ted Sorensen, John Kennedy's wordsmith and chief policy advisor, for help on the speech. *I'm not asking you for me; I'm asking you for him.* Sorensen mumbled that, yes, he'd do what he could, and turned in a masterpiece—but it was a masterpiece of unfettered grief, a lament for the irreplaceable loss of a leader whose vision and courage we will not see again in our lifetimes, and a near confession of inadequacy: "Though I cannot fill his shoes, I must occupy the desk he earned," Sorensen had written, and Johnson smiled mirthlessly as he struck the line out of the draft. He'd done more; he'd reached out to John Barlow Martin, Adlai's favorite writer, he'd even placed a call to Dick Goodwin, the kid—he wasn't even thirty!— who'd backstopped Sorensen on the Kennedy campaign. And most significant, he brought in Horace Busby, who'd been with him even before he got to the Senate, who could write words that fit Johnson like a custom-made suit, and who understood him as well as any man. *I want it short*, he'd told Buzz, *and I want it to put us back on our feet. You can mourn some, but if I give the Sorensen speech, people are gonna be throwing themselves off their roof. Make it brief, tough, plain, blunt.*

But the moment that mattered, the moment that splashed across every front page in America, every front page in the world, for that matter, came before he'd said the first words of his address, when the House doorkeeper,

Fishbait Miller, intoned: "Mistah Speak-ah, the majority leader of the United States Senate!" and Lyndon Johnson walked into the chamber with Jacqueline Kennedy on one arm and Robert Kennedy on the other. For a long moment the three of them stood motionless, Jacqueline in her widow's weeds, the two-piece black button-front jacket and dress—the same dress she had worn to the christening of her infant son John six days earlier, Bobby in a black suit, white shirt, black tie held in place with one of his brother's PT-109 tie clips. The applause which had begun with the doorkeeper's announcement stopped in a heartbeat; the chamber was utterly, impossibly still as the trio walked through the well of the House, to the steps that led up to the rostrum. Then the applause began again, and did not stop for ten full minutes; no cheers, no shouts, just the clapping, on and on, until Johnson beckoned to the two men seated behind the rostrum . . . and Vice President Richard Nixon and Speaker Sam Rayburn came down to the well to embrace the two Kennedys. Johnson then shook Bobby's hand, gently pressed Jacqueline's hand between his own and escorted them to two seats in the front of the chamber where members of the Cabinet sat during State of the Union addresses. Just before he turned to go to his seat, Robert Kennedy leaned back to Johnson and said, "This is for him, you know. It's all for him."

"I know," Johnson said. "I know."

How had it happened? At some point the night before John Kennedy's funeral, Johnson had called Joseph Kennedy, Sr. Whatever was said, whatever was promised, Joe had called Bobby with a message strong enough to bring the widow and the oldest surviving brother to Johnson's side. Its essence was simplicity itself: *No one has more reason to hate the son of a bitch than I do. He called me a goddamn Nazi sympathizer when he was running against Jack. A month from now, you can start planning to take him down in '64. But right now this country needs you and Jackie to do this.* In fact, it did not take much persuasion from Joe; there was a message America had to deliver to the world, and the Kennedys understood that, understood what it would signal if the First Family of America was supposed to have seemed to be denying the legitimacy of the President they now had to have, if only by their absence. So Jackie and Bobby took their seats, and when the Speaker intoned, "I have the high honor, the distinct privilege, to introduce the majority leader of the United States Senate," they rose with the rest of the chamber to applaud.

"All that I have," Johnson began, "I would have given gladly not to be standing here at this moment. An American hero has fallen—and we are the lesser for it. Two other American heroes—his wife and his brother—have come tonight to say that we will not let John Kennedy's death turn us from the course he was charting—and we are the better for their courage and their love of country.

"And I have come here to say that we will never forget the spirit, the vision, the energy John Kennedy embodied . . . and to say that while the leader we chose may have been taken from us, the government he would have led so brilliantly lives . . . and our system that the founders shaped nearly two centuries ago will survive and endure and prevail.

"This dark hour demands nothing less than a clear, honest explanation to our countrymen, and to a waiting world, of where we will go from there, and how we will get there. It is true that never before have we had to choose a President under these conditions. But our Constitution is more than equal to the task. And tomorrow, America and the world will see this for themselves.

"When I leave this chamber, I will go to the White House, along with the leaders of the Congress from both parties, and with Vice President Nixon. There, President Eisenhower, along with Presidents Truman and Hoover, will detail the course we will follow. It will, to the best of our ability, reflect what we believe to be the will of the American people. And it will demonstrate to every nation, whether it wishes us well or ill, that while our hearts have been broken, our will has not."

An hour later, Johnson, Nixon, the leaders of the Congress, and two former Presidents stood behind Eisenhower as he talked about what would happen the next day: how those Presidential electors whose states did not bar them from acting as independent agents would cast Presidential votes for Lyndon Johnson, and Vice Presidential votes for Hubert Humphrey; how those votes would force the House of Representatives to choose the President, and the Senate to choose the Vice President. Eisenhower and the others took no questions; when the statement was over, he and Johnson went together into the Oval Office for hours of conversations with the world leaders who had come to Washington for Kennedy's funeral. For eight years, the two men had forged a close working relationship, and now the departing President was signaling, as clearly as he could, that the transition of power would be seamless.

Not that there was national unanimity. Robert Welch, a retired candy manufacturer who led a two-year-old organization in Belmont, New Hampshire, the John Birch Society, fired off telegrams to his members urging them to oppose "a blatant coup d'état to destroy our system of government.

"As you know," he wrote, "I have long argued that both the U.S. and Soviet governments are controlled by the same furtive conspiratorial cabal of internationalists, greedy bankers, and corrupt politicians. If left unexposed, the traitors inside the U.S. government would betray the country's sovereignty to the United Nations for a collectivist New World Order managed by a 'one-world socialist government.' Now that betrayal is about to be complete."

A thirty-five-year-old editor of a five-year-old conservative magazine, William F. Buckley, Jr., went on NBC to urge Republican members of Congress to oppose this "flagrant effort at political manipulation. It is no disrespect to the dead—indeed, it is, rather, respect for our system of government—to note that it is by no means apparent that John Kennedy was legitimately elected to the Presidency. No Constitutional exegesis would permit such a rendering of the Framers' intent." There were grumblings on the Left as well: Walter Reuther, head of the United Auto Workers, and Joe Rauh, who led Americans for Democratic Action, had spent an anguished hour on the phone, sifting through ways to deliver the Presidency to Humphrey, or to Stevenson or to someone besides the Senate majority leader whom they had tried unsuccessfully to drive off the Democratic ticket back at the Los Angeles convention.

In the end, these were futile flailings. Even if the country had been prepared for an uprising over succession, there were no mechanisms to organize one. There was, for instance, no readily accessible list of Presidential electors; only the state election officials and political parties had such lists, and there was no quick, easy way to find phone numbers, addresses, names of officials. More important, there was no efficient mechanism for countless numbers of disaffected individuals to communicate with like-minded citizens, no way to arouse potential sympathizers. Long-distance telephone calls and telegrams were expensive, unwieldy; and on television, three networks dominated the conversation. For example, when William Buckley finished speaking, a roundtable of heavyweight historians and analysts dismissed his argument, warning of the fragile state of the American body politic. A citizen at his home in Rockford, Illinois, or Boulder, Colorado, could read a newspaper, listen to a radio, or watch the round-the-clock coverage on television, but he had no way of connecting with those who shared his views. Nor was there a quick, readily available tool for an ordinary citizen to gather information on his own. In 1960, communication was a one-way street, and information was fundamentally inaccessible. The whole idea of summoning up data or reaching thousands of individuals with the touch of a finger was a science-fiction fantasy. The mass media world was, as one observer defined it, the "simultaneous transmission to anonymous multitudes," and what those multitudes heard was that the men who governed America had charted a course designed to bring us through the horror that was John Kennedy's death.

MEASURED PURELY BY civic calculations, the elevation of Lyndon Johnson and Hubert Humphrey went as smoothly as possible. On December 16, the day after Johnson's speech to the Joint Session of Congress, 535 electors gathered at the fifty state capitols. One hundred Kennedy electors voted for Johnson for President; two hundred of them, along with seventy-five Nixon electors, voted for Hubert Humphrey for Vice President after Richard Nixon publicly urged them to do so (Senator Eugene McCarthy of Minnesota, known for a wicked wit that spared no one but himself, offered a paraphrase of Shakespeare: "Nothing in Nixon's political life became him like the leaving of it—we may devoutly hope").

On January 3, the new Congress gathered in joint session to tabulate the results. In a thoroughly choreographed sequence, Speaker Rayburn and Senate Minority Leader Dirksen rose to suggest that Kennedy's electoral votes should not be counted, on the ground that electors could not legitimately choose a dead person. The session promptly recessed; the members of the Senate and House retreated to their respective chambers; and they returned an hour later to report that the members had agreed to the objection. With Kennedy's votes discounted—and with furious objections from freshman Congressman (and John Birch Society member) John Rousselot gaveled out of order, the presiding officer, Vice President Nixon, declared that no candidate had received an electoral majority for President. The House of Representatives would decide the matter, with each state having one vote, determined by a majority of each state's delegation. (Nixon also invoked "a point of personal privilege" to offer up a tribute to the wisdom of the Founding Fathers, and to rework a line from Jefferson's first Inaugural address: "Today, we are all Democrats; we are all Republicans." Reporters promptly dubbed it "the opening speech of the 1964 campaign.")

That same evening, meeting in an extraordinary evening session, the House of Representatives voted to make Johnson President. From a hundred microphones, a thousand typewriters, came the same invocation: "The system worked!"

Unfortunately, the resilience of a late-eighteenth-century political mechanism no more measured what was happening in America than would an effective plumbing system in a house infected by the plague . . . in this case, a contagion of the spirit.

"A melancholy has settled on our land," wrote *New York Times* columnist James Reston the Sunday after the electors had met, and if the prose was tinged purple, the sentiment was sadly accurate. The ascension of John Kennedy had a consciously generational cast; the oldest President would be succeeded by the youngest ever elected, who had promised "a new generation of leadership"; a frail septuagenarian with a wife out of a Helen Hokinson *New Yorker* cartoon replaced by a President and a First Lady who could stir sexual fantasies; the World War II commanding general succeeded by one of the thirteen million who served under him in that war. Surrounding the forty-three-year-old onetime naval officer had been a corporal's guard of impossibly young men: His campaign manager–brother was thirty-four; his closest advisor was thirty-two; his press secretary was thirty-five; his *de facto* Chief of Staff was thirty-six. Beyond the statistics was the sound of a new generation coming to power. A photo that appeared just after the election had captured John, Bobby, and Ted, all toothy grins and compact bodies, a virility that all but crackled.

And now that was gone, obliterated in an instant of smoke and fire. Lyndon Johnson and his colleagues had done all that could have been asked of them to bring a measure of reassurance to the country, their work had brought them praise from editorial pages across the country, and from the men who sat at anchor desks, and in offices and coffee shops and at family gatherings, the conversation was filled with such sentiments: *Thank goodness the country's in good, responsible hands.* What Johnson and his colleagues could not do was to ease the palpable emptiness of the spirit, a sense that something important, something of limitless possibility, had been lost. Lyndon Johnson was fifty-two, young by Presidential standards, but there was nothing young about him at all. His face, with cheeks and jaw descending like a basset hound, his $400 custom-made suits, the senators who surrounded him (young men did not become Congressional leaders; you made it through seniority, so those around him in the pictures and TV news film were in their sixties, seventies, eighties), all reflected solemnity, gravitas. The idea of Lyndon Johnson throwing a football or skippering a sailboat or tussling with a child at a backyard barbecue was almost literally inconceivable. He was a man born for back rooms; chandeliered, wood-paneled offices thick with the smell of tobacco and whiskey, filled with men of furrowed brows and whispers behind hands that covered mouths. It was not his fault, he had done all that anyone could ask of someone thrown into such uncharted waters; but the very fact that he, Lyndon Johnson, was there, was about to step into John Kennedy's job, seemed in itself evidence that something had gone wrenchingly, horribly wrong.

At a meeting in mid-December of Kennedy's campaign staff, Dick Goodwin wordlessly passed out copies of a quotation from T. E. Lawrence, better known as Lawrence of Arabia. It read:

> We lived many lives in those swirling campaigns, never sparing ourselves any good or evil; yet when we had achieved and the new world dawned, the old men came out again, and took from us our victory, and remade it in the likeness of the former world they knew. Youth could win, but had not learned to keep, and was pitiably weak

against age. We stammered that we had worked for a new heaven, and a new earth, and they thanked us kindly, and made their peace.

It quickly found its way into Mary McGrory's *Washington Post* column. "Goddamnit!" Johnson exploded when he read the quote, "I didn't take a damn thing away from Jack. He wouldn't have won without me! A lunatic blew him up!" But for countless men and women of Kennedy's generation, it seemed to say everything. Indeed, Johnson's senatorial office and the Democratic National Committee both reported a steady stream of telephone calls from around the country, asking that their applications for jobs in the new administration be returned. The idea of picking up stakes and setting out to conquer the New Frontier suddenly seemed a lot less appealing.

Even the weather conspired against the nation's spirits. That vicious winter snowstorm that had hit the Northeast on the day John Kennedy was murdered kept tens of millions snowbound in their homes, unable to escape outdoors to relieve the grief pouring into their living rooms from their televisions. It stayed unusually cold throughout December all through the East and Midwest, and in mid-December, the steady encroachment of darkness by mid-afternoon fed and reflected the national mood. And, of course, it was the Christmas season; so the holly and the decorations, the displays in department store windows, the carols and seasonal songs on the radio, had an almost mocking quality. If you said "Merry Christmas!" to a passerby on the street, you were more than likely to be answered with pursed lips and a slow shake of the head.

On New Year's Eve, the crowds that usually jammed New York's Times Square and the downtowns of dozens of other cities were little more than dispirited clumps of indifferent celebrants. Even the frenzy that normally surrounded the climax of National Football League season was affected; when the Philadelphia Eagles met the Green Bay Packers at Franklin Field for the championship (pushed back to early January to make up for the games canceled on the day Kennedy had died), the game began with a moment of silence for Kennedy, and the halftime ceremonies were dedicated to his memory.

There was, curiously, one exception to the sense of numbed indifference.

Just a few days before Kennedy's murder, a new musical had opened on Broadway, written by the Lerner-Loewe team that had created *My Fair Lady*. It starred Julie Andrews and Richard Burton, and was set in the court of King Arthur: *Camelot*, it was called. While the reviews were mixed, the audience responded to the doomed romance of Guinevere and Sir Lancelot with an intensity that astonished the show's creators; audiences routinely wept as if at a funeral, then cheered for endless minutes.

"It's almost like a catharsis," director Moss Hart said, "as if they were seeing a mythical version of what's been taken from them." That catharsis, unfortunately, was limited to a few thousand people a night in a single Manhattan theatre. For the rest of the country, the aftermath of the killing infected the spirit. Elvis Presley's "Are You Lonesome Tonight?" a top-selling single the week Kennedy was killed, now took on a far more consequential meaning; it was played incessantly on the radio—almost as much as Ferlin Husky's "Wings of a Dove" (". . . He sends His pure, sweet love / A sign from Above / On the wings of a Dove"). Toward year's end, a new song began receiving major airplay on the nation's top forty AM radio stations that then dominated the airwaves. The Kingston Trio, among the most popular acts in the increasingly popular folk song genre, had recorded a song called "The New Frontier" just days before Kennedy's death, a rousing anthem celebrating what had become the candidate's catchphrase. The release was canceled, and replaced by the Trio's reworking of an old Irish anti-war song, "Johnnie, We Hardly Knew Ye." Its dirge-like melody in a minor key, and its mournful lyrics only thickened the funereal atmosphere of the holidays. ("We were marching out to the New Frontier / Now all we can do is shed a tear / And weep that you're no longer here / Johnnie, we hardly knew ye.")

The impact of the murder was not confined to matters of the spirit. The mood and the weather combined to heavily dampen the gift-giving frenzy of the season. Retailers reported a 35 percent drop in sales, taking a measurable bite out of the economy. For some enterprises, the death of Kennedy was a special blow. Viking Publishers had signed up a British-born writer named Ian Fleming, who had authored a series of spy thrillers featuring a dashing, debonair secret agent named James Bond. The Bond books had never sold well in the United States, but a Viking executive had picked up a rumor that John Kennedy was a special fan of the series. "If we can get that word out, it's going to be a gold mine!" a Viking marketing executive exulted. After Kennedy's murder, little was heard of Fleming or James Bond again. A New York stand-up comedian named Vaughn Meader, who had begun to gain notice with his pitch-perfect impression of Kennedy, saw his bookings canceled within days of the killing.

This was the climate in which Lyndon Johnson put together his Cabinet and his White House staff. He began with a blend of prudence and audacity. He would, of course, keep J. Edgar Hoover at the FBI and Alan Dulles at CIA—Kennedy had announced those decisions the day after his election, and there was no reason to roil those waters—and he kept McNamara at Defense and Dillon at Treasury. Putting two Republicans at those posts was exactly the right signal to send to Wall Street and the world. But for Secretary of State? The *Washington Post* had leaked the impending selection of Dean Rusk the very Sunday Kennedy was murdered, but for Johnson, the former career diplomat turned Rockefeller Foundation President was a symbol of the past. He knew whom he wanted in the job; he'd lobbied JFK hard to pick Arkansas Senator J. William Fulbright.

"Johnson and Fulbright were 'backyard pals' and Fulbright had a reputation in academia and the press as a big-time thinker, sagacious," recalled longtime Johnson aide Harry McPherson, and Kennedy was leaning toward the idea. But Kennedy's liberal advisors like Harris Swofford had persuaded Kennedy to reject Fulbright because of the race problem; Fulbright, along with almost every other Southern senator, had signed the infamous 1954 "Southern Manifesto" opposing the Supreme Court's decision outlawing school segregation. Kennedy couldn't see how Fulbright could succeed when the U.S.–Soviet competition for friends in Africa and Asia was so intense. Fulbright said as much to Johnson when he was offered the appointment.

"Now let's take a look at the way things will play out," LBJ told Fulbright. "When I go out and announce you for State, who's going to be standing right by my side? Hubert Humphrey, my Vice President, and there's no better friend the Negroes have had in the Senate. And when I announce you, somebody else is going to be named right with you: Congressman William Dawson, from Illinois. I need a Postmaster General with good political smarts, just like Roosevelt had with Jim Farley. And I have to think that Roy Wilkins and Whitney Young just might want to be in that room when the first Negro ever is named to the Cabinet."

He failed in his Cabinet hopes only once, when he tried to persuade Washington lawyer Abe Fortas to become Attorney General. No one was closer to Johnson than Fortas, who'd been at his side from his 1948 Senate race, when Fortas had persuaded his old friend Supreme Court Justice Hugo Black to put Johnson's name back on the ballot after a federal judge had invalidated Johnson's 87-vote primary victory. And no Cabinet post was more sensitive, involving as it did decisions about which powerful companies and individuals to prosecute, which investigative roads the Justice Department and the FBI should or should not travel.

"I can't do it," Fortas told Johnson flatly. "Caroline [Agger, his wife and fellow lawyer] would make my life a living hell if I found myself working for $22,000 a year."

It was when Johnson turned to the White House staff that the full dimensions of what he would face came into sharp, stark focus. He knew he wanted his own team around him—Busby, McPherson, Jim Rowe—but he also knew he had to have some of Jack's men, too. For one thing, they were simply better than his guys; hadn't they proved that in the 1960 campaign? So he called in Kennedy's team—O'Donnell, Sorensen, O'Brien, Salinger—telling each of them, "I need you more than he did," but he knew as he did that it was a futile effort. They had driven Kennedy's campaign, but they had only begun to plan for his Presidency when he was killed. It wasn't as if they had been in the White House for two or three years, with staffs of their own, experience with the levers of power and a taste for the heady life that came from being on the inside. What they had done, in fact, was to run a campaign against Johnson for the nomination; and no one knew better than Johnson that intra-party grudges die hard. Ted Sorensen agreed to help him with the Inaugural, and the others promised to think about it, but none of them seemed to be able to look him in the eye. He chalked it up to grief, until he asked Robert Kennedy to come to his office for a conversation in early January, and he got his first glimpse of what was in his Presidential future.

They met in Johnson's seven-office suite that occupied the entire northwest Senate wing on the Capitol's third floor. Kennedy glanced at the crystal chandelier, the frescoes on the ceiling of boys carrying baskets of flowers, young maidens reclining on couches; a Roman emperor's banquet, the life-sized portrait of Johnson that hung over the mantel fireplace. Once they entered LBJ's inner office, the two sat facing each other; Johnson, half a foot taller than Bobby, leaned forward, chin on hand, elbow resting on his knee, his face inches from Kennedy. *I know we got off on the wrong foot,* Johnson began, *and I know we said things about each other that we might like to take back, but this isn't about us. It's about the country. I need you here, by my side, fighting for what Jack wanted. There's no job, no position, you can't have.*

He said this knowing that the idea of Robert Kennedy as Attorney General would threaten a mass outbreak of cardiac arrest among his political supporters and campaign contributors. But as he talked, as his jabbing finger grew closer to Kennedy's chest, he told Kennedy, "I want us to leave this room and announce you'll be here, working for his ideas every day. There's a room full of reporters waiting, and I'd like it very much if we could come to an agreement about what you'll be doing to fight for all those ideas." The younger man put up his hand and shook his head.

"That's not going to happen, Lyndon. I'm going back to Massachusetts to take Jack's Senate seat. The family's decided this." There was a long moment of silence as Johnson glared at Kennedy, as if he could will Bobby to un-speak the words.

"You mean your father's decided this," Johnson finally said.

"I think you've said more than enough about my father," Bobby replied. "But we don't need to have an argument about this. When Joe Jr. was killed in the war, Jack took his place; I'm going to take his. I don't know if I'm cut out to be a senator . . . from what I saw on the Labor Rackets Committee, it's a lot of nice words and angry words and more words. But I'll have two years to decide that. For now, I think that's where I belong, and I hope I can be helpful to you there. Besides, Lyndon"—everyone else was already calling him "Mr. President," but the runt was still acting as if his big brother were going to be running things—"you need your own people with you. It wouldn't be fair to you to have you surrounded with people you don't know, and who don't know you. If you'd like, we can meet the press together, and you can tell them this is what you've encouraged me to do. Or if you'd rather, I won't say anything right now, and we'll make the announcement back in Boston."

They chatted inconsequentially for a few minutes more, so that the reporters staking out the Senate would not write that their conversation had only lasted a few minutes, that something must have gone awry. But as they talked about federal aid to education, and a health care plan for the elderly, and help for the impoverished of Appalachia, Johnson could only think of one thing: *A goddamn government in exile, that's what Bobby's going to have here. And that's why all his people couldn't look me in the eye when I asked them to join me; they knew goddamn well they were all going with Bobby.* And the next morning, Robert Kennedy stood on the steps of the state capitol in Boston, surrounded by Jackie, Ethel, Ted, Eunice, Jean, Joe, and Rose, and announced that he was accepting Governor Furcolo's appointment. Furcolo and the Kennedys ardently disliked each other; John had actually backed his opponent, commenting that "sometimes party asks too much," but if the soon-to-be ex-governor Furcolo had refused to appoint Bobby, he'd have been lynched. And Johnson stood before the microphones and cameras in Washington and welcomed the appointment, said he was looking forward to Kennedy's voice and vision in the Senate, to his wise counsel in helping Johnson make John Kennedy's dreams a reality, and he almost choked on the words.

"Rematch?" the tabloid headlines screamed the next day, and "Bobby in '64?" Within forty-eight hours of Bobby's announcement, T-shirts were in the window of Times Square and Washington, D.C., tourist shops, picturing John Kennedy in heaven gazing down on his brother.

All through that season, Lyndon Johnson worked the phones, summoned the leaders of business, labor, education, agriculture, huddled with governors, senators, leaders of the House, Democratic Party chieftains who still controlled big-city machines and state organizations in New Jersey, Indiana, Missouri. In these counsels he was as masterful as he had been as the Senate's puppet master. Yes, they told him, they would heed his pleas for forbearance, they would not press their demands too insistently. Yes, said Roy Wilkins and Whitney Young, they would do all they could to damp down the passions of the young Negro firebrands, the John Lewises who were threatening to board intercity buses in the North to challenge the segregation that was in place in the South. Yes, the Chamber of Commerce said, they understood he'd be pushing for federal aid to education and medical care for old folks, and they'd try to turn down the thermostat when they fought him; surely they knew he had their interests at heart, he was the best friend business could have in the White House. Yes, labor leaders said, they knew Lyndon had to watch the budget, had to work with hawkeyed scrooges like Wilbur Mills and Howard Smith, men who ran their committees like absolute monarchs; yes, he'd fight for a higher minimum wage, but it couldn't be that much higher—hell, they had to know he was the best friend labor could have in the White House (hadn't he learned all he had to know about the fat cats and bankers from his granddaddy, who'd taught him, "They lived off our sweat and even before airconditioning, they didn't know what sweat was. They just clipped coupons and wrote down debentures we couldn't spell and stole our pants out from under us"?).

It was his playing field, this inside game, and no one did it better. The problem, as the Inauguration approached, was that the Presidency wasn't an inside game, or at least, not only an inside game. He'd had a taste of that when he'd gone up against Kennedy for the nomination, relying on his allies in the Senate to deliver him the delegates, but it was as if those delegates were listening to a message he could neither deliver nor even hear, so that when he matched his experience, his legislative triumphs, his masterful ability to guide a bill through Congress like a riverboat captain who knew every sandbar and current on the Mississippi, and matched it against the thin-gruel record of a show horse running on his good looks and his daddy's money, the people who made the decisions had simply tuned him out, put him aside like yesterday's paper. And now, as he used all of his skills to hold the fragile country together, as he pleaded and promised and cautioned and maybe even threatened a bit, as public opinion polls reported stratospherically high approval ratings, he sensed—no, he knew—that at some primal level he was not connecting.

A big part of the problem was television. By 1960, the medium had come to full maturity, had come in fact to domination over the political process. Johnson had seen it take hold back in '52 when Eisenhower's backers had watched on TV as the convention, wired for conservative hero

Bob Taft, began to roll over Ike's delegate challenges; they then swamped the convention with telegrams until the party wheel horses surrendered, gave the disputed delegations, and thus the nomination, to Ike.

He'd seen Richard Nixon a few months later, his Vice Presidential nomination hanging by a thread amid charges of financial chicanery, go on TV for a half hour, talking not of bills or proposals, but of his savings accounts, his mortgage, his wife's cloth coat, his kids' dog, for God's sakes. And it had worked; this personal, face-to-face appeal had saved his career, and this past November he'd damn near won the White House. And he'd seen John Kennedy, with his angular face, his incandescent smile, his modulated voice and gestures, coolly project the image of a thoughtful, mature leader. It was a medium made for Kennedy; for Johnson, it was a nemesis. The intense lights deepened the furrows on his face, emphasized the jowls, enveloped him with a sense of weight, gloom, authority (visitors who met him for the first time in person were invariably struck by how handsome, how electric he was). In part, his trouble with the medium was a case of self-inflicted wounds. He was in face-to-face conversation animated, funny, acute. But he did not trust himself on the tube, thought he came off as vulgar, an uneducated rube. So he measured out his words . . . slowly . . . ponderously. It reeked of insincerity, which only deepened his self-consciousness, which only turned his public persona into the sort of stuffed-up, pompous political figure that had been the object of ridicule going back to Will Rogers, Mark Twain, Artemus Ward.

On January 4, 1961, the day after the new Congress had made it official, President-elect Johnson sat down in front of television cameras for an unprecedented conversation carried on all three networks. Negotiations over the ground rules were intense; one network executive said later, "It'd have been a lot easier if Khrushchev and Mao had been on the other side of the table." Johnson's emissary, the advertising and public relations man Jack Valenti, flatly rejected live coverage. Eisenhower's press conferences were never broadcast live, he argued, and for good reason; there was no way the President-elect was going to risk the consequences of an untoward word ("Don't you think the Russians will be watching?" Valenti said). He also insisted on final approval before letting the tape of the interview hit the airwaves ("What happens if you say no?" an NBC executive asked.

"Have Perry Como on standby," Valenti said). They bickered about how long it should be. Was an hour too brief? Was two hours too long? And they fought for days about where to do the interview. Johnson's pasha-like Senate offices? No, he was the President-elect, and a Senate setting would diminish him. A television studio? Worse—he was the incoming leader of the free world, not some TV pitchman. Well, the White House, then. No, he wasn't yet the President; that would be arrogant. Don Hewitt, a young CBS producer who had supervised the Nixon-Kennedy debates, broke the impasse by suggesting Blair House, the town house just across the street from the White House, where world leaders sometimes stayed, and where incoming Presidents slept the night before they were inaugurated. He also resolved the issue of length: "Sixty minutes," Hewitt said, "would be perfect."

But who would sit down with the President-elect? Television may have come into its own by 1960, but Lyndon Johnson's feet were planted squarely in an earlier era, where the newspaper columnist was king; they were the men whose words were read all around the country, digested over breakfast by anyone who mattered. Maybe Ed Murrow was in their class, but he was leaving CBS to run the U.S. Information Agency, a leaving made inevitable after the man who owned CBS, Bill Paley, had publicly emasculated him when Murrow had dared to slap the industry in public for its greed (on Election Night 1958, Murrow, the man who had brought Americans the news from London every night during the Blitz, the man who had challenged Joe McCarthy at the height of his power, was banished from the anchor desk, perched on a catwalk, reporting returns from a wall display). And even if you could get Murrow, you'd then have to have men from the other networks, and Lyndon Johnson wasn't about to sit down with David Brinkley, the NBC smart-ass who palled around with the Kennedys and who had called Lyndon's whistle-stop tour "the Cornpone Special," words that had come straight from Hyannis Port. So on that January night, Johnson sat down with James Reston of the *Times* and Walter Lippmann of the *Post*, with Howard K. Smith from CBS moderating the conversation, a TV man chosen by lot. The questions were respectful, even deferential, and Johnson spoke only in the broadest of generalities. Was the conflict between America and Russia basically irreconcilable?

"I've always believed," he said, with an attempt at a beatific smile, "that the hopes and dreams of a man who tills the soil are about the same whether he lives on the banks of the Colorado or on the banks of the Danube."

And what about the challenges here at home, about which John Kennedy had spoken throughout the campaign? Here Johnson sounded a very different note. "I've always thought," he said, "that what the man in the street wants is not a big debate on fundamental issues. He wants a little medical care, a rug on the floor, a picture on the wall, a little music in the house, and a place to take Molly and the grandchildren when he retires."

The reviews were fine, the editorial pages of the papers all pretty much struck the same note: that the country should be grateful that in these trying times, after the terrible trauma of Kennedy's violent death, we had a sober, experienced man at the nation's helm. But at some primal level, Johnson could sense that, while the people were reassured, while they knew he was fully capable of managing the government, while they respected him, he simply did not inspire affection, warmth, emulation, aspiration.

LATE ON the freezing cold morning of January 20, 1961, the dignitaries began to gather on the steps of the Capitol's East Front for the inauguration of Lyndon Johnson. Eight inches of snow had fallen the night before, paralyzing the city, turning the streets impassable, marooning hundreds of motorists, shutting down National Airport. By morning the temperature was 22 degrees, and the eighteen-mile-per-hour wind gusts made it feel more like zero. It was the kind of weather that had killed William Henry Harrison in 1841 (he'd come down with pneumonia after giving the longest Inaugural speech in history). Had it been a normal Inaugural, the weather would have created a social disaster, with dozens of parties and dinners canceled. But this was no normal Inaugural; for many of the Democrats who would have come to celebrate Kennedy's triumph, the whole idea of ball gowns and tuxedos, dance orchestras and champagne dinners, was too jarring after the two months unlike any they had lived through. Indeed, the Inaugural Eve snowstorm itself was a cruel joke of fate, invoking the storm that had hit the capital the day John Kennedy was killed. There would be dinners and dances later that night—the world had to know that America wasn't in some kind of comatose state, that it could mark the beginning of a new Presidency with pomp and circumstance—but among the powerful assembling on the Capitol steps the mood was dutiful, not joyous.

Shortly after noon, Lyndon Johnson and his wife, Lady Bird, stepped out of the Rotunda and made their way to their seats. The night before, he'd gathered at the White House with Eisenhower and former Presidents Harry Truman and Herbert Hoover—as strong a signal of continuity as could be mustered. Now, as he sat in the January chill, he glanced through the Inaugural address one last time and reassured himself that he and his speechwriters had made the right decision. He'd asked Sorensen to send him the drafts of what was to be Kennedy's Inaugural, and Ted had agreed, but had warned, "I'm not sure this is a good fit." And as soon as he read it, Johnson saw that Sorensen was right. It wasn't just the cadence, with its metered, almost poetic rhythm and high-flown language ("now the trumpet summons us again . . ."); it was that the whole theme was framed around Kennedy himself. Why, that language right near the beginning— "the torch has been passed to a new generation of Americans"—couldn't possibly come out of the mouth of a man whose personality and character so clearly marked him as one of the old generation of leaders. And he knew he could never deliver that climactic call: "Ask not what your country can do for you; ask what you can do for your country." Johnson's whole public life was rooted in what *he* could do *for* the people: bringing electricity into their farms and homes, roads into their towns, books into their schools.

So after Reverend Billy Graham delivered the invocation, Chief Justice Earl Warren delivered the oath, and the Marine Band played "Hail to the Chief," Johnson delivered a speech that walked a fine line between the rhetorical demands of an Inaugural and his own nature.

"We gather under brilliant sunshine this day, but a shadow lies across our hearts," he began.

"It is fitting and proper that we mourn the loss of the man we chose to lead us, but it is from John Kennedy's own words that we will find solace and strength. On this winter's day, we remember what he said on a summer night: 'We are not here to curse the darkness; we are here to light a candle.' He invoked the scriptural admonition to 'be strong, and of good courage; be not afraid [nor] discouraged.'

"For a hundred and seventy years, this nation has met every challenge to its future; we won our freedom from the most powerful empire on earth; we healed from the conflict at home that tore us from each other; we overcame economic calamity that threw millions into poverty; conquered a madman's lust for conquest that enveloped the world into war. Today, as we struggle to preserve peace and freedom in a dangerous world, we make this promise to John Kennedy: We will not succumb to the temptation to yield to our grief."

He took a few lines from Sorensen's draft, shaping them to his simpler style ("We will not negotiate out of fear, but we'll never be afraid to negotiate"), and added a pointed reference to civil rights. After warning America's allies to stay united because "a house divided against itself cannot stand, and the house of freedom must not fall," he turned toward home and said, "We cannot claim to be defenders of freedom around the world if millions here at home are denied the fruits of freedom because of the color of their skin."

It was by far the boldest statement any incoming President had ever made about the race issue, and it would have been the dominant story of the day . . . except that the moment that galvanized the country, the photo that was on the front page of every paper in the country, was the image of Senator Robert F. Kennedy, seated on the Inaugural platform next to Jacqueline Kennedy, watching the ceremony with tears streaming down his face.

Later that night and into the next morning, as Johnson obsessively watched the TV coverage and scanned the morning papers, the conviction grew that would guide him through the rest of his Presidency.

"I took the oath," he told a confidant later. "I became President. But for millions of Americans, I was still illegitimate, a naked man with no Presidential covering, a pretender to the throne, an illegal usurper . . . and then there were the bigots and the dividers, and the Eastern intellectuals, who were waiting to knock me down before I could even begin to stand up."

From that first day, Lyndon Johnson was determined to win not just the respect of the country, but its love; he would show them, the Harvards, the snobs, the smug Georgetown set, that a poor boy from the hardscrabble world of southwest Texas, using the skills he had mastered over a lifetime, could deliver more, far more, than a manufactured hero. He knew every lever of influence and how to pull it; he could sense the strength and weakness of every man he'd ever met; and by the time his Presidency was done, he would have done more, given more to the American people than anyone since FDR . . . and by then, they would learn to love him.

And for a while, it seemed to work.

HE KNEW IT as surely as he knew the contours of the land where he was born, as surely as he'd known the men he'd led in the Senate: at the heart of what ailed the country, at the heart of his own ambitions for himself and his region, was race. It was what divided the South from the rest of America; it was for almost every politician from the South both sail and anchor. You played on the deepest fears of whites and rode those currents into office, but you could never really hope for the ultimate prize; you were held fast by the chains of color. Even as he had abandoned his youthful liberalism when he sought the Texas Senate seat in '48, he'd always believed that the real hope for his region—and his Democratic Party—was to bring the black man and the white working man together. He loved to tell the story of the Southern politician who mused, "Just once before I die I'd like to go home and hear a real Democratic speech. All they ever hear down there now is 'nigra, nigra, nigra.'"

And the way to do that, Johnson knew, was with the vote. He understood the Negro hunger for respect; he'd watched the Montgomery, Alabama, boycott in '55 bring a whole colored community together risking jail, the loss of jobs, enduring the physical burdens of walking miles a day so as not to patronize segregated buses, elevating a young preacher to national prominence. He'd seen the sit-ins take root in '60, beginning in February, when four students at North Carolina A & T walked into an F. W. Woolworth's in Greensboro, North Carolina, bought school supplies, then sat down at the segregated lunch counter and tried to order Cokes. It was a brilliant tactic: the Negro boys and girls dressed in their Sunday best, sitting quietly at the counter, reading their textbooks, while a gaggle of slack-jawed white boys cursed them, doused them with ketchup and mustard. By late spring, the sit-ins had spread to dozens of cities, and in the

North, sympathizers were picketing the Woolworth's from New York to Los Angeles. The national chains were starting to feel the heat.

And yet, Johnson knew that at some level, the demand for respect at the lunch counter was touching the exposed nerve of the Southern white: *You let them sit next to you, and the next thing you know, they'll be in your schools, showering with your sons, threatening your daughters.* There was no telling where this fear might lead, what response it would produce, but his own fear deepened in 1961, on the day after his Inaugural, when seven blacks and six whites boarded Greyhound and Trailways buses in Washington, D.C., bound for points throughout the South, where they intended to challenge the segregated seating in Southern bus terminals. In Alabama, mobs of whites organized by Police Commissioner Bull Connor and Sergeant Tom Cook savagely beat the protesters in Anniston, and then in Birmingham, as FBI agents stood and watched. The next day, Johnson called Vice President Humphrey to the Oval Office. "I'm telling you, this is the wrong goddamn fight! Never mind that it's giving us a black eye all over the world; never mind that God knows how many Africans will see those pictures and decide, hell, maybe the Russians have a better idea. Never mind that some of those riders almost died. They're aiming at the wrong target.

"Yes, Hubert," he said, "I want all those things—buses, restaurants, all of that—but the right to vote, with no ifs, ands, or buts, that's the key. When the Negroes get that, they'll have every politician, north and south, east and west, kissing their asses, begging for their support."

No one knew better than Johnson that getting a voting rights bill through the Congress was just about impossible. You could get it through the House of Representatives—that was a cinch; civil rights bills had passed any number of times, where the majority could do pretty much what it wanted. But the Senate was designed to slow things down—"the saucer in which you pour your coffee to cool it," George Washington had said of it—and in 1961, Southern senators held a death grip on key committees, and had long ago mastered the rules of the chamber, where you could talk a bill to death unless two-thirds of the chamber voted to stop it, and where a single senator could bring the whole enterprise to a screeching halt. In '57, he'd steered a civil rights bill through the Senate, the first since

Reconstruction, but it was largely for show, and it accomplished almost nothing. It was supposed to help Negroes vote, but in 1960, fewer blacks had voted in the South than they had in '56. So what to do? He found the answer in a favorite tactic of his idol, FDR. Whenever Eleanor would bring his liberal friends to the White House to complain about the slow pace of action, Roosevelt would always tell them the same thing: *You have to put some pressure on me.*

So two days after the first "Freedom Rides" had ended in violence, he placed a series of calls to the NAACP's Roy Wilkins, the Urban League's Whitney Young, and to the young preacher Martin Luther King.

"I need you to come to Washington and start civil-righting," he began every call bluntly. And he laid out exactly what he had in mind, as though he'd been studying three-dimensional chess—which, in a sense, he had been doing all his life.

"It's like I said to you right after Jack Kennedy was killed," he reminded King. "You win the vote, and everything else falls right into place. You can take the most bigoted man from Mississippi, the man who's sure that if a Negro drinks a cup of coffee next to his wife, he'll be raping her by sundown, but if you ask him if he really thinks it's fair that a man can't vote for his President or his congressman because he was born with black skin, he's gonna stop and swallow hard"—Johnson gulped a couple of times at this point—"and he'll be rocked back on his heels. And the way I need you to come down here and fight for that vote is with the biggest march this town has ever seen. Your man Bayard Rustin said it back in '59: 'If a hundred thousand people come to Washington, the President will meet with its leaders and the Congress will sit in special session.' He was right: You need a march so big you'll scare the daylights out of Washington. Hell, I might have to say something about my concern about disruption and violence. And you need your speakers to beat me up a bit, too."

His message to Wilkins and Young had a slight variation. *You know what they're saying, the young Turks in Harlem and Chicago, and in the colored colleges all over the South: they're saying you're over the hill; they need new blood. You and I know it's not true; hell, you've done more for the race than any fifty people I know. Reverend King has the newspapers and the magazine covers and the TV cameras, but you've got your friends in labor and business who can make this happen. And maybe you can show the young Turks what a couple of old tigers can do.*

Within a week, a civil rights coalition announced plans for a major demonstration at the Lincoln Memorial to take place in April 1961, with a single demand: the right to vote. The younger, more militant wing of the civil rights movement was torn between tepid support of the march and a determination to continue the freedom rides across the South. In public, President Johnson expressed pro forma support for the right of demonstrators to come to Washington, but cautioned the organizers to avoid any words and deeds that might create an atmosphere where violence or disruption might occur, and urged officials and private citizens alike to avoid any acts of provocation. In private, he offered a very different view to Special Assistant Bill Moyers.

"Every time Bull Connor cracks a head open, every time Huntley and Brinkley put on a picture of a well-dressed colored boy with blood on his white shirt, I'm one step closer to a voting bill I can pass. Now, I don't want to see anyone die on one of those buses, but I think I know something about the way the world works, and I don't know that there's ever been a revolution without a martyr or two."

He pressed the point to one of his closest confidants, CBS president Frank Stanton, whose frequent visits to the White House rarely showed up on the official visitors' log.

"You need to put those pictures on the news every day, they're the biggest leverage I have. I know your stations in the South will black out those stories, but that's not where it matters—we need the people all over the country to see what's going on, so they'll start yelling at their senators to do something about it."

And when those images showed up night after night on the network news, when the AP and UPI pictures of bloody beatings hit the newspaper front pages—Johnson had quietly brokered sit-down interviews with Washington correspondents in return for the coverage—the President used the very images he had lobbied for when he called in the Southern senators for Oval Office conferences.

"I wonder," he began, "how many of you are planning to send money to the Communist Party of Russia, so they can pay their stooges in Europe and Africa and South America to poison the people against the United States. Of course you wouldn't do that, there's no group of men in the Congress more against the Communists than you." His face turned sorrowful, his chin almost grazing his neck. "And do any of you want me going off to meet with Khrushchev with a weight on my shoulders so heavy I could barely walk into the room? I know you don't want to bear me down with that weight. But you have to know that every time Adlai stands up at the UN and starts talking to the Russians about freedom, they just hold up something like this"—he threw the front page of the *Washington Post* on the table in front of his chair—"and just laugh in our face. We're in a death struggle with the Communists—you know, they have a whole university in Moscow, where they bring young people in from every country in Africa and Asia and God knows where else, to teach them why they should sign up with the Communists. And this"—he slammed his fist down on the front page of the *Post* with enough force to rattle the coffee cups—"is their biggest goddamn argument. 'If you were American,' the Communists tell those Africans, 'you wouldn't be allowed to vote in your own country. And if you tried, you'd be killed.'"

"If those outside agitators and their left-wing friends in the press—" Senator John McClellan of Arkansas began.

"I know all about those agitators," Johnson interrupted. "I get memos from Edgar Hoover every day. You think I don't know what they're up to, them and the press? You think I don't know they want to embarrass me and my Presidency, make me out to be a redneck rube, prove a man from the South has no business in this office, so that Bobby has a reason to go against me? But that's not what's at stake here. I know what you need to do to make the folks at home happy, but I want you to know that I'm going to do what I have to do. I'm under tremendous pressure from the fire breathers to do a Second Reconstruction—I mean, they want me to put troops in every bus station and five-and-dime south of the Potomac. I'm trying as hard as I know how to keep them on the fight for the vote, so maybe we can keep the pressure off the lunch counters and the public swimming pools."

When the gathering ended, he motioned Georgia's Richard Russell to stay behind. Johnson sat down across from him, close enough so that their knees grazed each other.

54　　　　　　　　　JEFF GREENFIELD

"I want you to know, Dick," the President said to the man he'd treated as a father in his years in the Senate, "I'm not going to compromise on this. If I have to, I'm going to run right over you."

"You may do that," Russell said. "But by God it's going to cost you the South and the election."

"So be it," Johnson said. "But if I don't do it, you'll be running on a ticket in '64 with Hubert, or maybe Bobby Kennedy at the top. There're Democrats from New York to California who can't wait to put one of their own in my place, and this is the only way to stop them."

If he was the stern but sympathetic voice of authority for his fellow Southern Democrats, he became a blend of Santa Claus and Uncle Sam when he came to deal with Ev Dirksen, the Republican Senate leader. Johnson didn't have to do the arithmetic; he'd lived it and breathed it every day. There were thirty-two Republicans in the Senate; he needed two dozen of them to break a filibuster. But for years, conservative Republicans and Southern Democrats had formed a powerful alliance of convenience— Southern Democrats blocking legislation to strengthen labor unions or increase social spending, Republicans standing with Southern Democrats to protect the filibuster on civil rights bills. If he could not bend Dirksen to his will, his audacious gamble would fail.

"I want you camped out in the Senate," Johnson told Vice President Humphrey. "I want you talking with Dirksen, buying him lunch, drinking with him" (when it was over, Humphrey told a friend, "I would have kissed Dirksen's ass on Main Street if I'd had to."). Through Humphrey, Johnson urged the more militant liberals—Phil Hart, Joe Clark, Bill Proxmire—to smother Dirksen with praise, seek out his counsel. Humphrey himself went on *Meet the Press* to call Dirksen "a great American, a patriotic American, who I know will do what is right."

But it was Johnson himself who took the lead with Dirksen, with a joint appeal to his political venality and his vanity. Every conversation they had in those months between the spring and fall of 1961 began with a favor: a patronage appointment, a judgeship, a few million dollars in the form of public works.

"You want that ambassadorship for your man?" Johnson asked Dirksen.

"Well, he's a good fellow," Dirksen said.

"I don't care if he's a good fellow; I want to know if you want him for that job. If I'm going to put a Republican in, I want to make damn sure he's your Republican."

For all that those favors meant to Dirksen—ambassadors and judges were known to disgorge campaign funds for their patrons, as did the industries that grew richer from the government contracts and public works— they paled next to the political and historical wonders Johnson laid out for Dirksen to imagine.

"You're a Republican from Illinois," Johnson said. "You stand for the right to vote, and you will be standing for the next hundred years right beside the first Republican from Illinois: Abe and Ev, the two great emancipators. You'll be on the cover of every liberal magazine in the country, and they'll be hanging your picture next to FDR in those sharecropper shacks from Macon to Hattiesburg. Hell, Ev, the only reason I'm sitting here instead of Nixon is that Jack and Bobby had the mother wit to call Dr. King and his wife when he was locked up in that county jail in Georgia. Jack and I took Pennsylvania with 2.5 percent. Michigan? Two point one percent. New Jersey? Eight-tenths of 1 percent. Illinois?

"I know, I know," Johnson said, waving Dirksen off, "but it wouldn't have been close enough to steal without the Negro vote. You stand up for the vote, bring those senators with you, and I'll be having to fight you tooth and nail for every Negro vote in '64. Now," he said, moving effortlessly from civic greatness to political calculation to a pointed reminder of indebtedness, "you've bled me for every last dollar the government has; my budget director is threatening to quit on me, 'cause I told him that river-dredging you wanted had to be funded. Now go on and do something for your party and your country."

All through the first weeks of his Presidency, Johnson was laying the ground for the battle that would come that autumn for the vote. He had no mandate from the electorate for the fight; nor he could he claim to be fulfilling the vision of the martyred Jack Kennedy, since Kennedy had said as little as possible about the civil rights struggle in his Senate years, and in his campaign. Hell, when Jack's aides had first reached out to Mrs. King after her husband had been jailed, Bobby had hit the roof, screaming at them that they had probably cost his brother the Presidency. Only later did

Bobby understand that it had turned enough of the Negro vote around to have won Kennedy the White House. But Johnson was reaching for every lever he could find, so he called Bobby to the White House for a conversation. After a desultory exchange about the Senate—Kennedy's frustration with the pace of the place was evident—Johnson got to the point.

"I want to make the voting rights bill a memorial to Jack," he said, "and I want you to be a principal sponsor, and I want you to help floor-manage it. I know you're not the master of the rules of the place, and we'll need some heavy lifting behind you on that, because Bobby Byrd and Sam Ervin can recite the rules in their sleep. But every time the people watch the news about the bill, I want them to think about Jack, about what they owe him for what happened. I'm sorry to put it that way, but it's gonna take guilt to get this through, and if they won't feel guilty about blocking a black man's path to the voting booth, then they have to sure as hell feel guilty about a young man who never got the chance to be President, never got the chance to see his kids grow up."

Johnson did not need a mind reader to understand what Bobby Kennedy was thinking as he looked up at the President. What kind of cynical son of a bitch would use the death of my brother to get a bill through the Congress? He also knew the one argument that would close the deal, it was the same as he'd told Dirksen: "When this bill passes, every Negro that walks into the courthouse to register will be thinking of Jack; his picture will be on every sharecropper's shack from Macon to Hattiesburg." And there was no way for Bobby to say anything but yes.

For all of Johnson's skill in working the machinery of inside leadership, it was a series of three interconnected events that brought the civil rights revolution of 1961 to fruition. The first was the March on Washington for the rights of Americans. On Saturday, June, 3, 1961, more than 150,000 marchers paraded through the streets of the capital from Union Station and the West Front of the Capitol, up Independence and Constitution Avenues, to the Lincoln Memorial.

There'd been pressure on the organizers about the focus of the march: The young leaders of the Student Non-Violent Coordinating Committee wanted a call for the immediate desegregation of all public facilities; labor leaders like George Meany and Walter Reuther, whose unions funneled tens of thousands of dollars into the March, were pushing for themes of economic justice: a higher minimum wage, medical care for the elderly. But the organizers of the March kept the focus on one single issue: the right to vote. The speeches had few words of praise for the President, who kept a public distance from the event he had birthed. In fact, Roy Wilkins and Whitney Young made pointed references to Johnson's record in the Senate. Martin Luther King, Jr., the thirty-one-year-old preacher who had helped organize the Montgomery, Alabama, bus boycott six years earlier, roused the crowd with a speech that invoked the words of America's founding document.

"Our nation was founded on the principle that 'life and liberty' are among the unalienable rights of every man. But in our own land, those who seek to exercise their liberty put their lives at risk. We proclaimed at our birth that 'taxation without representation is tyranny.' But that tyranny today binds down every citizen who walks through the courthouse door to pay his taxes, but finds that same door blocked with clubs and guns when he seeks to cast a ballot."

The live coverage of the March, coupled with footage of the violence against earlier civil rights demonstrations, dominated the news coverage that Saturday evening. But what happened the next morning turned a major news story into a national crisis. At 10:22 a.m., a few hours before a voter-registration organizing meeting was to begin, a bomb exploded under the steps of the Sixteenth Street Baptist Church in Birmingham, Alabama, ripping the building apart, killing four young girls who were attending Sunday school classes. The news reached the Negro leaders as they were sitting down to a post-march celebratory breakfast at the Willard Hotel in Washington. Roy Wilkins of the NAACP, often derided by more militant activists for his counsels of prudence, immediately sent off a telegram to President Johnson, warning that unless the federal government offers more than "picayune and piecemeal aid against this type of bestiality," Negroes will "employ such methods as our desperation may dictate in defense of the lives of our people." Had he waited a half hour, he would have saved himself the cost of delivering the telegram; at noon, the March leaders were summoned to the White House.

I will be making an announcement in an hour from the White House, the

President told them. *I want you standing behind me when I say what I have to say.* Before any of them could raise an objection—did they want to be "co-opted" by the President?—he told them what he was going to say, and they agreed without a moment's hesitation. His message was short and direct: He was summoning the Congress into special session in seventy-two hours. He wanted them back from vacations, fact-finding trips to Europe, business meetings, or anything else. If necessary, he would ask the Congress—"ask" in the case of President Johnson was a laughingly inadequate verb—to order the sergeant-at-arms to bring the members to the Congress by force. This was, he said, nothing less than a national emergency.

The Speech—that's what it was labeled in the months that followed, simply "The Speech"—was less than fifteen minutes long. "I am a man of the South," he said, "and its history and its traditions are in my blood and the blood of my closest friends and colleagues in this chamber. But I speak tonight of the blood that ran through a church in Birmingham, Alabama, last Sunday—the blood of four little girls who were savagely killed as they learned a lesson from the Good Book. They died," he said, "because in that church men and women were preparing to gather to seek the most fundamental right this great country grants its citizens: the right to choose their leaders. And I am here tonight to ask you to resolve that those children did not die in vain; that before this year is out, that right will no longer be denied anywhere in this nation because of the color of a man's skin."

He did not mention lunch counters, or restaurants, or bus terminals; he talked only of the vote, and why it made us different from the adversaries we were fighting all over the world, about how on that one day of the year, the dirt farmer in his dusty overalls, driving to the county seat in his battered pickup truck, was the equal of the banker who held the mortgage on his land, and was driven to vote in a chauffeured limousine. There is no day when we are prouder to be Americans, he said; and there is no day when we should be more ashamed that we withhold that right from millions of our fellow citizens. "And my fellow Americans," he said, "that day of shame is over."

For a moment, there was silence in the House chamber. Then the applause began, built, and built, and most of the members were standing; in the gallery, the guests were cheering, embracing each other, many with tears flooding down their cheeks. Johnson stood, motionless at the podium, and when the cheers and applause finally stopped, he spoke only a little while longer. He would, he said, send a bill to the Congress the next day "to enforce the clear command of the Constitution, and the clear demand of simple justice." It would place sweeping power in the Department of Justice to guarantee the right to vote. "Let me speak plainly to those who claim the mantle of 'states' rights' to shut the voting booth to the Negro. Our Constitution wisely divides power between Washington and the several states. That has been and is a bulwark against tyranny. But there is no state right—no right of any government at any level—to deny the vote to any American citizen." And he held up his hand to forestall the wave of applause he knew was coming. He paused for a long moment. Then he said:

> "And if there is anyone in this chamber who would argue that any state has such a right, if there is anyone in this house who thinks it just when cowards who mask their faces burn homes and murder little children, let him come to this rostrum now."

His eyes swept the chamber; for an instant, Mississippi Senator Jim Eastland seemed to rise, but he looked over and caught the eye of Senator Richard Russell, who shook his head urgently, *No, no, this will do you and us no good*, and Eastland settled back into his chair.

On June 15, a vastly toughened Voting Rights Act of 1961 was introduced into the Senate by Robert F. Kennedy of New York, and Al Gore, Sr., of Tennessee, who acknowledged later that he had been moved to put his political future on the line after his twelve-year-old son, Al Jr., asked him why he thought it was fair that someone with black skin shouldn't be allowed to vote. By June 20, the Senate voted to cut off debate. The Voting Rights Act of 1961 was passed a day later, and President Johnson signed the bill on July 4, at the foot of the Lincoln Memorial.

"However long Lyndon Johnson remains in office," the *New York Times* editorialized the next day, "it is almost impossible to believe that any moment of his Presidency will be as remotely consequential as this one."

If only that had been true . . .

. . .

HE HAD BEEN THRUST into the Presidency knowing little about the world beyond his country's borders, and caring less. In the Congress where he had spent half his adult life, in the Senate he had made so thoroughly his own, he knew better than anyone else the interplay between the men and women who spoke for their districts and their states, and the pressures that would gain or lose him their votes. He knew that the textile mills in the Carolinas made protectionists out of the most ardent free traders, that defense plants in California could make the most pacific of politicians zealous defenders of bombers that could not fly and would not defend an inch of American soil. He knew where a federal judgeship could mean a floodtide of contributions to a senator's reelection, and where it was little more than a personal favor to an old friend. And he believed at his core that the crafting of a bill was not simply the means to an end, but the end in itself. As his long-suffering aide George Reedy put it: "[he believed] that for every social ailment there is a self-acting legislative nostrum. In his mind, the passage of an anti-poverty bill should cure poverty; the passage of an education bill should cure illiteracy . . ."

But when it came to the wider world, Johnson could see it only through the narrow frame of his own reference. His longtime aide Harry McPherson once said of him, "I think that everywhere he looked in rural Asia, what he saw was Johnson City and the surrounding country, and I think that he believed that the same panaceas that could be applied to Johnson City could be applied to Accra or to the rural areas of Thailand . . . But I don't believe that the complexities of Asian history and Asian thought ever came through to him. I don't think that he ever really understood the fact that these people thought differently than Americans do." Leaders might be moved by the prospect of a dam or electricity; that Johnson understood. But the notion that a leader would "send thousands of his countrymen to die, month after month, year after year, for an idea, a belief, was utterly, totally alien to him."

He brought to the Presidency the same set of assumptions that defined most of the leaders of his time: that Communism was a global phenomenon and a global threat; that a Communist victory anywhere was a threat to free nations—or those that allied themselves with free nations—everywhere. In this he was not that much different from the man who was supposed to be President; as a young congressman, John Kennedy had joined the "Who lost China?" hysteria, had helped hound good men out of the foreign service because they had dared to suggest that Chiang Kai-shek was not the George Washington of Asia. Unlike Kennedy's, however, Johnson's beliefs were not tinged with subtlety. In 1947, he had told his constituents: "Whether Communist or fascist or simply a pistol-packing racketeer, the one thing a bully understands is force and the one thing he fears is courage . . . if you let a bully come into your front yard, the next day he'll be up on your porch and the day after that he'll rape your wife in your own bed. But if you say to him at the start, 'Now hold on, wait a minute,' then he'll know he's dealing with a man of courage, someone who will stand up to him. And only then can you get along and find some peace again."

That same year, he had offered his own version of the domino theory when he said: "Where the Great Bear's shadow touches, all else is blotted out. If Italy's lost, Greece will be cut off and Turkey isolated. The bell has tolled for Rumania, Yugoslavia, Czechoslovakia. It is tolling for Finland, Norway, Sweden. Each toll of the bell brings closer the day when it will toll for you and me . . ." And in 1951, he had said that unless the Soviet Union changed its ways, we should "crush this tyrant once and for all . . . make peace, quit stalling, or we will hit you with everything we have . . . The next aggression will be the last. We will strike back not at your satellites—but at you." A year later, he could write the folks back home in a newsletter that "We should announce, I believe, that any act of aggression anywhere by any Communist forces will be regarded as an act of aggression by the Soviet Union . . . we should unleash all the power at our command upon the vitals of the Soviet Union."

What most defined Lyndon Johnson's understanding of the wider world, however, was a dangerous mixture of ignorance and indifference. Harry McPherson, who served Johnson for decades, said flatly: "Johnson was unprepared in the foreign policy area . . . [He didn't have] an interest in foreign affairs, in some foreign affair for its own sake, something that was not just the nose-to-nose confrontation with the Soviets in size of military force . . . One time in the Senate, a friend said to him, 'The leader of the largest party in India other than the Congress Party is here, a very distinguished man, and he'd like very much to see Majority Leader Johnson.' Johnson sent a note: Got my hands full. Sorry. LBJ. Well, I don't know what he was doing that day. What he was probably doing was trying to raise hell with the Air Force for closing down some air base in Texas."

Nor did Johnson think the Congress ought to be a prime player in foreign policy. "There's only room for one pilot in the cockpit," he said. "And you don't challenge the pilot while he's flying the plane."

The contrast with John Kennedy could not have been more dramatic. Kennedy's entire Presidential campaign was based on the argument that the way to defeat the Soviet Union in the global Cold War was to understand and harness the forces reshaping the world. He had called for Algeria's independence from France in 1956, looked with skepticism at the string of alliances the United States had made with dictators across Latin America whose anti-Communism was all the credential they needed to win Washington's favor. During the campaign, he'd proposed a program to send thousands of young people into the Third World to teach and build, and he meant to make that program a key part of his appeal to young Americans as President. Kennedy brought that same skepticism to his approach to the military. As a Lieutenant JG in the South Pacific in World War II, who almost died in the Solomon Islands when his boat was sunk, he had learned to be wary of the wisdom emanating from the chain of command, noting in letters home the military's "capacity to screw everything up." And late in the campaign, in Seattle, he'd made a speech where he said, "We must face the fact that the United States is neither omniscient nor omnipotent, that we cannot impose our will on 94 percent of mankind . . . that there cannot be an American solution to every world problem."

Johnson's combat experience was confined to a single reconnaissance flight in New Guinea in 1942—a flight of dubious danger, for which he was awarded the Silver Star. His instincts were to trust the military, and to trust the "wise men" who formed the more or less permanent Democratic Party foreign policy elite, men like Paul Nitze and former Secretary of State Dean Acheson. The two men had been the principal shapers of NSC-68, the 1950 report of the National Security Council, which described the conflict with the Soviets in near-apocalyptic terms. ("The issues that face us are momentous . . . involving the fulfillment or destruction not only of this Republic but of civilization itself.") They believed the Soviet Union would respond only to force, or the credible threat of it; that any identification with anti-colonial sentiments in the Third World was a betrayal of America's traditional and vital European allies. With Nitze installed as the key State Department policy planner, and Acheson as an *éminence grise* on more or less permanent call, one of John Kennedy's central notions—to position the United States as a friend of a democratic revolutionary spirit—died in the Palm Beach bombing. When Dick Goodwin, the young Kennedy aide who had agreed to help Johnson with speeches, broached the idea of the Peace Corps that Kennedy had proposed during his campaign, Johnson dismissed him with a wave of the hand.

"The last thing we need is a bunch of snot-nosed know-it-all college kids getting themselves in trouble in a dozen different countries they can't even spell. If they have that much time on their hands, they can go build a road or clean up a park in Kentucky."

But because he saw foreign policy through a political prism, he was acutely aware of what a major military entanglement would mean to his domestic ambitions. His father had taught him that America's entry into World War I had brought the Progressive Era to an end, ushering in a spasm of repression—dissidents by the hundreds rounded up, jailed, deported. FDR himself had proclaimed after Pearl Harbor that "Dr. New Deal" had been replaced by "Dr. Win the War," and with that war had come the incarceration of tens of thousands of Japanese-Americans in camps across the western United States.

With the Cold War and Korea had come the rise of McCarthyism, when an alcoholic tin-horn demagogue had terrorized the United States Senate, as good, solid Republicans like Bob Taft and Ev Dirksen decided: *Yes, he's a fear-monger, a liar, but he's bringing working-class Catholics to our party; let him be,* and when Eisenhower himself had been intimidated into silence as McCarthy defamed his longtime colleague, General George C. Marshall.

Those finely honed political instincts also taught him that when American boys were summoned to kill and die for a cause that could not be understood, it was a threat to political survival—especially his. In 1954, when French forces found themselves surrounded in Dien Bien Phu in the hills of northwestern Vietnam by the Communist Viet Minh, some of the most important voices in the Eisenhower administration called for American troops to help lift the siege. Admiral Radford of the Joint Chiefs, Secretary of State John Foster Dulles, Vice President Nixon, all said this was the domino whose fall would jeopardize the whole region; Thailand would be next, and Indonesia, and maybe Australia would be at peril. American planes were sent to the Philippines, with French markings on them to disguise their origins. But President Eisenhower hesitated; not without the British, he said. And Johnson, still feeling the political effects of the Korean War stalemate, helped convince Ike not to intervene.

So from the moment he assumed the Presidency, there was division in the House of Lyndon Johnson, between his political instincts and his assumptions, and between his advisors as well. Yes, Nitze and Acheson and the ultimate insider Democrats like lawyers Clark Clifford and Abe Fortas were locked into the consensus Cold War notions. But the man he'd chosen as his Secretary of State, Senator William J. Fulbright, was a confirmed skeptic about the use of American military power, and about the whole idea that the United States could remake the world in our image.

"Maturity," he'd said, "requires a final accommodation between our aspirations and our limitations." More pungently, he thought that America could be heavy-handed, even bullying in trying to persuade other countries to become more like us. "We are," he said, "still acting like Boy Scouts dragging reluctant old ladies across the streets they do not want to cross." (Fulbright could also be one stubborn Arkansas mule, Johnson knew; when Joe McCarthy was riding high, he'd been the only senator to vote against funding for McCarthy's investigations.) And then there was Johnson's successor as Senate Majority Leader, Mike Mansfield of Montana. In his younger days, Mansfield had spent years in the military and later in the Philippines and China, and his notions about the Communist Chinese regime were complicated enough to have almost cost him his first Senate race back in '52. He was convinced that you couldn't lump every Communist in the world into the same category, and was powerfully drawn to leaders in the Third World who were trying to break their nations away from old traditions—leaders like that young fellow in South Vietnam, Ngo

Dinh Diem (a lot of progressive thinkers, Justice William O. Douglas and Hubert Humphrey among them, embraced "the miracle man" who was saving his half of Vietnam from the Communists with land reform and economic development). And, like Fulbright, Mansfield was highly skeptical about the effectiveness, the wisdom, or the morality of using America's might to shape the world in its image.

It did not take long for this divided house to face its first internal clash: a clash with consequences Americans would be living with for generations.

WHEN FIDEL CASTRO and his guerrillas came down from the Sierra Maestra Mountains on New Year's Day, 1959, and seized power in Cuba, his victory was met with substantial approval in Washington. The man he overthrew, Fulgencio Batista, was a notoriously brutal and corrupt figure, even by the standards of Latin America, and the thirty-two-year-old Castro, with his beard and his green fatigues, was the very embodiment of the romantic revolutionary. Within a few months, everything had changed. His summary executions of his adversaries, his seizure of American companies and investments, his increasingly anti-American rhetoric convinced U.S. officials that he was a Communist, determined to foment revolution throughout the hemisphere. When Castro came to New York in September 1960 to attend the United Nations General Assembly meeting, he delighted in poking figurative sticks in Uncle Sam's eye. He stayed at Harlem's Theresa Hotel, where he met with Black Muslim spokesman Malcolm X, and broke bread with Soviet leader Nikita Khrushchev. On September 26, Castro delivered a four-hour speech attacking American "aggression" and "imperialism," and charging that the United States had "decreed the destruction" of his revolutionary government.

On this point, at least, Fidel Castro was absolutely right.

As early as March 1960, President Eisenhower had ordered the CIA to begin training Cuban exiles to overthrow Castro. The Agency responded by drawing up a top secret plan dubbed "Project 40"—whose goal was "to bring about the replacement of the Castro regime with one more . . . acceptable to the U.S. in such a manner as to avoid any appearance of U.S. intervention." When Washington suspended the import of Cuban sugar a few months later, delivering what would have been a crippling blow to the Cuban economy, the Soviet Union happily stepped in, confirming the idea that Havana was becoming a full-fledged partner of Moscow. By the fall, CIA plans for the landing of an exile army on Cuban soil were accelerating. As those plans were gaining force, so was the determination of candidate John Kennedy not to be tarred with the brush that had stained so many recent Democrats: the charge that its leaders were soft on Communism. A decade earlier, in 1950, a year after Mao Tse-tung overthrew Chiang Kai-shek, Democrats around the country had been damaged by the accusatory question: "Who lost China?" In 1952, Republicans summed up their campaign theme in three alliterative words: "Korea, Corruption, and Communism." As a candidate that year, Richard Nixon had struck the same rhetorical note when he condemned Secretary of State Dean Acheson for heading the "cowardly college of Communist containment."

Kennedy himself had been dealing all year with Nixon's attack on Kennedy's suggestion that the U.S. should have expressed "regrets" over Francis Gary Powers's U-2 flight over Soviet territory that had been shot down. He would make sure he was insulated from such attacks—which is why, just before the fourth televised debate, he had called for the U.S. to assist "democratic forces" in Cuba to overthrow Castro. Nixon felt he had no choice but to attack Kennedy's proposal as "reckless" and "dangerous," even though he was a principal advocate of precisely that course of action. He was also convinced that CIA officials, drawn from the upper class, Ivy League circles in which Kennedy moved so effortlessly, had tipped off the Democratic candidate about the invasion plans, forcing Nixon to seem less tough on Cuba than Kennedy. It was impossible to prove Nixon's suspicions, especially since Nixon was suspicious about just about everyone whose path he crossed. What was undeniable was that on November 16, Richard Bissell—the CIA's Deputy Director of Plans—briefed President-elect Kennedy about the plans for a Cuban invasion, one designed to depose Castro without leaving any American fingerprints. Bissell was the perfect person to deal with Kennedy: son of New England aristocrats, educated at Groton and Yale, he was a core member of the fashionable "Georgetown Set" that included such Establishment figures as columnist Joseph Alsop, *Washington Post* publisher Phil Graham, Justice Felix Frankfurter, Dean

Acheson, and a dozen others. Bissell had also been the driving force behind "PBSUCCESS," the project that overthrew leftist Guatemalan President Jacob Arbenz in 1954 by stirring up protests and unrest when Arbenz proved too unfriendly to American business interests.

Kennedy had every reason to trust Bissell . . . except that there was something Bissell wasn't telling the incoming President: The CIA did not believe for a minute that an invasion of Cuba could succeed without the direct intervention of American military forces. Indeed, on November 15, the day before Bissell met with Kennedy, a CIA memo prepared for Bissell had concluded: "Our concept to secure a beach with airstrip is now seen to be unachievable, except as joint Agency/Department of Defense action." The CIA, to put it simply, was planning to launch an invasion by Cuban exiles, watch it founder, and then watch the President call in the cavalry—the Marines and Air Force, actually—to wipe out the Cuban military and depose Castro. There was no way a President could let an invasion fail, the Agency was sure, without being branded a weakling who let a Communist dictator defeat the most powerful nation on earth.

John Kennedy never told Lyndon Johnson about the CIA briefing; whoever he might have shared this information with, it was certainly not the incoming Vice President, whom he was not about to entrust with any significant role in the shaping of foreign policy (nor had Bissell mentioned to the soon-to-be-President that the Agency was tapping into the talents of worthies such as Jimmy Rosselli and Sam Giancana, two of organized crime's most prominent players, who had suffered grievous losses when Castro closed down Havana's casinos). When Kennedy was killed less than a month later, the unprecedented collision of shock, grief, a Constitutional crisis, and the need to put together a government under emergency conditions fully occupied Johnson's time. It wasn't until the week before inauguration that Bissell managed to secure an appointment with Johnson to brief him about the operation. The President-elect squeezed Bissell in between meetings to plan strategy on a federal aid to education bill, and a push to get senior citizens medical care under Social Security. What Johnson wanted most from the rest of the world was quiescence, a period when nothing much happened that would distract him from making 1961 a year of major domestic achievements. On the other hand, the prospect of inflicting a major defeat on the

Communist empire was a very attractive possibility—one that could only be seen as a blessing for the new Johnson administration. So when Bissell came to see Johnson in his opulent Senate office suite, Johnson was distracted and intrigued and wary. He was also inherently distrustful of Bissell's background, bearing, credentials, and attire: the three-piece light gray pin-striped wool, the light blue oxford button-down shirt, the tie bearing the insignia of some college or club. Johnson signaled his attitude by conducting his end of the briefing from the toilet in his baronial bathroom, as Bissell stood as far outside the door as he could. *You sure you can do this without leaving our fingerprints all over it?* Johnson wanted to know.

"I can assure you," Bissell said, "we have the same team we had in Guatemala in '54. We've got one of our best staffers—Howard Hunt—on the case. Back then as soon as the demonstrations started, the army rose up and removed Mr. Arbenz. We firmly believe the same thing will happen this time. Even if Castro is not immediately toppled, the expeditionary force will simply melt into the Escambry Mountains, and begin doing to Fidel the same thing he did to Batista."

Dammit, come closer, Biss, I can barely hear you, Johnson shouted from the bathroom where he was seated. On that note, the CIA's Deputy Director for Plans hastily concluded his briefing and fled the office with dispatch. The plan, he assured the President-to-be, would be another feather in the Agency's cap, to go along with their successes in Guatemala and in Iran.

THE NEXT TIME Richard Bissell stood face-to-face with President Lyndon Johnson was just after midnight on April 18, 1961, when an agitated Lyndon Johnson, Vice President Humphrey, Secretary of State Bill Fulbright, and two members of the Joint Chiefs of Staff gathered in the Oval Office. It was the night of the annual Congressional Reception in the White House East Room, a highly formal occasion; the civilians were dressed in white-tie and tails, Chief of Staff Chairman Lymen Lemnitzer and Naval Chief Arleigh Burke were in full dress attire, their chests gleaming with medals. Bissell was wearing a rumpled suit and had sweated through his white broadcloth shirt. The Oval Office was suffused with a powerful aroma of cigar smoke and mutual recriminations.

From start to finish, the CIA's plan had gone straight into the crapper.

First, the "stealth" invasion had leaked like a rusty drainpipe. Between Cuban intelligence agents scattered across Latin America and throughout the Miami exile community, and the loose talk in bars and restaurants of half a dozen cities, word of an impending attack was everywhere. Radio Moscow had warned of a coming "criminal" act by the American government—a broadcast that confirmed what the CIA already knew, that Soviet intelligence was on to the plan (the Agency never bothered to inform President Johnson of this detail). Reporters from Miami to Tegucigalpa had picked up the stories of an impending American strike—they would have had to be equipped with the faculties of Helen Keller not to—and when the *New York Times*'s Tad Szulc asked the White House for comment about an invasion story he was preparing, it took all of Lyndon Johnson's persuasion-threat skills to get the paper to downplay the story.

("The blood of American boys will be on your hands," Johnson thundered to *Times* publisher Orville Dryfoos. "I thought there weren't any American boys involved," Dryfoos muttered—after the President hung up the phone.)

Second, every logistical detail that could go wrong went wrong; every bad piece of information, every miscalculation that could have fouled up the plan, turned from worst-case fears into reality. Was the Cuban military ripe for revolt, as had been the army in Guatemala? No. Castro had ruthlessly purged the army of anyone remotely suspected of disloyalty, and the government's own army of informants was seeded throughout the armed forces (and just about everywhere else in Cuban society, for that matter). Was the Cuban Air Force substantially crippled by attacks from exiled Cuban pilots? No. On April 15, eight Douglas B-26B Invader bombers had taken off from Puerto Cabezas, Nicaragua, and attacked three Cuban airfields. They inflicted only minimal damage, but reported back to their CIA handlers that they had struck grievous blows against Castro's fleet. The Agency took the pilots at their word, thus assuring that when the beach landing did come, the forces and their leaders would be moving under a wholly false set of assumptions about Cuba's ability to resist. Were the landings executed well? No. When the 1,300 members of Brigade 2506 arrived off of Playa Giron from Puerto Cabezas, they transferred from the Landing Craft Infantry ships into small aluminum boats, while those coming ashore at Playa Larga were moved into fiberglass boats, some of which were immediately disabled by mechanical breakdowns, others of which were damaged when they struck coral reefs whose presence was unknown to anyone who had planned the landing.

And because the Cuban Air Force, contrary to the exile pilots' optimistic reports, was essentially whole, Cuban jets attacked the invading ships, sending much of the arms and equipment on board to the bottom of the sea. An airdrop of hundreds of exiles, whose mission was to block the road down which Castro's forces would come, went wretchedly wrong. About thirty men from the parachute battalion of Brigade 2506, along with tons of heavy equipment, were dropped south of an Australia sugar mill on the road to Palpite and Playa Larga, but the equipment was lost in the swamps and the troops failed to block the road. Later that day, Osvaldo Ramirez, the chief organizer of the rural resistance forces, was captured in Aromas de Velázquez and immediately executed. That should have raised serious concerns about the likelihood of widespread anti-Castro uprisings, but didn't. That evening, a night air strike by three FAL B-26s on San Antonio de Los Baños airfield failed, reportedly due to incompetence and bad weather.

By nine p.m. on April 16, thousands of Cuban troops and militia—commanded by Fidel himself—had taken complete control of the Bay of Pigs, and the Agency's chiefs were now ready to play their last card: a Presidential decision to double down on the mission with the full, open involvement of the United States Armed Forces.

Except . . . they were confronting that divided house that was Lyndon Johnson's foreign policy universe. It wasn't that he had serious principled reservations about the use of force, especially in Latin America. Many of his longtime political and financial backers were men who had grown rich extracting oil, sugar, copper, and fruit from the hemisphere, and whose sole concern with the local governments were that they keep the streets safe and the labor markets cheap. In fact, when Dick Goodwin showed Johnson a draft of John Kennedy's Inaugural that pledged a "new Alliance for Progress" in Latin America, Johnson waved it away without a second thought. But that same need for tranquility on the foreign front, that same determination to use all of his energy to become the second Franklin Roosevelt, had tempered his enthusiasm for the invasion.

And there was also the increasingly dissident voice of Secretary of State Fulbright: *Whatever you do*, he repeatedly cautioned Johnson, *make absolutely certain this can't be traced back to Washington. I can't think of a worse way to begin your Presidency . . . it'll set us back a decade or more all over the world.*

Confronted with these conflicting voices—the CIA confidently promising success, his Secretary of State and his own instincts signaling caution—Johnson did what he had done at every stage in his political life: He split the difference. On the night of April 16, just before the invasion began, he told the CIA that he would approve the second wave of pre-dawn air strikes on Cuban airfields, but approved only half the number of sorties, to lessen the chances of compromising the U.S.'s "plausible deniability." That decision inflamed officials of the CIA, who argued fruitlessly that in this case, half a loaf was worse than none, that the Cuban Air Force would be able to defend against the smaller number of strikes. Johnson, for his part, was growing progressively angrier as reports of failure after failure flooded into the White House situation room. ("You people," he snapped at top Bissell deputy Tracy Barnes, "couldn't fart and chew gum at the same time. I thought you said yesterday that their Air Force was damn near wiped out.")

So at this midnight meeting, there was only one question left: Would Johnson order the American military to attack Cuba? Bissell spoke of the hundreds of exiles now trapped at the Bay of Pigs, whose freedom and lives were on the line. Chief of Naval Operations Arleigh Burke, who had moved the U.S. aircraft carrier *Essex* close to Cuba's shore, urged Johnson to let him move a destroyer close in to attack Castro's troops.

As the President thought for a moment, Bill Fulbright got up and walked to the other side of the Oval Office, motioning the President to join him.

"It's obviously your decision," Fulbright said. "But you need to know that if you order a strike on Cuba, it would violate every rule of international law . . . and it would be a disaster on every conceivable level. It would also make it impossible for me to remain as Secretary of State."

Johnson appeared stricken; he surreptitiously grabbed his side.

"Damn gallstones," he said. It was a classic Johnson moment; Johnson always seemed to suffer a sudden assault on his body when faced with a crisis that was building to a head. His decision was classic Johnson as well: to deny the Agency and the military the war they sought while handing the disappointed chiefs a crucial marker.

I won't do this, he told the small group around him, then turned angrily to Bissell. *You had your chance; I even gave you the air cover you needed. But you screwed up every single phase of this chicken-shit operation. And you managed to make this government, and me, look like a fool in front of the whole world. Poor Adlai up at the UN, holding that picture of the damaged "defecting aircraft"? Hell, you think there's anyone in the world with a brain larger than his balls who couldn't smell out that story? But it's the only one we've got left, and we have to play with the hand we're dealt. A shooting war with Cuba right now is just the last thing we—I—need.*

Shortly before three a.m., the meeting broke up, and Johnson summoned the White House physician to check with him about those gallstones.

The fallout from the doomed invasion was, to put it mildly, embarrassing. The ten-plus dead fighters from Brigade 2506, the 1,200 captured exiles paraded through Havana by a triumphant Fidel Castro, fed the picture of an American-made fiasco. The fallout at home was intense. Fed by sources in the Agency and the military, Republicans in Congress denounced the President for "pulling out the rug" from the chance to depose a Communist tyrant, as Joint Chief Chairman Lemnitzer put it. Intriguingly, one of the most notable criticisms came from freshman New York Senator Robert F. Kennedy. In his maiden speech in the Senate, Kennedy, channeling his brother's campaign rhetoric and his own highly unevolved Cold War beliefs, recalled how his brother "eloquently voiced the aspirations for freedom of all those who live under tyranny, and pledged that this nation would stand with the democratic forces fighting for a free Cuba. Let us hope that the disaster we have just witnessed does not tempt our adversaries into searching for *further signs of weakness in our leaders.*" Far more important, as it turned out, was what lesson President Johnson took from the failure; what lesson he determined to remember the next time he was faced with such a decision.

It wasn't hard to imagine what a different President—say, John F. Kennedy—might have taken from the Bay of Pigs. Kennedy's anger at the misinformation the CIA had deliberately and repeatedly fed him might have prodded him not just to shake up the Agency, but to bring even more skepticism to its casual assumption that it was entitled to topple governments, even those freely elected. And his skepticism about the military, drawn from his World War II experiences, might have led him to entertain serious doubts about its casual optimism about the use of force, as well as its indifference to potential responses by the Soviet Union in Berlin or elsewhere. A President like John Kennedy might well have been highly dubious about taking the military at face value when a crisis erupted.

But John Kennedy wasn't President. Lyndon Johnson was in the White House. And Lyndon Johnson took a very different set of conclusions from the Bay of Pigs failure. For Johnson, it was more proof that the high-society, aristocratic tea drinkers and cookie pushers, the kind of people who ran the CIA and threw the parties in Georgetown and put on tuxedoes to listen to chamber music, had screwed him five ways from Sunday. He couldn't give the Chiefs what they wanted, couldn't have a war with Cuba and worry about the Soviets taking Berlin, but he didn't blame them for their anger. And at some level, he even sympathized with their anger. It was, after all, Speaker Sam Rayburn, his fellow Texan and first mentor in Washington, who once said, "If we don't trust our generals, we've wasted a lot of money on West Point." Next time, he would be a lot more inclined to bend their way—if there was a next time.

AT FORTY MINUTES PAST noon on Sunday, July 16, 1961, President Lyndon Johnson stood on the red-carpeted front steps of the U.S. Embassy residence in Vienna, Austria, waiting to greet his guest. Behind him stood a phalanx of American diplomats and Soviet experts: Secretary of State William Fulbright; outgoing U.S. Ambassador to Moscow Llewellyn Thompson; his successor, Foy Kohler; State Department policy chief Paul Nitze. Below them, on the street, hundreds of reporters, photographers, and cameramen jostled for position, waiting to capture the first meeting between Johnson and his guest—Nikita Khrushchev, Chairman of the Council of Ministers of the USSR, and First Secretary of the Communist Party of the Soviet Union.

It was a summit meeting that almost didn't happen. Preliminary talks for the meeting had begun shortly after Johnson's inauguration, prompted in good measure by the still-shocking circumstances of Johnson's Presidency. Moscow had been preparing for months for the possibility of a John Kennedy Presidency; their "Americanologists" had produced reams of political, biographical, and psychological evaluations of the candidate. Johnson, though a vaguely familiar figure in Soviet circles, was barely given a second thought. Who cared about an American Vice President? Now that he was in the Oval Office, the thought on both sides of the East-West divide went, it was important that he and the Soviet leader get a clear understanding of each other, beyond the hastily prepared analysis by the KGB—Moscow's secret police—that characterized Johnson as a friend of monopolists and militarists whose views were essentially no different from those of Richard Nixon's.

The Bay of Pigs debacle almost consigned the summit notion to the dustbin of history. Just as Khrushchev had blown up the 1960 summit in Geneva after President Eisenhower had tried to lie his way out of responsibility for the U-2 spy plane shot down over the Soviet Union, so he was bristling with anger at the covert U.S. attempt to overthrow the first Marxist revolutionary who had come to power in Latin America. As Khrushchev put it in his characteristically pungent way, "You don't shit in your neighbor's yard and expect an invitation to dinner." There was also reluctance in some of the inner councils of the Johnson administration, a reluctance fueled by concerns that the President's indifference to foreign policy might leave him at a disadvantage in dealing with the mercurial, wily, and fiercely determined Soviet leader. With an ambitious domestic program taking shape, and with his voting rights effort already underway, Johnson's aides feared the focus and energy required to prepare for a face-to-face summit might be one burden too many.

It was Johnson himself who pushed hard for the meeting. "I've been studying up on Khrushchev and his people," he told a surprised Averell Harriman one May afternoon in the Oval Office, when FDR's wartime ambassador to Moscow came to call.

"They don't have the least understanding of our system. They think I'm nothing but the front man for a bunch of oil billionaires and munitions manufacturers, part of the, what do they call it, 'reactionary ruling circles.' It might mean something if they come to realize that my hero is Franklin Roosevelt—they worship Roosevelt, right?" he said to the diplomat who'd been Roosevelt's envoy to Joseph Stalin during World War II. "And besides, I think Khrushchev and I have a whole lot in common. We walked the same roads to get where we are. I mean"—Johnson added with a grin at the multimillionaire Harriman—"neither of us had a daddy who owned a railroad . . . or made a Wall Street killing, like Jack's."

Indeed, both of the men who now had the power to wipe out most of the planet's life had walked hard roads. Both were raised without money. Johnson's father, Sam Ealy Johnson, had lost what he had through bad cotton trading, and Johnson's early life in Stonewall, Texas, in a farmhouse on the Pedernales, was far from easy. Nikita Khrushchev came from Kalinovka in the Ukraine, grandson of a serf, son of a miner. Both found their way out through political skills.

Johnson began attaching himself to older, powerful men from the time he was a student at Southwest State Teacher's College in San Marcos, Texas, when he made himself indispensable to the school's president. He leveraged that work into a job in Washington, where his obsequious attention to his colleagues soon made him the most influential aide in the House; a body to which he was elected at twenty-nine. Khrushchev joined the Communist Party at twenty-four. A few years later, he entered the Donets Industrial Institute, a worker's school run by the Soviets, where he became secretary of the school's Communist Party Committee. He graduated in 1925 to full-time Party work, and while working in Yuzovka, he became the protégé of Lazar M. Kaganovich, the secretary general of the Ukrainian Party's Central Committee and a close associate of future Soviet leader Joseph Stalin. Johnson worked himself into the orbits of House Speaker Sam Rayburn, and Senator Richard Russell. Khrushchev was pulled into the orbit of Stalin, for whom he executed—often literally—purges in the Ukraine, and whose growing madness he survived. Khrushchev not only made it through the Stalinist era, but also beat back every rival to become the dominant—albeit not the absolute—power figure in the Soviet Union (Johnson, of course, was propelled into power by the act of a lunatic).

And there was one other strikingly similar trait the two men shared: Both were acutely conscious of their lack of first-class education and breeding; both knew that others in their ranks condescended to them, sneered at them behind their backs for their social clumsiness, their often crude vocabularies. Both were more than willing to flaunt their language and their customs in public. While Lyndon Johnson never banged his shoe on a desk at the United Nations to protest a speaker, as Khrushchev had done in the fall of 1960, he was more than capable of performing the most basic of functions—including excremental—in the presence of others. (Richard Bissell was not the only highborn official to be summoned for a colloquy with the President seated on the toilet.)

As Johnson waited for Khrushchev, he mentally rehearsed the strategic and tactical guidance he'd been given by the men who'd briefed him over the last days. Harriman and Ambassador Thompson had given him almost identical advice: Do not get into an ideological debate about the merits of Communism and capitalism. Khrushchev spent years being drilled in Marxist dogma, they told him; what's more, he believes it. When he starts hammering away, Harriman said, laugh it off; make him get down to specifics. This was the kind of advice that was right in Johnson's sweet spot: He held no strong ideological convictions, he wanted to make life better for people who needed his government's help, and he wanted to know what kind of ideas he could get people to support. He was sure it was the same whether you were talking about money to bring electricity to the rural South, or the resolution of a border conflict, or arms control. From Paul Nitze and especially from Dean Acheson came the perspective they'd shared from the first days of the Cold War: The only thing the Russians respect is strength, firmness. Khrushchev has to know you're prepared to fight for the vital interests of the United States. The Bay of Pigs made us—you—look weak, indecisive in his eyes. You must disabuse him of this quickly. And he reminded himself one last time of his own certainty: *Put me face-to-face with a man, give me enough time, and I can reason with him, deal with him, bend him to my will.*

At 12:45 p.m., a black ZIL limousine pulled into the circular gravel driveway of the embassy. Khrushchev emerged from the car and walked quickly up the steps to shake hands with the President. The photographers body-slammed each other for the best angle of the handshake; it did not go unnoticed by any of them that the head of the five-foot three-inch Soviet leader barely reached the chin of the six-foot three-inch President. (*One for our side,* Secretary of State Fulbright noted silently.)

The two men retreated with their aides to the red, gray, and gold music room and sat side by side on a rose-colored sofa. Facing them stood Johnson's team and Khrushchev's court: Foreign Minster Andrei Gromyko, U.S. Ambassador Menshikov, diplomat Anatoly Dobrynin. When the pool photographers were dismissed, the men began with some forced small talk.

"I hope Gromyko doesn't make you too uncomfortable, Mr. President," Khrushchev said with a smile. "There are many in Moscow who think he looks very much like Mr. Nixon."

"In my country," Johnson said, smiling back, "we work across party lines. It is easier for you—you only have one party. Sometimes I envy you that."

Khrushchev saw his opening and ran with it; he immediately launched into a forceful denunciation of the Cuban invasion. *You always claim to be on the side of "freedom," but whenever a nation tries to be free in a way you do not like, you want to snuff that freedom out . . . like you did in Iran, like you did in Guatemala, like you tried to do in Cuba. You called Fidel a Communist; I think you made him a Communist when you cut off his oil and tried to starve his people. We believe socialism will triumph through the force of its ideas, but your country doesn't seem to trust anyone who wants to travel a different path.*

Khrushchev's attack was premised on the Soviet view of Johnson as an ally of the more "conservative and reactionary views," as the KGB analysis of the new President had put it. But it was precisely the kind of attack Johnson had been cautioned about, and he played it just as planned.

"Mr. Chairman," he said, leaning closer to Khrushchev and putting his hand on the Chairman's knee with just a bit more pressure than was fully comfortable, "I think both of our peoples have too much at stake here to watch us spend our time in debate. We have our interests, and we are determined to protect them; you have yours, whether it be in Warsaw or East Berlin or Budapest"—pointedly noting three cities where Soviet armies had ruthlessly suppressed uprisings in the 1950s. "But I doubt I am going to make a capitalist out of you, and I am reasonably sure all of your eloquence is not going to make a Communist out of me; so why don't we see if we can make this a slightly safer world before we go home? Why don't we see if we can take some of the billions we both spend on machines to kill and bring that money back home to build dams and roads and schools?"

It was a ploy aimed squarely at one of Khrushchev's most ardent—and controversial—passions. He'd been pushing the Politburo to cut defense spending, arguing that it was time to do something about the lines that wound through every street in the Soviet Union as housewives waited for bread and meat; it was an idea that triggered intense hostility from the armed forces, and from some of the old Stalinist bulls in Moscow. Johnson's words put Khrushchev on the defensive, and he protested loudly to the President that the aggressive posture of Washington—ringing the Soviet Union with missiles in Turkey, Greece, and Iran, for instance—forced Moscow to build ever-more-powerful weapons.

The conversation lasted until lunch—beef Wellington was the main course—and when the talks resumed, Khrushchev turned to the most urgent matter on the agenda: the status of Germany, and specifically, Berlin. World War II had ended with Germany divided; East Germany was a totally controlled satellite of the Soviet Union, a grim, gray gulag of a nation that had been stripped of much of its economic power by a Soviet Union determined to avenge the twenty million war dead. West Germany was an ally of the West with one of the most vibrant economies in Europe (French and British visitors in particular were inclined to ask, after a cursory look around, "Didn't *we* win the war?"). For years, East Germans had been voting with their feet; more than two and a half million had decamped to the West in the last decade or so. It was how they fled that made Germany the most likely terrain for armed conflict between East and West. The city of Berlin, nestled 110 miles into East Germany, had also been left divided after the War; while the four allied powers had sliced up the city, the real division was between East and West. For years, Moscow had been threatening to undo the postwar arrangement that had guaranteed the West access to Berlin; in 1948, they had shut down all rail and auto routes in an attempt to starve West Berlin into accepting Soviet control. A year-long airlift of 4,000 tons a day of food and materiel succeeded in breaking the blockade, and had birthed a different Soviet stratagem, one Chairman Khrushchev raised at irregular intervals. *It is time for this artificial construct to end,* he would thunder. *If the West will not agree to opening up all of Berlin to East German and Soviet forces, I will sign a separate peace treaty with East Germany, and turn over total control of Berlin to them.*

That was the argument Khrushchev began making to President Johnson immediately after lunch. And it would lead to the most dramatic clash of the summit, one that the Americans at first saw as a major victory, and one that triggered unimaginable consequences.

As Khrushchev talked about Berlin, about the logic of ending the postwar arrangement, he grew emotional. Why, he asked, should so sensible a proposition produce such hostility? It would be madness to start a nuclear war, kill tens of millions of people, over a matter of diplomacy. Or is it true, Khrushchev asked bluntly, as some of my advisors believe, that your generals and admirals believe the U.S. could emerge from a war as the conquerors of the planet? Do you really have such madmen in your councils of authority? Do they not know each of us has the power to utterly destroy the other?

It was at this point that the President asked Khrushchev if they could dismiss their aides and diplomats, and talk between themselves, with only their interpreters and a single notetaker from each side present. The Soviet leader raised his eyebrows, and asked if Johnson was going to try to persuade him to defect.

"I thought if we let you come to Disneyland this time, you might change sides," Johnson quipped, referring to the Premier's 1959 visit to the U.S., when his desire to see the theme park was turned down on security grounds. "No, Mr. Chairman, I just think we might find a real conversation more fruitful." When the subalterns had left, Johnson leaned in close to his counterpart, as he had done countless times in the Senate, often using his size to—literally—bend his targets backward as he bored in.

"Nikita Sergeyevich," Johnson began, using the patronymic common to Russians, but rarely employed in diplomatic conversation, "I'm going to speak very frankly, very bluntly to you. We are both men who came from hard times; we both know what it means to watch our fathers try to feed their families, to end the day with dirt on our hands, to feel the contempt of our own countrymen who think they are better than we are. So I feel I am talking to a kindred spirit when I offer you some wisdom from the folks I grew up with in Texas: Nikita Sergeyevich—*Never shit a shitter.*"

Khrushchev's interpreter turned beet-red; he groped for the right euphemism.

"No," Johnson said. "Tell it to him the way I said it."

The interpreter stumbled his way through the few words; the notetaker dropped his pencil; Khrushchev's face flushed deep red. This was the way *he* talked; this was the way *he* threw other people off-balance. Now this American President was using his own shock tactic against him.

"You know there are people in both of our countries who are under the delusion that they can win a nuclear war; you know that this is madness, that millions of your citizens and mine, and millions of others all across Europe, would die horrible deaths in another world war. But"—and here Johnson leaned so close to Khrushchev that their foreheads almost touched—"you also know what I know: that there is no real equivalence in what we have. The war hawks in my country are indeed mad if they think anyone can really prevail in a nuclear war, but they have reason to believe that their misguided beliefs are based in fact. They know my running mate, John Kennedy, was wrong when he talked about a missile gap. Yes, there is a gap, but it is not on our side. That's why, Mr. Chairman, it is imperative that we do nothing to encourage these people to put any pressure on me to act on this imbalance. As far as I'm concerned, the fact that you could wipe out millions of Americans and Europeans is deterrence enough. But you do not want—and I don't want—to create a crisis where the war hawks start to demand that we play this deadly numbers game."

The Soviet chairman sat mute for a long moment. Johnson's words struck like a dagger to the heart. His entire diplomatic posture, and much of his political stature at home, depended on the illusion that Soviet and U.S. forces were in rough equivalence. If the West thought that much of Moscow's nuclear might was a Potemkin village, how seriously would they treat Soviet diplomatic demands? If his own military thought the United States had gained a strategic advantage during Khrushchev's reign, how secure would his position be at the top of the USSR's unstable political pyramid? And if Washington threatened once again to overthrow the outpost of socialism in Latin America, how credible would Soviet promises be if Washington did not put real credence in the power of Moscow to match the U.S. kiloton for kiloton?

After a moment, Khrushchev put on a truculent face.

"Mr. President," he said sternly, pointing a finger in Johnson's face, "if you are living under the delusion that you are stronger than we, then I am afraid we will have to present evidence that even your ineffectual Central Intelligence Agency won't be able to miss. And I want to caution you in the clearest possible term: We will either reach an agreement on Berlin by year's end, or the Soviet Union will sign a treaty with the German Democratic Republic, and the postwar arrangement will end."

"That, Mr. Chairman, will be unacceptable to the United States and to Great Britain and France. I hope you will reconsider," said Johnson. "Perhaps we might move to a more hopeful arena." And they spent an hour going through the motions of possible cooperation in outer space. But the rest of the day—indeed, the rest of the summit—was a matter of putting the best face on a non-meeting of the minds. Through the state dinner at Schönbrunn Palace, through the opera, the ballet, and a truncated second-day gathering at the Soviet Embassy, and the very correct joint press briefing celebrating a "frank and fruitful discussion," it was clear that nothing of any substance had been accomplished. The impassive expression on President Johnson's face, the dour frown on Khrushchev's, spoke far more eloquently than the pro forma words.

The really consequential words were those spoken by Khrushchev to Gromyko on the long train ride back to Moscow.

That son of a bitch believes he holds the whip hand, Khrushchev thundered. *We need to show him that he cannot bully the Soviet Union.* Before the train had arrived back home, he ordered his military to resume nuclear testing with the biggest hydrogen bombs possible—30 megatons, 50 megatons, big enough to put the fear of God into Johnson and his monopolist friends. But the most significant conclusion he drew from Johnson's words he kept to himself.

He had to move as quickly as possible to redress the imbalance between Moscow and the West. He had to find a way to make the United States as vulnerable as was the Soviet Union. And he had to do it in a way that would answer the disparate pressures that were closing in on him. China had become an increasingly painful thorn in his side; its leaders were openly signaling their dissatisfaction with Khrushchev's denunciation of Stalin,

with his campaign to drain money away from the military in favor of satis-
fying consumer demands, and with his talk of "peaceful co-existence." His
enemies in the party and the government were striking the same chords.
The East German leader, Walter Ulbricht, was demanding that his Moscow superiors do something about the ceaseless flight of citizens to the
West. He wanted something dramatic, perhaps a wall, to pen in his disaffected subjects. And his favorite Marxist, Fidel Castro, never stopped
warning of a second American attempt to overthrow him, never stopped
urging Khrushchev to provide protection.

It was not immediately obvious what he could do, but it would have to
be something bold, something dramatic, something that would shock the
West into recognizing that it had to deal with the Soviet Union as a genuine superpower, fully capable of inflicting as much damage as the United
States could inflict on the Motherland. It took months, but by the summer
of 1962, it had come to him. Summoning five of his closest advisors, and
swearing them to absolutely secrecy, he said, "It is time to throw a hedgehog at Uncle Sam's pants."

THE AUTUMN OF 1962 was the season of President Lyndon Johnson's
content. The American economy, always the key to a President's political fortunes, was in full bloom. Fifteen years into the post–World War
II boom, the United States held the commanding heights of the world's
economy, and Americans were coming to believe that an unbroken rise
in their standard of living was something close to a law of nature. More
than half of Americans owned their own homes; well over half had savings
accounts that held six months' salary or more; the eight million veterans of
World War II who had gone through college on the GI Bill were now part
of the thriving middle class. The core American dream—that we would
live better than our parents, and that our children would live better than
us—was morphing from aspiration to reality.

With unemployment dropping below 5 percent, with the postwar inflation now a receding memory, with economic growth hitting nearly 10 percent a year, President Johnson was presiding over a government that could
simultaneously offer balanced budgets and expanded benefits. He'd pried

the first federal aid to education bill out of Congress last November—signing the law in a one-room schoolhouse he'd attended back in Stonewall, Texas—and a health-care program for old folks was almost within his reach. It was bottled up in the Senate by that coalition of Republicans and conservative Democrats, but if the midterm elections went the way he thought they would, he'd have enough allies on Capitol Hill to pass it. And, with a month to go, those elections were looking to make the kind of history beyond Johnson's fondest dreams.

Not since 1934, when FDR was presiding over the New Deal, had a party holding the White House actually gained seats in the Congress. Now, some of the prehistoric Republican bulls in the Senate—Wiley of Wisconsin, Capehart of Indiana, Bottum of South Dakota—were in danger of falling to a new breed of young Democrat: Birch Bayh, Gaylord Nelson, and that ex–bomber pilot in South Dakota, George McGovern. Even the South was showing some promising signs; yes, a lot of angry white voters would be looking to take their anger out on Democrats—"backlash," they were starting to call it—but there were also hundreds of thousands of Negroes who were already registered to vote, and that was already bearing fruit. A few dozen cities and small towns had elected Negroes to town councils and magistrates' courts—hell, there were even a handful of black sheriffs in Mississippi and South Carolina and Georgia—and with those men in power, the night riders and Klansmen were rapidly fading into history. Even without a federal law to desegregate restaurants and lunch counters and hotels, local authorities feeling the pressure of newly enfranchised Negroes were changing the law on their own. And would anyone, a few years back, have imagined that Senator Strom Thurmond, the "Dixiecrat" candidate for President in 1948, would have hired three Negroes to help staff his field offices in South Carolina? Or that George Wallace of Alabama, who'd lost a governor's race to a hard-shell segregationist in 1958, would be on the verge of unseating that governor in the Democratic primary with the help of the new Negro vote? It was an achievement striking enough that some of the leading liberal voices, the UAW's Walter Reuther and columnist Walter Lippmann among them, were beginning to talk about "a third Roosevelt Presidency." And more and more, the memory of John Kennedy—the President who never was—was dimming.

As for his prospects for election in 1964, it was looking more and more likely that the Republicans were heading into their second full-scale civil war in a dozen years. Back in 1952, the permanently simmering clash between Eastern internationalist liberals and Midwest isolationist conservatives had turned the Republican convention into Gettysburg. Not even the landslide victories of Eisenhower had dimmed the fury of the true believers who felt their tribune, Ohio Senator Robert Taft, had been cheated out of his due. Now these warriors were rallying behind Arizona Senator Barry Goldwater, a conservative who shared their dreams of repealing the New Deal and carrying the Cold War to the doors of the Kremlin. And while the more liberal Republicans were looking to New York Governor Nelson Rockefeller, Johnson had a surprise in store for them; right after the elections—Rockefeller was cruising to a second term—he was going to offer Rockefeller the number three post at State, with the implied promise that he would succeed Fulbright as Secretary (international affairs was always Rockefeller's favorite arena; as he put it, "Building a thruway is not exactly my idea of making history"). If Rockefeller saw the writing on the wall—that Johnson's reelection was unstoppable—he would save himself a few million of his grandfather's dollars. Meanwhile, some other governor—Michigan's George Romney, or Pennsylvania's Bill Scranton—would carry the liberal Republican banner. And if Goldwater prevailed at the convention and split the party? As Johnson said to his increasingly influential aide Bill Moyers, "If I run against Barry, I'd get four hundred electoral votes if they caught me getting a blow job from a secretary in the Oval Office."

It wasn't that the waters were totally calm. His closest aide from his Senate days, young Bobby Baker, had stayed on as Secretary to the Democratic caucus under Mike Mansfield—Johnson liked having a set of eyes and ears back at the Capitol—and the Republicans were digging into some nasty stories about just how the young man on a government salary had accumulated a town house, some pricey country real estate, and three luxury cars. Earl Warren's Supreme Court was stirring up a lot of anger among blue-collar folks with its decisions about dirty books, and keeping prayers and Bibles out of public schools, and letting criminals go free because the police hadn't treated them with kid gloves. He was pretty sure that his first pick for the Court—Connecticut Governor Abe Ribicoff—would follow the liberal line, but Johnson figured the goodwill he'd earn by putting a second Jew on the bench would be worth it.

The more serious trouble, of course, was coming from the world beyond America's borders . . . but then, wasn't that where trouble was likely to come from? Some of it turned out to be little more than noise: For months after the Vienna Summit, Khrushchev had hurled one threat after another about signing a separate peace treaty with East Germany, walking away from the prewar understanding about Berlin, and letting Walter Ulbricht's forces control the rail and road corridors to West Berlin. But 1961 ended, and that treaty never did happen. Khrushchev must have gotten the message at Vienna about who held the whip hand when it came to military might, because while he ordered up an impressive show of force (exploding those 30- and 50-megaton H-bombs he'd talked about at the summit), the rumors of a "wall" around East Berlin to stem the flood of refugees turned out to be just that—rumors. A series of troop movements around the Brandenburg Gate, suggested by Dean Acheson, among others, got the message through. The East Germans sharply increased border patrols, even shot and killed a few dozen would-be refugees—but they (at the direction of Moscow) seemed unwilling to test the West's resolve. If Khrushchev did indeed call West Berlin "the testicles of the West," he had decided not to squeeze.

In fact, so massive was the American stockpile of nuclear weaponry that some thinkers in the defense community were starting to wonder whether a more subtle approach to their potential use was needed. Current U.S. strategy, embodied in the Single Integrated Operational Plan (SIOP-62) called for "massive retaliation," the unleashing of the full U.S. arsenal, in the face of a Soviet attack. Perhaps this was excessive; perhaps a more limited deployment of weapons, aimed at Soviet military targets, could lessen the destructive impact of a nuclear war. A bright young German refugee at Harvard, Henry Kissinger, had made just such a point, and within the Pentagon and Defense Department–funded think tanks, there was much interest in a policy that could keep potential American deaths in the low millions—not counting European and Soviet casualties, of course.

There was, to be sure, pressure from the Reds, but it was coming from the other side of the world. In South Vietnam, infiltrators from the North and guerrillas in the South were assassinating officials in hamlets and villages, and making life miserable for the underpaid, disorganized soldiers of the South Vietnamese Army. And that was making life increasingly uncomfortable for Lyndon Johnson, because his military advisors were pressing him to move and move hard into the South. Not so much McNamara; the Defense Secretary was crunching numbers, ordering up computer simulations, looking for the most measured possible American policy. But the Joint Chiefs of Staff? They and the commanders on the ground in Saigon were champing at the bit, calling for a massive increase of support, 100,000, maybe 200,000 Americans, "surgical" bombing strikes at the North, assuring Johnson that China wouldn't enter the fight. ("That's what MacArthur thought in Korea," Johnson said. "This is different," they replied.) They reminded the President that if waves of the Chinese did come in, well, that's what tactical nuclear weapons were for. Once again, Johnson found himself pulled in two different directions. He believed, heart and soul, in the "domino theory": Lose South Vietnam, and Thailand, Cambodia, Indonesia, maybe even Australia, were put at risk. He believed that a show of force was what Communist predators understood and respected. But he also remembered his own refusal as Senate leader to stand with Nixon and John Foster Dulles in '54 when they wanted to commit American lives when the French were falling to Ho Chi Minh's forces in the North. He knew that General Douglas MacArthur, the hero of the American right, had warned for years about committing American combat troops into a land war in Asia. And he knew what such a commitment had historically meant to liberal dreams at home.

So Johnson split the difference. He authorized 15,000 Army and other military personnel into the South, as trainers and combat advisors, giving them the authority to "take all action necessary" to defend themselves if attacked. If that meant they would be patrolling the perimeters of their bases aggressively, increasing the chances that they would engage Communist guerrillas, well, he'd take that chance. What he would not do, at least not yet, was to send American bombers to attack the North, or to insert massive numbers of combat troops. Not only would that disrupt the whole terrain of the midterm elections, it would put large numbers of Americans into harm's way thousands of miles from home; something that the

American voter was historically reluctant to support, unless it was a Pearl Harbor situation. "Johnson always, always sees foreign and military policy through a totally political prism," one of his closest aides said at the time—which is why he was especially focused on a trouble spot far, far closer to home.

"Cuba is the bone in America's throat," Khrushchev had once said, and America's political class had been choking on it ever since the Bay of Pigs fiasco. As Fidel Castro moved closer and closer to the Soviet Union—as he declared on December 2, 1961, "I am a Marxist-Leninist and shall be one until the end of my life"—the slow burn of the United States grew hotter. This bearded pipsqueak was taunting the most powerful military force on earth, and doing it, in the endlessly repeated mantra, "only ninety miles from our shores." More ominously, Cuba's symbol of romantic revolution, Ernesto "Che" Guevara, was promising "two, three, many Cubas," working with insurrectionists across Latin America, from Honduras and Guatemala to Bolivia and Paraguay, and the Soviet Union had put hundreds of advisors onto the island to train the Cuban military. This was more than an ideological embarrassment; it was a frontal assault on the Monroe Doctrine itself, the 150-year-old assertion that the United States was effectively master in its own hemisphere (Monroe hadn't exactly said that, but that's what a succession of American Presidents and politicians had drawn from it). Running against the party in the White House at a time of widespread prosperity, Republican candidates for the House and Senate in the midterms were growing increasingly critical of the Johnson administration for its "vacillation and weakness" in the face of a Communist enemy just ninety miles, etc. Johnson was a veteran of political wars, and was not precisely shocked at the Republican attacks. What did drive him to near distraction were the shots across his bow coming from Massachusetts Senator Robert Kennedy. Ever since Kennedy's less-than-subtle criticism of the Bay of Pigs failure, Bobby had become a hero to the increasingly vocal Cuban exile community.

They brought him stories of political repression, of Soviet influence, of Castro's efforts at subversion in the hemisphere—some of them baseless rumors, others rooted in fact. And, while never explicitly attacking Johnson, Bobby would frequently express his "earnest hope" that the

administration "would remain vigilant in the face of the clear and present danger posed by the Castro regime." More recently, he had been raising questions about "the increasing and disturbing pace of Soviet military
activity," including what seemed to be the positioning of surface-to-air
missiles across Cuba, designed to shoot down hostile aircraft. It was all
phrased in politically appropriate terms, all surrounded by expressions of
confidence in the President, but Johnson knew full well what the little runt
was up to: *Make me look weak, make him look like the toughest guy on the block,
just in case there's a chance for a nomination fight in '64. Well, let him try; he
won't know what hit him.*

So it was a reasonably content President Johnson who looked up from
his morning newspapers on Tuesday, October 16, 1962, when his National
Security Advisor, McGeorge Bundy, knocked on his bedroom door and
entered with two oversized photographs in his hands.

"I'm afraid we have a problem, Mr. President," Bundy said.

"How big a problem?"

"They don't get any bigger."

FOR NIKITA KHRUSHCHEV, the decision to place nuclear-armed weapons into Cuba was a masterstroke, the most daring decision yet in a political life defined by unpredictable, audacious decisions. It was, he thought,
exactly the right move on so many fronts. Was the United States convinced
of its overwhelming strategic superiority, with its 1,000+ delivery systems,
compared with Moscow's puny arsenal of 10 to 20 operational missiles
and a couple of hundred mechanically suspect bombers? Then move a few
dozen missiles into Cuba, with ranges of 1,000 and 2,000 miles, and the
effective offensive power of the Soviet Union is doubled, putting ninety
million Americans under the shadow of nuclear annihilation. Had the U.S.
encircled the Soviet Union with bombers and missiles at its very doorstep,
from Iran to Turkey? Then let the Americans see how they liked it, with
the enemy camped at their doorstep. At the very least, it might persuade
Washington to remove those missiles as part of a grand bargain, or to think
twice before threatening to bring those missiles into play.

Was the U.S. projecting its power thousands of miles from home? Now

the reach of the Soviet Union would extend to one of the most consequential continents in the worldwide geopolitical chess game. If, in fact,
Fidel and Che were successful in bringing revolution to other nations in
the region, these new revolutionary regimes would know their socialist
experiments would be protected from the counterrevolutionary machinations of Uncle Sam by a close-at-home nuclear umbrella. And then there
was Cuba itself, fulfilling one of the fondest hopes of Khrushchev and the
aging fathers of the October Revolution that had brought the Bolsheviks
to power in 1917. For all of the betrayals of the Revolution's ideals, for all
of the horrors perpetrated by Stalin, these men still held to some of their
youthful illusions. Fidel and his khaki-clad insurgents seemed proof that
their hopes were still capable of fulfillment. For the first time, a Communist
uprising had succeeded without the Red Army or Soviet resources as the
key. At first, Moscow was highly dubious that Castro was a Marxist revolutionary at all. Now the Kremlin was determined not to let Washington
crush the Cuban experiment before it had a chance to begin. It had tried
once at the Bay of Pigs; and every indication, from the sabotage of Cuban
mines and factories, to the ceaseless rumors in the Cuban exile community,
to the military exercises up and down the East Coast of the United States,
to the speeches in the American Congress, convinced Khrushchev and his
intelligence services that it was only a matter of time before Washington
tried again. The revolution in Cuba had to be protected, and a massive
deployment of nuclear force was the only way to provide a genuine deter-
rent to Yankee aggression. The more he remembered President Johnson's
boasts at the summit, the more he was convinced that audacious action was
imperative.

Khrushchev kept his gambit a secret from all but five of his closest
advisors. Indeed, secrecy was the key to his strategy, and given the scope
of the plan, secrecy was going to be very hard to maintain. Several dozen
medium- and intermediate-range ballistic missiles would be shipped to
Cuba by sea during the summer and early autumn, each missile capable
of carrying a 1-megaton warhead. To protect against U.S. attacks on the
missile sites by air, or an invasion by sea, Moscow would also ship surface-
to-air missiles, and Il-28 light bombers. Most astonishingly, Khrushchev
also decided to ship to Cuba tactical missiles with nuclear warheads, each

packing a 5- to 12-kiloton punch. Each tactical missile could wipe out whole battalions of invaders. (What this meant, of course, was that any U.S. assault on Cuba was all but guaranteed to become a nuclear confrontation between the superpowers. That was something that apparently never occurred to Khrushchev or his associates.) Finally, more than 40,000 Soviet soldiers, pilots, and support forces would be deployed to Cuba to man the missiles, guard the sites, and provide protection against attack. All summer long, Soviet ships, disguising their real cargo by displaying machinery and motor vehicles on deck, sailed from ports in the Crimea and in the North. By September, the first R-11 and R-14 missiles (SS-4s and SS-5s, as they were known in the West) had arrived, along with cruise missiles and several dozen nuclear warheads.

By October, the Soviet freighter *Indigirka* reached Mariel with a cargo of forty-five 1-megaton warheads, twelve 2-kiloton warheads for the tactical weapons, six 12-kiloton bombs for the Il-28 bombers, and thirty-six 23-kiloton warheads for the cruise missiles. By mid-October, the first medium-range missiles had been deployed at San Cristobal, forty miles southwest of Havana. Now only one step remained for Khrushchev's plan to work: maintaining secrecy until the missiles were fully operational. Once they were in place, by mid-November, Khrushchev would personally reveal their existence—perhaps during a visit to Cuba, perhaps during a speech to the UN, perhaps at a summit with President Johnson. He liked that notion best; it would give him no small pleasure to watch the face of the oversized Texan when he realized the U.S. was now as fully vulnerable as the Motherland.

Unfortunately for Khrushchev, reliance on secrecy was a delusion. The sheer length of the missiles (seventy feet), and the logistics necessary to transport them from ports to their sites around Cuba, made secrecy no more possible than concealing the movement of dinosaurs. The trucks ferrying them along Cuba's narrow, winding roads kept knocking down telephone poles and mailboxes, and riding roughshod over roadside stands and shacks. Word of these strange doings soon reached the ears of American intelligence, prompting the CIA to end the suspension of U-2 flights over Cuba, a suspension Secretary of State Fulbright had pushed for, in order to create a better atmosphere for negotiations with the Soviets on Berlin and other issues. When the U-2 returned after photographing the scene 70,000 feet below at San Cristobal, it did not take long for analysts to decipher the meaning of the photos. It was that message that National Security Advisor Bundy was bringing to President Johnson this Tuesday morning in mid-October.

AT 11:45 A.M. on October 16, fifteen men sat around the long oblong table in the Cabinet Room of the White House. In the middle, flanked by the American flag and another bearing the Presidential seal, sat President Johnson, chin cupped in his hand. Vice President Humphrey sat at his left, his face white, his hands folded over each other to keep the slight tremble hidden. From State came Secretary Fulbright and Undersecretary George Ball; from Defense came McNamara and Paul Nitze, who'd moved over from State at Johnson's request. The Chairman of the Joint Chiefs, Maxwell Taylor, came, accompanied by Air Force Chief Curtis LeMay, whose cigar never left his mouth. CIA Director Richard Helms, along with Mac Bundy, the National Security Advisor, sat at a far end of the table. So did a man with no public office whose judgment Johnson trusted: former Secretary of State Dean Acheson.

"There's no doubt what these pictures show, is there, Mac?" the President asked Bundy.

"No, Mr. President," he said, gesturing toward Helms. "Dick's team says their length leaves no doubt."

"Can they be launched right now?" Johnson asked.

"We simply can't answer that," General Taylor answered. "This type of missile can be launched very quickly. And remember, sir, these pictures come from a very small part of the island. There could well be other sites, and those could be operational right now."

"How long before we get complete information about the rest of the island?"

"Could take weeks, Mr. President," Helms said.

"Weeks?"

"For complete coverage of a cloud-covered island, yes."

Johnson looked around the room, moving his gaze slowly from face to face.

"Do any of you," he asked, "want to suggest any option other than taking these missiles out?"

"I think we owe it to ourselves," Bundy said, "to think through a political track, at least for forty-eight hours: blockade the island, keep any more weapons and warheads from reaching Cuba, and be prepared to strike if we don't have a clear signal from the Soviets that they're prepared to get those missiles out."

"Do we have any way of knowing whether we can take every missile out?" Fulbright asked.

"Seems to me, General Taylor, you've just made it awfully clear that we can't know that . . . and if there's a nuclear missile standing after we hit them . . . a blockade would give them time to think about what they've done."

A fist slammed on the table. It belonged to Air Force Chief of Staff Curtis LeMay. LeMay had organized the incendiary B-29 bombing attacks against Japan that had devastated the island nation, killing somewhere between a quarter and a half a million civilians, and quite possibly saving millions of lives that would have been lost in an American invasion of the island. During the Cold War, he had organized the Berlin Airlift that had broken the back of the Soviet blockade of Berlin in 1948. LeMay had made no secret of his belief that nuclear war between the U.S. and the Soviet Union was inevitable within a matter of months or a year or two at the outside.

"We don't have any choice except direct military action," he said. "If we don't do anything to Cuba, they're going to push on Berlin and push real hard, because they've got us on the run. So I see no other solution. 'Blockade,' 'political action' I see leading us into war. It'd be almost as bad as the appeasement at Munich. We need direct military intervention right now."

"If I may . . ." The voice belonged to a man who appeared to have stepped from the pages of a magazine pictorial on the life of an upper-class Englishman. At sixty-seven, Dean Acheson was a portrait of certitude: his impeccably groomed moustache, his three-piece gray pin-striped suit set off perfectly by a tie bearing the insignia of his beloved Yale. As Truman's Secretary of State, Acheson had been the target of withering assaults by Joseph McCarthy, Richard Nixon, and other Republican zealots who saw in him the apostle of accommodation. In fact, Acheson was wedded to the notion that he understood better than anyone what motivated the Soviet Union, and what would cause them to alter their aggressive impulses. Acheson as much as any single individual embodied the Democratic Party's post–World War II mind-set about international relations. It was a mind-set that had been subject to hints of challenge by newer, younger Democrats, John Kennedy among them. For Lyndon Johnson, however, it was at the heart of how he saw the world. Focused on domestic concerns, he had long ago concluded that what was good enough for Harry Truman, George C. Marshall, and Dean Acheson was good enough for him. He would listen to Fulbright and Mansfield, he wanted the counsel of those who lived in the political arena, but he had a kind of reverence for the men who had led the country through the first dangerous days of the Cold War.

"Mr. President," Acheson said, "what I propose is a prompt, measured response to this provocation. I understand the impulses for an all-out assault; it may yet come to that. My own preference would be for a surgical strike at every missile site we can identify, as soon as possible, accompanied by a clear statement by you that we expect the Soviets to remove all of their offensive weapons."

"And if they do, in fact, have operational ballistic missiles in place?" Secretary McNamara asked.

"There isn't a chance in the world they would use them against the United States," Acheson replied firmly. "They are not suicidal. And they clearly understand spheres of influence. They would no more risk their survival over a country thousands of miles from their borders than we would have sent troops into Budapest in 1956. It is possible, perhaps, that they will hit our missiles in Turkey."

"And then . . . ?"

"Then, in accordance with NATO policy, we would strike at one of their bases inside the Soviet Union. At that point, it is hoped that cooler heads will prevail and everyone will stop and talk. But the far stronger likelihood is that a swift, targeted air attack by the United States on a non-populated area of Cuba would be seen not as an attack on the Soviet Union, but on something—not people—in Cuba. This would hardly call for a reflex attack on the United States that would mean the destruction of the Soviet Union."

The President got up from his chair.

"Excuse me for a moment," he said, and walked back to the Oval Office. A visitor was waiting for him: the man Lyndon Johnson regarded as the wisest, most prudent of counselors, the man who had mentored him through his rise in the U.S. Senate, whose friendship had survived even the battle over voting rights. He listened while the President sketched out the arguments he'd heard in the Cabinet Room.

"I know LeMay is a bit of a loose cannon, but I think the general's right, Mr. President," Senator Russell said. "It seems to me we're at a crossroads. We're either a first-class power or we're not. The Secretary says, 'Give them time to think'? Hell, they'll just use that time to get better prepared. I think we can't afford to stop with a strike at the missiles. I think we should assemble as speedily as possible an adequate force and clean out the situation. I don't know whether Khrushchev will launch a nuclear war over Cuba or not, I don't believe he will. But the more we temporize, the more surely he is to convince himself that we are afraid to make any real movement and to really fight."

The President nodded, thanked Senator Russell for coming by, and walked back into the Cabinet Room.

"Mr. President," Secretary Fulbright said, "I just want to make sure the political option isn't off the table. If we blockade every Soviet ship heading for Cuba, and a deadline—"

"For God's sakes," General LeMay said, "if we hadn't listened to you a year and a half ago, we wouldn't be dealing with Russian missiles!"

The room was engulfed in silence. Not since Douglas MacArthur had defied President Harry Truman's Korean strategy had a military man openly challenged civilian authority.

"I think we could use some time to think this through," the President said after a long moment. "Let's all be back here at nine a.m. Meanwhile, Dick," he said to the CIA Director, "I want every reconnaissance plane we have over Cuba. We have just got to know where those missiles are. I think Dean's right; Khrushchev can't be wanting a nuclear war over Cuba—but I want to make sure we take out as many as we possibly can."

It was a perfectly sensible, rational suggestion. And if events, and decisions, had proceeded along a sensible, rational course, it wouldn't have led to what happened.

THAT TUESDAY NIGHT, President Johnson's sleep was disturbed by dreams. All his life he had been plagued by visions of helplessness in the face of impending danger. As a young man, he'd been haunted by a recurring nightmare: He was sitting in a big straight chair, in the middle of a great open plain, helpless in the face of a cattle stampede coming straight at him. As a young Congressional aide, and into his Senate days, he saw himself chained to a desk, doomed to answer an endless stack of mail, trapped as he watched other men and women heading home to their families. In his first days as President, he dreamt that he was alone, imprisoned in a small cage, surrounded by dust-laden books, and when he looked in the mirror, he saw a twisted, bent old man. This night, he saw himself in the White House, somehow transformed into Woodrow Wilson, paralyzed by a stroke as others moved around him tending to the nation's business—a fear fueled by the near-fatal heart attack he'd suffered in 1955. By morning, he had decided on a course of action; given his character, his experience, the lessons he had taken from his decades in public life, it would have been almost impossible for him to have taken any other path.

> —He held fast to the assumption that the principal players—
> Khrushchev and Castro—were acting from the same fundamen-
> tal set of beliefs as himself. It was simply impossible for him to
> believe that anyone would risk the lives of millions of people for
> an idea, an abstraction.
> —He had never developed an interest, or much knowledge, about
> the wider world. He could sit in a room with a dozen lawmakers
> and calculate in moments how a decision on a bill or a govern-
> ment policy would affect their districts, their states, their politi-
> cal futures. But he was incapable of understanding how a leader
> from an utterly different political system might think or react to
> an American move in a genuine crisis.

—He had succeeded in life by identifying powerful elders, then emulating them, making himself indispensable to them, never by challenging them. Had John Kennedy lived to enter the White House, after besting his elders in the fight for the Presidency, he might have had a less reverential view of their wisdom. For Johnson, however, the words of Dean Acheson and Richard Russell carried enormous weight.

—He had succeeded by developing an acutely sensitive set of political receptors. He knew that a failure to act decisively would render him defenseless to attack. The midterm elections were barely three weeks away; a setback would cripple his efforts to pass his legislative program, leaving him something of a lame duck—and leaving him open to attacks from within his own party at the hands of the uncrowned Prince of the Restoration. Robert Kennedy would use his Massachusetts Senate seat as a staging area for assaults on the emasculated Lyndon Johnson.

—And he had always, always governed himself by the principle that reasonable men, sitting down together, could find a middle path. He had never been a man who thought in broad concepts or policies; in that sense, he was a classic legislator, leaving it to the man in charge to create the vision, employing his skills in fitting that vision into the practical realities of a body of men and women relentlessly pursuing their narrow interests. Now that he was the man in the cockpit, he still thought as he always had. In the welter of suggestions for what to do about the missiles in Cuba— negotiate, blockade, take them out, invade—Johnson's most fundamental instinct was to find the middle ground. He would take the path that demonstrated resolve, one that showed the Soviets that America meant business, but that would also clearly signal his intention not to trigger a wider war, to let Khrushchev know that there was a reasonable resolution to this crisis. There were U.S. missiles in Turkey that were obsolete; they could talk about removing them. There were nuclear test ban agreements they could reach. Once those missiles were out of Cuba, there was no need for a full-scale invasion, no need to go to the brink of war. He and Khrushchev could reason together, like reasonable men.

It was a perfectly sensible conclusion for President Johnson to reach, except for what he, and every other man in that Cabinet Room, did not know.

—They did not know that there were tens of thousands of Soviet troops and support personnel who had come to Cuba that summer and early autumn, to guard the missile sites, watch over the nuclear warheads, man the tanks that had been sent to protect the island from a U.S. invasion. So any strike at the missile sites would be an attack that would inevitably kill hundreds of Soviet citizens.

—They did not know that dozens of tactical nuclear weapons had been sent to Cuba, along with the medium- and intermediate-range ballistic missiles, greatly increasing the likelihood that any U.S.–Soviet confrontation would "go nuclear" almost immediately. Nor did they know that dozens of nuclear warheads, for strategic and tactical weapons, were already in Cuba, hidden in caves, but capable of being moved on short notice to the launch sites.

—They did not know that Soviet commanders in Cuba had been receiving conflicting signals from Moscow about just how free they were to use these weapons, signals that a military man could read as authorizing the use of tactical nukes if there was evidence of an all-out attack on the island.

—They did not know that Fidel Castro, certain that a Yankee invasion was coming, was putting enormous pressure on the Kremlin to take strong action against any incursion of his airspace by American airplanes . . . or that Soviet military officers on the ground in Cuba would be responsive to Castro's urgings.

All Wednesday, President Johnson and his team of officials and advisors met to hash out the details of the U.S. response. At sundown on Thursday

evening, U.S. fighter-bombers would take out the missile sites in San Cristobal and Remedios, with a limited number of sorties to minimize civilian
casualties. At nine p.m., the President would address the nation—and the
world—to announce the discovery of the offensive missiles, the surgical
strikes against them, and the tentative imposition of a blockade against
Soviet ships heading to Cuba. The speech would also contain a direct
appeal to Premier Khrushchev, and a pledge to stop all military activity in
return for a Soviet promise to remove the missiles. The Joint Chiefs were
instructed to move troops, planes, and ships in preparation for an invasion, but there would be no invasion if the Russians proved responsive to
the more limited use of force. And, in response to the urgings of Secretary
Fulbright, and former Soviet Ambassador Tommy Thompson, who knew
more about the Russians than any other American, the President agreed to
an extraordinary gambit: a direct conversation with Khrushchev. Johnson
would confront the Premier with the fact that the missiles had been discovered, and offer him the chance to resolve the crisis peacefully (this gambit
infuriated the Joint Chiefs of Staff, who were certain the Soviet leader
would simply stall for time. "I'm giving him twenty-four hours," Johnson
said to JCS Chairman Maxwell Taylor).

Reaching Khrushchev was no easy task: There was no direct communication link between the White House and the Kremlin. Although there
had been talk for years about establishing just such a "hot line" to deal with
fast-moving crises, neither teletype nor telephone nor computer communications had ever been established. It was two o'clock on Wednesday
afternoon—ten p.m. Moscow time—when the President, the Chairman,
their aides, and their interpreters gathered around speakerphones in the
Cabinet Room and the Chairman's office.

"We have discovered the offensive weapons you have deployed in Cuba,"
the President began. "We regard them as a blatant violation of international law, a deliberate act of deception, and a direct threat to the national
security of the United States. If you do not begin to dismantle and remove
these missiles within twenty-four hours, we will take all appropriate action
to defend ourselves."

Khrushchev's first responses were by turns defensive and truculent.
Those missiles are not there to attack you; only a madman would start a war

with these monstrous weapons. They are there only to protect the Cuban people from your aggression. You are no more threatened than we are by your missiles that surround us, from Turkey to Iran to Italy.

Tommy Thompson scribbled an urgent note and passed it to the President.

"Suggest that a trade for Turkey might be possible once he gets his missiles out," he wrote.

Johnson nodded, and began to speak when Richard Helms took a note from a grim-faced aide, and signaled the President to mute the call.

"Mr. President," he said, "we've just learned that one of our aircraft has been shot down over Cuba—pilot's presumed dead."

"Mr. Chairman," the President said into the phone, "I think we are done talking for now."

WHEN KHRUSHCHEV DECIDED TO dispatch tens of thousands of Soviet military personnel to Cuba, he didn't ponder long over who would command them. Issa Pliyev was the Grand Old Man of the Soviet military, although he was only fifty-nine. He'd been in the Red Army for forty years, commanded the 50th Cavalry division in the Great Patriotic War, fought in the defense of Moscow and Stalingrad, led the invasion of Manchuria. He was a beloved figure in the Red Army, and his judgment was considered sound enough, prudent enough, to be trusted to oversee the vast arsenal of nuclear weapons that had been dispatched to Cuba. Still, the men around Khrushchev were not that confident about the possible deployment of any nuclear weapons, so they instructed Pliyev not to use any tactical nuclear weapon unless Cuba was under clear assault. Khrushchev had also given orders to avoid any "provocations" against the United States.

It is unclear what Pliyev would have ordered had he been informed that an American U-2 spy plane had been spotted near Guantánamo. But when an antiaircraft unit got word of the sighting, Pliyev was not at headquarters to answer the urgent call of Captain N. Antonyets. Pliyev's top two deputies, Lieutenant General Grechko and Lieutenant General Garbuz, were certain that the U-2 was taking photographs in preparation for an imminent American invasion—an invasion, Castro had been insisting, that was coming within days, perhaps hours. Knowing that the aircraft would be out of range in minutes, the two Soviet generals ordered Captain Antonyets to fire his SA-2 rocket; the explosion sent the plane plunging to earth, and pilot Rudolf Andersen was killed. When General Pliyev reached his headquarters, he was told of his aides' decision to shoot down the U-2. An "operational-strategic necessity," General Gretchko called it. Pliyev nodded his assent. Clearly the United States was preparing to strike the island; clearly the U-2 flight was part of the pre-invasion preparation. He and his team were not about to leave the island, or for that matter the 40,000+ Soviet troops on Cuba, without protection. While the instructions from Moscow were less than crystal clear, they clearly did authorize him to use the weapons at his disposal to defend against an attack—all of his weapons. So when, a few hours later, urgent communications began to reach his headquarters about incoming American fighter-bombers, Pliyev had no hesitancy in using every weapon at his disposal.

The American attack was confined to conventional weapons, but it was massive. Squadrons of F-100 and F-101B fighter-bombers had attacked the missile sites at San Cristobal and Remedios; another squadron was minutes away from Sagua la Grande. The R-12 medium-range ballistics missiles had been destroyed, and hundreds of Soviet personnel were dead or dying. If this did not qualify as an all-out assault on the island, what did? Nor did it matter to Pliyev that the weapons he was about to deploy were nuclear in nature; the employment of battlefield nuclear weapons had been part and parcel of Soviet military planning for years. Moments after receiving word of the American assault on the missile sites, Pliyev ordered half a dozen KFR missiles—"Frogs" in the American parlance—fired at the Guantánamo Naval Base, the U.S. military installation on Cuba's Eastern shore. Each missile carried a warhead with 5- to 10-kiloton power. The force of the attack created an immense fireball over the sky of Eastern Cuba; virtually all of the 9,500 sailors and Marines were killed instantly, as were thousands of Cuban nationals who were still working at the base, despite the steadily escalating tensions between the U.S. and Cuban governments. The blasts also killed several hundred members of the Cuban armed forces, including Raul Castro, brother of the President, who had gone to lead the forces that would resist Marines seeking to move out from the base to aid in the expected invasion. For the first time since the end of the Second World War, nuclear weapons had been employed in a military conflict. For a generation, men at the commanding heights of military and civilian power had committed tens of billions of dollars, countless thousands of hours of thinking, about the possibilities and the consequences of such an event. And now that it had happened, it was surrounded by an impenetrable fog of confusion.

A FEW MINUTES AFTER six p.m. on Thursday, October 17, they had begun to gather in the International Situation Room, a 5,000-square-foot complex in the basement of the West Wing of the White House that had once housed a bowling alley. After the Bay of Pigs fiasco a year and a half earlier, National Security Advisor McGeorge Bundy had successfully lobbied for a facility to gather real-time information as quickly as possible during any international crisis. Now, in mid-October 1962, teletype machines linked to the communications systems of the State Department, Defense Department, the CIA, and the National Security Administration brought information directly into the center. President Johnson sat at the end of an oblong mahogany conference table, flanked by General Taylor and the other service chiefs, and a dozen civilians: Vice President Humphrey, Secretaries Fulbright and McNamara, Deputy Defense Secretary Nitze, and two State Department Counselors, Llewellyn "Tommy" Thompson and Chip Bohlen, who held much of the country's institutional knowledge about the Soviet Union and its leaders.

Dean Acheson had proposed he not be included in the gathering; holding no official post, he argued, it would be inappropriate for a private citizen to be offering policy guidance on so fundamental a matter as war and peace.

"Does anyone have a Bible?" Johnson asked. Charles "Chuck" Enright, the CIA official who served as night duty officer, produced one, and Johnson promptly swore Acheson in as a Special Assistant to the President.

"We'll get you the certificate later," Johnson said with a smile. "Now, sit down, Dean."

The facility was a far cry from the science-fiction-like fantasies of mid-century Hollywood: no giant video screens, no instant visual links to a worldwide reporting system, just teletype links to civilian and military centers, and, potentially most critical, to the U.S. Embassy in Moscow and the Soviet Embassy in Washington—the closest thing the two superpowers had to real-time communications.

They had come to the Situation Room with two purposes in mind: first, to follow the progress of the attacks on the Soviet missile sites in Cuba; second, to maintain communications with the Kremlin, so that there was no misunderstanding about the intentions of the United States.

"We have got to have Khrushchev understand," Johnson said, "that this is a limited, targeted strike on their missiles; it is not the beginning of an invasion, or an attack on Russia. I know you would prefer a different course of action," he said to the military chiefs, "but if we can get those missiles out this way, it's going to save a whole lot of killing."

"Or put the United States in mortal peril," muttered Naval Chief Lymen Lemnitzer. Joint Chiefs Chairman Taylor put a restraining hand on Lemnitzer's shoulder. This was, he thought, not an especially good time to even hint at a military challenge to civilian control.

Over the last thirty-six hours, the military had raised its alert level from DEFCON-5 to DEFCON-2—one level short of war. Navy and Marine personnel by the thousands had been loaded onto ships on the West Coast, and were heading east, through the Panama Canal, to be positioned for a potential invasion, while destroyers, aircraft carriers, and battleships on the East Coast were steaming south. More ominously, members of the House and Senate had been told to pack bags, and ready themselves for relocation to the Greenbrier Hotel in White Sulphur Springs, West Virginia. There, in 1959, the government had created an underground facility to house Congress in the aftermath of a nuclear holocaust. It included a dormitory, kitchen, hospital, and a broadcast center for members of Congress. The convention center, used by the Greenbrier guests for business meetings, was actually built above a disguised workstation area for members of Congress, complete with hidden thirty-ton blast doors. The walls of the bunker were made of reinforced concrete designed to withstand a nuclear blast in Washington, D.C. Many of the House and Senate members rejected the notice—"If anything happens," they said, "I'm going to stay here with my family"—but Johnson argued that if war did break out, the government had to keep running. By this Thursday evening, several dozen Congressional leaders and committee chairs had reluctantly agreed to relocate (Acheson and Nitze privately scorned the precaution as "alarmist," insisting again that the Kremlin would never risk nuclear war over territory so far beyond their reach).

That was clearly the expectation of Johnson and the men who surrounded him that evening. With the first word that the American fighter bombers were on their way to the missile sites, the White House informed the Kremlin, via cable to the Soviet Embassy, that this was a tightly controlled, limited strike to protect vital American national interests; that no further military action was underway or contemplated; and that the United States urged immediate negotiations to defuse the crisis, with every issue, including the future of U.S. missiles along the Soviet border, open for discussion. President Johnson's speech to the nation, scheduled for nine p.m., would make the same points.

It was a prudent, rational approach, designed by prudent, rational men. Once again, President Johnson had returned to the most deeply rooted instinct of his life: He had split the difference.

And then, at 7:35, as the group was arguing about the points UN Ambassador Stevenson would make in the Security Council the next morning, Chuck Enright was handed a piece of teletype from the Defense Department link. He passed it to Mac Bundy, who read it twice in disbelief.

"They've hit Guantánamo," he said. "And . . . they appear to have used a nuclear weapon. They've obliterated the base—nothing left."

Johnson turned angrily to CIA Director Helms.

"I thought we had every one of their ballistic missile sites under twenty-four-hour surveillance. I thought it was impossible for them to launch without at least a few minutes' warning."

"As the Chiefs and I said," Helms began, "we could never be certain that we had located every one of those—"

"Maybe it wasn't a ballistic missile," Paul Nitze said. "Maybe it was tactical."

"What the hell difference does it make?" said Curtis LeMay. "We've been attacked by a nuclear weapon by the Soviet Union. There've got to be thousands of dead American boys. For all we know, there's a missile headed right for Washington, right now. Mr. President, you need to give us the order, and we'll hit them with everything we've got."

"It might make all the difference," Tommy Thompson said. "Was there an order given by Khrushchev? Was it a rogue officer on the ground who panicked, or took matters into his own hands? I agree it can't go unanswered, but we need to do everything we can—now—to find out what this represents."

"What do you suggest, Tommy?" the President asked. "Lodge a protest with the UN? Cancel a tour by the Philharmonic?"

"There may be a response that will keep some options open," Secretary McNamara said.

From the moment he'd taken the post, he'd been intrigued by the idea of an alternative to the massive retaliation policy that was the core American strategy of the Eisenhower years. He'd devoured the monographs of the RAND Corporation, the books by young Harvard thinkers like Carl Kaysen and Kissinger. Maybe, he thought, it's worth a try.

"We've just been hit by a tactical missile launched from an ally of the Soviet Union," he said. "What if we launched one of our Jupiters from Turkey or Iran, targeted to Sevastopol. It would destroy the Black Fleet, take out at least as many Russians as we lost at Guantánamo—but make it clear that we want no further hostilities."

"And then we can sit here and let ourselves be burnt to a cinder while they take out New York and Chicago and Miami," LeMay said. "That is suicide—not to mention treason, Mr. President. Our strategy has kept the peace for a decade—they hit us anywhere, we hit them everywhere."

"And what if it is a rogue commander?" Vice President Humphrey asked. Every head turned in surprise. The Vice President rarely spoke up in any significant gathering; under President Johnson's stern discipline, the once-voluble Humphrey had turned into the near mute of the Johnson administration. Now his jaw was set, his fists gripped tightly in front of him.

"It's not out of the question," he continued, looking sharply at LeMay and the other generals, "that some hothead took it on himself to do this. For all we know, Khrushchev is having a fit. I can't see us plunging into a world war if this was a ghastly mistake; and if it isn't, then that missile's already on the way. Yes, they'll have to pay for this with a lot of Russian lives—but I'd rather lose a few thousand of ours and theirs than twenty or thirty million."

"And maybe you'd rather see our country become Soviet America," LeMay thundered. "Mr. President, let us do what we must, or go down in history as the President who lost the United States."

The men in the room waited for the President to speak. And at that moment, as it had over and over in his life, Lyndon Johnson's body betrayed him.

Throughout his career, at every critical moment, his primal fear of political death had triggered serious physical afflictions. As a twenty-nine-year-old candidate for the U.S. House of Representatives, he was struck by an appendicitis attack two days before Election Day; he was rushed to a hospital, underwent emergency surgery, and remained there for two weeks (his opponents accused him of faking his illness to gain sympathy). As a new member of Congress, his obsession to succeed had turned him into a nervous wreck; a severe rash broke out all over his hands, forcing him to wrap them in bandages. In his first campaign for the U.S. Senate, in 1941, he heard the devastating news that the popular Texas governor had decided to jump into the race; he was promptly hospitalized with what was labeled pneumonia, but was more likely a case of deep depression. In his second Senate campaign in 1948, Johnson was attacked by a powerful case of kidney stones, a condition he tried to conceal from the press. When his political ally John Connally insisted he come clean, he drafted and almost released a statement withdrawing from the Senate contest.

After a contentious clash with Senate colleagues in 1955, he suffered a heart attack that almost killed him. And now, at the most critical moment any President had ever had to face, Johnson's body betrayed him one more time. His face drained of all color, sweat covered his brow and face, and he fell forward in his chair, his face striking the table with a thud.

"Jesus, it's his heart!" Bundy shouted. "Get the medics in here now!" As the medical team rushed into the Situation Room to tend to him, Secretary Fulbright motioned to Humphrey.

"We need a decision, Mr. Vice President. Do we launch? Do we wait?"

"With respect, Mr. Secretary," Maxwell Taylor said, "on what authority do we presume the Vice President now exercises Presidential authority?"

"There is none," Dean Acheson said. "At least, not in any law. The Constitution says when the President dies, his authority 'devolves' on the Vice President. But Lyndon—the President's not dead—is he?" he asked the medical team, frantically working on Johnson. One of them shook his head uncertainly. "But logic suggests—"

"Logic suggests we should be executing SIOP-62," Lemnitzer said. "And 'logic' suggests we should be de-camping to Mount Weather—now!" Mount Weather was the top-secret Emergency Operations Center in Bluemont, Virginia, fifty miles west of Washington. The immense underground complex was the emergency operations center, designed to keep the Executive Branch of government functioning in the event of a disaster—or a war.

"The helicopters are on the West Lawn now," Bundy said. "We should—"

"No," Humphrey said. "If we board those 'copters, we'll have no chance to communicate with the Kremlin. We have to see if there's a way to keep this contained."

"For all we know," Nitze said, "Khrushchev's not even in control anymore. The hawks over there have been out to remove him ever since Vienna."

"I have to take that chance, General," Humphrey said to Taylor. "I think you need to go to Mount Weather. If it turns out we need to . . . we need to move to DEFCON-1, you can execute that from there." The generals rose to take their leave; LeMay could be heard muttering to Taylor: "If we don't hear anything in fifteen minutes, we're going to have to take matters—"

"Enough, Curtis," Taylor snapped.

The medical team had President Johnson on the floor, as they tried to bring breath into his body; Vice President Humphrey clutched the phone, listening for the signal that told him that a connection to the Kremlin had succeeded; Cabinet members, advisors, and military personnel scanned the teletypes, looking for reports that Soviet troops were marching into West Berlin, that Russian missiles were streaking westward, into Europe, or heading over the oceans toward the continental United States. What they did not know had, quite literally, become a matter of global life and death.

·   ·   ·

IN THE END, it came down to blind luck. When the telephone rang in Khrushchev's fifty-by-thirty-five-foot office in the Kremlin, he was stuffing a briefcase filled with top-secret papers as his security team was urging him, along with his highest-ranking advisors, to vacate; a helicopter was waiting in Red Square to take them to the massive underground complex just outside Moscow, one of the many facilities built to shelter top government and party leaders in the event of nuclear war.

Had Lyndon Johnson been on the other end of the line, Khrushchev would very likely have refused to take the call. The attack on the Cuban missile site had convinced him that the American President was firmly in the camp of the Pentagon war-makers. Had the Soviets ever taken any military action against the nuclear missiles that were encircling the Soviet Union? Did that cowboy not understand what a provocation a U-2 overflight would look like to the Soviet military commanders in Cuba? (Thank God he'd retracted his order authorizing those commanders to use tactical nuclear weapons; there was no telling what one of those hotheads might do.)

"It's not the President, Mr. Chairman," his private secretary said. "He has apparently been taken ill. It's Vice President Humphrey."

Khrushchev paused. He had met Humphrey back in December 1958 when then-Senator Humphrey was on a trip to encourage cooperation in scientific and medical research. What began as a courtesy call turned into an eight-hour marathon conversation; the two men talked of everything from farm issues to family matters to diplomacy. Humphrey, the Kremlin's American experts had explained to the Premier, was a leading figure in liberal circles, an ardent proponent of disarmament and a nuclear test ban. So what did it mean that at this moment of crisis, Humphrey, and not Lyndon Johnson, was speaking for the United States? Based on his decades of surviving Stalin's purges and the Kremlin's sometimes murderous office politics, Khrushchev did not believe for a minute that the American President had been "taken ill." Clearly, the war-makers in the Pentagon, the CIA, and the military-industrial complex had, at least for now, lost power, and the American government was in the hands of progressives.

So he took the call. Even through the interpreter, there was no mistaking the anger, and the fear, that was coming from Vice President Humphrey.

"Mr. Chairman," Humphrey began, "you have put the world on the brink of war . . ."

"It is your government, Mr. Vice President, that chose to invade Cuban airspace with your spy plane. How could you think we would not defend our ally—"

"I am talking about your decision to use a nuclear weapon that has killed thousands of Americans," Humphrey replied.

"What kind of bullshit is this?" Khrushchev exploded. "I have specifically forbidden my commanders on the ground to use any nuclear weapons without my personal authorization."

There was a brief pause; for a moment, Khrushchev feared the always-erratic electronics inside the Kremlin had failed.

"Are you telling me," Humphrey's interpreter said, speaking as slowly and deliberately as Humphrey had, "that you do not know that Guantánamo has been wiped out by your tactical nuclear weapons?"

Now it was the American's turn to sit and wait through what seemed like endless moments of silence.

"This is . . . impossible," the weak response finally came. But even as he spoke those words, Khrushchev was thinking: *Those lunatics. Did they not receive my instructions—or did they simply choose to ignore them?* Now Humphrey's interpreter was speaking again, rapidly communicating the message Humphrey was delivering in between urgent consultations with Tommy Thompson.

Mr. Chairman, if you really did not know that your commanders attacked our base at Guantánamo, if this was not your decision, we may be able to avoid a Third World War. But you must understand that we cannot allow Guantánamo to go unanswered; our military, and our people, would not stand for it. We are launching a strike at Sevastopol; it will kill thousands of people, and wipe out much of your fleet. If you do not respond, we will launch no further missiles, and will call our bombers back. But we need your answer now.

This time, the Soviet Premier did not hesitate. His assent brought an end to what came to be called the "Sixty-Minute War." No authoritative casualty count was ever established, because the thousands dead at Guantánamo and the tens of thousands dead at Sevastopol did not include the numberless dead who died of the effects of radiation: in Cuba, the Dominican Republic, southern Florida, the Crimea, and the nations bordering the Black Sea.

Nor were the political effects fully clear. Barely three weeks after the Sixty-Minute War, the midterm elections in the U.S. yielded the lowest voter turnout in modern American history; barely 13 percent of the voters went to the polls, producing wildly conflicting results. In Massachusetts, Senator Robert Kennedy barely survived a third-party challenge from forty-six-year-old Harvard University professor and longtime peace activist H. Stuart Hughes. Hughes, arguing that Kennedy's "inflammatory rhetoric" had helped push the great powers to "the brink of extinction," wound up with 38 percent of the vote, finishing only a few points behind Kennedy. In California, by contrast, the strong foreign-policy credentials of Richard Nixon propelled him to victory in the governor's race against incumbent Edmund "Pat" Brown, immediately lifting him into contention for the Republican Presidential nomination in 1964. There were also two prominent figures from the Right that were all but certain to run: Arizona Senator Barry Goldwater and General Curtis LeMay. The general had resigned his Air Force post with a furious denunciation at the "appeasers, the cowards" that had prevented the military from "ending the Communistic threat once and for all."

Those political considerations were quickly overshadowed by the clouds of confusion that surrounded the White House. President Johnson, it was clear, had suffered a major heart attack in the White House Situation Room that had left him severely weakened, physically and mentally. For years, Constitutional experts had warned of just such a possibility, had pointed back to the time when it had become reality, when a stroke-weakened Woodrow Wilson had had his Presidency taken over by his wife Edith and an advisor. For years, Constitutional amendments had been proposed, clearly spelling out the conditions under which a Vice President could assume the duties of the President, even against the wishes of a President. No such amendment had ever been adopted, or even sent to the states by the Congress. In its absence, only an informal understanding among Humphrey and the members of Johnson's Cabinet kept the essential machinery of the Executive Branch operating. In the absence of Johnson's formidable leadership skills, and the severe economic and emotional impact of the Sixty-Minute War, Johnson's ambitious domestic program—"a blueprint for a Great Society," he'd called it—withered. And, like the nation at large, the administration was divided between those like Humphrey who wanted to push for a major arms-reduction deal with the Soviets, and those who believed that only massive, unquestioned superiority could prevent another disaster. (Even if there had been unanimity on policy, the prospects for a deal with Moscow turned bleak in the spring of 1963, when Premier Khrushchev was removed from office by a coalition of Kremlin hard-liners, who accused him of temporizing in the face of "naked imperialist aggression." The coup, in turn, brought praise from Peking, putting a rapid end to what some had seen as a widening Sino–Soviet split.)

The hammer blows of bad news combined to make the optimism of early 1962 seem like a fantasy. So it was no surprise when the Gallup Organization in its most extensive survey ever, found "a deep, abiding sense of national pessimism . . . a growing conviction that America's best days are behind us. It is safe to say," Gallup concluded, "that America has never offered up a darker picture of its national mood than the portrait we see today, November 22, 1963."

Reality Reset

On December 11, 1960, Jacqueline Kennedy did come to the door of the Palm Beach mansion to bid John Kennedy off to church; she came holding her daughter Caroline.

Richard Pavlick did not want to kill John Kennedy in front of his family, so he put the triggering device down; he would wait for another time. Four days later, as he was staking out St. Edward's Church, local police—who had been looking for Pavlick—spotted the license plate of his car, and arrested him.

John Kennedy was inaugurated on January 20, 1961, and guided the nation through the Cuban Missile Crisis. His decision to employ a blockade, rather than a strike against the missiles or an invasion, has been widely credited with averting a possible nuclear war. After his assassination on November 22, 1963, Lyndon Johnson's leadership helped calm a shaken nation. In the years that followed, the Texas-born President engineered the passage of two landmark pieces of civil rights legislation, including the Voting Rights Act of 1965, that effectively ended the Second Civil War. But the escalation of the Vietnam War in early 1965, and the growing racial tensions throughout the country, turned Johnson's White House into a beleaguered fortress. By 1968, he was being challenged for the Democratic nomination by peace candidate Eugene McCarthy, and by his longtime adversary, New York Senator Robert Kennedy. By June 1968, Johnson had withdrawn from the race; Martin Luther King, Jr., had been assassinated in Memphis, Tennessee; Vice President Hubert Humphrey was far ahead in the race for Democratic convention delegates; and Robert Kennedy was fighting for his political life in the California primary.

AMBASSADOR HOTEL, LOS ANGELES, CALIFORNIA

— ★ ★ ★ —

JUNE 4, 1968, 11:45 P.M.

He was restless, energized, moving from the living room to the two bedrooms, down the narrow hallway of the Royal Suite on the hotel's fifth floor, now and again summoning an aide or a friend into a bathroom—the only space that afforded quiet and privacy in the steadily increasing tumult of this Tuesday night.

He had hoped not to be here at all, hoped to avoid the crowds and the ceaseless demands for his attention. As the California primary ended, he'd made it to the tape on fumes; last night in San Diego he'd faltered in mid-sentence, sat on the stage in near collapse, then been escorted to the bathroom, where he'd thrown up. He'd spent this Primary Day at the beachfront home of director John Frankenheimer, who, with Dick Goodwin, had made those effective TV spots, filmed glimpses of him on the campaign trail, answering questions, talking without a script (he was death on prepared scripts, couldn't make them look anything but stiff, phony). He'd recharged, hitting the ocean with his kids—he'd had to pull David to safety when the fifteen-year-old had gotten caught in the undertow— then crashing for hours, looking so drained that when Goodwin saw him slumped across two poolside chairs, motionless, he froze in fear. ("I suppose none of us will ever get over John Kennedy," Goodwin thought.) He'd wanted to watch the returns at Frankenheimer's home, make his victory statement from there—or, in the event he lost, his withdrawal from the Presidential race. But the networks said no, they'd set up camp at the Ambassador, that's where their cameras and correspondents were, so he'd come to the Ambassador in the early evening, driven by Frankenheimer in his Rolls-Royce Silver Cloud, the director so keyed up that he'd missed the freeway exit.

"Take it easy, John," he had said. "Life is short."

So now he worked the rooms in the Ambassador's Royal Suite, mingling with old pros like California Assembly Speaker Jess Unruh, one of the few pols who'd urged him to run, back last fall, and with old Kennedy hands Salinger, Sorenson, O'Brien, all of whom had counseled him not to challenge Johnson months earlier, all of whom were now working for him. He chatted with New York columnists he'd gotten close to: Jimmy Breslin of the *News*, Jack Newfield of the *Voice*, Pete Hamill of the *Post*, whose anguished letter to him earlier in the year ("if you won, the country might be saved") helped propel him into the race. There were other journalists there: Teddy White, of *The Making of the President* chronicles; Stan Tretick, the *Look* magazine photographer. There were allies from the streets, César Chávez and Dolores Huerta of the United Farm Workers, John Lewis from the Southern Christian Leadership Conference, who'd almost been killed on one of the Freedom Rides back in '61. There was Budd Schulberg, the screenwriter who'd written *On the Waterfront*, about a corrupt labor union; by coincidence, most Americans had first learned about Robert Kennedy a decade before this primary, as the intense thirty-one-year-old staring across a Senate hearing room at Teamster boss Jimmy Hoffa.

"Well, of course, you know who won this election for you," Schulberg said.

"You're going to give me that speech about the 85 percent or 90 percent black vote, and the Chicanos practically 100 percent."

"Bob, you're the only white man in the country they trust," said Schulberg.

Schulberg was right—but the picture was more complicated. The huge, historically unprecedented turnout in black and Latino districts had clearly given him the victory, overcoming the strong support for Senator Eugene McCarthy in middle- and upper-income suburban districts. (There was an independent slate of delegates, more or less understood to be for Vice President Humphrey, but many of his supporters had voted for McCarthy, knowing that a loss in California would end Robert Kennedy's campaign.)

But something else had happened in California, as it had happened earlier in Indiana and Nebraska, as it had happened this same day halfway across the country in South Dakota. He had won votes in small towns, in farm communities, in blue-collar neighborhoods, where voters had chosen him despite his views about the war in Vietnam and race. These were voters who'd felt, in some almost indefinable way, that the country was slipping out of control, that the war and the riots in the streets and on the college campuses needed someone tough enough to deal with it. Maybe it was Alabama Governor George Wallace; maybe it was the tough little Mick. If he could somehow wrest the nomination away from Humphrey, if he could somehow hold the fraying coalition of blacks and blue-collar whites together in the fall, there was a chance to win this thing, and then a chance to hold the country together . . .

The suite was buzzing now, electric. The network projections were saying he'd get 49 or 50 percent of the vote, but Jess Unruh had cautioned him, no, our vote's just about all in, the later numbers will shrink your margin, the networks will call it "inconclusive." Still it was a victory that would bring him all 174 California delegates to the convention in August. Coming a week after he'd lost the Oregon primary—the only loss ever suffered by a Kennedy in any contested election—it would keep him in contention, perhaps convince Chicago Mayor Richard J. Daley that he was more electable than Humphrey.

"Daley's the ball game," he had said when his campaign had begun, suddenly, improvisationally, in a spasm of energy after months of indecision, months when Minnesota Senator Eugene McCarthy, an indolent dilettante of a candidate in Bobby's mind, had taken the anti-war banner and ridden it to 42 percent of the vote in the New Hampshire primary, driving President Lyndon Johnson out of the fight for the party's nomination. Now, with Humphrey steadily accumulating support from party leaders in delegate-rich states without primaries, Daley was his best, no, his only hope of keeping the contest open. Once the New York primary was over—two weeks away in his adoptive state, where McCarthy sentiment was high among the educated liberal elites—there would be no more primaries, no more battlegrounds where the crowds, the passion, the family money, could win delegates and show those who controlled the nomination that he was all that stood between Richard Nixon and the White House. New York was going to be tough—"a bloodbath," he'd predicted earlier—but he could not afford to be pinned down in New York for the next two weeks; he had to begin trying to shake loose some of those states where Humphrey's allies had been locking up enough delegates to bring the Vice President tantalizingly close to the nomination.

That was the theme of the network coverage blaring from the half-dozen TV sets scattered throughout the room. All of the analysts were noting that the big winner of the primaries was the candidate who hadn't campaigned in a single one of them; Humphrey, they said, was within reach of a first ballot victory. CBS's Roger Mudd kept returning to this theme when he sat down for a brief interview with Kennedy.

"Are the delegates 'squeezable'?" he asked.

"Roger!" Kennedy said in mock outrage. "Your language!"

In fact, Mudd was exactly right. Somehow, he had to continue the fight even if there was no formal arena for the fight.

"I'm going to make him debate me," he said to *Look* magazine's Warren Rogers. "I'm going to chase his ass all over the country."

The first step, he knew, was to get McCarthy out of the race, or at the least, persuade his supporters to move. On every TV interview this night, he'd made the same point over and over:

"I can only win," he said, "if I have the help and assistance of Senator McCarthy and/or those who support him." Otherwise, he said, Humphrey will be the nominee—"and the policies about the war and the cities will not change."

The night before, journalist Jack Newfield and one of Kennedy's young speechwriters had gone to McCarthy's hotel to talk about unity after the primary. They found strong resistance—the bitterness over Kennedy's leap into the race just after New Hampshire was still deep—but one of the most significant of their number, Sam Brown, the Harvard Divinity student who'd organized the New Hampshire youth brigades, was clearly signaling yes, it was time to join forces. There'd been other hints of unity; in Colorado, Kennedy and McCarthy forces had combined to win two-thirds of the delegates. But McCarthy himself was likely to be a different matter; he was already telling the press that he thought Oregon was a far more significant test than California, an observation sufficiently detached from reality to suggest that his imminent withdrawal was not likely.

As for the future . . . well, there was some good news on the Daley front. True, when Kennedy'd announced, Daley had proclaimed his support for President Johnson, had used the term "Judas" to label the challenger. But Daley had also reached out to an old Kennedy loyalist, University of Chicago Professor Richard Wade, who'd been serving on the city's planning board. "Let's meet after every primary," the Mayor had said, adding meaningfully, "the primaries count . . . the primaries count . . . the primaries count." After Kennedy had lost in Oregon, Daley had summoned Wade to another meeting, where he'd waved off the loss, saying, "the primaries cut everything; if he's all right in California, he's going to be all right." On this primary night, Bobby had talked to longtime ally Kenny O'Donnell, who was watching the returns in Washington with Illinois Congressman Danny Rostenkowski. "I do what Daley says," Rostenkowski had told O'Donnell. "You win California and he's with you, we'll all fall into line."

So there was a chance, but with the primaries ending, he had to change the dynamic of the campaign. For that matter, there had to be a campaign shakeup fast; he'd jumped into the race so quickly that there'd been no time to build a structure. There was tension between the old John Kennedy hands, and his own Senate staff: Walinsky, Edelman, Mankiewicz, Dolan. There were fights about message: He had to stress his crime-fighting credentials as Attorney General, crime was a growing issue for middle America, but his younger aides were hearing that as a pander. The older hands in turn wanted the firebrands from his Senate staff off the road; they wanted him away from the frenzied crowds that unsettled older and suburban middle-class voters. *My problem*, he said, *is that I don't have anyone to do for me what I did for Jack.* More and more, he thought that Steve Smith, his brother-in-law, had to be given the reins of the campaign. Speaking of which, he thought, he should be out front and center, doing press interviews, he should come with me down to the ballroom for the speech. Where is he?

IN A FIFTH-FLOOR ROOM across from the Royal Suite, Steve Smith worked a quartet of telephones, jotting down numbers from precincts across the state. Several times during the evening, he'd resisted the pleas of

Dutton, Mankiewicz, and others who were urging the candidate to head down to the Embassy Ballroom for a victory speech. We're losing every voter on the East Coast, they said. He doesn't need to talk to California; the voting's over. Smith kept pushing back: We need to wait for Orange County, he said. We don't want any premature victory statements. Remember "Dewey Defeats Truman"? Now they'd lost the East Coast, and the Midwest as well, for that matter. It was almost midnight in California, but he knew now that the numbers would hold, that Kennedy had won, but without that magic 50 percent. It was going to be a forced march through the summer, and a costly one as well. When Bobby threw himself into the Presidential race, his brother Ted had said, *Bobby's therapy is going to cost the family five million dollars.* That was a conservative estimate; but then, Smith thought, *The family never does anything easily.*

Smith had married into the family twelve years ago, after meeting Jean Kennedy at Georgetown. He had good looks, an athletic, wiry body, and family money; his grandfather, who'd worked the ships along the Erie Canal, had founded Cleary Brothers, whose tugboats and barges plied the Hudson River. He'd quickly earned the trust of the insular family—Jack Kennedy had dubbed him "cool"—and was now guiding the investment strategy of the family's $300 million fortune, working out of the 200 Park Avenue address that housed Joseph Kennedy Enterprises. More important, Smith had been at the epicenter of the family's political rise. He'd run Jack's 1958 Senate reelection campaign, then moved to New York's Esso Building, where he'd become the logistical overseer of Kennedy's 1960 Presidential effort. Everything from the list of some 40,000 contacts to the scheduling of *Caroline,* the family-owned Convair twin-engine plane, fell under Smith's control. There was something about Smith's quiet confidence, his willingness, even eagerness, to remain out of the spotlight that kept him on the receiving end of more responsibility.

He'd been dispatched to set up Ted's 1962 Senate race, and Bobby's New York Senate run two years later, and now, he'd learned this Primary Day, he was being tapped to bring order out of Bobby's chaotic insurgent Presidential run after the primary season had ended. *This is going to be a real walk in the park,* he thought. *O'Brien and O'Donnell are feuding, they both think Sorenson is empire-building, the Senate staffers don't trust any of Jack's*

guys, who think the Senate guys are bomb-throwers, and I figure we have about
seventy-two hours before Humphrey wraps this up.

Well, tomorrow the senior campaign team would gather in Smith's bungalow on the grounds of the Ambassador. On Thursday, Bobby would fly
back East, stopping in Missouri for a meeting with convention delegates,
and then Friday he'd be in Niagara Falls, to launch the battle for New York.
After that . . . ?

He checked the numbers one last time. There was no room for doubt, it
would be a clear win, not overwhelming enough, not 50 percent, not what
they wanted or needed, but it would keep him in play. Soon the candidate
would go downstairs to claim victory. In fact, there was a commotion outside the door, the sound of a crowd moving down the corridor to the elevators. *I'd like to go down with him,* Smith thought. But he was in his stocking
feet, and maybe it wasn't worth the clutching and grabbing. Maybe he'd
catch up with him at the victory party tonight . . .

HE STOOD WITH the waiters, busboys, janitors, cooks, and cleaners in
the narrow pantry way that led from the Embassy Ballroom to the kitchen.
He'd come here on a last-minute impulse, but in another sense, he'd come
here driven by a lifetime of rage. He was twenty-four years old, short
enough to have dreamt of a career as a jockey, dark-haired, olive-skinned—
dark enough to be shunned by his blond, blue-eyed classmates at John
Muir High School and Pasadena City College. (When his parents told the
twelve-year-old they were leaving their native Jordan for the United States,
he'd asked them if that meant he would become a blue-eyed American.)
He worked odd jobs—a stable boy at the Santa Anita racetrack, a clerk at a
health-food store—but he spent many rootless days watching television, or
at the Pasadena Public Library, or practicing his shooting skills at a range
near his family home. And always, always, the fate of the Arabs at the
hands of the Zionists was his obsession.

They had driven him and his parents from their land, forced them
to Jordan, where there was no work, no life for them. The power of the
Jews over the financial and political life of the United States had seen to
it that Israel was armed with weapons far superior to those of their Arab

neighbors. A year ago, in June of 1967, they had seized the Holy City of Jerusalem, and now as the one-year anniversary approached, they were gloating, rubbing the Arabs' noses in their defeat and humiliation. Earlier this day, in fact, he'd seen a huge billboard announcing a march down Wilshire Boulevard to commemorate the first anniversary of the Six-Day War. He was sure the Zionists, the Jews, were celebrating that they'd beat the hell out of the Arabs. And he knew as he headed for the Ambassador Hotel that he was about to strike a powerful blow for his brothers, a blow that would avenge their shame and suffering.

He had admired Robert Kennedy, liked the way he spoke up for the underdog, the man at the bottom. But then he saw Kennedy at an Israeli Independence Day celebration, and . . . he was wearing a yarmulke! And he heard a radio report of Kennedy at a synagogue, saying ". . . in Israel—unlike so many other places in the world—our commitment is clear and compelling. We are committed to Israel's survival. We are committed to defying any attempt to destroy Israel, whatever the source. And we cannot and must not let that commitment waver." He'd run out of the room, clutching his ears.

And that's when he wrote in his diary, over and over, "RFK Must Die, RFK must be assassinated, must be assassinated, assassinated."

Now, a few minutes before midnight, Sirhan Sirhan was standing on a low-rise tray stacker in the pantry way just off the Embassy Ballroom. On his right arm was a rolled-up Kennedy poster. Inside the poster, clutched in his right hand, was a fully loaded .22 caliber Iver Johnson Cadet revolver.

As he heard the commotion outside his room, Steve Smith hesitated, then quickly slipped into his shoes. He knew how chaotic the victory celebration would be, knew how utterly exhausted his brother-in-law would be. Someone had to provide adult supervision, he thought, and it was a role he had more and more come to assume himself.

"Curiously enough," he said later, "for some reason I can't explain, during the course of the campaign, whenever I was with the Senator, I made it a point to place myself in front of him, and sort of move as if I were clearing a way. I think it helped expedite his getting from one place to another." On this night, Smith

knew, it would be crucial to get Kennedy from his speech to his press conference to bed. So he opened the door, squeezed himself inside the crush of people, and rode down next to Kennedy, keeping himself close by until he found himself just behind Bobby on the stage of the Embassy Ballroom.

"Ah, ruthless Steve Smith, always going for the limelight," Kennedy cracked.

"Somebody has to keep you away from your adoring public," Smith said. "Now give your speech and let's get the hell out of here."

THE EMBASSY BALLROOM was packed, hot, feverish with energy; the crowd had been gathering for hours, and as midnight came, there were conga lines dancing through the hall, random shouts and cheers. He spoke for fifteen minutes. He congratulated Los Angeles Dodgers pitcher Don Drysdale, who had broken a major league record for the most consecutive scoreless innings. He thanked everyone from his dog Freckles to his wife ("not necessarily in that order") to his brother-in-law Steve Smith: "ruthless, but effective." He said America could heal its racial and generational divisions, and then said, "Now it's on to Chicago and let's win there!" (*God, he thought an instant later, I forgot to mention the New York primary!*)

The stage was too crowded, as all stages are when a candidate claims victory. There was Ethel, Jess Unruh, Dolores Huerta—he'd wanted César Chávez with him, but he could not be found—Paul Schrade of the United Auto Workers. Bill Barry, the former FBI agent serving as his only security, waited to guide him through the crowd; so did former Olympic athlete Rafer Johnson and LA Rams lineman Roosevelt Grier, who were volunteer bodyguards during the California campaign. (The campaign had refused the protection of the Los Angeles police, in part because Kennedy and Los Angeles Mayor Sam Yorty cordially despised each other, Kennedy viewing Yorty as a racist demagogue, Yorty viewing Kennedy as a spoiled rich kid turned subversive.)

Kennedy instinctively recoiled against security measures, insisting on an open car when he campaigned through some of the most dangerous streets in America, upbraiding his staff when they picked up threats and tried to move him in and out of venues through underground garages. That morning, at Frankenheimer's house, he had said flatly, "If someone with a rifle wants to kill me, there's really not that much that can be done about it." Weeks earlier, after Martin Luther King's murder, he'd told a civil rights veteran, "There are guns between me and the White House." From French novelist Romain Gary to Jacqueline Kennedy to *Newsweek* columnist John J. Lindsay came flat predictions that he would not live through the campaign.

So far, at least, the principal danger to Robert Kennedy had come not from his enemies but from his most ardent supporters. They tore at him as he motorcaded through streets, grabbing for his cuff links, his PT-109 tie clasp, his shoes. They left his hands and forearms red and bleeding, pulled at him so enthusiastically that at one point he was yanked from his car, chipping his teeth. To ride with Robert Kennedy was to see something more than the adulation of a celebrity, something more than enthusiasm for a politician; it was to see, to feel, an energy, a desperation so intense as to pose a danger to the very object of their passion.

And that may be why Fred Dutton, the old Kennedy hand who'd become the de facto campaign manager, who'd inherited unbidden power over campaign themes, scheduling, and logistics, who was often seen in the convertible holding Kennedy's legs as he rode through the streets, made a snap decision not to bring Kennedy through the ballroom crowds, not to subject him to another victory speech before the overflow crowd assembled one floor below in the Ambassador Ballroom, but to send him through the kitchen to a freight elevator that would take him to a press conference in the hotel's Colonial Room. Bill Barry, who'd begun to clear a path through the crowd, scrambled to regain his place near the candidate as Kennedy stepped down from the platform and was guided through the gold curtains to a back exit by the hotel's assistant maître d'hotel Karl Uecker, into the long, narrow pantry that would lead to the freight elevator. Kennedy was engaged in an on-the-run interview with Andrew West, a reporter for the Mutual Radio Network, who was asking how he was going to wrest the delegates away from Vice President Humphrey.

"It just goes back to the struggle for it . . ."

And Steve Smith, standing behind Kennedy, strode in front of them, looking to clear the way, which is why he glimpsed the fury in the eyes of a short, dark-haired young man who suddenly jumped down from a low-rise tray stacker and rushed toward the Senator, screaming, "You son of a bitch!" Smith, who'd played

in so many of those rough-and-tumble touch football games on the Cape, threw
himself at the attacker, who was knocked to the floor just as he fired one shot from
his revolver. The bullet grazed Smith's shoulder. By then, Roosevelt Grier and
Rafer Johnson had pinned the attacker against the wall, immobilizing his shoot-
ing hand, while half a dozen people surrounded Robert Kennedy, pulling him
and Ethel to safety.

HAD SIRHAN BISHARA SIRHAN stayed home that night, or had the
candidate left the stage through the crowds in the ballroom, it is highly
possible—make that probable—that the California primary would have
marked the high point of Robert Kennedy's Presidential campaign. Fred
Dutton was right when he reflected much later, "We had been losing alti-
tude." Back on March 31, when President Johnson had suddenly, shockingly, withdrawn from the race, some around Kennedy thought, *That's it,*
he's the nominee. But when he and his aides began calling Democratic office-
holders and kingmakers, they found widespread hesitancy about throwing
their support to the young upstart who'd challenged a sitting President in
the middle of a war.

Some of it was due to grievances old and new; the Kennedy campaign
had played very rough back in '60, and nobody played rougher than Bobby.
His clumsy entry into this Presidential race, hours after Eugene McCarthy's near victory in New Hampshire, had added potent fuel to Bobby's
"ruthless" image. Some of it was about the deep divides that were already
beginning to fracture the New Deal coalition. Big-city white ethnics and
Southerners were more and more resentful and fearful of black demands
and Robert Kennedy had become the tribune of black frustration and
anger. For many Southern Democrats, for whom segregation was the
defining cause of their political lives, Bobby Kennedy as Attorney General had been the embodiment of Northern aggression. Throughout the
country, culturally conservative Democrats were more and more repelled
by young protesters with filthy words on their placards and drugs in their
pockets; World War II veterans who believed in the lessons of Munich,
saw appeasement if not surrender in the opposition to the Vietnam War.
And Bobby Kennedy had criticized the war, even questioned its morality,

standing with the longhairs and the draft card burners. Some of it was
about affection for Hubert Humphrey's work as a champion of liberal
causes from labor to civil rights. Some of it was about fear; what would a
vengeful Lyndon Johnson, who still held the reins of the Presidency, do to
those who dared support his nemesis?

In the two months since Johnson's withdrawal, Humphrey's lead had
lengthened even as he avoided every state where a primary might test
his voter appeal. Instead, he relied on his allies in big-city Democratic
machines and in organized labor to line up delegates in states where there
were no real primaries at all. Kennedy's campaign had miscalculated here,
a costly consequence of the hasty, last-minute disorganized plunge into the
race. They'd decided to stay out of Pennsylvania, with its 130 delegates, and
what happened? Philadelphia Mayor Tate and Pittsburgh Mayor Barr had
organized an unscheduled delegate meeting in mid-May and locked up
just about every convention vote for Humphrey. They'd kept Kennedy out
of New Jersey, and Governor Richard Hughes had committed his favorite-
son delegates to the Vice President. All across the South and Southwest,
delegations were lining up for Humphrey, a powerful bloc of votes that
numbered more than 600. Even if Mayor Daley threw his support and the
118 delegates he controlled to Kennedy, would that be enough to persuade,
or cajole, or threaten the party's Old Bulls to reconsider?

But when Steve Smith knocked Sirhan Sirhan to the floor of the pantry
in the Ambassador, when the country learned that Robert Kennedy had
escaped from an attempt on his life, a wholly new dynamic emerged. And
it began in the first moments after the Los Angeles police burst into the
kitchen hallway to handcuff Sirhan and speed him away to police headquarters in downtown LA.

"Is anybody hurt, is everybody all right?" Kennedy asked the men around
him once he'd disentangled himself from their grasp. Yes, they assured him,
Steve Smith had been grazed, he was being taken to Central Receiving
Hospital on West Sixth Street, but it was nothing serious. We need to get
you back upstairs until we know there's no one else . . .

Kennedy motioned them for quiet. "We're going to the hospital to check
on Steve. I want to do a statement for the press; I have a feeling they'll be
there. Then we'll do a full-fledged press conference tomorrow morning."

"Senator, you do understand there was just a direct attempt on your life," Bill Barry said, still shaken by the last-minute change of plans that had left him powerless to protect Kennedy. "That man was firing a loaded weapon at you. For all we know, there are others, maybe outside the hotel, maybe—"

"So the sooner we leave for the hospital, the better," Kennedy said. "There's no way anyone could be waiting there."

"All right," Barry said. "But"—he pointed to a phalanx of Los Angeles police officers, whose helmets, leather belts, and boots gave them the appearance of a paramilitary guard in a Latin American police state— "those guys are escorting us. Either that, Senator, or you find yourself a new chief of security."

Kennedy paused, then nodded once, and the group moved out. If Kennedy noticed that he was completely surrounded by campaign aides, police, and the reporters who had rushed into the kitchen when news of the attack filtered into the Colonial Room, he said nothing. Indeed, the press and the public heard nothing until 1:45 a.m., when Kennedy climbed on top of a police car to speak to the hundreds of reporters and supporters who had found their way to the emergency room entrance of Central Receiving.

"I just want to say that Steve Smith is in very good shape. He suffered only a minor wound to his shoulder. Thankfully, no one else was injured. I will be meeting with the press at eight a.m. tomorrow at the Ambassador Hotel, where I will try to answer your questions. Right now, I have only one announcement: If I'm elected President, I intend to propose a Constitutional amendment to impose severe criminal penalties on anyone telling brother-in-law jokes."

That quip did not make the morning papers on the East Coast. But it led all the morning wake-up shows on TV, and all the hourly news updates on the radio. And at 11:00 a.m. eastern time, it was the tape all three networks used to begin the live news conference, along with the breaking news that President Johnson had ordered Secret Service protection for all Presidential candidates. The light-hearted remark, the grace under pressure, made a powerful impression.

("If you can laugh in the face of a threat to your life, I don't care if you're Jane Fonda or Ronald Reagan, people are gonna like you," one reporter said.)

Kennedy's press conference was dominated by the same handful of questions, asked a dozen different ways, answered with all the patience the candidate could muster. No, there was no inkling of what motivated the attack. No, he did not think the attempt on his life was a result of the frenzied nature of his campaign. Yes, he'd heard from all the other candidates, and from President Johnson, and was grateful for their good wishes. Yes, he understood that under the President's order, he was compelled to accept Secret Service protection, but hoped his campaign and the Agency could come to an agreement that would permit him to campaign as close to the voters as possible.

"Let me just note," he added, "that I've appeared in public from one end of the country to the other, from Bedford-Stuyvesant to Gary and Hammond in Indiana to Oakland and Watts and East Los Angeles here in California. This . . . happened in the middle of a luxury hotel. So perhaps the lesson here is for me to spend more time in the streets of poor and working-class neighborhoods, where I seem to be perfectly safe. And yes, I will be flying to St. Louis tomorrow to meet with convention delegates from Missouri, and then to Niagara Falls to begin my efforts in New York."

There was no scientific, quantifiable way to measure the effect of Robert Kennedy's appearance on the national stage just hours after the attempt on his life. There is no way to know how many Americans, indifferent to Presidential politics, saw the lithe, composed young man on their television screens and thought: We almost lost him. There is no way to measure the sense of relief, even exultation, felt by citizens whose most indelible memories of any public event were shaped by November of 1963, when reports of "shots fired at President in Dallas" were quickly followed by news of John Kennedy's death. Indeed, just eight weeks earlier, the first bulletins about an attack on Martin Luther King's life were replaced by confirmation that he had died. Those events had triggered anguished silent pain, overwhelming grief, violent rage. This time, it wasn't just that the intended victim had been spared: They had been spared. This time, fate had dealt salvation.

The response was nowhere more passionate than in the black community. Despite the strong support for Robert Kennedy, there were memories of his earlier temporizing on civil rights, and affection for Hubert Humphrey's long embrace of the cause. Just a few weeks ago, columnist Drew

Pearson had broken the story—with information eagerly supplied by FBI Director J. Edgar Hoover and Lyndon Johnson—that Robert Kennedy had authorized the wiretapping of Martin Luther King's phone (it was a potentially devastating rumor, made more dangerous because it was true; Kennedy was looking for evidence that one of King's close associates was a member of the Communist Party).

So, while Robert Kennedy had won the overwhelming majority of black votes in Indiana, California, and the District of Columbia, Vice President Humphrey could claim the support of Cleveland Mayor Carl Stokes, and other black elected officials. Civil rights leaders like the NAACP's Roy Wilkins and the Urban League's Whitney Young, who had long worried that the anti–Vietnam War sentiment would divide liberals and weaken support for a liberal domestic agenda, had stayed studiously neutral throughout the primaries. Now, however, Robert Kennedy's brush with death triggered a firestorm in black America. He was fighting for us, and he almost got killed. In black churches the following Sunday, countless ministers preached about the "divine intervention" that had saved Robert Kennedy. ("If John Kennedy is the twentieth century's Abraham Lincoln, cut down in his prime," said Martin Luther King, Sr., "then Robert Kennedy may be the twentieth century's Franklin Roosevelt, who escaped an assassin's bullet to become the greatest President of our time!")

Those black officials who had thrown their support to Humphrey found themselves confronted with angry constituencies. Within seventy-two hours, Mayor Stokes had announced that he was "reassessing" his support for the Vice President. It was left to Dr. Kenneth Clark, the Columbia University social scientist whose work on the effects of segregation had helped shape the Supreme Court's school desegregation decision, to explain the political impact of Kennedy's escape.

"The only way to appreciate what is happening," Clark wrote, "is with a mind game: imagine, decades into the future, that a black candidate for President is competing against a white candidate with a strong civil rights record. If that black candidate were to become a genuine contender, those blacks who had backed the white candidate would find themselves under enormous pressure. In effect, however much his campaign would have it otherwise, Robert Kennedy is the black candidate—at least, in the black community."

The impact of the near miss, however, went beyond black America. It had a significant impact on the American Jewish community as well, one which was to have a major impact on the shape of the battle for the Democratic nomination.

The skepticism about Robert Kennedy among many American Jews stretched back a generation. His father, Joseph Kennedy, Sr., had been a leading voice of appeasement when he served as Ambassador to Great Britain in the years leading up to World War II, declaring at one point in 1940 that democracy in Britain was "finished." He vocally opposed American efforts to aid in resisting Hitler's advance across Europe, and his anti-Semitism—casually referring to "kikes" and "sheeneys" in conversation—was a matter of record.

Robert Kennedy's early work for Senator Joseph McCarthy had stirred strong suspicions within the overwhelmingly liberal American Jewish community. More broadly, the zealousness with which he went after his targets in labor unions, and the humorless intensity of his work for Jack in 1960, had left lingering uneasiness, especially among well-educated professional Jews who were instinctively drawn to more cerebral political figures like Adlai Stevenson and now Eugene McCarthy.

Then there was the matter of his religion. Unlike Jack, who seemed to wear his Catholicism lightly, Bobby was by every reasonable measure a true believer—his ten children testified to his embrace of the Church's teachings on birth control. ("Remember," one of his own Jewish speechwriters said, "there's something to the old adage that 'anti-Catholicism is the anti-Semitism of the intellectuals.' Besides, Bobby always reminded me of the parochial school kids in my neighborhood who used to chase me home from school, demanding to know why I had killed their Lord.")

For his part, Kennedy could sometimes express exasperation with the repeated demands of American Jewry for expressions of support for Israel. It was, in fact, this pressure that had sent Kennedy to the Nevev Shalom Synagogue in Los Angeles for a speech that Sirhan Sirhan had watched with increasing rage. A few weeks earlier, after receiving one too many disparaging comments about the depth of his commitment, Kennedy had turned to a claque of aides—Walinsky, Edelman, Mankiewicz, Greenfield—

and said, "when I'm President, I'm going to sign a separate peace treaty with Egypt and Jordan—and I'm going to make you all be witnesses!"

But when Los Angeles police searched Sirhan Sirhan's bedroom in his family's modest frame cottage on East Howard Street, began questioning those who knew him, and then found his diary, the news of what had propelled the young Arab immigrant to murder Kennedy became the only topic of conversation among politically engaged American Jews—which is to say, every American Jew over the age of four. Sirhan was a passionate believer in the Arab cause, a zealous, obsessive anti-Zionist and anti-Semite. He railed that Jews "sucked the lifeblood out of America," believed they controlled every American politician with their money and their control over the media. He had written of his urge to kill UN Ambassador Arthur Goldberg, but transferred his fury to Kennedy when he'd seen him wearing a yarmulke, celebrating Israeli Independence Day, offering full-throated support for the Jewish state against "any attempt to destroy Israel, from whatever the source . . ."

The response to this news was as powerful as it was simplistic: "Robert Kennedy was almost killed because he spoke out for Israel!" In the less affluent, less liberal Jewish neighborhoods of Brooklyn and Queens, local Democrats could almost feel the surge of sentiment for the almost-martyred Kennedy. That surge turned into a flood tide a few days later, when Kennedy gave a long-scheduled commencement address at New York's Yeshiva University, where he was introduced by former Supreme Court Justice and UN Ambassador Arthur Goldberg, who had endorsed Kennedy two days earlier. When he walked onstage at the Lewisohn Auditorium, the audience gave him a five-minute standing ovation, chanting, *"L'chaim! L'chaim!"* ("To life! To life!") In his speech, Kennedy reaffirmed his support for Israel, but also spoke of the need for reconciliation, so that "the children of Abraham, Jew and Christian and Arab alike, may at long last live out their lives free of terror and privation." Two weeks earlier, any hint of sympathy for Palestinians might have subjected Kennedy to criticism. Now, there were only cheers.

For the Presidential campaign of Senator Eugene McCarthy, the reports of Sirhan Sirhan's motivation could not have come at a worse time.

On Friday, June 7, as Kennedy was flying to Niagara Falls to launch his New York primary campaign, a dozen senior staff members of McCarthy's campaign, including youth organizer Sam Brown, announced that they were endorsing Kennedy as "the only peace candidate with a credible chance to win the Presidency and stop the war in Vietnam. We will never lose our admiration and respect for the courageous battle Senator McCarthy waged," they said, "but we cannot permit that admiration and respect to let us ignore the clear political reality: Robert Kennedy is the only candidate for President who stands a chance of ending this disastrous war." It was hardly a unanimous sentiment within the McCarthy campaign, where resentment against Bobby Kennedy still ran high—"If we have to have an opportunistic Red-baiter as President," one said, "let's elect Richard Nixon and get the real thing!"—but it was a hit the campaign could ill afford.

What happened next, however, was one of the odder events in contemporary American political history: a combination of a self-inflicted wound and an exercise in political subterfuge that would be replicated again and again in years to come. Its roots lay in one of those offhand arsenic-tipped observations for which Eugene McCarthy was famous—or notorious. His admirers had long enjoyed exchanging some of his cracks. Walking by two of the least popular members of the Senate in angry argument, he'd muttered: "Trouble in the leper colony." His bile was especially aroused by the Kennedys, whom he saw as less Catholic, less politically committed, and less intelligent than he. He often seemed to be suggesting that voting for Kennedy was a sign of lesser intelligence.

"[In Indiana] they kept talking about the poet out there. I asked if they were talking about Shakespeare . . . But it was James Whitcomb Riley. You could hardly expect to win under those conditions." Sometimes he skipped the subtlety, as when he pointedly noted that he was winning the support of the more intelligent, better-educated voters.

It was one other observation, made a few nights before his victory in the Oregon primary to a handful of reporters, that proved so consequential. Talking about the efforts of the Kennedy campaign to find a compelling argument in a state with little of his natural constituency, McCarthy quipped: "I'm sure in a few days they'll be leaking a story that somebody took a shot at him."

In an era when images were captured only by bulky film or videotape, when the concept of universal access to data via mobile computers was something out of *Star Trek,* there was every reason to believe that McCarthy's wisecrack would live on only in the memories of the handful that heard it, or at best as a piece of gossip shared over late-night drinks in a hotel bar. One of the reporters, however, was carrying a Norelco Carry-Corder 150, and discovered that evening that she had recorded McCarthy's quip: a tape she played a few nights later for a young operative for the Kennedy campaign with whom she'd shared three beers, a few tokes of Maui Wowie, and a bed. When the operative heard Kennedy press secretary Frank Mankiewicz angrily relate a reporter's account of McCarthy's crack, he said casually, "Yeah, I heard the tape." Mankiewicz had more or less forgotten the comment . . . until the morning after the attempted assassination, when he stopped in the middle of a telephone conversation with a Washington columnist, sat bolt upright, and said: "Holy . . ."

It took the better part of the morning for Mankiewicz to track the young man down; the California campaign had been so disorganized, so chaotic, so riven by internal feuds, that the idea of a master list of staffers was laughable. It took a series of conversations to convince the young man to reach out to his very temporary playmate. ("It was just . . . you know . . . a thing . . . not like . . . you know . . . we're *dating.*") It took about three minutes to convince the reporter that if she made a copy of the tape, she'd be fully credited when the story broke, propelling her into work far above her current employment as a stringer for a local Salem, Oregon, radio station. By Sunday evening, after passing through a series of cutouts insulating the campaign from the recording, the tape was in the hands of a reporter for the *New York Post.* The *New York Times* was never seriously considered; it was a paper firmly in McCarthy's corner, a paper so instinctively resistant to the Kennedy appeal that Bobby was inclined to chalk it up to snobbish anti-Catholicism. The *Post,* by contrast, was the longtime voice of New York liberalism, owned by heiress Dorothy Schiff and edited by James Wechsler, a Kennedy admirer. The *Post* had endorsed McCarthy early in his campaign, which made the venue for the story even more compelling. Mrs. Schiff had an occasionally mercurial temperament when it came to political judgment; back in 1958, she ordered a last-minute retraction of the *Post*'s endorsement of New York Governor Averell Harriman because of an offhand remark. Now, viewing McCarthy's wisecrack through the prism of a genuine assassination attempt, she was horrified.

"McCarthy Mocked RFK Danger," a front-page *Post* headline proclaimed on Monday morning. That same day, both all-news radio stations in New York had somehow gotten copies of the tape, which they played throughout the day and into the evening rush hour, where hundreds of thousands of commuters heard it on their car radios. Among McCarthy's campaign insiders, the remarks spurred a lengthy, increasingly acrimonious debate between political veterans, who urged McCarthy to express regrets, and his inner court of friends and hangers-on—dubbed "the Astrologers" by campaign veterans—who thought the whole controversy a contrivance fed by Kennedy operatives and a cynical press core. The Senator himself did not help matters when, braced by a scrum of reporters and cameramen as he entered his Manhattan hotel lobby, he recycled one of his better-known quips.

"I used to think of the press as blackbirds," he said with a small smile. "One flies on the telephone wire, they all fly on; one flies away, they all fly away. It seems I may have been ornithologically imprecise. 'Vultures' might perhaps be more accurate."

In fact, McCarthy's earlier assessment of the press proved all too accurate; the tape had created an appetite for "McCarthy in Trouble" stories. *Newsday*, the dominant Long Island newspaper now published by onetime Johnson press secretary and Kennedy admirer Bill Moyers, ran a series of stories about the alliance between McCarthy and Humphrey supporters that had formed in the days just before the California primary, about the appointment of Tom Finney, a former CIA official, as McCarthy campaign director. Because *Newsday* was read by almost every resident of Nassau County, the reports of a Humphrey–McCarthy alliance to stop Kennedy had a major impact among one of McCarthy's key affluent suburban supporters. When the *New York Post* recycled those stories, and switched its endorsement to Robert Kennedy, it cost McCarthy heavily in New York City. (The *New York Times*, for its part, reaffirmed its backing of McCarthy, chastising him for "unfortunate and regrettable remarks," chastising the press for its "overwrought reaction," and raising the possibility that "the Kennedy forces had used their money and influence to publicize a remark clearly intended as a private remark. A remark," they added, "of a piece with McCarthy's admirable reliance on the intellectual quip, the witty aside, the reflective understatement—and poetry.")

On the night of June 18, Kennedy won at least 150 of the 175 New York convention delegates. (The numbers were inexact, since in this first-ever New York Presidential primary, only the names of delegates were on the ballot.) Eugene McCarthy gave a terse concession speech, celebrating the victories in the snows of New Hampshire and the Oregon spring, noting that "those who retreated from the first battles, only to come down from the hills and shoot the wounded, would have to answer to their consciences, and to history." He did not congratulate Robert Kennedy or answer questions about the future of his campaign—perhaps because it was clear that there was no future.

That night, as he had two weeks earlier, Robert Kennedy was restless, energized, moving through the Presidential Suite at New York's Sheraton Hotel in midtown Manhattan. (This time, the Presidential Suite, the Knickerbocker Ballroom, the elevators, and every other venue where Kennedy might visit were under Secret Service protection.) The mood of the campaign did not reflect the outsized New York victory; they'd known it was coming for days. What the campaign knew, what the Humphrey campaign knew, what the press knew, was that one number mattered, and it wasn't how many delegates Kennedy had won that night, or how many primary votes Kennedy and McCarthy had won.

The number was 1,312.

That's how many delegates it took to win the Democratic Presidential nomination. That's the number all the networks were featuring on their tote boards. And while there was no way to tabulate precisely how many delegates the candidates now had, the networks were pretty much in agreement that Humphrey had well over 1,000. But in sharp contrast to the analysis that had dominated the coverage two weeks earlier in California, the coverage this night reflected the uncertainty that the foiled assassination attempt had created.

"With the primaries over," ABC's Bill Lawrence was saying, "everything we know about Presidential politics tells us that the winner was the candidate who did not compete in any of them: Vice President Humphrey. With the backing of President Johnson, whose dislike of Senator Kennedy is as intense as Kennedy's of him; with the support of elected Democratic officials in many if not most of the big industrial states, as well as in the South; with the strong backing of AFL-CIO President Meany, Mr. Humphrey should be on his way to an early ballot nomination, perhaps on the first ballot. The question is: Has Senator Kennedy's escape from that attempt on his life changed the equation? If not, do these Kennedy wins in the two biggest states provide him with a lever—or a club—with which to move Democrats? There was evidence in New York that the attempt on the Senator's life had an impact among voters. The problem for Mr. Kennedy is that there are no more voters—or to be more precise, no more contests where voters can speak."

It was that dilemma that Kennedy spoke to when he claimed victory that night: "The primaries are over, but the campaign is not. In every state where Democrats have had the chance to speak, they have voted overwhelmingly for a change of course, for new policies, for an end to the war, for reconciliation at home. I intend to give Democrats in every state the chance to choose between the course we are now on, and a new direction. I fully intend to abide by that choice, but to deny Democrats the right to choose is to deny our heritage, and to ensure our defeat in November."

Millions heard Robert Kennedy that night. But no one was listening more intently, no one was more determined to respond to that challenge, than one Democrat in particular . . .

HE PACED back and forth, watching the three color television screens in the Oval Office, flicking the remote to change the audio from one set to the next. Every few minutes he would wander over to the Associated Press and United Press teletypes, ripping the paper out of the machine, scanning the latest updates as if hoping to find different numbers, a better story.

Two weeks ago, he had been awakened by Walt Rostow, his national security chief, to be told of the attempt on the life of Robert Kennedy. He had immediately ordered Secret Service protection for all Presidential candidates, called Kennedy in California to offer some words of thanks that

he had not been harmed. Whatever else he had been feeling—his longtime
aide Harry McPherson observed much later that "he must have been filled
with a hundred conflicting emotions"—he had kept strictly to himself.
Tonight, watching Kennedy bask in the adulation of his supporters, there
was no ambiguity about what he was feeling: *This is my worst nightmare.*

It was the literal truth. All his life he had been haunted by dreams of
helplessness, abandonment, impotence in the face of threats. Over the last
three years, those nightmares had turned into a real, living hell. He had
wished all his life for the power to do good, to bring material balm to his
people, especially to the poor. For a time, after his landslide victory in 1964,
after the second emancipation of black Americans, after the launch of the
War on Poverty, he believed, along with much of the country, that he would
preside over a nation where the blessings of liberty and prosperity touched
everyone . . . and where he would become the most beloved leader since
Franklin Roosevelt.

Then it all started to come apart.

The Negroes in city after city began to destroy their own neighborhoods, looting, shooting, killing, dying, stirring anger and resentment
among white working- and middle-class Americans. *How could they do
this after all I have done for them?* he wondered, because he knew to a certainty that it was aimed at him. The college kids, whose daddies could send
them off to school with new clothes and new cars, were disrupting classes,
parading across campuses with filthy clothes and filthy words. Didn't they
know millions and millions of Americans would have given their right arm
for the chance to send their kids to college? And then there was the war,
that goddamn war. He'd known from the beginning it would be a disaster,
known it in the marrow of his bones. He'd spent hours on the phone with
Dick Russell, the biggest hawk in the U.S. Senate, who was as sure as he
was that it was the worst damn mess anyone could imagine, a war there
was no way to win, but a war he couldn't end. He'd been there in the Senate when China fell to the Communists in '49, when Korea turned into a
stalemate; he'd watched Harry Truman and Dean Acheson, stalwart anti-
Communists, branded as appeasers, cowards. If he'd pulled up stakes in
Vietnam, it would all start again.

"And this time," he told a confidant, "there would be Robert Kennedy

out in front leading the fight against me, telling everyone that I had betrayed
John Kennedy's commitment to Vietnam. That I had let a democracy fall
into the hands of the Communists. That I was a coward. An unmanly man,
a man without a spine. Oh, I could see it coming, all right. Every night
when I fell asleep, I would see myself tied to the ground in the middle of
a long, open space. In the distance, I could hear the voice of thousands
of people. They were all shouting at me: 'Coward! Traitor! Weakling!' . . .
Moscow and Peking would move in a flash to exploit our weakness . . . and
so would begin World War III . . ."

So he'd widened the war, not as much as his generals and admirals had
wanted, but splitting the difference, sitting up late into the night, picking the targets, reading over the casualty lists, watching as his popularity
shrank and the protests mounted, and even loyal political allies like Dick
Daley in Chicago told him the war was a disaster, that it would rip apart
the Democratic Party.

And always, always, there was the specter of Robert Kennedy, distanc-
ing himself from the war his brother had set in motion, calling his efforts
for the poor inadequate, looking for the chance to reclaim the throne. From
the very beginning in the summer of '60, when Bobby had shown up in his
hotel suite in Los Angeles, trying to force him off the ticket, the little runt
had tried to undermine him, contemptuously attacking his work as Vice
President on the Equal Employment Opportunity Commission, cutting
him out of White House meetings. In November of '63, as Senate Republicans began to zero in on his longtime Senate protégé Bobby Baker, Kennedy began leaking damaging information to Senate Republicans, hoping,
Johnson was certain, to force him off the ticket in '64. One of the key
inquiries was set to begin on the afternoon of November 22 . . .

Those first days after Jack's death had poisoned things between them
irrevocably. Bobby seemed to hold him responsible for the murder of his
brother; he'd look across the table at Cabinet meetings and see a usurper, an
impostor. He'd tried to force himself on the ticket as Vice President in '64,
hoping to stampede the convention with an emotional tribute film about
Jack (Johnson made damn sure that movie was shown *after* the nominations were done). And in the years since, Bobby had relied on the immense
network of Kennedy loyalists in the government to feed him information,

rumors, anything to undercut the President. (When he and Bobby got into a shouting match over stories that Kennedy had brought back a Vietnam "peace feeler" from Europe, Kennedy had said, "It was your State Department that leaked the story." "It's not my State Department," Johnson had replied, "it's *your* State Department!") It was of a piece with his conviction that there was no end to the power and reach of the Kennedys, that whatever plagued his administration was inevitably, certainly, linked to his enemy. In 1967, he'd said to Supreme Court Justice Fortas, his longtime private lawyer who continued as part of Johnson's inner circle after he joined the Court, "I believe that Bobby is having his governors jump on me, and he's having his mayors jump on me, and he's having his nigras and he's having his Catholics. And he's having them just systematically, one after the other, each day, go after me."

And when Bobby did enter the Presidential race, it was for him the final straw. The thing he had feared from the first day of his Presidency was actually coming true. Robert Kennedy had openly announced his intention to reclaim the throne in memory of his brother, and the American people, swayed by the magic of the name, were dancing in the streets. It was unbearable to him.

And so he followed an impulse he had wrestled with all of his life: He quit.

He'd almost done it in '48, locked in a vicious Senate primary battle with Governor Coke Stevenson, hospitalized by kidney stones, unwilling to acknowledge his condition to the press and the voters. He'd thought hard in '60 about just walking away from his public life, starting over in a new place, maybe with a new woman. In '64, he'd told some of those closest to him that he would go to the Democratic Convention in Atlantic City, a convention ready to shower him with love, and tell them, no, he'd thought about it, but maybe the party and the country needed a different man at the top. And the answer came back from his staff and his political allies and his wife: *No, no, you can't do that, Mr. President, you've led America back after Dallas, there's no one else who could do the job, you're the leader we need.*

He knew that some of those around him thought that was what the threats to quit were all about, and maybe that was true in part, but this time it was different; the anger was too white-hot, the divisions too wide, and there was a question of personal survival as well—could his heart, weakened from his near-fatal heart attack in '55, take the pressure, or would another of his nightmares come true, would he end up like Woodrow Wilson, immobilized by a stroke, while those around him struggled for the power he could no longer exercise?

So he'd gone before the TV cameras on March 31 to announce a new move for peace in Vietnam, a partial halt to the bombing of the North, an invitation to negotiate an end to the war. And at the end, in a section held back from the advance text, he said, "I shall not seek—and will not accept—the nomination of my party for another term as your President." (It was almost worth it to watch the faces of the know-it-all TV commentators, gasping for a few coherent words, looking like a bunch of fish that had just been pulled out of the water.)

Bobby had come to see him a week or so after, and they'd exchanged a few patently insincere words—Bobby saying maybe the breach was his fault, telling the President, "you are a brave and dedicated man," the words coming out so quietly he'd made Bobby say them again. When Bobby had asked him of his intentions in the campaign, he'd waved Kennedy off, saying that wasn't what he was focused on right now. And in the three months since, he'd surprised his advisors by staying out of the battle between Kennedy and his Vice President. (He did not share with these advisors that his real choice for President was a Republican: New York Governor Nelson Rockefeller. He'd urged him to run during a White House dinner in April, pushed the Indiana industrialist J. Irwin Miller to start a "draft Rocky" committee.) He seemed detached, indifferent to the outcome of the Democratic primary, waving off polling data from Indiana and Nebraska, almost resigned to a Kennedy restoration, even asking one of his aides rhetorically, "Well, what's wrong with Bobby?" You could almost believe that he was no longer obsessed with Bobby . . . unless you picked up the *Washington Post* on May 24, and read Drew Pearson's column charging that Bobby Kennedy—the great tribune of black America—had ordered wiretaps on Martin Luther King, Jr., back in 1963 . . . and unless you knew that the Oregon primary was just four days away, a state with a long, rich tradition of supporting civil liberties (a state where back in '48, Tom Dewey had defeated Harold Stassen in the Republican Presidential primary by arguing that the Communist Party should not be outlawed) . . . and unless you knew that a Johnson aide had asked J. Edgar Hoover's top aide for information about the wiretaps on May 17, a day before Drew Pearson met with the President.

The story had hurt Bobby in Oregon, no doubt about that; he'd lost to McCarthy by six points, but Kennedy's hold on black America was too strong. Civil rights leaders bought the idea that Kennedy had been trying to protect King from Hoover's charge that he was surrounded by Communists, and in California, a huge turnout in Watts and East Los Angeles had been the key to his victory. When he survived the assassination attempt, he had become politically invulnerable as far as Negroes were concerned. In fact, that near-death experience had changed the game in ways no one could really measure. The nomination that had been about to fall into Humphrey's lap might now just be up for grabs.

Well, the President thought as he watched Kennedy rally his supporters, *there's a lot more where that King story came from. A lot more. And if there was anyone who despised Bobby Kennedy more than me, it's Edgar Hoover. Let's see the little runt squirm his way out of what's coming next.*

On June 19, the morning after the New York primary, Richard J. Daley reached for the telephone at his desk on the fifth floor of Chicago's City Hall. He paused for a moment, looked out of the floor-to-ceiling windows to the cars and pedestrians on LaSalle Street, then placed a telephone call to Robert Kennedy.

Daley was in the thirteenth year as the city's mayor, his fourteenth as Chairman of the Cook County Democratic Party Central Committee. At sixty-six, he had spent more than two-thirds of his life serving the people of Chicago, and the Democratic Party, not necessarily in that order, although in his mind, the two were inseparable. He had worked his way up the greasy pole not with personal charisma or blazing intellect—he was portly, jowly, with a shaky command of language, and his outward affect reflected the plodding nature of his mind—but no one worked harder, no one better mastered the intricacies of budgets or voter habits, no one more thoroughly committed himself to making the arcane, mind-numbing work of government function smoothly, efficiently to ensure that a grateful electorate would keep the party in power.

He had lived all his life within boundaries physical, cultural, and political; he lived in a bungalow in the working-class Bridgeport neighborhood just blocks from where he was born. He sent his children to the same parochial schools, stayed faithfully married to Eleanor, a girl from the neighborhood. His roots were planted firmly in the Eleventh Ward, where he still served as its committeeman. His climb began there, when he signed on as secretary to a famously indolent alderman, Big Jim McDonough, followed him to the city treasurer's office, went to Springfield as a state senator and director of state revenue, came back to Chicago as deputy controller, the county clerk, then used his power as party chairman to unseat Mayor Kennelly in 1955. He was a man who believed in the structures he had been born into: you got a job because you knew the right people, and you paid for it by turning out the votes on Election Day; you lived in the neighborhood where your kind felt welcome, Irish here, Poles there, blacks and whites kept separate by choice, by design, and by public policy; it was no accident that the fourteen-lane Dan Ryan Expressway cleaved the city by color. And when Martin Luther King, Jr., had come to Chicago in 1966, he'd met with him, signed an agreement to push integrated housing that had all the force of a raindrop on the Chicago River, and watched as King folded his tent and left.

So the tumult and upheaval of the late 1960s troubled him, offended him, threatened his sense of order. When black neighborhoods exploded after King's murder in April, he ordered his chief of police to "shoot to kill" an arsonist, anyone with a Molotov cocktail, and "shoot to maim any looter." He shared the contempt of his working-class contemporaries for the anti-war protests of the radical, arrogant young; it was treasonous behavior, never mind their dress and their language. When a huge anti-war demonstration in May turned chaotic, when the police used clubs on some of the demonstrators, he had leapt to the defense of authority. Now, with the Democratic National Convention two months away, he was mobilizing police and calling for the National Guard to protect Chicago against the radicals' threats to immobilize the city. Maybe they weren't really planning to put LSD in the Chicago drinking water, but you couldn't be too careful.

Such a man would seem to have little in common with the anti-war, civil rights passions of Robert Kennedy, a figure who had committed the ultimate heresy of challenging the sitting President of his own party. The reality was different. First, there were family ties that went back a generation. Joseph P. Kennedy, Sr., had built the Merchandise Mart, the retail behemoth on the far side of the river that was the city's largest private employer, one of its biggest property taxpayers, and one of the party's biggest (if private) benefactors. There were also ties of blood. Daley was forever proud of what he did to help put the first Irish-Catholic in the White House, backing Jack at the 1960 convention over Illinois's own Adlai Stevenson, then on Election Night helping to ensure that the state's twenty-six electoral votes would wind up in Kennedy's corner. When he heard the news from Dallas on that November 22, he'd been inconsolable for days.

But the impulse that drew Daley to Robert Kennedy ran deeper than affection for the family. There was the war. For Daley, it was a visceral wound. Every week, the coffins were coming back: to the Irish in Bridgeport, to the Poles on Milwaukee Avenue, to Greektown, to the towering housing projects where the coloreds lived on the South Side, coffins carrying all that remained of the kids too poor, or too patriotic, or too removed from the safety of college deferments to shield them from combat. One of those coffins held the mortal remains of Joseph McKean, a golden boy of the Bridgeport streets, one of the few graduates of De La Salle to make it to Harvard. McKean had enlisted in the Marines, gone to Vietnam—and three weeks later he was dead.

The war was a political matter, too: He could see the faith of voters in their government ebb as the war dragged on, as the light at the end of the tunnel seemed more and more like the headlight of an oncoming train, as the war's purpose and outcome became more and more remote.

That's why he asked a colleague: "And for what? For real estate?"

That's why he'd told Johnson's people at the White House back in '66 that the war was going to be a disaster for the Democratic Party, why he'd said bluntly: "When you've got a losing hand, you throw in your cards and get up from the table." And when they'd asked, what about prestige, he'd said, "You put your prestige in your back pocket, get up from the table, and walk away."

He knew that the country wanted the war to end, and they'd likely vote for the candidate who seemed most likely to end it. Richard Nixon, who seemed on a glide path to the Republican nomination, was promising "a new policy . . . an honorable end to the war in Vietnam," and while that was all smoke and mirrors, it might sound better than anything coming from Hubert Humphrey, who appeared paralyzed by the thought of what Lyndon Johnson might do if his Vice President sought to distance himself from the war. Bobby, on the other hand . . . there was no doubt that Bobby meant to end the war.

And about the blacks . . . yes, Bobby seemed at times too sympathetic to the troublemakers and the rabble-rousers, too eager to berate his white audiences about all the terrible things happening to the coloreds, as if it was the white man's fault that they kept having babies without being married, as if it was his fault that they couldn't keep their neighborhoods clean, or keep their kids out of gangs, couldn't get off welfare and find a job like everyone in his family and his neighborhood had done. After King had been shot, they'd gone nuts; he'd had to call out 2,000 National Guardsmen, and by the time it was over eleven were dead and a twenty-eight-block-long stretch along Madison Street had been charred or burned. It was anarchy, sedition, pure and simple.

But there was also this: blacks were now 30 percent of the city's population—they'd only been 14 percent back in '50—making them as powerful a voting bloc as any; and Bobby had their ear, their hearts, their trust. If he went with Bobby, that would make a big difference when he ran for mayor again. And Bobby was talking in a way that whites could understand, talking about how destructive the welfare system was, about how big government was not the answer, about how private enterprise had to be encouraged to come into black neighborhoods, so jobs would be there, so those neighborhoods would prosper. (He'd almost laughed out loud when he watched the California debate and saw Bobby telling Gene McCarthy that it wouldn't work to move 10,000 Negroes into Orange County.)

Then there was politics, pure and simple. The top of the ticket mattered to Daley, and to his organization, because that's what helped pull in your slate, that's what kept your legislators and councilmen in power, that's what won you the State's Attorney office, the job that came with subpoena power, to put every municipal contract, every patronage job under the withering light of a grand jury. A good party leader would do almost anything to make sure the top of the ticket was a sail, not an anchor. Back in '48, Daley had watched as Jake Arvey, the city's Democratic leader, grappled with a string of corruption charges and growing public anger. That year, Arvey slated University of Chicago economist Paul Douglas for U.S. senator, and downstate patrician diplomat Adlai Stevenson for governor—two of the most impeccably corruption-free public figures in the state. Both men had won, and the Cook County organization retained its power.

Now, twenty years later, Daley could see, no, he could feel, the new threat: the cracking of the Democratic Party coalition born in FDR's New Deal. Crime was infecting the white ethnic neighborhoods, turning them to the law-and-order campaign of Nixon, and to the harsher message of Alabama Governor George Wallace. (He'd seen a "Wallace for President" yard sign around the corner from his own home!) Big Labor was banging the drums for another escalation in Vietnam, while the reformers and intellectuals had turned solidly against it. And could Humphrey really hold this coalition together? He liked Hubert—hell, everybody liked Hubert—but where was the strength, where were the balls to make a voter feel that this was the leader who could hold it together, who could talk to black anger and white fear, maybe find some common ground between the races and the generations?

Now Bobby—he'd won the blacks and the blue-collar whites in Indiana, the farmers in Nebraska and South Dakota, the Mexicans in California, and with McCarthy going down the tubes in New York (Daley couldn't stand that smug, smirking, "I'm so much cleverer than you are" faker), the reformers and the college types who hated the war really didn't have any other place to go. As for Daley's standing, going with Bobby might cost him some with the labor guys, but with the construction booming all over Chicago, they'd forgive him quickly, and his Ward committeemen and council members were loyal, they'd follow his lead. Johnson might make trouble for him with poverty money, but, hell, the Mayor was already screaming at the White House about funding those thugs with Community Action money. Besides, backing Bobby would do him a world of good with the blacks, who were starting to raise real noise about being left out of the jobs-and-contracts pie.

And maybe if Daley backed the candidate who was against the war, maybe the demonstrations at the convention wouldn't be quite so big, quite so nasty. He thought of the pictures from earlier in the spring, the April 27 march by the Chicago Peace Council when 6,000 of them marched from Grant Park to the Civic Center Plaza, with his police wading into the mob, pushing them into the Civic Center fountain, clubbing the protesters with their nightsticks. Bad enough as it was on the front page of the *Tribune* and the *Sun-Times* and the *Daily News,* it would be awful for the city if it happened in the middle of the convention. Christ, the whole world would be watching.

So he picked up the phone, called Bobby, said he'd noticed Kennedy had been in Philadelphia, Cleveland, Detroit, thought maybe it was time he came to Chicago, maybe find time for a good old-fashioned Democratic rally in downtown around noon, when the lunchtime crowds would be out on the streets, and maybe if he liked, the Mayor could introduce him with a few words, talk a bit about old times and times to come and how the Democrats could keep Nixon out of the White House. And Bobby said, yes, he thought he could find the time, could move a few things on his schedule, and how would next Monday work, could the Mayor put something together that soon?

And Daley thought about the 35,000 people on the city payroll, the sanitation workers and building inspectors and firefighters and cops, and said, yes, he was pretty sure that would work.

So when Kennedy's campaign announced on Thursday that the Senator would be going to Chicago for a noon rally on Monday, everybody knew what that meant. You didn't campaign in the middle of that town in the middle of the day unless Mayor Daley wanted you to, unless he was in your corner. And when Kennedy stood in the middle of North LaSalle Street, with 300,000 spilling into the side streets, with Daley himself introducing Bobby as "the next President of the United States!" everyone knew that the campaign had just turned a very big corner of its own.

JUST AFTER NINE P.M. on Thursday, July 4, Robert Kennedy stood on a bunting-covered platform in the middle of the Jefferson National

Expansion Memorial in St. Louis, a ninety-one-acre park on the west bank of the Mississippi River that marked the start of Lewis and Clark's expedition to the West. The massive Gateway Arch towered 630 feet above him; surrounding him were some 75,000 spectators, drawn by the candidate, the promise of fireworks, and by the celebrities who had come to entertain them: Sammy Davis, Jr., Andy Williams, the Jefferson Airplane—("Don't tell me we can't put a broad-based coalition together!" one aide cracked)—Bill Cosby, Gregory Peck, and a cluster of famous athletes. "The bad news," Kennedy began, "is that the great Cardinal pitcher Bob Gibson will not run with me as my Vice President. The good news is, he says I can run with him as his Vice President." It was the same joke he'd told about Alabama football coach Bear Bryant in Alabama, the same joke he'd use about any famous sports figure in any state. But it always went over well. He was in a buoyant mood that evening, because he'd spent the day traveling across Missouri by train, joining Independence Day celebrations in a dozen small towns, reviving the old political tradition of the whistle-stop, as he had in the primary states. It proved to be one of the most consequential tactics of his campaign, in ways neither he nor his key advisors could have fully imagined.

It had begun back in Indiana, the first primary test Kennedy would face. One of his old friends, Indiana-born writer John Barlow Martin, suggested that Bobby campaign by train, retracing the route of the famed Wabash Cannonball. *If you're going to win this primary,* Martin had argued, *you'll have to win over small-town Indiana, and this is the best way to do it; besides, it'll make for great television.*

But it turned out to be more, a lot more than a campaign stunt or a catchy visual. For one thing, it connected Kennedy, a symbol to many of unsettling change and frenzy, to an older, slower, more comfortable time. For the men and women of Kokomo and Marion and Bedford, the railroad depot had been at the center of life and commerce before the interstates and the malls had passed them by, hollowed out their towns, left the storefronts around the town squares vacant. There was also something flattering in the notion that a serious contender for the Presidency, a Kennedy, no less, a man who had not lived a moment of his life in a small, Midwestern town would come to them, the people the TV cameras and celebrities never visited, and ask for their votes. More than his presence, though, was a connection that Kennedy had begun to feel with the weathered faces of farmers and laborers; the same sense of "outsiderness" that he sensed almost viscerally in the faces of Negro children in urban ghettoes, Hispanics who worked the fields in California's Imperial Valley. Speaking without a text, often unpolished, sometimes groping for words, he had communicated the kind of unvarnished, no-frills presence that struck a chord with these classic Hoosiers. On Primary Day, May 7, Kennedy won every rural county through which the Wabash Cannonball had traveled. So he'd repeated the whistle-stop in Nebraska, and it was one of the campaign's best days. He was increasingly at ease in his speeches, and began mocking the pandering of conventional campaigners.

"I'm doing more for the farmer than any of them," he said of his rivals, "and if you don't believe me, just look down at my breakfast table. We are consuming more milk and bread, more eggs, doing more for farm consumption than the family of any other candidate!" He would mockingly "instruct" his listeners on proper politically useful behavior.

"Break out in spontaneous applause whenever I make a point." And when the clapping broke out, he demanded, "Did anyone over twenty-one clap?" At Ogallala, he asked, if other candidates had appeared. "No!" the crowd shouted, and he said, "Remember who was here first . . . In fact, when I was asked why I wanted to campaign in Nebraska, I said, 'Because I want to go to Ogallala.'" And on May 14, Kennedy won by huge margins all along the route of his train, from Kimball to North Platte to Lexington. By the time he campaigned by train through California's San Joaquin Valley, he had ratcheted up his humor, explaining to a crowd in Fresno that he had decided to enter the primary so that he'd have an excuse to visit the Fresno Mall.

"Because after you've seen the Pyramids of Egypt and the Taj Mahal, what is left but to visit the Fresno Mall?" What might have sounded like an insult became a shared joke—candidate and audience mocking the platitudes.

Now, with the primaries over, a new factor had entered the equation. In many of the big states, the old-line politicians supporting Humphrey were based in the big cities, heirs to the once-invincible, still-significant machines that had installed Democrats in power decades earlier. Small-town Democrats often felt like red-haired stepchildren when it came to the spoils of office, yet by the rules of most state parties, they had votes in county and statewide gatherings out of all proportion to their share of the population. To the strategists around Kennedy, desperately looking for ways to pry delegates away from Humphrey, a show of strength in rural and small-town America could mean as much as huge rallies in the streets of the big cities. In fact, it could mean more, because Kennedy would be surrounded by people and images that reassured rather than unsettled the TV audience.

The decision to campaign through small-town America was yielding other political benefits as well: Governor John Docking of Kansas, Governor Harold Hughes of Iowa, and Senator Quentin Burdick of North Dakota, watching Bobby connect with their kinds of voters, were signaling that they just might be lining up behind Bobby.

"I'd like to claim credit for our brilliant insight," one top aide later said, "but the truth is, we were looking at the footage from those states and it hit us that we'd somehow signed up Norman Rockwell as our scenic designer." Another aide put it more pungently.

"Look at them!" he shouted as he watched the news coverage from Nebraska. "They're so *old*! They're so *clean*! They're so fucking *white*!"

So on the morning of July 3, Kennedy spoke to a crowd of some 5,000 outside Kansas City's Union Station, the fifty-four-year-old Beaux Arts masterpiece. Then he boarded "the Arden," the Union Pacific's best private railroad car owned by the family of the line's founder, E. R. Harriman. (It had taken a transatlantic phone call to Averell Harriman, negotiating a Vietnam War settlement in Paris, to get the car for Kennedy's use in Nebraska.) With its wood paneling, private dining room, and an open rear platform surrounded by a polished grille, it was the perfect accommodation for a whistle-stopping candidate; local politicians, contributors, influential journalists, and traveling companions could be courted between speeches, and the campaign was spared the trauma of Ethel Kennedy's fear of flying (an understandable fear, since she had lost her parents in a plane crash).

All that day, the *"Show-Me" Special* rolled across Missouri, through Warrensburg, Sedalia, Jefferson City, Hermann, through towns that had not seen a Presidential candidate since Truman, or Coolidge, or Grover Cleveland. The high school bands were there, the drum majorettes in thigh-high skirts, the gold-tasseled uniforms and brass instruments gleaming in the sun, the mascots—Eagles, Lions, Vikings, Wildcats—on hand to greet the candidate. He spoke from the rear platform of the Arden, or he'd motorcade a short distance to the town square, ringed with American flags and bunting. He joked with them, teased them ("How many of you have read my book?" "We have! We have!" "You lie!"). And he quoted Missouri's most illustrious son as he challenged the Democratic Party not to choose a nominee who had ducked the primaries:

"Harry Truman once said, 'It's not the hand that signs the laws that holds the destiny of America, it's the hand that casts the ballot.' The millions of Americans who have cast their ballots this year, have voted overwhelmingly for a new course; now it is time for those of you who do not have a chance to cast ballots to make your voices heard."

(Some in the press did not fail to note the irony of Robert Kennedy quoting a man who had fought hard to keep his brother out of the White House, who despised primaries as a threat to party discipline, who regarded a challenge to a sitting President's renomination as treason, and who had said of Bobby, "I just don't like that boy and I never will.")

By eight p.m.—just about two hours late—the *"Show-Me" Special* pulled into Union Station in St. Louis, once the busiest station in the world, whose gold-leaf Romanesque arches dominated the Great Hall, now dingy from years of neglect. A clutch of Missouri politicians traveled with Kennedy on the last leg of his journey, a significant sign given that the state's Democratic governor, Warren Hearnes, was solidly behind Humphrey. One of those most valued by the Kennedy campaign was the thirty-nine-year-old Lieutenant Governor Tom Eagleton, who was mounting a spirited primary challenge to Senator Edward Long, a Teamsters' mouthpiece who had frequently attacked Robert Kennedy for overzealously prosecuting the union.

By nine p.m., Kennedy had mounted the platform under the arch, and was speaking to the crowd that had been entertained during its long wait by the singers, comedians, and other celebrities.

The crowd was juiced, ready to scream its enthusiasm. What they heard was a Fourth of July speech that struck a note Kennedy had been sounding since his first days in the Senate, but which was a frontal challenge to Hubert Humphrey and to the orthodoxies of the Democratic Party.

"We celebrate today our independence from a powerful empire that had ceased to honor the rights of the individual. At the center of this campaign—and that of my colleague, Senator Eugene McCarthy—is the belief in the power of the individual to shape his own destiny, to be part of a renewed citizen participation in our civic life. But if we are to genuinely honor those who built this great nation, if we are to be true to its spirit, then we must reassert some fundamental truths that we have at times forgotten, as a party and as a nation . . . one of the elements of the 'new politics' is to halt and reverse the growing accumulation of power and authority in the central government in Washington, and to return that power of decision to the American people in their own local communities . . . the answer to our problems is not just another federal program, another department or administration, another layer of bureaucracy in Washington. The real answer is in the full involvement of the private enterprise system—in the creation of jobs, the building of housing, in training and education and health care.

"There is nothing 'liberal' about a constant expansion of the federal government, stripping citizens of their public power—the right to share in the government of affairs—that was the founding purpose of this nation. There is nothing conservative about standing idle while millions of fellow citizens lose their lives and hopes, while their frustration turns to fury that tears the fabric of society and freedom."

The speech in fact used the same language Kennedy had been using throughout his Senate years. ("When I go into the ghetto," he told a federal education official at a Senate hearing, "the two things people most hate are the public welfare system and the public education system.") But for some in the press, hearing it for the first time in the context of a major speech, it was another sign that "Bobby was appealing to the Right." In Sacramento, Governor Ronald Reagan, in the midst of his own stealth pursuit of the Presidency, joked, "He's sounding more and more like me." And in the days to come, Vice President Humphrey would tell audiences at labor union gatherings and party conventions that he, not Kennedy, was the true liberal in the race.

"I don't believe Democrats want a nominee who appeals for votes by running down the great works of Franklin Roosevelt and Harry Truman and Lyndon Johnson and, yes—John F. Kennedy. Did Social Security 'strip us of our power'? Did Medicare? The minimum wage? The civil rights laws? We don't want a candidate who talks like FDR one day, and Barry Goldwater the next!"

It was an effective message to the more traditional liberals who had long seen Humphrey as their champion, the kind of message that would work to hold those big-state delegations in place as the convention grew closer. It would take an even more powerful argument to shake those delegations loose; as it happened, the argument the Kennedy campaign seized on was rooted in what had become the central fault line of the Democratic Party for the last four decades.

NECESSITY MAY BE the mother of invention, but it was something more like desperation that gave birth to the trap that snared Vice President Hubert Humphrey. On Saturday, July 6, half a dozen men sat by the pool at Robert Kennedy's sprawling home off Hickory Hill Road. It was the same pool that was the setting for some of the more boisterous parties during John Kennedy's Presidency, including one where some of the formally clad guests had wound up leaping, or falling, or pushing one another into the water. There was, however, nothing boisterous about the gathering this Saturday noon, apart from the play of Kennedy's dogs: Freckles, the cocker spaniel, and Brumus, an enormous black Newfoundland with the habit of depositing saliva on the suit jackets of Kennedy aides and associates. (When one Kennedy aide was mocked by reporters for walking Freckles on a campaign stop, he replied, "To you, it's dog shit; to me, it's an ambassadorship.") These men had guided John Kennedy's fight for the 1960 Democratic nomination, but back then they had had two years to plan their strategy, and they were not challenging the President of their own party. So they sat this Saturday in lounge chairs, legal pads and papers on their laps, all looking at the same numbers: one hundred delegates, one hundred goddamn delegates. As best as they could measure, if the Democratic convention were balloting today, they would lose to Humphrey by a hundred delegates.

They had made up ground since the attempt on Kennedy's life, no doubt about it. Almost all of McCarthy's delegates had defected to Bobby, and there was even a chance that in Minnesota, Humphrey's home state, the anti-war passions would bring most of that delegation to his side. There were promising signs in Ohio, and the Kennedy–McCarthy coalition in Colorado had become Bobby's. In Washington State, Jim Whittaker, the mountain climber who'd led Bobby up to the summit of Mt. Kennedy, had turned out to be a first-rate tactician, and that delegation might yield a pleasant surprise from its 38 delegates. All well and good, but the men gathered around the pool had spent too many years in the infantry work of politics to be capable of self-delusion. Steve Smith, Dave Hackett, O'Donnell and O'Brien, Fred Dutton, Robert Troutman (who'd run the convention operation for JFK in '60, and who would do the same for Bobby) could see the reality beneath the crowds Bobby was drawing in the big cities and the small towns: they were a hundred goddamn delegates short.

Daley had helped, of course; there was no better barometer of lunch-bucket, no-bullshit Democratic Party thinking than the Chicago mayor, and every councilman, state assemblyman, ward committee chair, and sewer inspector from Newark to Detroit to Denver knew what Daley was saying when he'd backed Kennedy: *Hubert can't win; Bobby can.*

The problem was that for too many other players, old ties to Humphrey, old wounds from the Kennedys, and the power of organized labor counted at least as much as Daley's signal. Humphrey was a familiar, reliable, pliable Democrat, who had stood up for civil rights and organized labor from his first days in public life, and who was also firmly committed to the orthodoxies of the New Deal and the Great Society. Bobby was playing with the very forces that could threaten their hold on power: angry blacks, zealous young hotheads, "reformers" with no understanding of how politics really worked, no respect for the system that provided jobs and services in return for votes. If Bobby was going to empower people in their own neighborhoods and school districts, then where was the leverage for mayors and governors, where was the ability to trade contracts and jobs for votes?

Then there was organized labor. For Democrats, unions represented both fuel and machinery. Millions of dollars came into their coffers from

the political action committees of unions, money for advertising, direct
mail, and logistics. Millions more were spent by unions to tell their members who was on their side and who was not. Labor manned the phone
banks that called union households on Election Day, that lined up transportation and babysitters and poll watchers. Take labor out of the equation, and the Democratic Party would be consigned to permanent minority
status. And for most of the party, organized labor meant George Meany.

At seventy-three, the onetime New York City plumber had spent a lifetime in the labor movement. He'd been its top dog since 1955, when he
took the American Federation of Labor into the merger with the Congress
of Industrial Organizations. He was a crusty, blunt-spoken man whose face
wore a constant scowl, whose prominent jowls and ever-present cigar gave
him the look of one of those monopoly capitalists caricatured by left-wing
artists. And his politics, while liberal, had a conservative streak, especially
when it came to foreign policy. He'd spent years kicking Communist-
dominated unions out of the Federation, and there was no bigger hawk
when it came to facing down the Soviet Union and Communist insurgen-
cies around the world. When his key rival in the union movement, the
Auto Workers' Walter Reuther, turned on the Vietnam War, Meany argued
for its escalation. He had, in other words, no use for Robert Kennedy's
Vietnam views, and while he had kicked the Teamsters Union out of the
Federation after the Senate hearings Bobby led, Meany had a suspicion
that there were plenty of other unions Bobby might like to go after. And
when Bobby talked about "jobs" for all those Negroes in the ghettoes, it
sure sounded as if Bobby was going to take on the tradition where men
passed on construction jobs to their sons and their nephews, which kept
those high-paid jobs in the hands of white union members and their families. So Meany and his loyal allies in the union movement had thrown their
clout behind Humphrey's Presidential bid; even those old-line Democrats
inclined to go with Robert Kennedy had to think long and hard about
turning on one of their most consequential benefactors.

One final, immense obstacle separated Robert Kennedy and those hundred goddamn delegates: the South. More than 600 delegates came from
Southern and Southwestern states, and even if Bobby could count on support from black Democrats in those states, they'd be of little help, thanks to

a venerable parliamentary device. In an effort to maximize their clout, most Southern states had long lived by the "unit rule": however a majority of a state's delegation voted, all the votes of that delegation would be cast the same way. Maybe there were four, or ten, or twenty delegates who *wanted* to vote for Bobby, but under the unit rule, their votes would automatically be counted for Humphrey.

So the men sat around the pool at Hickory Hill, picked at their tuna sandwiches, sipped their iced tea, debated the wisdom of a visit to foreign capitals, and settled into that uncomfortable silence that spoke volumes about their options, or lack of them, when Robert Kennedy began tapping his prominent front teeth and asked a simple question:

"What about Mississippi?"

"I hear it's beautiful this time of year," someone said. A glance from Kennedy—whose "steely blues" had the power to freeze the blood— silenced the chuckles. Then he explained:

Four years earlier, during the coronation of Lyndon Johnson at the '64 convention in Atlantic City, the only controversy involved the composition of the Mississippi delegation, an all-white collection of segregationists, white supremacists, and other worthies who made no secret of their intention to abandon the national ticket that fall. An insurgent multiracial delegation had challenged the official delegation; one of its members, a thirty-seven-year-old heavyset black woman named Fannie Lou Hamer, mesmerized the credentials committee—and a national TV audience— with accounts of the beatings and jailings she suffered for attempting to register to vote. The conflict infuriated President Johnson, who feared losing Southern white voters, and he dispatched Hubert Humphrey to resolve the dispute; it was, in effect, Humphrey's Vice Presidential audition. After an acrimonious debate, the Mississippi Freedom Democratic Party was offered two non-voting seats, and a promise that in the future, only racially representative delegations would be seated.

Now, in 1968, Mississippi was coming to the convention with a delegation that included all of one black delegate and one black alternate. Its leaders were the staunchly segregationist Senator John Stennis, and the blatantly white-supremacist Governor John Bell Williams, who made no secret of their intentions this time around to support the third-party

Presidential bid of Alabama's George Wallace. This time, a "loyalist" delegation, half black and half white, was challenging the regulars. And this time, Robert Kennedy was asking, wouldn't a frontal assault on the Mississippi regulars raise some other possibilities?

"You know," Dave Hackett said, "it's not just Mississippi. There's a good chance that if the credentials committee takes a look, they'll find that Alabama and Georgia and maybe some others are out of compliance with the rules. If Humphrey has his people back the challenges, we have a real shot at picking up some of those delegates. If he has his people vote with the regulars—"

"He burns his bridges with whatever friends he has left with the blacks and liberals," O'Brien said. "And how can Meany have his labor people vote with the segregationists? I mean, he's no friends of the blacks, but he did put a hell of a lot of money into the March on Washington." O'Brien grinned as he shook his head.

"It'll drive Lyndon absolutely crazy."

"Call it a side benefit," O'Donnell said.

David Hackett held up a cautionary finger.

"I'm not sure it would be enough to turn things around—not as long as those states have the unit rule. Hell, they could put twenty blacks on the Georgia delegation who'd all vote for us, and they'd still wind up counting every vote for Humphrey." He paused for a second. "Of course," he said, "we could take on the whole idea of the unit rule. 'Let every vote count,' that sort of thing."

"Um, David," Larry O'Brien said. "Don't we have a small problem with the California delegation? You know, Bobby got 46 percent of the vote, and 100 percent of the delegates. We can't afford to lose one of them."

"Maybe we won't have to," Kennedy said.

THE FOLLOWING MONDAY, KENNEDY called a press conference at his Washington headquarters. "I am asking those delegates who support me to seat the loyalist Mississippi delegation at the convention, and to weigh carefully the challenges to other delegations as well. We cannot claim to be 'the party of the people' if we permit those who speak in our name to deny representation to Democrats based on the color of their skin.

"I am also asking my supporters to vote to abolish the unit rule at this convention. By requiring every member of a delegation to vote the same way as a majority, it undermines the foundation of free choice—it mandates that delegates vote against their consciences. That may be the way things are done in Moscow; it should not be the way things are done at the most important gathering of the Democratic Party. In the interests of consistency, I am releasing my California delegates, chosen in a "winner take all" primary, from their legal commitments to me. If they choose to vote for Vice President Humphrey or another candidate, they should feel free to do so."

("Weren't you worried that you'd lose some delegates?" a reporter asked him later.

"Not with Rosey Grier in the delegation!" he replied.)

"Twenty years ago," Kennedy concluded, "Hubert Humphrey became a national hero by calling on Democrats to 'walk out of the shadows of states' rights, into the bright sunlight of human rights.' I call upon him to step out of the shadows of closed-door politics, into the bright sunshine of free choice and fair representation. While we compete for the nomination of our party, let us walk together in the name of fairness and justice."

The nature of the trap Kennedy had laid for Humphrey became evident within forty-eight hours. The Humphrey campaign had long planned to back the integrated Mississippi slate challenging the regulars; the "official" delegation was packed with segregationists who'd be standing side by side with George Wallace's third-party campaign in November. But the logic behind throwing out the Mississippi delegation extended to other states: Alabama, maybe Georgia. (A twenty-eight-year-old Georgia state senator, Julian Bond, who'd been expelled from the legislature for his anti-war views, only to be put back in office by a unanimous Supreme Court, was raising serious questions about the delegation, in particular, its governor, Lester Maddox, whose claim to fame was his threat as a restaurant owner to use an ax handle on Negroes seeking service. Bond, in turn, drew the ire of more traditional Georgia Democrats, including a state senator from Georgia named Jimmy Carter.) And deposing those official delegations could be costly to the Vice President: the official delegations were lined up solidly with Humphrey; the challengers were likely to have in their ranks a lot more Kennedy backers.

As for the unit rule, it was as fundamental to Southern Democrats as grits and Friday night high school football. It was the mechanism by which Southern delegations exercised power out of all proportion to their numbers, the device that kept them as players after Democrats had thrown out the "two-thirds to nominate a candidate" rule in 1932. By coming to the convention with a united slate, a state guaranteed that its voice would be heard on matters ranging from platform plans to potential Cabinet posts. So it was hardly surprising that by four p.m. on the day Bobby announced his challenge to the rule, a telegram arrived at Humphrey headquarters signed by eight Southern governors, stating flatly: "If You Want Us to Stand with You, Stand with Us on Unit Rule." It was duly noted that one of the signers was Texas Governor John Connally, one of President Johnson's closest political allies. It was not exactly a major leap of intuition to see Lyndon Johnson's fine hand in the pressure coming down on the Vice President.

Unfortunately for Hubert Humphrey, it was not just Southern states that saw fundamental issues at stake in these looming credentials and rules fights. For Democrats in the North and the industrial Midwest, anything that raised the specter of a civil rights issue stirred the blood. The party had been split as far back as 1924, when a platform plank denouncing the Ku Klux Klan had divided the emerging big-city Catholic Democrats from the Protestant Southern wing of the party. The civil rights plank Hubert Humphrey had championed in '48 had driven hundreds of Southern delegates to walk out of the convention and fall in behind the white supremacist third-party campaign of South Carolina Governor Strom Thurmond (now a U.S. senator and a Republican). The Civil Rights Act of 1964, sponsored by John Kennedy and guided into law by President Johnson, was a key reason why five Southern states, once reliably Democratic, had given their electoral votes to Barry Goldwater that year, and why the independent Presidential campaign of George Wallace was threatening to win enough electoral votes from the South to throw the choice for President into the House of Representatives.

Beyond politics, civil rights was the issue that had brought countless young people into politics in the first place; until the escalation of the war in Vietnam, it was for liberals the most emotionally compelling of all political

causes. More than a few of the men and women now beginning to move
into public and party offices had been foot soldiers for civil rights. They'd
gone South to help register blacks; they'd picketed Woolworth stores in
support of the sit-ins. Whoever these delegates preferred for President,
they were not about to sit back and give their sanction to a segregationist delegation from Mississippi or anywhere else—especially when they'd
made an explicit promise at the *last* convention to bar any such delegation.
Given their bedrock distrust of Southern political machinations, it was a
small step to convince them that the unit rule was just another device to
perpetuate the power of the reactionary whites.

On principle alone, then, liberal-minded Democrats would have
brought heavy pressure on the Humphrey campaign. There was also some
not-so-subtle political maneuvering at work. All through the spring and
early summer, supporters of Robert Kennedy had been at work in the big
non-primary states, trying to find fault lines in Hubert Humphrey's support. In Michigan, United Auto Workers chief Walter Reuther, officially
neutral, had been staging a rearguard action, pushing back against strong
support within his own union for Humphrey: the dependable liberal, the
longtime friend of labor. Now, with a new convention battle brewing,
Reuther saw a target of opportunity. His union's executive council, proud
of its longtime financial support for the civil rights cause, and well aware
of the growing number of blacks within its ranks, unanimously backed
Reuther's proposal to let the Humphrey campaign know its mind.

"We are confident," the union's press release said, "that Vice President
Humphrey will not turn his back on twenty years of courageous fights for
civil rights and fair representation. No temporary political advantage could
possibly be worth the damage to his reputation, and to the Democratic
Party's principles." A strikingly similar statement came from a joint statement signed by 175 of the 200+ black delegates who would be attending
the Chicago convention, many of them from states whose leaders had committed themselves to Humphrey. ("It's a nightmare," one pro-Humphrey
governor told a *New York Times* reporter. "If we don't get 90 percent of the
black vote, we lose every election. Hell, if the black vote even stays home
in any significant number, we lose. So how the hell do I vote with the same
redneck bastards who sicc'ed police dogs on people who were trying to

register? But if I stand against them, if I vote to seat the insurgents, that means forty, fifty, who the hell knows how many delegates for Bobby on the first ballot. That could mean no first ballot nomination for Hubert, and after that . . . who the hell knows what?")

All through late July and August, the Kennedy and Humphrey campaigns struggled for every tactical advantage, every uncommitted delegate, using every weapon in their political arsenals. In late July, Kennedy forces staged a "mock primary" in Pennsylvania, hoping to prove to the political machines in Philadelphia and Pittsburgh that their support for the Vice President did not reflect the sentiments of rank-and-file Democrats. Instead of dismissing the mock primary as a "cheap political stunt," the Humphrey forces almost pulled off a coup: the Steelworkers Union, along with the organizations controlled by Philadelphia Mayor Tate and Pittsburgh Mayor Barr, fired up their Election Day machinery and sent tens of thousands of their troops to flood the polling places. Only a huge turnout from the black neighborhoods of Philadelphia and a big Kennedy vote from smaller towns in Pennsylvania turned the primary into a dead heat. ("Fine with us," said Kennedy spokesman Pierre Salinger. "We'll settle for half the delegation." "It's a deal," replied Humphrey co-chair Walter Mondale. "As long as you settle for the 46 percent of the California delegation you won instead of the 100 percent you got under the rules.")

Another Kennedy stratagem was more successful. For weeks, the campaign had been planning a summer trip abroad, to demonstrate that Robert Kennedy already had the stature of a world leader, and to suggest that his election would improve America's battered international prestige. When the State Department—and by inference, the President—made it clear that they did not want to see Europe turned into a staging area for a Presidential campaign, Moscow, Berlin, and London all turned down the proposed visits. The *New York Times* editorial page agreed, condemning "Senator Kennedy's single-minded and self-interested intention to sacrifice diplomatic tradition to his boundless ambition." Kennedy did manage a thirty-six-hour trip that took him to two nations: first to Czechoslovakia, where 500,000 cheered him as he spoke from the steps of Hradčany Castle, praising the liberal reforms of "Prague Spring" as the reformist leader, Alexander Dubček, stood by his side; then he flew to Warsaw, where he paid a visit to the new young Cardinal Karol Wojtila. In both cities, his message was the same: "Every great power—whether it be my own country or the Soviet Union—must respect the desire for freedom and independence that is the birthright of every citizen. Freedom," he said, "is not America's gift to the world; it is God's gift to the world." (This last comment brought a sharp rejoinder from a young Texas congressman, George Herbert Walker Bush, for "injecting religion into the sensitive arena of international relations.") Others asked about the political implications of the visit: when reporters noted that a large number of Polish-Americans lived in Milwaukee, Toledo, Pittsburgh, and Grand Rapids, a campaign aide responded: "No kidding. I guess you learn something new every day."

Both campaigns played their strongest assets: Humphrey appeared before union-organized rallies, hammering home his argument that he was the only candidate devoted to the cause of organized labor. ("I don't support right-to-work laws like George Wallace does; I didn't vote for Taft-Hartley like Richard Nixon did; and I don't think you help the poor with child labor schemes!") The Kennedy campaign staged a series of receptions at the family compound in Hyannis, where delegates met in small groups with Bobby, while their wives were guests at teas hosted by the Kennedy women. (Bobby's mother, Rose, regaled them with tales of Bobby's mischievous behavior as a young boy.) Yet for all the struggles within the Democratic Party, the most significant midsummer impact on Robert Kennedy's campaign would come from the *Republicans*.

IT WAS LATE on the night of Wednesday, August 7, in the sixteenth-floor Penthouse Suite of Miami's Hilton-Plaza Hotel. Richard Nixon finished his supper—cheese omelet, milk, ice cream—and dispatched a message to the two dozen men who had just engineered his first-ballot Presidential nomination.

"I would appreciate it," he wrote, "if you could meet with me tonight in my room . . ." He was summoning them to hear them out about his running mate. In fact, he had already made up his mind. And what he was going to tell them would require every ounce of his persuasive ability. It was Bobby Kennedy who had pushed him to this decision; and it was Bobby

Kennedy who was his best hope of convincing Republicans that he simply had to do what he was about to do—because Robert Kennedy was emerging as a clear threat to the central premise of one of the most remarkable comebacks in American political history.

From his first days in public life, Richard Nixon had embodied the idea that he was the spokesman for "the forgotten American." "Nixon is one of us," proclaimed his first campaign ad for Congress in 1946. When George Wallace was a freshman legislator in Alabama sounding moderate notes on the race issue, when Ronald Reagan was an enthusiastic New Deal Democrat looking to salvage a fading acting career, Richard Nixon was winning office by tapping into the grievances of what came to be called middle America. He was speaking for the GI just home from World War II looking to start a small business, but entangled by the red tape of Washington bureaucracy, for the young couple unable to drive their new car for the gas rationing that still governed the land, for the college-bound veteran whose GI Bill money was stuck somewhere in the file cabinets of the Capitol.

He'd saved his political career in 1952 by going on TV to talk directly to the country about charges he was living high on the hog off a secret "rich man's trust." No, he'd told his audience, here's what I've saved, here's what my mortgage costs me, here's how much insurance I have. He'd stuck it to Stevenson—"I believe that it's fine that a man like Governor Stevenson, who inherited a fortune from his father, can run for President"—and yes, at the end, he'd described another gift: "It was a little cocker spaniel dog in a crate . . . sent all the way from Texas. Black and white spotted. And our little girl, Tricia, the six-year-old named it Checkers. And you know, the kids, like all kids, love the dog and I just want to say this right now, that regardless of what they say about it, we're gonna keep it."

Oh, the eggheads and the liberals had gone nuts about that line, but the telegrams and phone calls had come into the Republican National Committee, they'd come from his people, shopkeepers and insurance salesmen, real-estate brokers and middle managers, the Rotarians, Kiwanis, the vets from the Legion and the VFW, the people who played by the rules, kept the lawns in their suburban tracts neat, and they'd said, *We believe him, this is our guy, don't you dare kick him off the ticket,* and at age thirty-nine he was Vice President of the United States. For eight years he'd stood loyally by the side of Ike, the national hero, the beloved father figure who never extended a hand to him, barely stirred himself to campaign for him, and so he lost by the narrowest margin in history, one-tenth of one goddamn percent, and he knew as surely as he knew the sun rose in the East, that the Kennedys, with their money and their pull and their friends in the Mob, had stolen those votes in Chicago while Lyndon's people stole those votes in Texas, and stole his Presidency right out from under him.

So he'd written his memoir—*Six Crises*—and waited for the next opening. He thought he saw it in California in '62, but when he went back home, he realized quickly it had been a dreadful mistake. He'd had no business running for governor—hell, he couldn't have cared less about budgets for roads and schools; his mind was fixed on Khrushchev and Castro, Mao and Nehru, the world and its complex geopolitical forces. He'd lost by a quarter of a million votes, and on the morning after Election Night, he'd shaken off his aides, stormed into the pressroom at the Beverly Hilton Hotel and told the stunned press corps, "You won't have Nixon to kick around anymore because, gentlemen, this is my last press conference." Five days later, ABC News broadcast "A Political Obituary." And whom did they invite to be one of the happy mourners? Alger Hiss, a goddamn Communist traitor!

Now, more than five and a half years later, he was on an easy path to the Republican Presidential nomination. It had been a combination of fate, luck, and the kind of dogged perseverance that had characterized his life from his first days as the child of a financial failure. Michigan Governor George Romney, the favorite of the Rockefellers and the Scrantons and the Eastern elitists, had imploded, withdrawing from the field even before the voters of New Hampshire could punish him for his stupendously dumb comment that he had been subjected to "the greatest brainwashing ever" on Vietnam. Rockefeller had given every indication that he would jump in, then held a press conference in April to say . . . no, he *wasn't* going to run. (Ted Agnew, the governor of Maryland who was a big Rockefeller fan, had gathered friends and supporters to watch the announcement. He was blindsided, furious enough to reach out to Nixon and say, *I'm with you, now*.) Three weeks later, Rockefeller said, on second thought, yes, I'm in, but he had more than enough enemies in the party to make his nomination almost impossible.

There was Ronald Reagan, of course, the self-described "citizen-politician" who'd made a powerful speech for Goldwater in '64, had been recruited by a gaggle of California millionaires to run for governor, had used the hippies and the campus radicals and the criminals as targets of opportunity, and had beaten Governor Brown, the man who'd defeated Nixon in '62, beaten him by almost a million votes. Reagan would have leapt right into the Presidential contest, but a scandal involving homosexual members of his staff had sidelined him, and now Reagan's only hope was to conspire with Rockefeller to deprive Nixon of an early-ballot win, and then let the two survivors battle for the spoils. And with Senators Strom Thurmond and John Tower firmly in Nixon's corner, he had a firewall against a conservative defection to Reagan.

As for November . . . Richard Nixon was perfectly positioned as the alternative to President Johnson: the experienced, tested leader who would restore traditional American values to the White House, who would blend strength and diplomacy to achieve peace with honor in Vietnam, who would put the authority of the President on the side of the police, not the criminals, who would simply not permit chaos in the streets and stalemate a half a world away. The billboards in the primary states proclaimed the theme with admirable concision: "Feel Safer with Nixon." And there he was, in white shirt, tie, and suit jacket, gazing thoughtfully into an open briefcase. He need risk nothing specific about his plans: as the alternative to a President who had lost the confidence of the country, that was more than enough.

Now Johnson was gone, leaving the battlefield just as the trumpets were sounding. And now there was Bobby Kennedy, making a real contest of the Democratic nomination. There was no way to challenge his experience, hell, he'd been in effect the Assistant President of the United States for nearly three years, had been there during the most dangerous thirteen days in American history, that Cuban Missile Crisis. (Yes, he and his brother had blundered into it, with Jack's timidity at the Vienna Summit with Khrushchev and all those comic-opera CIA plots to kill Castro, but there was no way to make that case in public.) And as for change? Well, you couldn't exactly link Bobby to LBJ when the two hated each other as much as any two men can, when Bobby had run against his own party's President.

And there was something else, something Nixon found impossible to admit to anyone, and almost impossible to admit to himself: the Kennedys spooked him. Maybe it was their money, or their ease with perfect strangers, or the effortless charm (too bad nobody seemed able to show just how charmed the women around Jack—and maybe Bobby—had been, but the press wouldn't touch it with a ten-foot pole). When Bobby campaigned in Indiana and Nebraska and California, he never missed a chance to tweak Nixon.

"Have you seen those billboards?" he would ask the crowds. "What's in that briefcase? Maybe it's his seventh crisis." (Curious that Bobby would pick up on the briefcase as a symbol of the stuffed-shirt bureaucrat, just as George Wallace would mock the "pointy-headed bureaucrats" who carried around their bologna sandwich lunches in their briefcases.)

The longer the Democratic nomination remained unresolved, the more complicated Nixon's strategy became. If he were running against Humphrey, he could still run as the candidate of undefined change. If Bobby were the nominee, he would run as the candidate of reassurance, of bedrock American values, speaking to what one of his speechwriters, Ray Price, had labeled "a country caught in this terrible complex of fear, unstructured fear, amorphous fear . . . you will be the candidate of dynamic stability." And there was another possibility: what if Bobby lost the nomination, but joined Humphrey's ticket as his running mate? It was far from impossible; Nixon had been told that one of Bobby's key aides, Fred Dutton, had said, "Of course he'd take the Vice Presidency. Bobby's a Roman; he'll go where the power is."

And so the specter of Robert Kennedy on the ticket weighed powerfully on the choice he had to make in the next several hours—the choice of a running mate. Left to his own devices, he would have chosen Robert Finch, the lieutenant governor of California, who had served Nixon's political operations for more than decade. But Finch said no, it would smack of cronyism, and besides, he simply wasn't ready for a post that might propel him into the Presidency at a moment's notice. There was Spiro Agnew, "Ted" everyone called him, the sleek, silver-haired governor of Maryland, who'd put Nixon's name in nomination earlier that evening. Agnew had won the governorship in 1966 with crucial backing from the state's independents and

Democrats, who recoiled at the right-wing Democratic nominee's blatant appeal to racial fears. More recently, though, Agnew had become a conservative hero; after much of Baltimore went up in flames when King was murdered, Agnew had called out the National Guard, slapped a curfew on the city, summoned black leaders to a meeting where he'd denounced militant blacks as "circuit-riding, Hanoi-visiting, caterwauling, riot-inciting, 'burn America down' type of leaders." "I call on you to publicly repudiate black racists," he said. "Thus far, you have not done so." It was the kind of in-your-face push back that Nixon admired, and that could play just fine among the working-class and lower-middle-class whites his campaign was working to pull away from the Democratic Party of their fathers, and from the third-party campaign of Governor George Wallace.

More and more, though, Richard Nixon had begun to conclude that his running mate had to act as a rebuttal to Robert Kennedy. He had to be young, energetic, with credible connections to the cities, to balance Nixon's strength among voters who at root wished that urban America might be walled off from the rest of the country. He had to have the ability to connect with Negroes, without the driven intensity Bobby possessed that made suburban voters uneasy. And that was how he had come to the jaw-dropping conclusion that his running mate might just have to be . . . New York City Mayor John Lindsay.

Had Nixon not been convinced that Bobby Kennedy was going to wind up on the Democratic ticket, the idea of Lindsay would have been ludicrous. The forty-eight-year-old Lindsay was a walking, breathing symbol of WASP aristocracy: tall, lean, with cheekbones angular enough to slit open an envelope, and a thousand-megawatt smile. He'd fit fine as the congressman from Manhattan's wealthy East Side—the so-called silk stocking district—but he was miscast as the Mayor of a city ripe with ethnic and tribal clans that had warred with and against each other for a century. It was a city where even Republicans had to honor the custom of a municipal ticket featuring an Irishman, an Italian, and a Jew (hence, the immortal 1961 Republican jingle: "You'll be safe in the park / every night after dark / with Lefkowitz, Fino and Gilhooley"). Only massive disaffection with New York's rising crime rate and its burgeoning municipal scandals had enabled Lindsay, running on a "fusion" ticket, to win a narrow victory in 1965.

By one measure, he was a fish out of water as a mayor; he had no feel for the grievances and frustrations of the white working class, the cops, the firefighters, the sanitation workers, the lower-middle-class homeowners of Brooklyn and Queens. His stiff-necked posturing had helped trigger a crippling bus and subway strike in the first minutes of his administration, while his love of the cultural splendor and bright lights of Manhattan did not endear him to the residents of Fresh Pond Road and Bay Ridge.

By another measure, he was by mid-1968 the nationally recognized champion of urban America. Along with Robert Kennedy, Lindsay was one of the only white politicians who could reach the ghetto, who could convincingly argue that he meant not just to hear their grievances, but to act on them. On the night Martin Luther King was killed, while Kennedy was quoting Aeschylus to the blacks of Indianapolis, Lindsay was walking the streets of Harlem and Bedford-Stuyvesant, and he was there again the next night and the night after; and while dozens of cities burned, New York was not one of them.

There was also a tensile toughness about Lindsay. Just as Nixon admired the way Ted Agnew had called out the National Guard, and called out the Negro leaders of Baltimore, Nixon liked the way Lindsay had said no to the powerful municipal unions of New York, the way he'd pushed back against the sanitation workers earlier in the year, getting in Governor Rockefeller's face, demanding the Guard be called out to clear the streets of garbage. There was a touch of Calvin Coolidge in that move, Coolidge who, as governor of Massachusetts in 1920, had crushed a police strike, declaring, "There is no right to strike against the public safety anytime, anyplace." (Come to think of it, that's how Coolidge wound up on the ticket with Warren Harding in 1920.)

It was no easy task to persuade the power brokers he met with that night to accept the idea. The liberal Republicans loved it, of course: Percy, Hatfield, Scranton. And the House Republicans had already signaled their overwhelming backing of Lindsay. One of his law partners, Len Garment, raised a Constitutional problem; since both Nixon and Lindsay were legal residents of New York, the Republican electors from New York would not be permitted to vote for both men in the unlikely event that the Nixon–Lindsay ticket carried New York. (That problem was easily solved when

Nixon changed his voter registration back to California.) As for the conservatives who'd stood with him against the Reagan challenge—Strom Thurmond, John Tower, Barry Goldwater—it was Robert Kennedy who turned out to be Nixon's ace in the hole.

"Look," he said to the group after the venting had settled down. "I happen to think it's a fifty-fifty shot that Bobby's the nominee, and a near certainty that he'll be on the ticket. You think he'll decline on principle? For God's sake, he did everything he could four years ago to be Johnson's running mate, and you all know how much he despises Lyndon. So what does that mean?" he asked rhetorically. "First: the places where Lindsay might hurt us most—Florida, Texas, Tennessee, the Carolinas—are exactly the places where white voters will flee from Bobby like the plague. In fact," he chuckled, "I'm sure that the President and Governor Connally will go all out in Texas to help make sure a ticket with Bobby on it will crash and burn. The Deep South? Forget it, that's Wallace country. Worst case, Lindsay means Wallace takes South Carolina. But second"—he held up two fingers—"if Lindsay can help us keep the black margins down in Detroit, Philly, Cleveland, Newark, even Chicago, and he's as gangbusters in the suburbs as I think he'll be, he adds up to a plus with a hundred electoral votes. Maybe he can force the Democrats to spend some time and money in New York—wouldn't that be a hell of a bonus?"

"Have you considered the risk of a floor fight?" Barry Goldwater asked. "You're talking about a guy who's totally against the war, totally for civil rights, wants to spend billions of dollars—"

"Look," Nixon said sharply. "Did the liberals keep Johnson off the ticket in '60 once Kennedy picked him? Besides, I happen to know something about the Vice Presidency. I can promise you—John may think he's going to be the champion of the cities; he even sent Teddy White to me with a note explaining how if I picked him he'd feel free to speak out on any issue he wanted. Well, if John Lindsay thinks he can use the Vice President's office to attack his President, he's going to have to take public transportation to do it. I need him to win, not to govern. I owe you one promise: not to die in office.

"Also," he added, "just imagine the grief this is going to cost the *New York Times*."

They grumbled, they protested, but in the end, they gave their grudging consent. "My 'Bobby' insurance," he called it. What he didn't share with the power brokers was a growing feeling that Bobby's presence on the ticket would provide him with another source of significant support—from the man now living at the same house he planned to occupy in January.

"MY GOD, *it's a war zone!*"

It wasn't *one* delegate, or alternate, or reporter, or TV technician who said it; it was just about everyone—campaign staffer, TV producer, curious passerby—who had the chance to check out Chicago's International Amphitheater in the weeks leading up to the Democratic National Convention. The thirty-four-year-old, 255,000-square-foot structure on Halsted and 43rd Street, right next to the Union Stock Yards, had hosted everything from cattle auctions to the Ringling Brothers Circus to Elvis (he first wore his gold-lamé suit here) to the Beatles to four earlier national nominating conventions. It was here, at the fractious Pier Six brawl that was the '52 Republican convention, where Senator Everett Dirksen, battling on behalf of the conservative hero Robert Taft, pointed his finger at New York Governor Tom Dewey, champion of the Eisenhower liberals, and thundered, "We followed you before and you took us down the road to defeat!" Never, however, had convention participants seen a venue like this one. The arena was surrounded by a seven-foot-high chain-link fence, and, inside, a catwalk ninety-five feet above the Convention floor had been built to accommodate police with walkie-talkies and rifles to patrol the proceedings. Across the city, 7,500 armed soldiers had been mobilized to join nearly 12,000 cops and the 300-man Cook County riot squad; the mayor of one of America's great metropolitan cities was taking seriously the threat of a confrontation that would throw a huge shadow over whoever emerged as the Democratic nominee.

The convention wasn't even *supposed* to be in Chicago in the first place. The Republicans had chosen Miami Beach for their '68 gathering, and there was a lot of sentiment for putting the Democratic convention in the same city. That sentiment was particularly strong among the TV networks— ABC, CBS, and NBC—who would each save a few million dollars in production expenses if they could wire one hall instead of moving the miles of cables, the $40 million worth of equipment, the hundreds of workers 1,379 miles—half a continent—away. But then, in early 1967 Mayor Daley had chatted up President Johnson at a White House meeting, explaining that Democrats had done badly in the midterm elections because the faithful had stayed home, explaining what a powerful encouragement it would be to the party if the convention were to be held in Chicago, where President Johnson would be guaranteed a rapturous reception when he came to be renominated. Little more than a year later, the whole idea of a Chicago convention had turned into a logistical and political nightmare. The telephone workers were on strike, so the candidates and the press would be without most of their communication tools; the taxicab drivers were on strike, so the whole transportation network of Chicago would slow to a crawl. The restaurants and nightclubs in Chicago were six miles from the convention site; without cabs, the free-spending pols and their financial benefactors would be far less likely to enrich the city's economy.

Those problems, though, were dwarfed by the threats of disruptions that no convention of either party had ever faced. Months earlier, with President Johnson certain to be the party's 1968 nominee, protesters of all persuasions were planning huge demonstrations during the convention, including the promise (or threat) to march on the convention site itself. On March 23, the National Mobilization Committee to End the War had met outside Chicago to coordinate the protests; more than a hundred groups, left and right—more precisely, left and far left—had attended. At the same time, the Youth International Party—the "Yippies"—proclaimed that they would bring 100,000 followers to Chicago. Their front men, Abbie Hoffman and Jerry Rubin, were Marxists who owed more to Groucho and Harpo than to Karl. They threatened, among other things, to taint the city's water supply with LSD, turning millions of people and a few thousand convention delegates into hallucinating freaks, and to set thousands of nubile young women to baring their bodies, the better to lure delegates into compromising positions. Among those who took these threats seriously was Mayor Daley, who dispatched whole platoons of cops to patrol the city's reservoirs. But it was Daley himself who acted as a magnet for demonstrators. When Chicago exploded after King's death, and he ordered his police to "shoot to kill" arsonists and "shoot to maim" looters, it was a red flag not just to the folks who preferred to march under a red flag, but to more mainstream activists as well. (Daley himself—with his jowls, his scowl, his clumsy mauling of the English language—was a walking cartoon of Thuggish Authority.)

So it was understandable that anyone looking at the logistical and political terrain of Chicago in the weeks before the convention would see not just a war zone, but the likely possibility of something like a war breaking out in the streets of the second biggest city in America. Indeed, had Steve Smith not slammed Sirhan Sirhan to the floor of the kitchen at the Ambassador Hotel back in June, had Democrats prepared to convene with the certainty of a Hubert Humphrey nomination, that possibility would have become a near certainty.

But now Robert Kennedy was very much alive, very much a candidate.

And Mayor Richard Daley was *backing* Kennedy; Daley was throwing all of his considerable weight behind a candidate who was *against* the war, who was promising to *end* the war, who was pounding away at conditions in the ghetto, who was taking on the leaders of his own party. This held no weight with the radicals at the Mobilization; to them, Kennedy was another agent of the corporate state, another coat-and-tie liberal working for the system. ("The worst thing to happen to the movement in years," radical lawyer William Kunstler told an interviewer, "was that Sirhan missed. If he'd been luckier, we would have been spared one more false prophet standing between America and a revolution.") But for the foot soldiers who had left their studies behind to campaign for Eugene McCarthy in New Hampshire and Wisconsin, for the veterans of the sit-ins, teach-ins, marches on Washington, voter registration campaigns in the South, petition drives for anti-war candidates, Mayor Daley had suddenly become, if not a hero, then an ally. The idea of disrupting a city whose leader was on their side seemed . . . *ludicrous,* a point that prominent youth organizers like Sam Brown had begun to press almost from the day Daley had stood in downtown Chicago with Bobby.

"If you want to help end the war," Brown and several dozen anti-war figures declared in a joint statement, "if you want to help turn America around, organize your neighbors, your town, your city; let the Democratic Party hear from the grass roots."

By the weekend before the convention began, fewer than 3,000 protesters had come to Chicago. The small number, in turn, had given Robert Kennedy's campaign the ammunition with which to persuade a very reluctant Mayor Daley to ease the draconian edicts he had imposed earlier. It had taken days of increasingly urgent conversations between Steve Smith and Daley's lieutenants, followed by a face-to-face conversation between the Mayor and Robert Kennedy, with Bobby urging Daley to think about how much better Chicago would look to the nation if it did not resemble a police state, and repeating to Daley much the same points he had made to the Ohio delegates back in May: *I'm a Democrat, I believe in the organization, I have no intention of damaging what you've built here.* (Later—much later—these reassurances would come back to cause Kennedy no end of grief.) Reluctantly, Daley agreed to grant the Mobilization a permit to rally in downtown Grant Park, agreed to scale back police presence in and around the convention site, even agreed to take down the seven-foot-high chain-link fence. There was a clear message these decisions were designed to convey to the country: *Do not identify the Democrats as the party of disruption and chaos.*

That was a message every Democrat could embrace—except, as it happened, the most powerful Democrat of all, who was about to disrupt the convention to its core.

THE THOUGHT HAD OBSESSED him for weeks: *Maybe it wasn't too late, after all. Maybe there was a way back, a way to reclaim the prize he had so publicly, shockingly abandoned four months ago.* Now, on this Sunday in late August, Lyndon Johnson was hours away from launching the most audacious gamble of his life, one that would take him ten thousand miles in forty-eight hours and end, he hoped, with his renomination for President of the United States.

He'd told everyone he was done with politics, that he'd stepped aside to devote his last months in office to ending the war in Vietnam. And it was true enough . . . for a while. But the more he watched Hubert Humphrey and Bobby Kennedy fight for the nomination, the more frustrated he became, the more he felt that in the deepest part of him there was a missing piece to this story, and that the missing piece was . . . him.

The very possibility of Robert Kennedy winning the nomination was loathsome. It wasn't just that he and Bobby had despised each other almost at first sight. It was that Kennedy's nomination would mean that the Democratic Party, the party he'd given his life to for thirty years, had repudiated all he had worked for, denounced the war, disdained the Great Society he had promised and done so much to make real. It was Bobby who would be hailed as a savior by the Negroes whose emancipation he, Lyndon Johnson, had made possible. It was Bobby's picture that would hang in the homes of the poor, the poor who owed their health care, their *food,* to his beneficence. It would also be a personal affront—for God's sakes, the whole *reason* for a convention set so late in August was so he could accept renomination on his birthday. So for Bobby to stand there in Chicago, cheered by thousands, while he, the President, was effectively banished from the hall? No, that was not going to happen if he had anything to say about it.

Yet the more Johnson watched Hubert Humphrey, the more convinced he was that Hubert just wasn't up to it. All through the summer, he'd been venting his dissatisfaction to anyone who'd listen.

"He cries too much," he'd told a visiting journalist. "That's it—he just cries too much." To his close aide Marvin Watson, he put it more bluntly. "Hubert squats when he pees."

He'd grabbed Agriculture Secretary Orville Freeman, a close Humphrey ally and fellow Minnesotan, to vent: *He's all over the place, he talks too much, doesn't he know that Connally and the other Southern governors are just about to throw Hubert over the side if he breaks with them on the credentials and rules fights? Doesn't he understand that he can't play footsie with Bobby on a Vietnam peace plank in the platform? I've told him a hundred times, the Communists will only come to the table if they're convinced America will stand tall!* It was the same argument he'd made to Hubert right to his face at a recent Cabinet meeting, reaming him out right in front of Rusk and Clifford and the others.

But there was one thing he *hadn't* said to Hubert.

A few hours from now, on this Sunday evening, he'd be on Air Force One, flying all night to Kiev in the Ukraine, the breadbasket of the Soviet Union. On Monday morning, he would be sitting down with Soviet Premier Kosygin for a follow-up to their summit meeting the year before in

Glassboro, New Jersey. For weeks, a small group of diplomats from the two nations had been shaping a far-reaching agreement that covered some real steps toward disarmament, and strict controls over the spread of nuclear weapons. On Monday evening, he would stand with Kosygin and Soviet Communist Party chief Brezhnev to announce the breakthrough . . . then board Air Force One for an all-night flight to Chicago, where he would take the podium to receive the cheers of his party, and a "Happy Birthday" salute as well. Mayor Daley might have thrown in his lot with Bobby, but Johnson was firmly in control of the convention. He had personally picked the chairman of every key committee—rules, credentials, platform—and the executive director of the convention, John Criswell, had been reporting back to him on a regular basis using the code name "Bert." Marvin Watson, now Postmaster General, who had served as the White House aide stoking the President's most paranoid fantasies about his enemies, headed a cadre that had been in Chicago for days, quietly encouraging Johnson's old allies to keep the President in mind as a possible candidate for a draft.

The President's surprise appearance would freeze all of the convention's business: the credentials fights, the rules fights, the dispute over the platform. He, the President, the leader of his party, would be standing before them, delivering tangible, undeniable evidence that firmness in the face of aggression was in fact the surest, no, the *only* way to ensure peace. And who knew what the convention dynamic might lead to? These gatherings had a life of their own. As a young congressman in 1944, he'd seen the Democrats force even as powerful a figure as President Franklin Roosevelt to dump his Vice President in favor of the more acceptable Harry Truman. In '52, he'd watched the Republican convention in the firm grip of conservative backers of Senator Robert Taft forced by a wave of public opinion to nominate the more moderate Dwight Eisenhower. If these delegates—or more accurately, the men who *controlled* those delegates—thought Bobby too hotheaded, too threatening, and thought Hubert too weak, too soft to beat Richard Nixon, well, maybe they'd turn to the one who'd actually *led* America for almost five years, who'd *delivered* for the very folks Bobby and Hubert were always yelling about.

And it wasn't just his summit-to-Chicago masterstroke he was counting on to put him within reach of renomination. No, he'd had a very productive conversation with J. Edgar Hoover a few days ago, and Edgar was preparing to put some fascinating material into the hands of columnist Drew Pearson, the same columnist who had exposed Bobby's wiretapping of Martin Luther King back in May. When the delegates and power brokers at the convention opened their morning papers on Wednesday—the day the convention was scheduled to pick its nominee—they'd find undeniable accounts about Bobby's efforts as Attorney General to cover up brother Jack's behavior with women, including Ellie Rometsch, a suspected East German spy, and Judith Exner, mistress of Sam Giancana, one of Chicago's most prominent gangsters. That story would share space with accounts of the President's summit triumph, and his surprise convention appearance, but this was one time when Johnson didn't mind giving Bobby Kennedy a ton of publicity. Bobby would be choking on his breakfast while the delegates were recalling Johnson's convention speech the night before: a classic Democratic speech, one that McPherson and Califano had been working on for weeks, extolling the Five Enduring Rights: health care, education, a good job, security, and justice, and pledging "that so long as I have breath in my body, I shall use it to encourage my country in its journey toward a freer, braver, more responsible and united America."

On this Sunday afternoon, Assistant Secretary of State William Bundy was preparing to send a secret diplomatic note to all the allies around the world, informing them of the surprise summit. Press Secretary George Christian was minutes away from summoning the White House pool to Andrews Air Force Base, for an unannounced trip to an undisclosed location. The President was on the phone to Marvin Watson, obsessively reviewing every detail of his convention arrival: how to make sure the sergeants-at-arms would pen Bobby's New York and California delegations back in the far reaches of the amphitheater when the President arrived to speak, when to let Mayor Daley know he would be expected to meet the President's helicopter at Meigs Field for the short drive to the amphitheater. Yes, Daley was backing Bobby, but the Mayor was a respecter of tradition and office; there was no way Daley would disrespect the President of the United States, and when he walked onstage with the President, wouldn't that throw the fear of God into the Kennedy campaign.

And then Soviet Ambassador Dobrynin called, asking for an urgent meeting. He told the President that the Soviet Union had received a request from Prague, asking for "fraternal assistance against forces of aggression"—Kremlin-speak for a full-fledged invasion of Czechoslovakia. Hundreds of tanks, and two hundred thousand soldiers from the Soviet Union and the Eastern bloc, were pouring across the Czech borders, shooting a dozen young protesters in Wenceslas Square, placing Prime Minister Dubček under house arrest.

How in God's name is this possible? Johnson thundered at National Security Advisor Walt Rostow, who stammered that no one could know for sure, that it was more than likely that the Soviet military had put the screws to Kosygin, maybe with Brezhnev's support; they'd likely argued that Prague's rapid drift away from Moscow, the promise of free speech and a multi-party election posed an intolerable threat to the Soviet Union's dominance over its Eastern European interests.

Well, there was no way Lyndon Johnson was going to any summit with Kosygin and Brezhnev while Czech blood was running in the streets of Prague, no way he was going to have any landmark peace agreement with Moscow to celebrate in front of thousands of Democrats at the convention. Maybe he could still go anyway, to mark his sixtieth birthday, perhaps spawn enough goodwill and fond memories of past triumphs to spark a genuine draft. He'd sleep on that, but one thing was clear: those stories about the Kennedy brothers and the women would have to be held for now. Without the cover of a summit and an arms deal, his appearance in Chicago just before Drew Pearson published those stories would be too much of a coincidence for anyone to accept. Maybe those stories would have to wait for the fall. If Bobby lost in Chicago, they wouldn't be needed. If he became the nominee . . . well, there *were* worse things than the thought of Richard Nixon as President—and the thought of President Bobby Kennedy was definitely one of them.

FOR ALL THE MILLIONS of dollars spent, the tens of thousands of miles traveled, the countless man-hours spent on the phone, in rented cars, in hotel rooms and union halls and coffee shops, for all the appeals to patriotism, justice, the national interest, and self-interest, it was an unplanned encounter, an accident of fate, that determined the Democratic Party's Presidential nominee.

It was Monday, August 26, the opening day of the Democratic National Convention. In downtown Chicago, a constant swarm of delegates, alternatives, favor seekers, trinket sellers, and the merely curious had turned the intersection of Michigan and Balboa Avenues into an impassible mass of humanity. The Conrad Hilton Hotel, where Humphrey's inner circle was bivouacked, and the Blackstone Hotel, where Robert Kennedy's forces gathered, faced each other across Balboa Avenue as if they were the fortresses of warring tribes. The Humphrey campaign was in feverish negotiations with its Southern supporters and with party leaders in the East and Midwest, trying to strike a balance that would satisfy both sides on the hot-button questions of seating virtually all-white delegations from the South, and on preserving the unit rule. Kennedy's inner circle was looking for pressure points to push the big pro-Humphrey states like New Jersey and Pennsylvania to their side on the same fights; they'd paid for prominent Negro leaders to come to Chicago for face-to-face confrontations. ("You vote with Eastland and Lester Maddox," a thirty-year-old Philadelphia activist named Wilson Goode yelled at Mayor Tate, "and you won't see one damn brother at the polls in November!")

Eugene McCarthy had come to Chicago as well, arriving with poet Robert Lowell, *Life* magazine essayist Shana Alexander, and a quartet of European journalists. He paused on his way to his suite in the Hilton to answer a reporter's question about the invasion of Czechoslovakia—"I hardly consider it a major world crisis"—and to speculate on a possible Humphrey–Kennedy ticket:

"If Hubert wants to be Jack, he'll need a Bobby to do with Bobby what Bobby did to Lyndon." The European journalists spent several minutes trying to translate and comprehend the comment.

Robert Kennedy was in the living room of his suite on the fourth floor of the Blackstone, a fifty-eight-year-old Beaux Arts building with roots deeply embedded in Chicago's political history. It was here in 1920 that Republican leaders had gathered in the notorious "smoke-filled room" to nominate Warren Harding as President. (Kennedy's campaign had respectfully declined the hotel's offer to put the Senator in that very suite.) It was here in '44 where Harry Truman learned he'd been picked as FDR's Vice President, and where in '52 Eisenhower learned he'd been nominated for President.

What would make the Blackstone Hotel so significant a player in the politics of 1968 was that the Kennedy suite had a picture-perfect view across Michigan Avenue to Lake Shore Drive, Lake Michigan, and Grant Park, where several hundred protesters were camped out. He was enjoying a rare few minutes of ease, lunching on a cheeseburger and a Heineken, when Frank Mankiewicz called up from the lobby to pass along a wild rumor that Lyndon Johnson might be coming to the convention.

"Well, it came from Jimmy Breslin, so I'm giving it zero credibility," Mankiewicz cracked, looking over at the *New York Daily News* columnist, whom he'd run into by chance.

"Is he with you?" Kennedy asked.

"Yeah, Hamill and Newfield as well."

"Bring 'em up," Kennedy said. "I could use a laugh or two." He enjoyed the byplay with the famously irreverent Breslin. After hearing Kennedy's impassioned talk about suicide among young Indians, Breslin had said, "I guess the only reason Jim Thorpe won the Olympics was because the rope broke." For his part, Kennedy once said, "I always thought growing up poor gave you character, Jimmy—then I met you, and now I'm beginning to wonder."

When the three writers entered the suite, they found Kennedy at the window of the living room, staring out at Grant Park. They could hear faint strains of the music playing over the loudspeakers from the stage that had been set up at the park's Buckingham Fountain: Country Joe and the Fish's "I Feel Like I'm Fixin' to Die Rag."

"We just came from the park," they told him.

"Who's over there?" he asked.

"A real mix," Hamill said. "Some hard-core types—Mao jackets, Vietcong flags. Some of them are looking for another summer of love. There was a dustup over the Czech invasion; Bill Kuntsler was arguing that no one should criticize a 'socialist' country, but there were a few signs that said 'the pig is the same all over the world.' Jerry Rubin's telling them to kill their parents. Abbie's threatening to send 'an army of studs' to the convention to seduce the wives of the delegates."

"They don't seem to be big fans of yours," Breslin said, goading him. "A couple of them said if I ran into you, make sure I ask you why you're afraid to come out and meet them face-to-face."

Kennedy nodded; then, as he so often did, said nothing, just kept looking out over Michigan Avenue to Grant Park. Dave Hackett, his oldest friend and chief delegate hunter, looked up from the desk he was working at over on the far side of the living room. There was a distinct edge in his voice.

"Senator," Hackett said, "I hope you're not thinking what I think you're thinking . . ."

What happened next might have seemed inexplicable behavior by a serious candidate for President; it was, however, consistent with one of the most powerful strains in Robert Kennedy's character: He loved risk, embraced it, sought it all his life, and especially after the death of his brother.

Maybe it was because he was the runt of the litter, a five-foot nine-inch scrawny kid in a family of three six-foot-plus brothers, a boy closer to his mother than to his bluff, take-no-prisoners father. He'd gone out for the football team at school, felt bitter disappointment that he had been too young for combat in World War II. He dove into freezing waters of Cape Cod, into dangerous white-water rapids in Colorado, into piranha-infested waters on a trip to Latin America. He admired physical courage and daring. It was why he was drawn to astronaut John Glenn, bullfighter El Cordobes, boxer Jose Torres; why he once had such enthusiasm for counter-insurgency in Vietnam and guerrilla tactics aimed at deposing Fidel Castro. And central to his embrace of risk was his willingness, eagerness, to face his critics, even his fiercest opponents, face-to-face. He and Teamster Union boss Jimmy Hoffa had exchanged angry words and poisonous glances across a Senate committee hearing room in the 1950s. He'd stood in packed halls and argued with student radicals at Waseda University in Japan in 1962, and in 1965, at Chile's Concepción University, he'd waded into a mob of Communist students, one of whom had spat in his face. All through this primary campaign, he'd gone right for the provocative encounters. He'd spent a long night in a coffee shop in Indiana with young supporters of Gene McCarthy, praising them for their involvement, regretting that his late entry into the race had lost him their backing. He told college students in every primary state that he opposed student draft deferments ("What about a boy who just wants to open a filling station after high school; why should he have to give up his plans and go off?"). When well-heeled medical students at Indiana University asked who would pay for his health-care plans, he answered: "You will!—You!—You!"

So it was hardly out of character when Kennedy motioned to the writers and said, *Come on, I'd like you to introduce me to your fine, patriotic friends. Dave, don't worry. Between the Secret Service and these three brave men, I'm sure everything will be fine. Besides, if I know Daley, about half of the people in that park are undercover Chicago cops.*

It took less than ten minutes for Kennedy, the three writers, and three extremely agitated Secret Service agents to leave the Blackstone through the parking garage, hop into a van, and wend their way up Michigan Avenue, across Congress Parkway, and over to the Buckingham Fountain at Grant Park. It took two minutes before Kennedy and his party found themselves surrounded by a dozen, then several dozen, then a few hundred of the crowd of protesters . . . and just about that long for the gathering to turn confrontational.

"Why did you work for Joe McCarthy?" "Why did you and your brother get us into Vietnam?" "You're in bed with Daley, whose pigs beat us up two months ago!" "Why won't you stand with the Black Panthers who want justice for their brothers and sisters!"

For a few moments, Kennedy tried to answer the questions. Then he held up his hands.

Well, you tell me something now, he said. *How many of you have spent one minute this summer working in a black ghetto, or in Eastern Kentucky, or on an Indian reservation? Just a ten-minute ride from here,* he said, pointing south, *there are thousands, maybe tens of thousands of children who go to crumbling schools, whose homes are overrun with rats. How many of you have spent* five minutes *doing something to make their lives better?*

They were shouting at him now, some of them, but he spoke over them.

You call police "pigs." Why can't you see that they put their lives on the line every day, in neighborhoods where they're seen as occupiers. We need more black men, men from the neighborhoods in our police forces and we can't accept police brutality, but who do you think crime hurts the most? You think there's something "heroic" about a gang that hits an eighty-year-old Negro woman and steals her rent money? He called them out on the Vietcong flags they were carrying, asking if they could name a Communist country where their counterparts would be permitted to march in protests in the streets of those cities, asking if they'd bothered to see the news from Prague. He talked about a young man named John Lewis, a man who almost died during a Freedom Ride, who had put his life on the line to change the country because he wanted to love it, not hate it. *And we are not far from the time when a man like John Lewis will sit in the Congress of the United States, and in your lifetime, if not mine, in the Oval Office as well.* (They howled with derision at that one.)

A few minutes later, when an orange went whizzing by Kennedy's head, one of the Secret Service detail took him by the shoulders, turned him around, and said, "Senator, it's time to leave *now.*"

Under other circumstances, it was a clash that would have stirred some conversation a day later when the New York writers devoted their newspaper columns to it. Conventions, however, were not ordinary events. For the television networks in 1968, they were the most crucial of all news events, a World Series, heavyweight championship match and royal coronation, where success or failure pretty much determined which network would claim news supremacy for the next four years. (Twelve years earlier, NBC had paired a stolid, no-frills anchor named Chet Huntley with a young, witty thirty-six-year-old David Brinkley, and their convention coverage had made NBC the dominant news network for a decade.) The networks each spent millions of dollars, dispatched whole brigades of correspondents, reporters, producers, and camera crews to record every event (NBC and CBS each booked 750 rooms in Chicago hotels for their armies). Conventions were covered gavel to gavel and beyond; a news conference, a rally, a rules committee dispute, was more than likely to interrupt daytime programming. With demonstrations promising to provide drama and conflict, if not actual bloodshed, it was no surprise that NBC and CBS had posted camera crews at Grant Park. Both networks captured the confrontation between Kennedy and the protesters.

Under other circumstances, the networks might well have cut live to the event, with the tape played back directly from the scene with Ampex Quadruplex machines, then microwaved back to the control room at the amphitheater. Chicago, however, was in the middle of a series of strikes by telephone and electrical workers. Only a fervent mix of pleas and threats by Mayor Daley had persuaded the strikers to let the networks set up any equipment at all so that the convention could be televised. There was, however, no give when it came to remote locations. If the networks wanted to show any event that took place beyond the convention site, they would have to wait for the tape to be driven to the amphitheater. Between the massive gridlock that gripped downtown Chicago, the snarled roads and highways that the bus and taxi strike had produced, and the endless lines of press people waiting to get their credentials checked, by the time the CBS and NBC crews got their tapes in the hands of the control room, it was almost time for the network evening newscasts to air.

"Good evening," Walter Cronkite intoned at 6:00 p.m. central daylight time, "an extraordinary confrontation between Presidential candidate Robert Kennedy and a mob of radical protesters took place today on the very day that the Democratic National Convention was about to begin. CBS's John Laurence was there." The twenty-seven-year-old Laurence, brought back from Vietnam for the convention, described the clash as "one of the most unguarded moments a major political figure is ever likely to have."

The piece ran for almost six minutes; an eternity by the standards of thirty-minute network news broadcasts. It was Cronkite himself who insisted on the length. Beneath the surface image of solid "Uncle Walter" objectivity, Cronkite was an ardent liberal. He had turned hard against the Vietnam War—his lengthy broadcast earlier in the year calling the war a stalemate was hugely influential. When he saw it, President Johnson supposedly said, "If I've lost Cronkite, I've lost middle America." He was also a personal friend of Robert Kennedy. Most important, he knew dynamite footage when he saw it. So, for that matter, did the top producers at NBC News, who also featured the footage as the lead of their newscasts. When Shad Northshield, the famously profane head of NBC's Nightly News, saw the tape, he yelled: "It's a goddamn *fuck-in!*"

In 1968, the network evening newscasts were something of a national ritual. With cable television little more than a string of community antennas in rural America, with all-news radio in its birth pangs and with computers the province of a few giant corporations and the military, the evening news was the only source of information available between the afternoon papers and the morning papers that hit America's doorsteps the next day. More than nine out of ten TV homes watched one of the evening newscasts; and more than sixteen million homes kept their televisions on to watch the conventions—gatherings which in those times actually *decided* who the nominees would be. And that night, as the convention began with a mind-numbing series of welcoming speeches, the networks repeatedly cut away for the far more riveting footage of Robert Kennedy confronting the radicals, running the tape three, four, five times during Monday's coverage. In an effort at balance, the networks also showed Hubert Humphrey—welcoming into his suite at the Conrad Hilton a stream of middle-aged and older overweight men in suits.

It was, then, a mass audience that saw Kennedy, shirtsleeves rolled up, tie loosened, sporting the shorter haircut demanded by his advisors, defending the virtues of his country in front of a long-haired, tie-dyed, bearded cluster carrying the flag of the enemy, wearing the American flag on the seat of their jeans. They saw him defending the police, insisting that criminal behavior and violence were intolerable. To the reporters who had followed Kennedy on the campaign, it was very familiar stuff; but to the millions watching at home, including countless voters who had thought of Robert Kennedy as the champion of militant Negroes and long-haired white radicals, it was a startling sight.

And they responded.

Telegrams of support began arriving by the thousands, addressed to the convention, to the Democratic National Committee, to politicians in residence; the volume grew so high, the addresses so vague, that a local Western Union executive had to track down a master list of convention-goers from a harried clerk in the bowels of the amphitheater. Telephone calls overwhelmed the switchboards at the Hilton, the Blackstone, the Ambassador, and dozens of other hotels. It is impossible to know whether these messages reflected the will of rank-and-file Democrats. A Harris poll published the Monday of the convention showed Robert Kennedy leading Hubert Humphrey by a narrow 41–38 margin, with the rest either undecided or favoring someone else. A Gallup poll showed a dead heat. Both polls showed Robert Kennedy running slightly better against Nixon than Humphrey did. What was clearly true was that the flood of messages had a powerful impact among the Democrats gathered in Chicago. Poll numbers are, by definition evanescent. *These* were yellow rectangles of paper, stacks of pink message slips. *Real people, lots of them,* had taken the trouble to pay for a telegram or a long-distance phone call. And overwhelmingly, they were lining up behind Robert Kennedy.

Sixteen years earlier, two outbursts of public reaction had shaped the politics of 1952. Viewers at home, watching the Republican National Convention on TV for the first time, deluged the convention with calls and telegrams protesting the machinations of convention insiders, demanding "fair play" for the Eisenhower forces; his delegates were seated, and Ike won the nomination. Two months later, Richard Nixon saved his place on the ticket—and his career—with his "Checkers" speech, when literally millions of letters, telegrams, and phone calls overwhelmed the Republican National Committee and the Eisenhower campaign.

Now, in 1968, on this Monday night in late August, something that looked very much like a grass-roots explosion was pounding the Democratic Convention, something that delegates, party leaders, and the campaigns were struggling to understand. Because of the telephone strike, communication between the campaign staffs and their lieutenants inside the hall were chaotic at best. In fact, the delegates and state party chairs inside the hall were themselves operating in a fog of confusion. All through the amphitheater, clusters of delegates grouped around small black-and-white portable TV sets, watching the tape of Robert Kennedy's confrontation in the park replayed over and over. Others raced for the pay telephones scattered throughout the building, calling home to ask if their families or business partners had any clue about what was happening. Loyal subordinates of top Humphrey backers left those phone calls to report glum news to their bosses back on the floor: *My guy says Bobby really put it to those punks!* In suite 2525A of the Conrad Hilton Hotel, Vice President Humphrey and his campaign team watched the TVs with growing fury.

"I hope those folks at the networks realize I'll be appointing the FCC Chairman when I'm President," Humphrey snapped. "We're going to investigate all this next year."

Within a few hours, Humphrey's campaign was facing the distinct prospect of a political meltdown. The mayor, governors, senators, congressmen, state chairs, indeed, every good politician had a powerful, primal ability to sense a threat to his survival. These telegrams, these telephone calls, had aroused their deepest fears. And they voted those fears. By the time the convention's Monday session adjourned, it was 1:15 on Tuesday morning. The Mississippi and Alabama delegations had been unseated, replaced by "loyalist" slates of roughly equal black and white members. Georgia's delegation had been cleaved in half, with a "regular" and "loyalist" slate dividing the forty-two votes equally. And when the "unit rule" came up for debate, it was Senator Walter Mondale of Minnesota, the co-chair of the Humphrey campaign, going to the rostrum to denounce the rule as "an anachronism, a relic whose time has passed." The signal from the Vice President's camp could not have been clearer: They had neither the inclination nor the power to prod their big-state liberal backers to stand with the most conservative forces in the party. The unit rule was abolished by a 3-to-1 margin. In itself, these decisions were a powerful tonic to Robert Kennedy's campaign. More significant was what these votes reflected and fueled: Hubert Humphrey's patience with Lyndon Johnson had reached the breaking point.

FOR MORE THAN a decade, they had been mentor and student. When Humphrey, the firebrand liberal, had come to the Senate in 1949, he had become a pariah by frontally challenging the powerful old lions who ran the place. Johnson, a fellow freshman but with years of experience in Washington, became a counselor to Humphrey, later assigning him legislative tasks. Humphrey in turn came to respect Johnson's skills, and had warded off a liberal challenge to Johnson's Vice Presidential nomination in 1960.

That dynamic abruptly shifted to something more like master and servant when President Johnson came to picking his running mate in 1964. He'd demanded a pledge of absolute loyalty, in keeping with his pronouncement that when he chose a running mate, he wanted "his pecker in my pocket." He'd put Humphrey through an agonizing, humiliating waiting game before announcing that he was in fact, the choice. When Humphrey raised doubts about the escalation in Vietnam in 1965, Johnson had cut him out of all deliberations in Vietnam for more than a year. And after the President had renounced another term, he began to openly scorn Humphrey's capacity for the job, as well as his manhood. There was no way all those disparaging remarks weren't going to get back to Hubert, and there was nothing Humphrey could do about them. His Presidential fortunes were tied to Johnson, who controlled the apparatus of the Democratic Party and the convention. Those 600 votes in the South and Southwest, he knew, were prepared to vote for Hubert in large measure because he was the only thing standing between Bobby Kennedy and the nomination.

Except . . . there were all these hints that Johnson might not really have left the field, that a part of the President's mind was fixated on the possibility that he might find redemption in Chicago. Humphrey had even called campaign chronicler Teddy White, to ask him if Johnson might try for the nomination—stark testimony to Humphrey's exclusion from any inner circle of information. He'd only been told of Johnson's intended flash summit meeting just before its intended announcement, before the Soviet invasion of Czechoslovakia had blown that idea up on the launching pad. Even now, after the convention opened, there was talk of a surprise Presidential appearance sometime in the next twenty-hour hours. And on this Tuesday morning, Johnson's people, who controlled every element of the convention machinery, were expressing their boss's cold fury at what had happened the night before at the convention.

"The President's not very happy about this," Marvin Watson said to Humphrey in the living room of his suite on the Conrad Hilton's twenty-fifth floor. "Connally told him you'd promised to be with his people on the unit rule." Watson was Postmaster General now, but for the last three years, he'd been Johnson's closest White House aide, the one who eagerly fed him the latest information and innuendo about the myriad alleged Bobby Kennedy conspiracies.

"Well," said Humphrey, as he nibbled on a slice of cheddar. "You tell the President that if I'd stayed with the unit rule, I'd have lost four hundred delegates. Does he understand that *I'm* the candidate? Or am I misunderstanding something."

Watson ignored the jab.

"The President wants to know about the Vietnam platform plank," Watson said. "He wants to make sure you understand that any loss of support for our policy is going to be seen in Hanoi as a sign of weakness; he asked me to call your attention to the statement of General Abrams."

In an unprecedented use—or misuse—of the military, Johnson's National Security Advisor Walt Rostow had solicited a statement by the commanding general in Vietnam that any halt in the bombing of the North would jeopardize American forces in the South. That statement had promptly been sent to House Majority Whip Hale Boggs, chair of the convention platform committee, for immediate public distribution.

"I'm aware of the general's statement. I'm also aware that there is significant dissent from that view in the Defense Department. And," Humphrey added, his face flushed with anger, "I'd like the President to understand that we're looking for platform language here that can provide an alternative to the Kennedy plank. We think a *conditional* bombing halt can defeat a call for an *unconditional* one. We think we can paint Bobby into a corner. But if the President thinks this convention is going to simply wrap its arms around what we're doing now, and if he thinks I can beat Richard Nixon without being my own man, then he isn't nearly as shrewd about politics as I think he is . . . assuming of course, he *wants* me to beat Nixon."

"Of course he does," Watson muttered. "But this is about the safety of half a million American boys. So let me say it again: The President believes anything other than support for our policy will be read as a sign of weakness in Hanoi."

When Watson left, Humphrey waved his associates away and sat alone for a long moment. He had sought the Presidency in 1960, and been crushed by the magnetism and the money of John Kennedy. He'd eagerly sought the Vice Presidency four years ago, assuming that Lyndon Johnson would spare him the indignities he himself had endured, from Kennedy, only to discover that Johnson was more than happy to inflict the same indignities on him. He had assumed he and Bobby Kennedy would be fighting for the nomination in 1972; instead, it was happening now. By June, he had become the insider, the candidate of the machinery, closing in on the nomination without winning a single vote. And then Bobby had survived the attempt on his life, and the campaign terrain had shifted out from under him.

Every instinct told him *this* was the time to break free, *this* was the moment for a declaration of independence. No sitting Vice President had won a Presidential election since Martin Van Buren in 1836, and if he were to break that pattern, he would have to stake his own claim on the office, and chart a course away from the disaster that was Vietnam. And every *political* calculation told him that following his instincts would be suicidal. His tormentor was also his most powerful benefactor; no one had to tell him what Lyndon Johnson would do if he saw his war repudiated by his own running mate. If he stayed with the course he knew to be a failure, he had a chance for the nomination, and then he could signal a change of course.

There was, however, one way to redeem himself.

And so he called Robert Kennedy, slipped away from his handlers, and that Tuesday night had a brief, urgent meeting. And they agreed on what each of them would do once the battle was over.

THE NOMINATING SPEECHES began on Wednesday at six p.m., after a two-hour recess that followed the debate on the platform. The Kennedy campaign had trimmed its sails some, offering a plank that called the Vietnam War a "tragedy" rather than a "disaster," praising the courage of the troops, calling for negotiations among "all parties" to achieve "a just peace" and "an independent South Vietnam," offering faint words of praise for President Johnson's decision "to halt the escalation and open the door to negotiations." The more temperate language came after a brief but intense dispute among Robert Kennedy's team, but it proved tactically effective. By a narrow 1370–1180 vote, with 70 abstentions, the plank was adopted, defeating language drafted by the White House that praised the President's "determined efforts to resist Communist aggression in Southeast Asia" and rejecting "dangerous concessions that would expose allied forces to increased danger." What was left unclear was just how many Humphrey supporters backed the softer language, in hopes of giving the Vice President running room should he be the nominee. When the nominations began, no one could say for sure whether Kennedy or Humphrey would prevail, or whether abstentions and favorite sons would push the convention to a second ballot for the first time since 1952.

The nominating speeches were predictable, save for one dramatic moment: Connecticut Senator Abe Ribicoff, seconding Kennedy's nomination, looked straight at the Texas delegation sitting directly in front of him and said, "With Robert Kennedy as President, we wouldn't have to witness flagrantly undemocratic politics at a Democratic convention!" The TV networks cut to a split-screen shot of Chicago Mayor Daley enthusiastically applauding Ribicoff, while Texas Governor John Connally shouted (as he later insisted he said), "You phony!"

Just after nine p.m., a tall blond woman named Dorothy Bush, recording secretary of the Democratic National Committee, stepped to the rostrum as she had done at every convention since 1944 and intoned: A-la-bam-a . . . thirty-two votes!" And as soon as Alabama ("the Yellowhammer state . . . home of the Camellia . . .") cast its votes, the full meaning of what had happened in the eighty-five days since that midnight in a Los Angeles hotel kitchen crystallized.

With the unit rule abolished, and an integrated delegation now seated, 12 of Alabama's 32 votes went to Robert Kennedy—twelve more than chief Kennedy delegate hunter Dave Hackett had estimated back in June on the day Sirhan Sirhan had taken his pistol into that hotel kitchen.

In state after state, the pattern was the same: a few more, in some cases a lot more, votes for Kennedy. Alaska, home of Senator Ernest Gruening, one of only two senators to vote against the 1964 Gulf of Tonkin Resolution that helped pull the U.S. further into Vietnam, cast 8 of its 28 votes for Kennedy. Georgia, whose delegation had been split in two by the credentials committee, gave him half of its 44 votes. Florida was solidly for Humphrey, but without the unit rule, 10 of its votes went for Kennedy.

Then Michigan reported, and the combined work of Walter Reuther and Detroit Mayor Jerry Cavanaugh—a white mayor in an increasingly black city—brought 50 votes for Kennedy. In Missouri, where Kennedy had whistle-stopped to celebrate the Fourth of July, a jubilant Tom Eagle-ton announced that 40 of its 60 votes were in Bobby's corner. ("I'm in shock!" he shouted.) In Minnesota, Humphrey's home, the anti-war forces that had rallied behind Eugene McCarthy put 25 votes in Kennedy's corner. Nevada gave 6 of its votes to Kennedy, which surprised everyone except the handful who knew that in June, the reclusive billionaire Howard Hughes had given a $25,000 cash contribution to Bobby's campaign, in hopes he would end nuclear tests in Nevada. Ohio, whose delegates Kennedy had wooed so intensely in May, gave him 60 more; and while Pennsylvania's big cities held for Humphrey, that vast middle of Pennsylvania, with its coal mines and steel mills, its farms and small businesses, went for Bobby, and 40 more votes fell to him. And in the press corps and among the shrewder number crunchers around the hall, a murmur began to grow: *Texas, Texas will do it, can you believe it, Texas!*

"Tex-as!" Dorothy Bush recited. "One hundred and four votes!" And now the cavernous convention hall quieted; the cameras focused in on the delegation positioned in a place of honor at the very front of the hall. There, at the microphone by the state's standard, was Governor John Connally, silver-haired, impeccably tailored in a custom-made pin-striped suit, his face set in full battle mode, and it was almost possible to read his thoughts: *I'll be goddamned if I let Texas put that little son of a bitch over the top.*

"Madam Secretary," Connally began, "Texas—the home of America's greatest President, Lyndon Baines Johnson"—cheers, boos, catcalls erupted—"Texas, home of the Alamo, where American patriots chose death before surrender . . . Texas, *voting under the unit rule*"—and the convention exploded in noise. Behind Connally was Senator Ralph Yar-borough, the ardent liberal whose blood feud with Connally had brought President Kennedy to Texas in November of 1963, who had been riding in the car just behind Kennedy and Connally when the shooting began. Now Yarborough was grasping for the microphone, yelling up at the rostrum, "Poll the delegation! Poll the delegation!" A thoroughly discomfited Carl Albert conferred for a moment with Dorothy Bush and the convention parliamentarian, then announced, "Since this convention abolished the unit rule, the Texas delegation will be polled. The roll call will continue."

When the last delegation was tallied, Robert Kennedy had 1,290 votes,

Humphrey 1,180. Had the unit rule survived, Humphrey would have had just enough votes to deprive Kennedy of a majority, and the faint hope that a second ballot might produce defections from Kennedy's totals. But when the cameras zeroed in again on Texas, they caught John Connally and dozens of the state's delegates storming out of their seats, up the center aisle, and out of the hall, and a jubilant Ralph Yarborough was at the microphone.

"Madame Secretary," Yarborough announced. "Texas votes as follows: thirty votes for Lyndon Johnson . . . sixty-five votes for Vice President Humphrey . . . and nineteen votes for the nominee of the Democratic Party, Senator Robert—"

Dave Hackett, camped in a command post trailer under the floor of the amphitheater, picked up the telephone and rang Suite 407 in the Blackstone Hotel.

"Bobby," he said, "it's Dave. I just have one thing to say to you—when you pick a running mate, don't fuck it up like you did the last time."

IT HAD BEEN ON his mind for days, weeks; it had in fact claimed a part of his thinking from the first moments he had decided to enter the contest. It stirred some of his most painful memories. Just as it was his brother's reckless behavior that had put his career in the malevolent hands of J. Edgar Hoover, just as it was his brother's fear of political defeat that had kept the United States entangled in Vietnam, it was his brother's decision to run with Lyndon Johnson in 1960, and it was Jack who had kept Bobby from forcing Johnson off the ticket that Thursday afternoon in Los Angeles eight years ago. There may well have been self-delusion about Robert Kennedy's belief; without Johnson on the ticket, John Kennedy might well have lost that election, and there was no way to know whether political pressures might have kept John Kennedy from leaving Vietnam in a second term. By 1968, however, Kennedy had come to believe that Lyndon Johnson was not just a failed President, but a dangerous one. And from that belief came a recurring sense of guilt that he and his brother had put this cowardly, dangerous man in the White House.

So he'd been worrying over a running mate long before Dave Hackett's

wisecrack at the moment he won the nomination. He knew his choice had
to be credible as a potential President—after what happened to Jack and
what had almost happened to him, the possibility of a sudden succession
to the White House was no dim abstraction. Beyond that were hard political calculations. He started by thinking about his top supporters. Senator
George McGovern ("the most decent man in the Senate," he'd called him
once, then amended it to say, "maybe the *only* decent man in the Senate").
But McGovern was up for reelection, and if he joined the ticket, Democrats
would almost surely be sacrificing his Senate seat. Senator Ralph Yarborough of Texas was tempting, if only for the grief it would cause President
Johnson, but Yarborough was too hot, too likely to stir uneasiness about
his finger on the button. Senator Al Gore of Tennessee would balance the
ticket geographically and generationally (he was sixty-one), but he'd voted
against the Civil Rights Act of 1964, and Kennedy remembered that his
Justice Department had sniffed out some troublesome financial dealings
between Gore and billionaire wheeler-dealer Armand Hammer, who was
more or less the Soviet Union's financial enabler in the West. Governor Harold Hughes of Iowa was a former truck driver, a recovering alcoholic with
a commanding presence and a blunt, no-bullshit approach. But Hughes
was also running for the Senate, a sure bet to win, and Kennedy might
well need that vote to get his program through. Besides, Hughes had a
streak of mysticism that would unsettle voters. One of Kennedy's Nebraska
coordinators had spoken with Eugene McCarthy's Nebraska treasurer, a
thirty-three-year-old financial wunderkind named Warren Buffett, who
was helping Hughes in his Senate bid. Hughes, Buffett said, had casually
mentioned having conversations with his brother—who'd been dead for
ten years.

"I love Hughes," George McGovern had said to Kennedy. "But picking
a running mate who even seems a little mentally unstable? It'd be political
suicide. You really have to be careful here, Bob."

Besides, it became increasingly clear to Kennedy and his advisors that
they would have to pick a running mate who had *not* supported him.
Whatever his young Senate aides might think about running with someone who had been hawkish on Vietnam, a divided Democratic Party could
not win in November.

"You write very nice speeches about a coalition government in Vietnam, and reconciling black and white and young and old at home," Kennedy chided one of his speechwriters. "Now you want to tell me that if somebody was for Hubert, they're beyond redemption?"

Some of Humphrey's most prominent backers could be eliminated very quickly. Maine Senator Edmund Muskie, New Jersey Governor Richard Hughes, San Francisco Mayor Joe Alioto, were all Catholics, and two on the ticket would be one too many. Senator Fred Harris of Oklahoma was a young, fresh face, but, at thirty-seven, he was too young to be running with a forty-two-year-old Presidential nominee. Besides, Ethel wouldn't stand for it; they'd more or less adopted Fred and Ladonna Harris, had them to Hickory Hill any number of times, and as soon as Hubert announced, Fred had jumped right on his bandwagon. *As my brother might have said,* he thought, *sometimes party unity asks too much.*

"In a perfect world," Larry O'Brien had said earlier in the day, "you'd find a Southerner with proven experience, who opposed your nomination, and who could help deliver a big state . . ."

"Do you think Lyndon Johnson would be interested?" Joe Dolan asked. "He *is* constitutionally eligible, you know."

Now, an hour after he'd won the nomination, he and his aides were gathered in the living room of his suite at the Blackstone. He'd taken the awkward pro forma call from Richard Nixon, the gracious congratulatory phone call from Hubert Humphrey, the stilted, formal call from Lyndon Johnson, who told him, *I'm sure Jack Kennedy is looking down tonight, and I'm sure he's proud of you.* Then, almost as an afterthought, Johnson said, *I know you don't need my advice, maybe you don't want it, but I'd take a hard look at Sanford down in North Carolina. I thought about him for myself four years ago, but I thought two Southerners would be overreaching.*

As the group worked through the possibilities, they kept circling back to Terry Sanford, the fifty-one-year-old former governor of North Carolina. Back in '60, when he was elected, Sanford had risked the wrath of local Democrats by backing John Kennedy for President. As governor, he'd been a symbol of "the new South"—sending his children to integrated public schools, pushing for more money for schools and colleges, leveraging his clout with the White House to create the Research Triangle Park that jump-started the economy of Raleigh-Durham. He'd signed on as Lyndon Johnson's campaign manager earlier in the year, then headed up the citizens' committee for Hubert Humphrey. Picking Sanford wasn't going to help him win North Carolina, they all agreed, but as Kennedy said, "With my views on tobacco, I couldn't carry North Carolina if Jesus was running with me, and then the *New York Times* would say I was alienating the Jewish vote." But it was the right signal to unhappy Democrats; it was a nomination that spoke directly to the challenge posed by George Wallace's third-party campaign, and the idea of Sanford in the Oval Office was reasonable.

It was left to Arthur Schlesinger, Jr., the resident historian, to note the unprecedented nature of the choice.

"I never thought I'd see the day," he said, "when a Southern governor would wind up on a Democratic Party ticket."

If that break with tradition was a surprise, it was matched on Thursday night when Terry Sanford finished his acceptance speech, motioned for the applause to stop, and said, "I am honored now to welcome the man who will introduce our nominee for President . . . a tireless champion for justice and equal rights, Minnesota's favorite son . . . ," and a roar erupted as a smiling, energized Hubert Humphrey bounded onto the stage. This was the gesture he and Kennedy had agreed to on their phone call: that whoever lost the nomination would come to the convention hall to introduce the winner.

"He looks liberated," said one newsman.

"He *is*," his colleague said. "I just hope the next time he goes to the White House mess he brings a food taster along."

"I had hoped to be here under somewhat different circumstances," Humphrey began, and launched into a podium-thumping celebration of the Democratic Party. He ended by bringing the convention to its feet when he thundered: "To those who believe that we Democrats cannot overcome our differences and unite in November, I have three words for them: *President Richard Nixon!* We've had a family argument," Humphrey concluded, "but it is time now to stand together, work together, for the American family. It is time for a President with the vision and the energy to heal our divisions. It is time for the next President of the United States: Senator Robert Kennedy."

He walked onto the stage slowly, almost solemnly, shook hands with Humphrey, and approached the rostrum. There were no waves at the crowd, no expansive gestures. Only a pointed reminder from Fred Dutton kept a smile on his face, his eyes level, instead of looking down at his feet. ("It makes you look uncomfortable, ill at ease," Dutton said. "I *am* ill at ease," Kennedy replied.)

He began with thanks to Humphrey ("I am grateful he did not get to speak *before* the balloting, because I might well have been out here introducing *him*"), paid fleeting tribute to Eugene McCarthy—*May his lecture fees increase,* he thought—and then addressed his other adversary.

"There were clear differences—profound differences—between the President and myself. There is no sense attempting to hide that truth— besides, when it comes to avoiding the truth there is no way any of us could compete with the Republican nominee. But when the history of our time is written, it will record that Lyndon Johnson was the Second Great Emancipator—who did more than any other President since Lincoln to make the promise of equality a reality. And for that, every American, black and white, owes him our profound gratitude."

And then Robert Kennedy gave what Theodore H. White called "the most unusual acceptance speech in American political history."

He talked about ending the war in Vietnam, not "to simply withdraw, to raise the white flag of surrender . . . but to end it in a peace for brave men . . ."

He talked about crime, an issue Richard Nixon was raising for the first time in any Presidential campaign, an issue that was rending the Democratic coalition of big-city whites and blacks. He talked about it as he had all through the primary campaign, to the uneasiness of some in his own camp.

"The real threat of crime," he said, "is what it does to ourselves and our communities. No nation hiding behind locked doors is free, for it is imprisoned by its own fear. No nation whose citizens fear to walk their own streets is healthy, for in isolation lies the poisoning of public participation."

He talked about welfare: "The answer to the welfare crisis is work, jobs, self-sufficiency, and family integrity; not a massive new extension of welfare, not a great new outpouring of guidance counselors to give the poor more advice. We need jobs, dignified employment that lets a man say to his community, to his family, to his country, and most important, to himself: 'I am a participant in its great public ventures. I am a man . . .' "

And he ended with words he had given before, words that had sparked something of an argument among his speechwriters and aides. *The press will say you're recycling old stuff,* they argued. *Well,* came the response, *there are sixty million Americans who've never heard it.* In the end, it was Kennedy who decided to include it: *I think this is at the heart of our problem—mine and the Democratic Party's problems. They think I'm too radical, and they think we don't feel what they're feeling.*

So he ended his speech by talking about "another great task before us: to confront the poverty of satisfaction—a lack of purpose and dignity—that inflicts us all. It is folly to believe that we can find such purpose and dignity in the mere accumulation of material things. Our gross national product is over eight hundred billion dollars. But the gross national product counts air pollution and cigarette advertising. It counts ambulances to clear our highways of carnage. It counts special locks for our doors and the jails for those who break them. It counts napalm and the cost of a nuclear warhead, and armored cars for our police who fight riots in our streets, and television programs that glorify violence to sell toys to our children.

"And for all that it measures, it does not allow for the health of our children, the quality of their education, or the joy of their play. It does not include the beauty of our poetry or the strength of our marriages, the intelligence of our public officials or the intelligence of our public debate. It measures everything, in short, except that which makes life worthwhile. And it can tell us everything about America except why we are proud to be Americans."

There was in 1968 a template for acceptance speeches: They were designed to rally the party, to elicit loud, long applause at frequent intervals; indeed, news reports tallied the number of interruptions as a gauge of a speech's power. Robert Kennedy's acceptance speech was interrupted just nine times. For long stretches, there was not just a silence but a stillness. Only later did one or two reporters recognize what was happening: These delegates, these fired-up partisans, had *listened.*

And from Bebe Rebozo's home in Key Biscayne, Florida, Richard Nixon was listening, too.

THE CENTRAL PREMISE OF Richard Nixon's campaign was gone, knocked into a cocked hat by Robert Kennedy's nomination. He'd begun his improbable comeback on the obvious assumption that he would be running against President Johnson. Never forget, he'd written his staff in one of his memos, that "we are the OUTs, and they are the INs." When Johnson withdrew, and Humphrey began piling up delegates from the non-primary states, he'd focused on pinning the Vice President to his unpopular President.

"Let's get ready to ask Humphrey to name any policy, any program, where he disagrees with what Johnson did," he'd written in one of his "RN" stream-of-consciousness memos. And arching over every speech, every TV ad, was the meta-theme: "If after all these years and all these billions, we're enmeshed in a quagmire of war abroad, and violence and disorder at home, I say it is time for new leadership."

Well, that argument was useless now. But that didn't mean there wasn't a different, maybe even more powerful one, an argument that had been plastered over all those billboards months ago: *Feel Safer with Nixon.* Maybe it wasn't the most eloquent theme in American history, but it was a perfect fit with the national mood—*What the hell is happening to my country?*— and with the right strategy, it would define Richard Nixon's opponents as the symptom of all that was unsettling the voters. George Wallace had tapped into the resentment of the folks who were just getting by, not poor enough for government aid, not affluent enough for material comfort or security. He'd gone beyond pure race-baiting—though, God knows, there was still plenty of that—to an attack on the Ivy League foundation executives, spending tax-free money on radical blacks, to pointy-headed bureaucrats forcing your children to travel miles from home to attend dangerous schools. Teddy White had told him of Wallace's visit to a big newspaper, where he'd said, "Your reporters will be for Bobby. Your publisher and board of directors will be with Nixon. *But your pressmen and truck drivers will be for me.*" But Wallace was too hot, too crude, too mean to be credible. (Presidents just do not threaten to run over protesters.)

And Bobby? Bobby *scared* an awful lot of voters. Those TV pictures of him driving through ghettoes, while black hands reached out to grab him, black faces with mouths wide open in screams of joy, the frenzy of long-haired college kids leaping and hollering; they were the kinds of pictures Nixon's people would *pay* the networks to put on their newscasts. Back in June, around the time Bobby had almost been shot, polls showed that more people thought him a divider than a uniter. And it wasn't just those pictures that scared people. He seemed at times to identify with the very forces that rattled the hardworking, taxpaying, law-abiding forgotten Americans Nixon had been talking about from his first days in politics. He'd gone to Berkeley and proudly proclaimed, "We dissent!" He'd talked at times as if he could *understand* why young black men robbed from their neighbors and set fire to their neighborhoods. He'd said a while ago there was nothing wrong with donating blood to the Vietcong, the people who were killing Americans in South Vietnam (the *Chicago Tribune* had called him "Ho Chi Kennedy" for that one). He'd talked about *understanding* that all Communists weren't the same, about the terrible American government driving Indians to suicide, and making migrant workers suffer, and letting Vietnam go Red because the government we were backing wasn't perfect.

The key to November, then, was to persuade enough voters that Bobby Kennedy was, at root, the candidate of "surrender"—surrender to the forces of Communism abroad, surrender to the forces of lawlessness and violence and upheaval here at home. If his campaign played it right, Richard Nixon would be the candidate of safety, order, and restoration—not of a family, but of a better time, when you could walk a street, or send your kid to school, or go to your job, with a sense of security, a sense that things would be the way they were supposed to be. For whites who had made it—just—into the middle class, Richard Nixon would be their champion, protecting them from the criminals who threatened their safety, from the judges who wanted their children forced into dangerous schools, from feckless policymakers who lacked the tensile strength to stand up against freedom's enemies.

And there was one other piece to this strategy: making sure that the President of the United States had no reason to work against a Richard Nixon Presidency. In fact, he was already taking some significant steps toward that end. He'd met with the President just after he'd won the nomination, a nice bipartisan photo op, but as they sat across from each other at a long table, he thought he'd seen something in the President's face as he sat, propping his chin in his hands. It was as if he was reexamining his longtime adversary, weighing the possibility that Nixon just might be a better guardian of Johnson's legacy than either Humphrey or Kennedy. And now that Bobby was in fact the Democratic nominee, he was going to test that possibility, by sending to the White House an emissary whose cover no one would think to question.

HE STOOD ON a platform in the middle of Cadillac Square in downtown Detroit, looking out at the crowd of 40,000 who had gathered on this Labor Day noon to begin the formal opening of the fall campaign. Democratic candidates had been coming here for decades; John Kennedy had stood here exactly eight years ago. Now, as Robert Kennedy prepared to speak, he could calculate the barriers between himself and the White House by what had happened in those eight years—here in Detroit and across the country.

> —In 1960, the specter of race riots was a fading memory from World War II; Negro protesters wore coats and ties and did their homework at lunch counters as white thugs beat them. Now the sight of cities in flames was commonplace; just five miles from here, a year ago, a police raid on an after-hours drinking spot exploded into a five-day riot that left forty-three people dead. It had happened in dozens of cities—indeed, John Lindsay was the Republican Vice Presidential candidate because it *hadn't* happened in New York—and beyond the violence, battles over political power, schools, and jobs had stretched the New Deal– New Frontier coalition of blacks and working-class whites to the breaking point. Yes, Detroit Mayor Jerry Cavanaugh and Senator Phil Hart and Coleman Young, a talented, ambitious black state senator, might all be standing together behind him, but the tensions between black and white Democrats were going to be fertile ground for the appeals of Wallace and Nixon.

—In 1960, there was a clear national consensus on foreign policy. International Communism and its containment was the focus; Democrats in Congress backed Eisenhower, and Republicans in Congress backed John Kennedy. The noxious poison of McCarthyism had died years before the Wisconsin demagogue had; except for the fever swamps of the John Birch Society, you challenged the wisdom of your opponents, not their loyalty. When 6,000 students staged a protest against nuclear weapons at the White House in February of 1962, they'd worn coats and ties, and the White House had sent out coffee. Now, with the Vietnam War in its fourth year of a full-scale combat, the increasing militancy of the anti-war movement had spawned an increasingly militant counterweight, and partisans exchanged epithets: "Baby killer!" "Traitor!" Among some of the young, the dress, hair, and language seemed designed to provoke from their elders not simply opposition, but revulsion.

—Finally, the Kennedy who'd stood at Cadillac Square in 1960 was a very different figure from the Kennedy who stood there in 1968. John Kennedy was at root a cautious politician, coolly measuring the dangers of overreaching. He stirred excitement on the stump, but never frenzy; in his appearances on the increasingly powerful medium of television, he was contained in speech and gesture.

Robert Kennedy's personality, and the seismic shift in the political ground, made him very different. His detractors—and indeed, some of his most devoted supporters—agreed with the signs that sprouted up at many of his appearances: "Bobby Ain't Jack." He was half a foot shorter, a bundle of barely contained passion. He was often awkward in public, uncomfortable with the emotions he stirred. His motorcades through black and brown neighborhoods had helped drive up votes in key primaries, but they did not play well in suburban neighborhoods. His rhetoric could at times be hot, disturbing; he'd asked on national TV whether America had the right to bomb Vietnam, killing civilians, so that Communism would stay 11,000 miles away from the United States instead of 10,000 miles. He'd once described the violence of young blacks in the ghetto as "a cry for love." And those who disagreed with Kennedy—on Vietnam, on spending, on race, on changing migrant labor laws—didn't just disagree with him, they *feared* him because implicit in his words and deeds was the unspoken footnote, *And I mean it.* That poll showing more people regarded him as a divider than a uniter said it all: If he could not overcome that sense that he was a divisive, polarizing figure, he could not win.

The speech he gave in Cadillac Square was aimed squarely at his central political dilemma. The argument Kennedy had made to hostile college kids—*Why should a boy who wants to open a filling station instead of going to college have to change his plans while you get protected on campus?*—hit a chord with the crowd of working-class blacks and whites with a high school education. It was a way of playing on their resentment while appealing to fairness, not repression. So did a theme he'd struck in his primary campaign: the tax laws that let multimillionaires pay less than 1 percent on their earnings, while workers on an assembly line paid a third of their income. So did his notions of trading medical school scholarships in return for a commitment to work in the poor urban and rural communities, or paying retired construction workers to teach a trade to young men.

"We must grasp the web whole," Kennedy said at Cadillac Square, the same phrase he'd used for the last few years, and it was central to his hopes for the Presidency. He had to persuade the country that his ideas *connected*—that he was not simply pandering to the blacks, or promising money to the poor, or turning to the right, or running on the memory of his brother, or pursuing a ruthless quest for power. And he had to do it in a time when the essential optimism of 1960, the belief that government did more or less the right thing most of the time, had withered in the face of war and division.

He ended this first speech of the fall campaign with the words he had used all through the primary, the words from George Bernard Shaw that cued the press that it was time to pack up and head for the buses, words that struck an optimistic chord: "Some men see things as they are, and ask *why?* I dream of things that never were, and ask *why not?*"

And as he was speaking, one of his most trusted aides was meeting with one of his most zealous enemies. It was a meeting that would have convinced any witness that, when it came to political self-preservation, the idea of a "ruthless" Kennedy machine was a lot more than a myth.

.   .   .

By 1968, J. Edgar Hoover had held more power for more years than anyone else, by some measures more than the seven Presidents he had served
under—or over. Yes, Presidents had the armed forces to command, but
their will could be frustrated by Congress, and the duration of their power
was limited by voters, and now by the two-term limit imposed by Constitutional amendment. Hoover, by contrast, was virtually immune from
the checks and balances that constrained courts, the Congress, and the
President. A compliant press had spent decades glamorizing and glori-
fying the work of the Federal Bureau of Investigation, and a worshipful
Congress that did not hesitate to subject Cabinet officers to withering
scrutiny treated Hoover's visits to Capitol Hill as something between a
royal appearance and a papal blessing. Even those inclined toward a more
skeptical assessment of the Director stayed mute, knowing that the FBI's
appetite for intelligence, or gossip, or rumor, or scandal ensured that reams
of such information on virtually every public person (and his family) were
secreted away somewhere in the Department of Justice. No one failed to
bow the head and bend the knee for J. Edgar Hoover.

No one but Bobby Kennedy.

Hoover might have expected something very different. He and Joe
Kennedy had been something of a mutual admiration society during Joe's
days at the Securities and Exchange Commission, and the two exchanged
notes of high regard when Joe was Ambassador to Great Britain. When
Jack was elected in 1960, his first announcement on the day after he won,
was that he was reappointing Hoover to head the FBI.

But Bobby? Everything about the young man appalled him: the infor-
mality of his office, the way he dressed, rolled-up shirtsleeves and no jacket;
the dogs and children that had free rein. He had also insisted that Hoover
report to him, the Attorney General, instead of reporting directly to the
President. Whatever the Justice Department chain of command said,
Hoover had never been blocked from direct access to the President. Much
more than Bobby's style, though, was his obviously low regard for the work
of the Bureau. The FBI prided itself on its clearance record, and on its
relentless pursuit of domestic Communism (*Masters of Deceit* was the title

of Hoover's best-selling book on the Red Menace). But Bobby disdained these achievements, demanding again and again to know what the Bureau was doing about organized crime, even though Hoover had proclaimed repeatedly that there *was* no such thing as the Mafia. *For heaven's sake, Bobby's own father had told him to lay off the organized crime crusade, and the kid just wouldn't listen.* To make matters worse, Kennedy was pounding at the Bureau to hire more Negroes, something that Hoover found personally repellent. Every year, at an elaborate ceremony, he'd shake the hand of every new agent, and . . .

Given Bobby's feelings, and the fact that he was more or less Jack's Assistant President, Hoover might have reason to fear for his job. Not so; for among the millions about whom the FBI had gathered intelligence was one John Fitzgerald Kennedy. And it was the kind of guaranteed employment insurance the Queen of England might envy. John Kennedy's sexual recklessness, his flagrantly adulterous conduct even as President, had offended Hoover profoundly. On more than one occasion, however, his dalliances had posed direct threats to the national security; and Hoover was diligent, even meticulous, in letting the Attorney General know what his minions had learned: that Kennedy was involved with a woman who was the girlfriend of Sam Giancana, a prominent Chicago gangster, or that he had been involved with Ellie Rometsch, a suspected East German spy. (No hard evidence was unearthed about her spying, but Bobby had been so unnerved he'd had the woman summarily deported.)

So Hoover and Bobby endured each other until November 22, 1963. It was Hoover who called Bobby at his home that noon, emotionlessly telling him his brother had been shot. Before President Kennedy had been buried, the direct line between Kennedy's office and Hoover's had been disconnected; Hoover was dealing directly with Johnson. As for the Director's view of a potential President Robert Kennedy? On the day Kennedy announced, Hoover's top assistant and closest companion, Clyde Tolson, said flatly, "I hope someone shoots the son of a bitch." Nor was there any doubt of Hoover's willingness, eagerness, to help Lyndon Johnson block Bobby's path to the White House. The story that Robert Kennedy had authorized wiretaps on Martin Luther King, Jr., had gone directly from Hoover to the Oval Office to columnist Drew Pearson. That revelation, though, was small change compared to the treasure trove Hoover had gathered about the conduct of John and Robert Kennedy: not just sexual misbehavior (though Hoover regarded President Kennedy as a "moral degenerate"), but the use of gangsters and violence in Bobby's zealous effort to topple Fidel Castro. For many of Robert Kennedy's most devoted followers, Hoover's potential for blackmail, especially in concert with Lyndon Johnson, was a political sword of Damocles; it was, for them, one persuasive explanation for Robert Kennedy's reluctance to challenge Johnson for the Presidency. (Much later, his longtime personal assistant, Angie Novello, acknowledged, "I wanted Bob in the White House so badly, but I didn't want him to run in '68 because I was afraid of what certain people in high places would do, I was afraid they would do something mean and unheard of . . .")

Given the toxic enmity between Hoover and Kennedy, it seemed inexplicable when one of Robert Kennedy's closest colleagues appeared just before noon on a late summer day at Harvey's Restaurant on Connecticut Avenue and handed a sealed envelope to the maître d' with instructions to deliver the note to Hoover's table. Even if Walter Sheridan had not been one of Robert Kennedy's most dogged investigators at the Senate Rackets Committee and at the Justice Department, he would have had no trouble locating the FBI Director: Every day of the week, Hoover and his deputy Clyde Tolson would lunch at Harvey's, at a table blocked off from the rest of the dining room by a serving trolley. In fact, Hoover and Tolson spent most of their lives together, on and off the job. They traveled together, vacationed together, went to ball games and horse races together, were so bound to each other that FBI agents had a nickname for the two: "J. Edna and Mother Tolson." *Time* magazine had pointedly noted some years back that "Hoover is seldom seen without a male companion, most frequently solemn-faced Clyde Tolson"—words that brought a full-field FBI investigation down on the writer. *Time* might have been even more pointed had it known that Tolson was Hoover's sole heir, and that the Director and his top associate had made plans to be buried next to each other.

No one ever learned what was in that 9-by-12 manila envelope Sheridan delivered to Hoover's table. No one ever knew why Hoover and Tolson canceled their traditional Labor Day trip to Los Angeles, where they would relax by the beach and bet the horses at the Del Mar racetrack. It is likely that fewer than half a dozen people ever learned of Walter Sheridan's Labor Day visit to Hoover's home on 30th Place a few blocks from Rock Creek Park. The words that passed between them—and the cardboard boxes that were exchanged—were whispered about for years, but they were no more than rumors. And in 1968, the mass media of the era were genuine "gatekeepers." There simply was no accessible means for injecting rumors directly into millions of homes. So the rumors remained nothing more than a low-grade hum. President Johnson's repeated calls to Hoover were met by silence, evasions, and on one occasion a not-so-subtle warning from the Director that "*every* President needs and deserves insulation from salacious rumors . . .￼" Much, much later, after a dinner with several bottles of wine and a glass or two of cognac, an old journalist friend asked Sheridan about what had happened.

"It was fortunate," Sheridan replied, "that Hoover and Bobby both learned enough Latin to understand the meaning of 'quid pro quo.'"

If the fear of scandal no longer hung over Robert Kennedy's campaign, a very different kind of fear did. Months ago, when the pressure for him to challenge Johnson for the nomination was growing, he would push back again and again with one core argument: *The President has enormous power to direct the flow of events,* he'd say. *He could change Vietnam policy on a dime, stop the bombing, or escalate the war to try and rally the country behind him.* Had Kennedy known of a private White House conversation in mid-September, he would have had good reason for that fear . . . very good reason.

THE REVEREND BILLY GRAHAM was one of the most admired men in America. At forty-nine, the jut-jawed, strikingly handsome evangelist with the richly timbered voice was the embodiment of "muscular Christianity," a man who had turned a small radio ministry in the mid-1940s into a sprawling empire of television appearances and "Crusades for Christ" rallies that drew tens, even hundreds, of thousands. His rise to prominence was fueled by media titans like William Randolph Hearst ("Push Graham," he instructed his editors in 1949) and Henry Luce, whose *Time* magazine put Graham on the cover in 1954. He was so magnetic a figure that NBC offered him a five-year, $5 million contract to appear opposite the most popular personality in broadcasting, Arthur Godfrey.

When it came to matters of race, Billy Graham was squarely in the liberal camp. He refused to preach before segregated audiences, bailed out Martin Luther King, Jr., when the preacher was thrown in jail for demonstrating, and openly supported Lyndon Johnson's landmark civil rights laws.

He was also an ardent anti-Communist, who came to admire Richard Nixon for his dogged efforts to expose the treasonous work of Alger Hiss. He grew so devoted to the former Vice President that he began ingratiating himself to Nixon by echoing some of his darker impulses. When Nixon would rant about the left-wing Jews in the media and business, Graham would note that he would often meet with leaders in the Jewish community, adding, "They don't know how I feel about what they're doing to this country . . . their stranglehold has to be broken or this country's going down the drain."

By 1968, Graham was wholly committed to a Nixon Presidency, which is why he came to the White House on September 15 to meet with Lyndon Johnson. It was more than a courtesy call, more than a social chat with a friend. Billy Graham had come as a courier, bringing a very specific message to the President from Nixon.

Nixon wants you to know, Graham said, *that he will keep his criticisms of you strictly on policy grounds; he intends to treat you and the office with respect. When a settlement to end the war is reached, he intends to give you a major share of the credit; he will ask you to take on major foreign assignments, so that your unique talents can be put to good use, and will do everything to make you a place in history.*

The President nodded, said nothing, and turned the conversation to lighter matters: *When are you and Ruth going to come visit Bird and me at the ranch?* The words that Graham had spoken, however, stayed with the President once the reverend had taken his leave. More than ever, he was convinced that his legacy would be determined by Vietnam. If the choice was between a Republican President who would honor his work and a Democratic President who would scorn it . . . well, that wasn't much of a choice at all.

. . .

"GODDAMNIT!" Richard Nixon shouted as he threw the *New York Times* halfway across the dining room of his Fifth Avenue apartment. "What is it about my running mates and the Negroes?"

Eight years ago, Henry Cabot Lodge had thrown a hand grenade into the campaign by pledging that Nixon would appoint a Negro to the Cabinet. It had taken days for Nixon to put out the fires among many of his Southern supporters. Now, New York Mayor John Lindsay was presiding over a meltdown that had just shut down the largest public-school system in the country, and had thrown a white, mostly Jewish teachers' union into a pitched battle with the black residents of an impoverished, dysfunctional Brooklyn ghetto. It had begun more than a year ago, when the Ford Foundation decided to fund an experiment to put more control over schools in the hands of local communities.

"And you know who runs the Ford Foundation?" Nixon asked his inner circle who had gathered around the table. "McGeorge Bundy. First, he screws up Vietnam. Now he decides to put a bunch of . . . thugs in charge of the schools!"

One of the three districts chosen for a decentralization test was Brooklyn's Ocean Hill–Brownsville, an impoverished ruin of a neighborhood with three-fourths of the population on welfare, the highest drug-addiction rate in the nation, with abandoned homes and stores that had the look and feel of postwar Berlin. A group of militant black organizers with a distinctly racialist outlook had gained control of the district's schools, and had summarily dismissed eighteen white teachers and administrators. When the heavily Jewish teachers' union challenged the dismissals, the dispute took on an ugly cast, with anti-Semitic language and threats of violence. A citywide strike had shut the city's schools down for two days, and now, in mid-September, a second strike was underway. Lindsay had canceled all campaign appearances, and was locked in a series of round-robin negotiations with the local school board, the city's Board of Education, and the teachers' union.

Nixon's instructions to his campaign team were blunt: *We need to push Lindsay to settle this strike fast; he needs to get those teachers back in those schools.*

It took two days of pleas, arguments, and threats, but Lindsay gave in, and the city's schools reopened; a three-day siege of the schools in Ocean Hill–Brownsville by black militants ended when 2,000 police drove them out. *That's the kind of TV we need,* a partially mollified Nixon said. *Shows our ticket means what it says about law and order.*

"But maybe I should have gone with Agnew," he mused later. "Just once, I'd like a running mate who was an asset, not a liability."

ALL THROUGH THE AUTUMN, Robert Kennedy's campaign grappled with the essential contradiction of their candidate's message: He was the candidate of change, the candidate who promised "a new America," who could trigger frenzy in the streets of dozens of American cities; but he was also the candidate of restoration, the man who could tamp the fires of disorder, and the broader sense that America had lost its moorings. He could not win unless the disaffected—the blacks, the Hispanics, the seven million young people on college campuses—were engaged enough to come to the polls in November, or to work on his behalf if they were too young to vote. ("Can we lower the voting age to eighteen?" Kennedy asked jokingly at a rally in Ann Arbor. "How about twelve?")

And he could not win unless the far bigger voting bloc—"the un-poor, the un-black, the un-young" as Richard Scammon and Ben Wattenberg called them—believed he was moved by *their* grievances, as their children were bused to dangerous schools, as their devotion to cultural traditions and decent behavior was being undermined on college campuses and on their television sets. This was the Robert Kennedy of the campaign's fall television campaign: Five-minute and half-hour broadcasts put Kennedy into suburban living rooms, clad in a dark suit from Lewis and Thomas Saltz, the high-priced Washington men's store, white handkerchief in his breast pocket, hair carefully trimmed above his ears, as he chatted over tea with a dozen women wearing their garden-party best. He stood on a stage in a small meeting room in front of a hundred women wearing flowered hats, smiling shyly as his mother Rose told of his mischievous boyhood, how she would discipline him with a ruler. He sat in a classroom, talking earnestly with a class full of fifth-graders about saving the redwoods.

At halftime of National Football League broadcasts, football fans in front of their televisions saw Kennedy standing at the Brooklyn Navy Yard or Ford's River Rouge auto plant outside of Detroit, talking with the men who built the ships and the cars, sometimes disagreeing with them, sometimes prodding them when they expressed admiration for the tough talk of George Wallace ("Do you really think people shouldn't be allowed to vote because of the color of their skin? Do you really want a President who promises to kill someone because they're demonstrating against him? Isn't that what used to happen to men who went out on strike?").

The Kennedy image that director John Frankenheimer and onetime speechwriter Dick Goodwin were presenting came in sharp contrast to the Robert Kennedy painted by Richard Nixon's campaign. Nixon himself was never seen directly attacking Kennedy; when he appeared on camera, it was at one of the many "town halls" he conducted, answering unscreened questions from friendly audiences. The format was the brainchild of twenty-seven-year-old talk-show producer Roger Ailes, who convinced Nixon that the town halls were the best way to escape the screen of a flagrantly biased press.

"Maybe one day we'll have a network that will be fair and balanced," Ailes said. "Until then, we have to let the voter see you as you are."

The one-minute Nixon spots were very different. Created by longtime J. Walter Thompson ad executive Harry Treleavan, and directed by Gene Jones, they were premised on a central theme Treleavan described this way: "There's an uneasiness in the land. A feeling that things aren't right. That we're moving in the wrong direction. That none of the solutions to our problems are working." Had Johnson or Humphrey been the Democratic nominee, a simple call for "new leadership" would have been enough. With Robert Kennedy as the nominee, Nixon's ads had to link Bobby with that uneasiness. So they featured a quick montage of dramatic, unsettling still images of burning cities, Vietnam combat, street clashes between demonstrators and police, intercut with shots of a fist-clenching, long-haired Robert Kennedy and some of his more provocative words.

"We dissent! We dissent! We dissent!" ran the clip from one ad, edited from a 1966 Kennedy speech at Berkeley. Then the voice of Richard Nixon was heard, solemnly intoning that "we must never confuse dissent with disruption and destruction." Another ad replayed a Kennedy speech where he said that for many Negroes "the law has been an instrument of oppression."

"May the day never come," Nixon said, "when an American President calls the law an instrument of oppression. The law is every American's protection—black, brown, or white. The first civil right is the right to be safe in our homes, our streets, our neighborhoods."

That theme, of course, was one of the prime messages of the campaign's wild card: George Wallace. And as the campaign entered its last two weeks, it became increasingly clear that the former Alabama governor was turning into one of Robert Kennedy's best, if wholly unintentional, assets.

The first sign of this came from Wallace's choice of running mate: retired Air Force Chief of Staff Curtis LeMay, chosen to shore up Wallace's nonexistent national security credentials. LeMay had been one of the heroic figures of World War II, directing the low-altitude incendiary bombing of Japan that had killed some half a million civilians; an invasion of Japan, he and others argued, would have killed twice as many. Besides, he said at the time, in war, "There are no innocent civilians." As Air Force Chief of Staff, he had been a formidable advocate of overwhelming nuclear force, clashing with Defense Secretary Robert McNamara over strategy and resources. His biggest, most consequential battle, however, was with John and Robert Kennedy during the Cuban Missile Crisis, when he all but demanded the bombing of missile sites. "Appeasement," he called the blockade. He joined the Wallace campaign not out of sympathy for the governor's views on race, but because he thought Richard Nixon was insufficiently committed to victory in Vietnam—and because he welcomed the chance to indict Robert Kennedy for his "near-treasonous" views on Vietnam.

Unfortunately for Wallace, LeMay's way with words was as blunt as his persona: the bulldog face, the cigar perpetually jammed in his teeth, the forceful, often blustering tone. When he talked of the need for Americans to overcome their fear of nuclear weapons, when he threatened to "bomb North Vietnam back to the Stone Age," voters heard the voice of General Buck Turgidson, the character played by George C. Scott in the movie *Dr. Strangelove.* And when he assailed Robert Kennedy for "caving in to Moscow and Havana" during the Cuban Missile Crisis, voters remembered how close the world had come to nuclear war. Robert Kennedy's book on the crisis, *Thirteen Days*, had just been published, and while Kennedy mentioned no names of those who had advocated other courses, he had no compunction about responding to LeMay at a press conference.

"The great advantage of General LeMay's advice," Kennedy said, "was that if we'd taken it, none of us would have been around to prove how wrong it was."

Wallace's second great, unintended gift to Robert Kennedy was the support of a united labor union movement. Kennedy's nomination was a grievous disappointment to AFL-CIO President George Meany. Kennedy's views on Vietnam were anathema to Meany, who had been fighting Communism since his earliest days as a union organizer. In the days after Robert Kennedy won in Chicago, Meany seriously pondered the possibility of staying neutral in the fall campaign. *Yes, Nixon's no friend of labor,* he argued with his Executive Council members, *but Bobby means surrender in Vietnam.*

It was Wallace's appeal to the blue-collar vote that proved decisive. The labor movement had first glimpsed the danger four years ago, in 1964. In a time of widespread prosperity and low unemployment, *before* the explosion of racial conflict, Wallace had entered the Democratic Presidential primaries in Maryland, Indiana, and Wisconsin, and had won more than a third of the vote in each state. Now in 1968, as a third-party candidate, Wallace was drawing alarming numbers among union members. And for organized labor, Wallace was a mortal enemy. He came from a state that was a home for runaway businesses fleeing the unionized North, a state where the "open shop" was law, where the whole principle of collective bargaining was under permanent legal siege, where wages were low and working conditions dreadful. Even if working-class whites came to Wallace's side out of fear of crime or black militancy or radical protesters, it would mean they were listening to a voice that could in time lure them away from loyalty to the union movement. And that was a possibility the movement could not survive.

That was enough to convince a reluctant George Meany to abandon the idea of neutrality, and endorse Kennedy. More important, labor embarked on a massive campaign to warn their members of "the Wallace threat."

More than fifty million pamphlets were mailed to members out of national headquarters; tens of millions more came from local affiliates all over the country. Twenty-five thousand men and women manned phone banks in the last weeks of the campaign. At Meany's insistence, most of the messages were aimed less at praising Robert Kennedy than at condemning George Wallace. Politically, it didn't matter; in the big industrial states, a union member who turned away from Wallace was almost certain to turn to Kennedy, not Nixon.

There was a third benefit Wallace provided: He spared Kennedy from a debate. From the moment of his nomination, the press began speculating about another series of Kennedy–Nixon confrontations. A hundred columns and television pieces revisited 1960, Nixon's sallow, drained, undertaker-like appearance in the first debate, John Kennedy's cool, composed demeanor that played well enough in the medium to neutralize Nixon's "experience" argument. Debating, however, was one arena where the "Bobby Ain't Jack" point was well taken. In his TV appearances, Robert Kennedy simply lacked Jack's smooth affect. He would run his hand up to his head, as if to run it through his hair; he would hesitate, pause, at times grope for a word. More and more, Robert Kennedy had come to see issues in shades of gray; not when it came to people who were suffering, God knows, but he was more comfortable with nuance than with packaged comments for the evening news—"sound bites" was the phrase they were beginning to call them. Last fall, he had appeared with California Governor Ronald Reagan in a satellite "town meeting" with an international group of students, most of whom were militantly Left, who excoriated America's Vietnam policies. Reagan's unswerving condemnation of North Vietnam played far better on television than Kennedy's more complex analysis. ("Never put me in that situation again," he snapped at an aide.)

Had 1968 been a simple Nixon–Kennedy clash, the Republican might well have forced the issue, demanding to know why Robert Kennedy was ducking a debate, quoting William F. Buckley on why Bobby wouldn't appear on his *Firing Line* TV show ("Why does baloney avoid the meat slicer?"). With Wallace on the ballot, however, the strategic implications were clouded. There had only been one series of Presidential debates—Johnson had refused to face Barry Goldwater in 1964—and the only tentative conclusion from 1960 (apart from the need for a really skilled makeup artist) was that the less experienced candidate had more to gain. Letting George Wallace stand on the same platform as the major-party candidates would elevate him even before a single word was spoken. That posed a direct threat to Nixon's prospects in Tennessee, South Carolina, and Kentucky. As for the Northern states, late polls suggested that the labor movement's bombardment of blue-collar voters, and General LeMay's intemperate remarks about nuclear weapons, had cost Wallace support: His prospective votes now were coming from traditional Democrats most concerned with crime and disorder—exactly the voters Nixon most needed to win the major battleground states.

Giving George Wallace the bully pulpit of a prime-time, three-network debate, then, was a chance Richard Nixon could not take. Republican allies in the House and Senate blocked the efforts to suspend the equal time provisions of the Federal Communications Act; the Democrats responded with pointed ads asking why "Richard Nixon is afraid to face Robert Kennedy and the American people."

By late October, Robert Kennedy had moved into a small lead over Nixon, but the race was clearly too close to call. Either Kennedy or Nixon could win—or, indeed, George Wallace could well succeed in depriving either candidate of victory, propelling the election into something close to Constitutional chaos.

"Any late-breaking development," a chorus of analysts proclaimed, "could decide the outcome."

And in the last week of the campaign, President Johnson decided it was time . . .

IT WAS ONE A.M. on November 1, and Clark Clifford lay awake in the master bedroom of his fifty-year-old house in Bethesda, Maryland, profoundly troubled. That would have surprised anyone who had worked with the sixty-one-year-old Secretary of Defense, who had spent a lifetime conveying a sense of serene assurance. It came from his six-foot two-inch, 180-pound frame, topped by a mane of wavy silvery hair. It came from the impeccably tailored double-breasted pin-striped suits, the soothing, cultured voice with the faint echoes of his roots in Kansas and Missouri. From his first days in Washington, something about him had gained him easy entry into the corridors of power. As a young naval aide at the Potsdam Conference in 1945, he had gone to Samuel Rosenman, one of Truman's top aides, asking for more work to do. *Let's keep that man at the White House,* Rosenman had said to Truman. It was Clifford who helped shape Truman's 1948 upset, urging the civil rights strategy that drove Southerners out of the convention but won critical liberal votes in the North, urging Truman to recognize the state of Israel that year even as Secretary of State George Marshall threatened to quit.

His calm demeanor—no one ever remembered him raising his voice or losing his temper—won him the confidence of everyone around him. Truman raised the idea of a Supreme Court appointment; admirers urged him to go back to Missouri and run for the Senate, but Clifford had another target in mind. In 1950, he opened a law firm in Washington and quickly became the highest-paid lawyer in the capital. His clients included TWA (Howard Hughes was among his first clients), AT&T, RCA, ABC, GE, DuPont, Standard Oil. He'd greet his clients in his paneled office on Connecticut Avenue, give them all the same speech about how he would not represent them before the President or his staff: "If you want influence," he would say, "you should consider going elsewhere. What we can offer you is extensive knowledge on how to deal with the government on your problems." And his clients would nod, *Yes, of course,* and think to themselves, *This man can open every door in this town.*

He was a trusted and discreet advisor to Presidents; he'd helped Jack Kennedy with his transition, "and all that he asked for," Kennedy said at a pre-election dinner, "was that we advertise his law firm on the back of one-dollar bills." Kennedy had put him on the Foreign Intelligence Advisory Board after the Bay of Pigs debacle, and Johnson had made him one of his closest counselors on Vietnam. Clifford had been a consistent voice for escalation, for increased military pressure on the North. Only air and ground power, he argued, would force North Vietnam to abandon its goal of conquering the South. So it was only natural that when Defense Secretary Robert McNamara seemed to be weakening in his resolve, seemed more and more to be doubting whether more bombs and troops could ever prevail, warned that further escalation "would be dangerous, costly in lives, unsatisfactory to the American people," and worse, seemed to be cracking under the pressure, seemed even to be feeding information to his friend Robert Kennedy, Johnson pulled McNamara out of the Pentagon, sent him to the World Bank (without telling him), and reached for the experienced hand who was unshakably committed to winning the war.

Except . . . almost as soon as Clifford arrived at the Pentagon at the beginning of 1968, the doubts began. The confident assertions of "progress" grew more ephemeral the harder Clifford pushed for real facts. At the start of February, one day after Clifford's confirmation, the Tet offensive showed that the Vietcong and North Vietnamese could strike at will just about everywhere in the South, including the grounds of the American Embassy. Yes, they suffered huge losses, but the television footage that demonstrated there were no safe havens in South Vietnam also seemed to prove that the light at the end of the tunnel was an illusion. General Westmoreland and his military commanders were asking for 200,000 *more* men in arms, on top of the half million already there. By mid-March, Clifford and the other "wise men" around Johnson were telling a stunned, angry President his policy was in ruins. By month's end, Johnson had reversed course, ordered a partial halt to the bombing, opened the door to negotiations and, to Clifford's shock, had taken himself out of the running for renomination.

In the months that followed, Clifford had begun to see more and more examples of the President's behavior that was puzzling, even mystifying. First it was a chill in the air between them, almost as if Clifford's reassessment of the Vietnam approach had been a personal affront to Johnson. It was harder to reach the President, and the invitations to dinner, to a weekend at the ranch, had all but ceased.

And now . . . there was another, darker cloud. What had happened was that an intense split now divided the highest figures in the Johnson administration. Clifford, along with chief Paris negotiator Averell Harriman, was pushing for the fastest possible end to the conflict. (Clifford was particularly dovish, writing in a private memo, "I do not believe we ought to be in Vietnam . . . I think our being there is a mistake. I'm disgusted with it all.")

By contrast, Secretary of State Dean Rusk, White House National

Security Advisor Walt Rostow, U.S. Vietnam Ambassador Ellsworth Bunker, and the military were holding fast to the view that only the use of intense military power would ever bring Hanoi to heel. And more and more, thought Clifford, the President was drifting back to the hawkish side of the argument. ("I think the White House is obsessed with bombing," he'd told a deputy.) He was appalled when Johnson permitted, maybe even encouraged, Rostow to extract a pro-bombing statement from General Creighton Abrams and pass it along to the chairman of the Democratic Convention Platform Committee. He almost became hoarse this past summer trying to talk Johnson out of that secret summit with the Soviet leaders, followed by the lightning trip to the Democratic convention, before the Soviet invasion of Czechoslovakia snuffed out that idea. Clifford still shuddered at the thought of what that would have done to an already fractious Democratic Party.

And all of this, Clifford believed, flowed from one source: the specter of a Robert Kennedy Presidency.

He had never been close to Bobby. Unlike Jack, Bobby was far too hotheaded, far too emotional for someone who held that much power, and who might hold even more. When Bobby and Ted Sorenson had come to the White House in March, proposing a commission to review Vietnam policy as the price of keeping Bobby out of the campaign, Clifford had thought it an unacceptable limit on Presidential power. While he had stayed clear of the fight for the nomination, he had rooted hard for Humphrey. Indeed, he was sufficiently skeptical about Bobby to have wondered just how "spontaneous" that confrontation with the radicals in Chicago had been.

What overrode those feelings was a far more powerful sentiment: Clark Clifford detested Richard Nixon.

His contempt stretched back more than two decades, back to Nixon's willingness, eagerness to assail the patriotism of some of Clifford's friends and colleagues; his silence when Joe McCarthy in effect called General George Marshall a traitor; his attack on Dean Acheson as "the dean of the cowardly college of Communist containment." It deepened when Nixon bathetically invoked his wife's cloth coat and his children's dog in that Checkers speech, and when he piously praised President Eisenhower's return to clean language in the White House (everybody knew Ike cursed like the lifelong military man he was). The idea of Richard Nixon in the White House was an affront to everything Clifford believed about the temperament and character of a President.

And it was because of his disdain, his contempt for Nixon, that Clifford, lying awake in his Bethesda home, was coming to a sickening conclusion: *Lyndon Johnson wanted Richard Nixon to win the Presidency.*

He knew as well as anyone how deep the enmity ran between Lyndon and Bobby. He'd heard the stories of Johnson's darker musings, about Bobby and the TV reporters and the Negroes and the Communists. In the end, Clifford had always thought that Johnson could not stomach the idea of a President Nixon, who'd smeared so many in his own party, who had so little feeling for the very people—black, brown, poor white—whose betterment Johnson saw as his legacy. Even now, Nixon was playing footsie with the Southern segregationists, was drawing on the fear of crime with his attacks on bleeding-heart judges. Now that didn't seem to matter to Johnson. *Nixon is far closer to me on Vietnam than Bobby is,* he'd said more than once, even told Charles Murphy, a key Humphrey aide during the nomination fight, that "it'd be better for the country if Nixon won." In fact, Clifford's feelings were strong enough that when chief negotiator Averell Harriman came back to the United States for a funeral, Clifford had shared with him his growing conviction that the President wanted Nixon to beat Bobby.

And Harriman, the seventy-seven-year-old veteran diplomat, the heir to a great railroad fortune who had been at Stalin's side in World War II, who had sought the Presidency for himself a decade and a half earlier, who had survived and flourished through power struggles at the highest levels of power, shocked Clifford with his response.

In the days since, Clifford kept replaying what Harriman had said. It was at the front of his mind all through this restless night. Johnson had convened a gathering of his Vietnam advisors later that evening, and Clifford did not know what was on the agenda. But he could not shake the feeling that whatever it was, it was designed to make sure that Robert Kennedy would not win the White House . . . which meant Richard Nixon would . . . which meant that the unflappable, imperturbable Clifford would be facing the toughest decision of his life.

. . .

KENNEDY HAD BEGUN this early November day in Newark, New Jersey, flown to Cleveland and Chicago, then to St. Louis before boarding the chartered 707 for the flight to San Francisco and a twenty-four-hour sprint through California. He was rallying the core in the last days of the campaign, risking a return to the frenzy that had surrounded his first days. It was a calculated, necessary risk. It was all coming down to Ohio, Illinois, Missouri, California. He and Nixon would split New England; he would take the Mid-Atlantic states, with only suburban-heavy New Jersey in doubt; Nixon and Wallace would divide the South and the border states; West of the Mississippi was just about solid Nixon, with a chance for him in Colorado and the Pacific Northwest. So the big Midwestern prizes, Ohio and Illinois, the weathervane state of Missouri, and the 40 electoral votes of California would decide it.

That meant a massive, hugely expensive effort to find votes in neighborhoods where turnout was historically low. It meant cluster-bombing neighborhoods with "walking-around" money—$100, $200, $300 a pop—to the assemblymen, council members, district leaders, funeral home directors, ministers, who would provide coffee, a sandwich, car fare to lure voters to the polls—or maybe they'd just pocket the money, no one could know for sure. It meant treading through the minefields of tribal wars in Polish, Irish, German, Jewish, black neighborhoods, ministering to the easily bruised feelings of local power brokers, while shielding the candidate from any association with the business at hand. (Kennedy aides still shuddered at a meeting in New York weeks before the primary, when a local leader asked Kennedy bluntly: "What's in it for me?" and was escorted from the room as Bobby shouted, "Don't you make any deals with him!")

His words were now stripped down; gone were the detailed programs and the crafted rhetoric; now it was the simple skeletal structure of the message: *I think we face significant challenges over the period of the next four years, but I believe we can also make significant progress. I believe we can help end the divisions. I ask for your help, I ask you to stand with me, and heal this country.* Now, as he sat in the forward cabin of the chartered jet, he seemed to be drawing more and more within himself, waving off briefing papers and speech drafts, staring off at . . . nothing.

He's exhausted, the reporters told one another. *He's thinking about Jack. He's thinking about what he'll do if he loses. He's thinking about what he'll do if he wins.*

Those who knew him best had a different idea. From the time a year ago when he had seriously wrestled with the prospect of challenging Johnson for the nomination, Robert Kennedy had been haunted by one reality, one he knew better than almost anyone else: *The President of the United States has enormous power to shape events to his will.* And nowhere was that more obvious than in the arena of war and peace. He had no doubt that, were it not for the Soviet invasion of Czechoslovakia, Johnson would have flown to the Chicago convention, summit agreement in hand, looking for a renomination. His "friends at court" had sent him notes on the President's musings about Richard Nixon.

So as he sat and stared out of the window, Robert Kennedy was not thinking about his brother . . . or about the prospect of victory or defeat . . . or about his plans for a better America.

He was thinking: *I wonder what the son of a bitch is going to do?*

THEY GATHERED in the Cabinet Room on the evening of November 1, the meeting room just off the Oval Office that overlooked the Rose Garden. A portrait of FDR hung over the mantel at one end of the room; a bust of John Kennedy stood in one corner. *Now, there's an irony for the history books,* Clark Clifford thought as he took his seat. Across the table, Dean Rusk and Walt Rostow sat side by side. Around the table sat the other members of Johnson's "Wise Men," the men who had counseled him on the war: retired General Max Taylor, ex–Vietnam ambassador Henry Cabot Lodge, ex–Treasury Secretary Doug Dillon, Supreme Court Justice Abe Fortas, whose elevation to Chief Justice was in serious jeopardy in the Senate. Dean Acheson, Clifford noticed, was not present; the longtime hawk had told the President days earlier that he was done with Vietnam, that it was no longer worth the candle. And UN Ambassador George Ball was gone; he'd resigned out of frustration with the war negotiations, and was out campaigning for Kennedy. Now, as they all stood to acknowledge the President's entrance, Clifford realized that none of those present shared his conviction that the war had to be stopped, and soon. His anxiety deepened when he saw Johnson take a folded piece of paper out of his breast pocket, slip on his spectacles, and begin to read.

"As you all know," he began, "we have been anxious to reach an agreement with North Vietnam on a bombing halt and the beginning of real negotiations. I have also been concerned that an agreement from the North could be part of an effort to deceive me; we know that with the Communists, they frequently do that. What I just must never do, however, is to agree to anything that would jeopardize the safety of the men in the field—whether a total bombing halt, the partial halt I ordered last March, or any other action. I have recently received a communication from our commander in the field, General Creighton Abrams, who has advised me"—he paused to look pointedly at the paper—"who has advised me that he can no longer assure me that his men are not endangered by the cessation of bombing at the nineteenth parallel."

"Mr. President," Clifford interjected, "as Secretary of Defense, I must note that this communication directly violates the chain of command that—"

"Clark," the President said, "as Commander in Chief, I believe I have the authority to request and receive information from *anyone* up or down the chain of command. Now," he said, returning to the paper, "I cannot and will not permit the safety of our fighting men to be put in danger by the continued actions of the North in bringing men and arms into the South under the protective umbrella of our bombing halt. Accordingly, I intend to announce tonight the immediate resumption of bombing. I will be holding a conference call with the three candidates for President, and I will once again urge them not to play politics with our country, and to be awfully sure they know what they're talking about before they throw themselves into the intricacies of these negotiations."

Perfect, Clifford thought. *This is a dagger right at the heart of Bobby's campaign. Wallace is irrelevant; nobody cares what he thinks about Vietnam. Nixon will piously agree to protect our fighting men, which means he can still be as vague as ever. And Bobby is out there with a policy the President and his general says will endanger our troops.*

And Clark Clifford, now certain that President Johnson was determined to see Richard Nixon win the Presidency, now certain that the lives of countless more Americans and Vietnamese were about to be lost in the cause of a domestic political power struggle, did what the wise men who serve Presidents never do.

He got up and walked out of the room.

THEY WERE A CONTINENT away from each other when the news broke, and at opposite ends of the emotional calculus as well. A half hour earlier, President Johnson had told them of his decision on a conference call. For Richard Nixon, moving through Bergen and Essex counties in New Jersey, it was a godsend, putting him on the side of America's armed forces. For Robert Kennedy, campaigning in suburban Los Angeles, it was the strike he had feared from the beginning, the power of the President to shape events to his will. Not only would the resumption of the bombing put him directly at odds with the commanding general, it would surely trigger a massive wave of demonstrations from the most militant, radical protesters. The TV images would dominate the airwaves in the last forty-eight hours of the election.

Kennedy was in the manager's office of the Los Angeles Farmers Market with a handful of campaign aides, waiting to speak to a huge outdoor crowd, when one of his advance men burst in.

"Turn on the TV!" he yelled.

They looked around and saw a ten-inch black-and-white portable with rabbit ears. When they turned it on, the reception was so bad that there were half a dozen blurry figures on the screen.

"Who is it?" Kennedy asked impatiently.

"Clark Clifford!" the advance man said. One of the aides grabbed the set and held it over his head, frantically moving the set back and forth.

"Perfect!" Kennedy said. "Don't move!"

"This decision reflects admirably on the President's willingness to listen, even to change his mind in the face of compelling evidence," Clifford was saying to an auditorium in the Pentagon packed with reporters and cameras. "My hope now is that it can help lead to the just peace we all seek. Thank you," he said, and walked off the stage.

"What did he say?" Kennedy asked. "What did he do?" At that moment, there was a frantic pounding on the door to the manager's office; a dozen reporters were trying to jam their way in.

"Your comment, Senator!" "What's your reaction?"

"I'd be happy to comment, if—this is off the record, please—if someone could tell me what the hell just happened?"

"Johnson changed his mind!" "He's stopping the bombing completely!"

There was a long moment of silence.

"Give me ten minutes," Kennedy said.

In fact, it took the Kennedy campaign half an hour to learn all that had happened. Defense Secretary Clifford had told the President he would resign effective immediately; he would publicly declare that he could not execute a policy he believed would lead "only to more death, more destruction, more war." For the master of the insider game to threaten such a move was not just unheard of; it was near unthinkable. (The last time a Cabinet member had "resigned on principle" was when William Jennings Bryan had quit as Woodrow Wilson's Secretary of State in 1915 to protest Wilson's war policies.) More startling was that Clifford told the President that his two lead Paris negotiators, Harriman and Cy Vance, would also be announcing their resignations—just as Harriman had told Clifford he would do if he thought President Johnson was shaping his Vietnam decisions to help Richard Nixon win the Presidency. ("The very idea of that vile man in the White House chills me to the marrow," Harriman had said.)

And then Clifford had called Richard Nixon directly, telling him in cryptic language that he knew of the dealings between the Nixon campaign and the South Vietnamese government.

"I just cannot believe," Clifford said to Nixon, "that you would have anything to do with undermining your government's negotiations to end this war. . . . I just know that there is no way you would countenance *any* of your subordinates committing what is damnably close to *treason*. So I know I can rely on you to support your President in this effort." Nixon assured Clifford of his complete innocence; then as soon as he rejoined the campaign, he gathered campaign aides John Mitchell, Bob Haldeman, and John Erlichman, and snapped, "When we get to the White House, you guys have *got* to learn how to cover your tracks!"

The President's reversal dominated every front page, every news broadcast on the Monday before Election Day. And all three candidates confined themselves to bromides, telling the nation that *we only have one President at a time.* Had Johnson resumed full-scale bombing, Kennedy would have found himself pushed onto the defensive, pushing back against the perennially potent charge that he was undermining American unity. Thanks to three consummate men of the Establishment, Kennedy would not be heading into Election Day bearing that burden.

SHORTLY BEFORE NOON, on January 20, 1969, the incoming President of the United States walked out onto the Inaugural platform on the East Front of the Capitol. It was cloudy and cool, about 35 degrees, a sharp contrast from the day, eight years ago, when he'd sat on the same East Front platform watching John Kennedy take the oath of office. A massive snowstorm had blanketed Washington the night before, and on Inauguration Day, it had been so cold that a heater had been placed under the podium. (It had started to smoke during Cardinal Richard Cushing's endless invocation.) The sun had been so blinding that Robert Frost could not read the special poem he had written for the day.

The new President could almost hear the television commentators reaching back to 1960, noting how many of those who had been on that platform had returned today: Ike, Johnson, Humphrey, and Nixon, the once and former Vice President. He remembered how incredibly close that 1960 election had been, how it could have been altered by any one of a dozen small twists of fate. As he took his seat, acknowledging the cheers, he smiled at the thought of how close this second Kennedy–Nixon contest had been, and how large the role of simple, random chance:

—If Steve Smith had not been there to repel Sirhan;

—If Eugene McCarthy had not been neutralized before the New York primary;

—If the Soviet Union had not invaded Czechoslovakia just before
President Johnson's attempt to reclaim the nomination;
—If the TV cameras hadn't recorded that confrontation in Chicago;
—If Clark Clifford had not turned so strongly against the Vietnam
policy he had helped to shape.

And as in 1960, it had been another long Election Night. New Jersey's
17 electoral votes fell narrowly into Nixon's column, its heavy suburban
electorate too unsettled by Robert Kennedy's intensity. The major Midwestern states were solid for Kennedy: Michigan, Minnesota, Wisconsin,
and Illinois, where Kennedy's 150,000-vote plurality stilled the idea of
"another stolen election!" In Ohio, concern over John Kennedy's Catholicism had helped Nixon to a comfortable victory eight years earlier; this
time, a huge push by labor put the state on Kennedy's side. He also captured Missouri, a state that almost always went with the winner. There,
as in Ohio, Illinois, and Pennsylvania, TV ads featuring his whistle-stops
through small towns and farm communities proved to be the difference.
In each of those states, the small towns and rural areas had given Kennedy
a surprising share of their votes, replicating the pattern of the primaries,
underscoring what NBC's Charles Quinn had found months earlier: voters
with deep hostility to Negroes and peace demonstrators "willing to gamble
on this man, maybe, who would try to keep things within reasonable order,
and at the same time do some of the things that they knew should really
be done." Elsewhere, the news for Kennedy was bleak: Nixon and Wallace
divided the South, and the Republicans swept the plains and almost all the
mountain West. (Kennedy won only in Colorado, where a thirty-one-year-
old lawyer named Gary Hart led an unprecedented organizing effort.)

In the end, it came down to California, where the voters had revived
Robert Kennedy's campaign, where that campaign, and his life, had almost
ended back in June. In 1960, his brother had lost California by the narrowest of margins, 35,000 votes out of 6.5 million, barely half of 1 percent of the
total vote. Because it was so likely that the state's 40 electoral votes would
decide the outcome, both the Nixon and Robert Kennedy campaigns broke
with tradition and spent Election Day in California. All that day, Kennedy
campaigned one last time through the streets of Watts and South Central

Los Angeles, through the barrios of East Los Angeles, cheering on the enormous lines massing outside the polling places. And that night, as the returns reported the record-high turnouts in the poorest neighborhoods and towns of the state, as the TV analysts explained that their computer models had been rendered worthless by the flood of new voters, that they would have to wait for the votes to be counted, he knew . . .

As KENNEDY GLANCED OVER at President Johnson, seated on the other side of the podium, he grudgingly acknowledged an unaccustomed emotion: gratitude. In the first days after the election, Johnson had averted what could have been something of a Constitutional crisis. He'd invited Kennedy and his closest aides to the White House. The threatened resignations of his Defense Secretary and his Paris negotiators had stunned him, infuriated him, but with the campaign over, the prospect of a division between the present and future President was simply too dangerous to permit—which is why Johnson had Clifford and Harriman at the White House meeting. Johnson began by greeting Kennedy as "Mr. President," then asserting bluntly, *You know, for all our differences, we did have one thing in common: Neither of us wanted the other fellow to occupy this office. But that's yesterday. I'm going to do everything I can to get this war off your back before you take office.* And then he had looked at Kennedy and said, *I need your help. We will get nowhere if Hanoi thinks it can just wait ten weeks and get everything they want from you.*

If Kennedy was at all angered by the implication in Johnson's challenge, he didn't show it, most likely because it was a concern he shared. Indeed, one of the lessons the often-impulsive Kennedy had learned in his White House years was the critical need to imagine yourself in the shoes of an adversary, and to help a potential adversary understand the pressures on you. As Attorney General, Kennedy had often met secretly with Georgi Bolshakov, the Washington head of Moscow's military intelligence unit, to ensure that Moscow fully understood President Kennedy's thinking. It was that ability that had resolved the 1962 Cuban Missile Crisis. Faced with a conciliatory first message from Soviet leader Khrushchev, and a belligerent second one, Kennedy had followed Soviet expert Tommy Thompson's idea, and convinced his brother to reply to the *first* letter ... and as he thought back to those anxious days and nights, he remembered another step he had taken, a step that few in the room, including President Johnson, ever knew had taken place.

In the most dangerous days of that 1962 missile crisis, Robert Kennedy had kept open a back channel to Soviet Ambassador Anatoly Dobrynin, meeting him in Dobrynin's third-floor sitting room of the Soviet Embassy near Dupont Circle, then in Kennedy's massive Justice Department office. In anxious, urgent tones—"I've never seen him like this before," Dobrynin cabled Moscow—Kennedy argued that yes, U.S. missiles would be removed from Turkey in exchange for the removal of Soviet missiles in Cuba, but the U.S. could not publicly acknowledge that because of political considerations. Kennedy had also cautioned Dobrynin that a swift resolution was a matter of supreme urgency, that pressures from the military, and from hawkish politicians, might force President Kennedy's hand if a resolution could not be reached quickly. Kennedy even fed the Soviet paranoia about the right-wing military, vaguely hinting at the possibility of a coup if the military thought that John Kennedy was weakening.

Now the newly elected President reached out to Dobrynin once more, inviting him to his Hickory Hill home, on conditions of the strictest secrecy. Hanoi, he knew, was far closer to Moscow than Peking, given the thousand-year enmity between Chinese and Vietnamese, and given Moscow's significant assistance in arms and materiel to Hanoi. *It is imperative,* Kennedy said, *that Hanoi understands my position. This was a close election. Between Nixon and Wallace, the conservative forces won as many votes as I did. You have been here long enough to understand the risks any President takes in dealing with any Communist country. In some ways, I have* less room *to reach an agreement than Johnson does. In the short term, there will be no agreement that does not preserve the security and independence of South Vietnam, and Hanoi should be under no illusion about my willingness to preserve that independence.* (Left unspoken was the footnote: *If Saigon can't protect itself in two or three years, so be it.*)

That silent sentiment was the same message that George Ball, Robert Kennedy's special envoy to Saigon, delivered to the Saigon government: *Do not make the mistake of thinking Lyndon Johnson can protect you from a negotiated settlement with the North.* But the leaders of that government had already gotten the message, or read the handwriting on the wall. On November 8, General Thieu and Air Marshal Ky resigned as President and Vice President. An interim government was cobbled together, composed of several figures who had led one regime or another since the fall of Ngo Dinh Diem in 1963. At the Paris peace talks, the Saigon government sat with the Americans, and the insurgent National Liberation Front sat with the North Vietnamese.

JUST AFTER NOON, he rose from his seat on the Inaugural platform, shook hands with a beaming Chief Justice Earl Warren ("If I'd had to swear in Nixon, I might have thrown up," the Chief Justice later said), and took the oath of office. He began by breaking precedent, thanking—on behalf of himself and the nation—the President who did so much to make this a more just land. ("I left out the part about how much he did to divide and weaken us," he said to Senator McGovern at the post-Inaugural Capitol lunch.) The speech itself was short, blunt, shaped by Adam Walinsky, Dick Goodwin, and Ted Sorensen, deliberately stripped of any stylistic or substantive link to John Kennedy's 1961 classic. His brother had spoken almost exclusively to the wider world in 1961; President Robert Kennedy was speaking to his own country.

"This is a great nation and a strong people," he said, then deliberately evoked FDR's Inaugural promise to speak candidly. "Any who seek to comfort rather than speak plainly, reassure rather than instruct, promise satisfaction rather than reveal frustration—they deny that greatness and drain that strength. For today as it was in the beginning, it is truth that makes us free . . ."

"Our ideal of America," he said, "is a nation in which justice is done; and therefore the continued existence of injustice—or unnecessary, inexcusable poverty in this most favored of nations—this knowledge erodes our ideal of America, our basic sense of who and what we are. It is, in the deepest sense of the word, demoralizing—to all of us."

When he spoke of the wider world, it was to argue that the world will heed America because "we are a people pursuing decency and human dignity in its own undertakings, without arrogance or hostility or delusions of superiority toward others; a people whose ideals for others are firmly rooted in the reality of the society we have built for ourselves.

"More than three hundred years ago," he concluded, "on a ship sailing to England, John Winthrop gathered the Puritans on the deck and said, 'We must consider that we shall be as a city set upon a hill, and the eye of all people will be upon us.' My fellow Americans, let us climb that hill, and build that city."

("Son of a bitch!" Governor Ronald Reagan said as he watched the speech with his Kitchen Cabinet in his Pacific Palisades home. "'City on a hill'? That's *my* line!"

"Not anymore," grumbled Lyn Nofziger.)

ON INAUGURATION DAY, the new President issued an executive order that went largely ignored in the news of the day, an order proposed by a frequent visitor to Kennedy's Senate office. Daniel Ellsberg was a thirty-seven-year-old ex–combat Marine, ex–State Department civilian in Vietnam. He had then worked for the RAND Corporation, helping compile a series of papers for the think tank that detailed America's conduct of the Vietnam War. Late into the transition, Kennedy had summoned his new foreign policy team and asked them about the papers.

George Ball, the incoming Secretary of State, worried about the release of so many classified documents.

"Hell, George," said his just-appointed deputy, former Johnson aide Bill Moyers. "They classify take-out menus at the Pentagon."

"Besides," said Undersecretary of State Dick Goodwin, "it's a little hard to argue that it's a state secret that we blundered our way into Vietnam." Then he turned to Kennedy.

"You should know, Mr. President, that these papers don't paint a pretty picture of any recent President—including President Kennedy."

"Well," Robert Kennedy said, "maybe we'll get some credit for openness. Besides, if they're like every other government document, people will fall asleep before they're halfway through. The only way they'll become big news is if we try to suppress them."

. . .

ONE OF THE MOST significant acts of Robert Kennedy's Presidency came before he ever took the oath of office (not counting the birth of his eleventh child on December 12, a daughter he and Ethel named Stephanie, after the brother-in-law who had saved his life). The private, very secret conversations with Anatoly Dobrynin at Hickory Hill convinced the Soviet ambassador that Kennedy was serious about his warnings to Hanoi not to rely on his opposition to the war for more favorable peace terms from the American side.

"You must understand the United States," Dobrynin told a group of top North Vietnamese officials at an urgently convened meeting in Hanoi. "The reactionaries *always* have the upper hand. They *always* manage to put the so-called liberals on the defensive. Look what happened back in 1960: Richard Nixon was the most notorious anti-Communist in the land, but it was John Kennedy who called for the overthrow of Castro; it was Robert Kennedy who prodded the CIA into attempts to depose, even kill Fidel; and it was the Kennedy brothers who took the world to the brink of war over those missiles in Cuba, even though they knew they did not really affect the balance of power. Why? For fear of being labeled 'soft on Communism.' Robert Kennedy *told* me if his brother had traded Cuban missiles for their obsolete missiles in Turkey, it would have been political suicide.

"And look at your own country. Johnson ran a 'peace' campaign against that madman Goldwater. And six month later, bombs were falling all over the North. Now? You probably would have been better off if Nixon had won. No one doubts his anti-Communist credentials. He could recognize China and get away with it. But Robert Kennedy *cannot* be seen as making too generous an agreement with you."

Hanoi had listened to Dobrynin, and not just because he had spent six years as Moscow's man in Washington. The Soviet Union was a principal supplier of aid to North Vietnam, and more important, solidarity with Moscow was Hanoi's best protection against China; hostilities between Vietnam and China had stretched back centuries. The leaders of the North had no intention of abandoning their goal of reunification. But if the nearly quarter-century battle had to be extended for a few more years, if an armistice permitted Hanoi to restack arms and replenish its depleted ranks, well, there was simply no way the U.S. would ever find the political will for a second war in Vietnam.

This was not the only way Hanoi signaled that it was indeed attuned to events in the United States. On January 19, after months of opposition to the idea, Hanoi agreed to a standstill cease-fire: "a gesture of goodwill," one Hanoi diplomat told Agence France-Presse off the record. So on the day Robert Kennedy took the oath of office, the guns were stilled, bombs were not raining down on the North, napalm was not torching the hamlets of the South, American TVs were not telecasting images of dead and wounded GIs at the dinner hour.

("It's like that Yankee pitcher Lefty Gomez once said," Ronald Reagan reflected as he watched the Inaugural with close aides at his Pacific Palisades home. "'I'd rather be lucky than good.' Fellas, make sure you cook up a good-luck omen when I take the oath in four years.")

On April 2, an interim peace agreement was announced in Vietnam. It was an unwieldy arrangement, premised on the idea—or fantasy—that Catholics, Buddhists, military commanders, guerrilla warriors, neutralists, ex-colonialists, and staunch Communists could form a governing coalition. No one could say with assurance that the peace would hold. But its impact on the home front was immediate and profound.

By early 1969, the war in Vietnam had exhausted America—not simply with its cost in blood and treasure but in the acrimonious divisions that had torn fathers from sons, brother from brother. Three hundred young men—boys, really—were coming home in body bags every week. Five hundred thousand were under arms 10,000 miles away; hundreds of thousands more lived their lives with a summons to combat hanging over their heads. Millions more were in a state approaching emotional combat. Many Americans were outraged by the refusal of their leaders to ends the conflict with a massive force of arms. *What are all our weapons for if not to pound the enemy into submission? We should win and then get out.* Some had grown to despise their own country so deeply that they were prepared to attack Army recruiting centers, government offices, government-funded research centers, with homegrown bombs.

"There is no telling," wrote columnist Walter Lippmann in April 1969 on the fourth anniversary of the escalation of the war, "what might be happening here at home if the war in Vietnam were to continue. Who would dare look ahead three or four years and confidently measure how much more violent the militant young might grow, how many centers of learning might become armed camps, how repressive the authorities might become in an effort to stem the violence? If Robert Kennedy's luck—and ours—holds, we will, thank God, not have to ponder this bleak future."

Had Walter Lippmann focused on Vietnam's next-door neighbor, his relief at what the war's end had prevented would have been far more profound. For years, Cambodia's mercurial, thoroughly manipulative leader, Prince Norodim Sihanouk, had been performing an intricate balancing act among North Vietnamese troops using his country as a staging area, homegrown Communist guerrillas (loosely organized under the "Khmer Rouge" banner), the hard-core anti-Communist Cambodian armed forces, and the U.S. military, eager to attack those North Vietnamese staging areas. As hostilities in Vietnam ceased, so did the pressures on Sihanouk. So when dissident general Lon Nol tried to organize a coup against Sihanouk's government in early 1970, he failed to enlist any backing—official or otherwise—from the Americans.

("I hope everyone remembers the last time the United States sanctioned a coup in Southeast Asia," President Kennedy remarked drily. "If we'd stayed on the sidelines, Diem might have kicked us out before we had a chance to stumble into a land war in Asia.")

With Sihanouk holding on, however uncertainly, to the reins of power, Cambodia became little more than a footnote. Later, when a Khmer Rouge leader named Ieng Sary fled to Thailand, he published an account of the Khmer Rouge's intentions called *Year Zero,* in which he claimed that the movement's chief, Pol Pot, had planned to "wipe out" the "corrupt" educated class of the nation. And if it cost two million lives, Pol Pot was quoted as saying, "That is a cost we can bear." The charges were dismissed by Harvard professor Henry Kissinger as "the delusional rantings of a paranoid."

IN THE UNITED STATES, the timing of the peace accord turned out to be another accident of fate. Across America, hundreds of gatherings had been planned for April 4 to mark the first anniversary of Martin Luther King, Jr.'s murder. In many cities, there was more than a little uneasiness at what those gatherings might trigger. Instead, they turned into solemn celebrations nationwide, marked by tributes to the man who had lost his life in the service of non-violence and justice. (At Kent State University, in Ohio, two leaders of the protest movement, Allison Krause and Jeffrey Miller, announced that a similar gathering would be held on campus every year to mark the end of the conflict.)

President Kennedy announced the agreement in a brief, somber television address. "The victors," he said, "are the young men who will not kill and be killed, the countless innocents, North and South, who will not die in the service of an illusion . . ." White House Press Secretary Mankiewicz was closemouthed when reporters asked what venue Kennedy would choose to commemorate Martin Luther King's death. Their questions were answered late that night when a small press pool was summoned to Andrews Air Force Base, with no further guidance. Twelve hours later, Air Force One and the press and staff plane landed at Tan Son Nhut Air Force Base just outside Saigon. From there, Kennedy and a small press contingent boarded three H-21 transport helicopters, accompanied by two H-1 Huey gunships, for brief visits to four bases across the South. At each stop, Kennedy greeted the men, and spent a few minutes thanking them for their service.

"The war divided our country," he said, "but on this much we are united: America's fighters put their lives on the line because that is what they pledged to do; and it is because we have men like you who keep that pledge, our security is never in doubt. History will judge whether the judgments of your leaders were sound; but you have written your own history about your courage and sacrifice." (Kennedy saw no need to address the other realities of what Vietnam had done to combat morale: the statistics on drug use, the stories of enlisted men attacking their own officers.)

He returned home to an American spring characterized by a collective sigh of relief and weariness. There would be no celebrations of victory, no ticker-tape parades, no iconic photos of young women dashing into the ranks of GIs to plant impassioned kisses. Nor would there be images of American fighting men fading away in silent retreat as an enemy's flag was hoisted in victory. Even as his opposition to the war deepened, Robert Kennedy had said, "We can't just run up the white flag," and he was speaking not just of domestic politics, but of the lessons America's adversaries would take from such a defeat. So the peace agreement was just that: an agreement between adversaries who jointly acknowledged that the costs of violence had grown too high. For ardent proponents of victory—Governor Reagan and General LeMay among them—it was "an ominous moment in American history." For most of the country, it was a welcome end.

(There was one event that did provide a moment of high drama; on April 28, the first contingent of American prisoners of war arrived at Andrews Air Force Base aboard a U.S. military transport. Leading them out of the plane was Lieutenant Commander John S. McCain III, a thirty-two-year-old naval pilot who had been the target of intense physical abuse—torture, really—when he refused to accept early release after the North Vietnam learned that his father was an admiral who had command over all U.S. forces in Vietnam. Three weeks later, as McCain mingled with the other freed POWs at a White House reception, he was summoned by a protocol officer into the Blue Room, where President Kennedy was seated with Admiral McCain, whom he had ordered home from his command.

"I have a feeling you two might want to get reacquainted," the President said. He started to walk out of the room, stopped, and said to the younger McCain, "When you're up and around, I'd like you to come into the White House and help me make sure the Vietnam vets get what they deserve." It would be the start of McCain's career as the Democratic Party's most formidable spokesman on military matters.)

Politics and popular culture joined in 1969 in turning away from the war. *Life* magazine had been working on a major effort to paint the war in starkly human terms: They had planned to run a multi-page spread of the faces of American GIs killed in one week's fighting. When the peace agreement was announced, the editors briefly considered gathering the photos from the last week of war, and then decided, "No one really wanted a last look at it." In Hollywood, director Robert Altman had begun shooting a black comedy about a Mobile Army Surgical Hospital in Uijeongbu, South Korea, clearly intended as an allegory to Vietnam. By the time the film was finished, 20th Century Fox found itself with a fine film that audiences shunned in droves. The movie grossed less than $4 million, and plans for a *M*A*S*H* television series were scrapped. Fox had similar bad luck with its much-anticipated *Patton,* starring George C. Scott as the larger-than-life World War II commander. Audiences, it seemed, simply wanted no part of any story that kept memories of war—any war—alive.

A more significant retreat—and one that strikingly demonstrated the law of unintended consequences—came from America's young. The 1960s had been (simplistically) viewed as a wholesale rejection of the "silent generation" of the 1950s. One of the enduring legacies of John Kennedy's Presidency was the Peace Corps, in which men and women, mostly in their early to late twenties, spent two years of their lives working in distant, impoverished countries. Even for those who never enlisted, there were enduring memories of the long lines of applicants that had snaked through campuses when the Peace Corps recruiters came to call. In 1966, *Time* magazine had chosen the "Under-25 Generation" as its "Man of the Year," proclaiming that "this is not just a new generation, but a new kind of generation, [promising to] infuse the future with a new sense of morality, a transcendent and contemporary ethos that could infinitely enrich the 'empty society.'" Hundreds of commencement speakers had showered praise on the young as "the most idealistic, most committed generation in history."

"What it seems to be turning out," wrote Jimmy Breslin, "was that they were idealistically committed to not getting their rear ends shot off in a jungle."

Not that all that many mourned the decline of the more radical antiwar elements, who marched with flags of the National Liberation Front, who chanted, "Ho, Ho, Ho Chi Minh; NLF is gonna win." When the National Mobilization Committee to End the War called for a demonstration to protest Kennedy's failure to order a unilateral withdrawal, only 3,000 people showed up; that was enough to persuade organizer Rennie Davis to cancel plans for a giant Washington demonstration later in the year.

"As Dylan put it," Davis said, "'you don't need a weatherman to know which way the wind blows.' Right now, there's not even a hint of a breeze." Even Kennedy's refusal to end the draft or to pardon draft resisters failed to stir strong dissent. Without the fuel of a shooting war, without images of American soldiers setting fire to thatch-roofed villages, the fantasies of a violent revolution led by middle-class liberal arts majors dissolved.

(Kennedy was adamant about the pardon issue. "How do you justify that to the millions who obeyed the law?" he asked. Indeed, when one of his very young speechwriters had told him during the campaign that he intended to refuse induction, Kennedy assured him, "I'll see you get treated right; I used to have a lot of influence over the federal prison system. Besides, a lot of the greatest men in history have begun their careers by spending time in jail.")

What also faded was the appetite of the young for *any* engagement with the wider world—unless there was great music, and corollary sensual pleasures to draw them. When Robert Kennedy first heard of plans for a three-day summer music festival in Woodstock, New York, he called in his younger aides.

"Shouldn't we be offering them something else to do with their time? Couldn't we organize a weekend to repair slums, or clean parks, or help fix up some schools?"

After an awkward silence, one of the braver aides spoke up.

"Well, Mr. President, you'd be offering them a choice between three days of hard, exhausting work in the middle of the summer or three days listening to some of the greatest rock bands in the world, along with drugs, and the very real possibility of frequent, uncomplicated sex. I don't think it's a fair fight."

The President nodded, and said, "I hope you realize that you've just made the most powerful argument for keeping the draft. I think we're going to persuade a hell of a lot more young people to sign up for a domestic Peace Corps if there's the chance of basic training in their future."

IN THOSE FIRST WEEKS and months, Robert Kennedy offered a down payment on his Presidency's promise. The issues of race, crime, welfare, poverty, and jobs were like old-growth trees whose roots ran deep and intertwined with one another. What he could offer from the outset were gestures, designed to demonstrate that his administration knew the challenge; and that meant throwing himself personally into the fight.

He began with a speech to a Joint Session of Congress in early February, where he said that "the conditions in the hidden corners of America demand nothing less than a fierce urgency of action, not to right every wrong immediately—that is neither possible nor wise—but to bring hope to millions who have lived without it for too long."

Ten days later, Kennedy embarked on the first of what his aides privately called the *I meant what I said* tours, revisiting some of the places he had visited in his Senate years. In mid-February, he flew into Lexington, Kentucky, a year to the day after he had first arrived in eastern Kentucky as part of a Senate committee hearing. In a one-room schoolhouse in Barwick, at the Letcher County Courthouse in Whitesburg, at the Prestonburg Library, the President brought with him the news that an emergency jobs program would soon put a few thousand unemployed miners to work repairing roads, schools, libraries, and courthouses across Appalachia and up into the southern tier of New York State. ("If anyone thinks it's an accident that President Kennedy's first trip was to a heavily white region," Washington columnists Evans and Novak wrote, "they are no doubt moving their lips when reading this column.")

At the end of February, he set out on a two-day blitz of urban America, beginning in Brooklyn's Bedford-Stuyvesant, where two years earlier he had organized a Community Development Corporation, locally controlled, aided by a blend of public and private resources, designed to rehabilitate housing and inject jobs into the largest black ghetto in America.

"The Community Development Corporation," he had argued in his campaign, "is at the heart of what I believe must happen to restore and renew the blighted neighborhoods of our cities." He took that message to Cleveland's Hough neighborhood, to Southside Chicago (with a not entirely thrilled Mayor Richard Daley in tow), to Detroit's Twelfth Street and Claremont Avenue, where the bloody riots of 1967 had broken out, to the Crenshaw District of Los Angeles. In each neighborhood, he announced the same kind of emergency jobs program he had brought to eastern Kentucky, pointedly noting that these were temporary measures; that only the vigorous, permanent engagement of private enterprise could provide a long-term solution. *And that will be a piece of cake,* he thought as Air Force One flew back from Los Angeles to Washington. *It only took my*

*staff eight months to fight through the turf wars in Bed-Stuy; we should be able
to put a nationwide program in place in, what, twenty-five years?*

IF REVENGE is a dish best served cold, then in the spring of 1969, President Robert Kennedy enjoyed a two-course meal at the expense of one of President Johnson's closest advisors.

For two decades, Washington lawyer Abe Fortas had served as Johnson's personal attorney and confidant. After 1965, when Johnson had all but ordered Fortas onto the U.S. Supreme Court, Fortas had continued to advise Johnson on matters ranging from Vietnam to politics; and on at least one occasion, he had at Johnson's behest tried to persuade his fellow justices to extract information about FBI wiretaps that would likely prove embarrassing to former Attorney General Kennedy. So Kennedy managed to restrain his grief when Johnson's attempt to elevate Fortas to Chief Justice in 1968 failed after Republicans and Southern Democrats mounted a protracted floor fight against him. A mix of Fortas's liberal opinions on civil liberties, his ties to the President, and some eyebrow-raising financial dealings was too toxic a brew.

Now the choice of a Chief was in President Kennedy's hands. The Washington insiders assured each other that the obvious choice was Harvard Law professor and former Solicitor General Archibald Cox; but a mix of political obligation, political advantage, and political fear led Robert Kennedy elsewhere.

Arthur Goldberg had regretted his decision to step down from the high court almost from the moment he had yielded to Johnson's demand in the summer of 1965 that he become Ambassador to the United Nations. To his admirers, Goldberg's move came from a willingness to do anything that might help end the war in Vietnam. To cynics, he made the move because Johnson had sat with Goldberg in the Oval Office and told him, "The man who settles this war will be sitting in this chair, and Arthur, you can settle that war." His tenure had been marked by frustration, by growing dissent from Johnson's Vietnam policy, and by his resignation in the spring of 1968.

Robert Kennedy owed Goldberg; his endorsement in June had been a significant help in the New York primary. There was also a clear political advantage in naming America's first Jewish Chief Justice, and in putting a second Jew on the Court. (A joke quickly made the rounds describing Goldberg's mother responding to the comment, "You must be so proud." "Yes," she supposedly said, "his brother's a doctor.")

There was another dimension to the choice, one that the White House was disinclined to discuss. Goldberg had been telling friends that he was seriously considering a run for governor of New York in 1970 against Nelson Rockefeller. Given Goldberg's minimal political charisma—"I spent a week listening to Arthur Goldberg last night," went one wisecrack— the prospect of Goldberg leading a Democratic ticket in New York was a nightmare no Democrat, those in the White House most especially, wanted to live through.

Goldberg's nomination sailed through the Senate despite halfhearted efforts by some Republicans and Southern Democrats to block the return of the liberal justice. As Georgia's Richard Russell later explained: "The idea of filibustering to stop a Supreme Court nominee would have the Founding Fathers rolling over in their graves."

Just as Goldberg was heading toward confirmation, *Life* magazine revealed that Justice Fortas had accepted a $20,000-a-year-for-life retainer from a financier entangled in legal difficulties. After a highly unconvincing attempt to explain away the arrangement, and under heavy pressure from his fellow justices, Fortas resigned. Once again the insiders assured each other that the choice was clear: Archibald Cox was headed for the High Court. And once again, political calculation pointed elsewhere.

While Democrats held a 58–42 margin in the U.S. Senate, those numbers were illusory; there were a dozen or more mostly Southern conservative Democrats with minimal enthusiasm for Robert Kennedy's domestic agenda. Among Republicans, there was an equal number of moderate, even liberal senators—Javits of New York, Case of New Jersey, Scott of Pennsylvania, Percy of Illinois, Hatfield and Packwood of Oregon—whose support could be critical. Moreover, given Kennedy's lingering reputation as a ruthless political partisan, an early move across party lines made good political sense.

So Kennedy turned to fifty-eight-year-old Californian Thomas Kuchel, whose sixteen-year career in the U.S. Senate had ended when he lost the Republican primary to the zealously conservative superintendent of state schools, Max Rafferty. (That major political event had gone all but unreported since it happened on the same night Robert Kennedy almost died.) Kuchel's GOP colleagues had chosen him as Senate Republican whip, making the thought of a confirmation battle out of the question. The President received muted praise from Republican-leaning newspapers, leaving it to columnists Evans and Novak to note that Kuchel had declined to endorse Nixon for governor, Goldwater for President, and Reagan for governor *after* they had won the party's nominations. ("My kind of Republican!" Kennedy said to his political team, and called Archibald Cox at Harvard to assure him he'd be next—"unless I can find a *really* impressive woman.")

JULY BROUGHT two pieces of good news to the Kennedy administration: one that had been nearly a decade in the making, the other in the form of a providential escape from disaster, both linked to his family.

On July 16, Apollo 11 blasted off with a three-man crew headed for the moon. Commander Neil Armstrong—"You sure his first name isn't 'Jack'?" cracked Press Secretary Mankiewicz—would step off from the lunar module onto the surface of the moon four days later. For Robert Kennedy, it was an event that put the legacy of his brother front and center.

Throughout the 1968 campaign, Kennedy's forces had pushed back against the idea of a "restoration." His advisors winced when they saw signs at rallies calling for "Camelot Again!" After early speeches that invoked Jack's "We can do better" mantra, Kennedy had been at pains to say, "We can't solve the problems of the 1970s and 1980s with solutions out of the 1960s." But the conquest of the moon was different. John Kennedy had embraced the challenge at a time when the Soviet launch of Sputnik had raised real doubts about America's vaunted technological superiority. It was John Kennedy who told a joint session of Congress in 1961: "I believe that this nation should commit itself to achieving the goal, before this decade is out, of landing a man on the moon and returning him safely to the earth." The Apollo 11 Saturn V rocket had blasted off from the Kennedy Space Center on Merritt Island, Florida.

So when the public relations teams from NASA and the White House convened to plan the stagecraft of the spacecraft's mission, Robert Kennedy walked into the Cabinet Room and heard of Armstrong's intention to pronounce, "One small step for a man, one giant leap for mankind." He said: "I've only got one small suggestion of my own: Tell Commander Armstrong that if he does not quote John Kennedy when he steps off the module, he will have to find alternative transportation back home." So when Armstrong walked onto the surface of the moon, he said: "We come here not under a flag of conquest, but under a banner of freedom and peace."

Kennedy watched the moon landing with a profound sense of relief. The risk of failure, or catastrophe, from lift-off to moon landing to return to splashdown, was a constant worry that would have troubled any President. Kennedy's relief, however, was more personal, with no connection to the moon mission. For several days, his brother Ted had been at the Cape to compete in the Edgartown Yacht Club regatta. He'd brought along four of Robert Kennedy's children—and that was what averted a near disaster. On the night of July 18, Ted Kennedy had ferried over to Chappaquiddick Island, to drop in at a party where several White House employees, young women who had bonded in Robert Kennedy's Senate office, were taking their first days off since the Inaugural. Sometime after eleven p.m., Ted Kennedy told the group he was driving back to Edgartown, and one of the women, Mary Jo Kopechne, asked for a ride back. As it happened, two of Robert Kennedy's children were also at the party—which meant that two Secret Service teams were also there. One of the agents, Jesse Colin, leaving on a shift change just moments after Kennedy and Kopechne left, spotted the Senator's car making a turn onto Dike Bridge road, and took off in pursuit; having surveyed the area around the party in daylight, the agent knew how rickety Dike Bridge was. ("I didn't know *what* Teddy was up to," Colin told colleagues later over a drink, "and I didn't want to know. But he was just going too damn fast for that bridge.")

Colin's fears were realized when he saw the 1967 Oldsmobile Delmont 88 plunge into Poucha Pond. Within seconds, the agent stripped to his briefs, dove into the water, and pulled Kopechne and Kennedy out of the car.

The incident might have remained private, except that Deputy Sheriff Christopher "Huck" Look was driving to his home just south of Dike Bridge, saw the flashing lights of Agent Colin's car, and "stopped to render assistance." The resulting police report provoked a spate of rumors and wisecracks, and in the weeks afterward, Massachusetts Republicans plastered their cars with bumper stickers reading: "TED'S ALL WET!"

THEY SAT AROUND the long rectangular table in the Laurel Lodge on a late July morning, summoned to Camp David to talk about The Issue That Dared Not Speak Its Name.

In the Kennedy history, China was far from its finest hour. As a young congressman, John Kennedy was an enthusiastic member of the "Who lost China?" chorus, questioning the patriotism of many of the "old China" hands at the State Department who had doubted the popularity of Chiang Kai-shek, and who were driven out of public life in the wake of Mao's triumph. As President, John Kennedy had dismissed the idea of recognizing the Communist government as unworthy of serious discussion. Nor were the Chinese offering any signals that an accommodation with the West would be welcome. They had scoffed at Soviet Premier Khrushchev's idea of "peaceful coexistence," scorned his retreat during the Cuban Missile Crisis. Mao himself had once said that if half the world perished in a nuclear war that ended with a Communist triumph, those two billion lost lives would be a reasonable price to pay.

By 1969, it was clear that the continued isolation of China from the West was no longer sustainable. With its six hundred million people and its massive army, China would be crucial to any hope of long-term stability in Asia. The more it was excluded, the more inclined it would be to support armed uprisings in the name of "national liberation." By contrast, a China engaged with the West opened up all sorts of possibilities. It could serve as a powerful check on the ambitions of the Soviet Union. And while China was still an impoverished, rural nation, the future prospect of a market that big would put a gleam in the eye of the most ardent capitalist.

The problem, of course, was political. For twenty years, a "China lobby" with a powerful presence in both parties and the media had effectively shut down even the semblance of a debate about China. It was, in fact, a measure of the lobby's power that Kennedy and his advisors had chosen as the site of their conversation one of the most secure facilities on earth.

"You remember what Ben-Gurion told me a couple of years ago?" Senior Counsel Ted Sorenson asked Kennedy.

"Something dramatic, right?"

Sorenson nodded.

"He told me that the peace of the world depended on you being elected President, and then traveling to China in secret to meet with Mao."

"Well," Kennedy said drily. "He's one-for-two. Can you imagine what our Republican friends would say about that? Not to mention *Time* magazine. Talk about a Manchurian Candidate . . ."

Dick Goodwin raised a finger.

"Mr. President, I've been wanting to bring this up, but I've been a bit afraid you'd either laugh me out of the room or have me shipped off to St. Elizabeth's for observation."

"Let me guess," Kennedy said to his Undersecretary of State. "You want to sneak off to Peking and meet with Mao like you did with Che in Uruguay?"

"Not me," Goodwin said. "And God knows not you—you'd be crucified. But"—he took a folded paper out of his jacket—"I'd like you to listen to this."

He began to read:

"'Taking the long view, we simply cannot afford to leave China forever outside the family of nations, there to nurture its fantasies, cherish its hates and threaten its neighbors. . . . In the long run, China must be brought back into the community of nations.'"

"Reasonable enough," said Secretary of State Ball. "Who wrote it?"

"You're not gonna believe it," Goodwin said.

Three months later, on a Thursday morning, Press Secretary Mankiewicz told the White House press corps and the networks that the President would be making "a major announcement" within the hour. Since there had been no hint of any impending appointment or policy change filtering through the White House, the speculation ranged from a White House shake-up to a Supreme Court retirement. No one was prepared for the sight of President Robert Kennedy walking into the East Room . . . with Richard Nixon at his side.

"Last August," Kennedy began, "we received indications from the People's Republic of China that they would welcome conversations with a representative of the United States about matters of interests to both nations. Because of his wide experience in international matters, I asked Vice President Nixon if he would serve as our envoy to Peking, and he graciously accepted. Let me ask the Vice President to report on his conversations."

"Well, gentlemen," Nixon began, flashing his painful grin, "this may not be my *last* press conference, but it is surely the most unexpected."

Then he was all business; detailing the role of Pakistan in acting as an intermediary; his trip to Karachi, ostensibly to negotiate a business deal on behalf of one of his law firm's clients; his flight to Peking aboard a Pakistani military jet; and three days of talks with Premier Chou En-lai, and other leaders of the government. The only revelation more shocking than the invitation to Robert Kennedy to visit China in 1970 were the photographs of Richard Nixon toasting the health of Mao at a private dinner.

"I also had the opportunity to visit some of the historic sites of China," Nixon added. "And I can say that it truly is . . . a Great Wall."

There was an angry response from some in the conservative movement.

"So He Was 'Tricky Dick' After All," read the cover of *National Review*. Barry Goldwater, newly returned to the Senate from Arizona, charged that "Richard Nixon has betrayed six hundred million Chinese, and his own professed principles."

For most Americans, however, the anti-Communist credentials of Richard Nixon insulated Robert Kennedy, especially when Kennedy announced at the press conference that Nixon would be traveling with him to Peking. (Kennedy kept to himself his plan to name Nixon as permanent envoy to China when limited diplomatic relations were established—just about when the '72 campaign was heating up.) Moreover, the sheer boldness of the move won Kennedy applause from some Republican voices. *The Wall Street Journal*, perhaps contemplating the business possibilities of a nation with hundreds of millions of unskilled workers, found comfort in the prospect "that a seasoned, prudent Richard Nixon would be a moderating figure who would, hopefully restrain the more impulsive instincts of the President."

The opening to China and the peace agreement in Vietnam were signal successes, achieved in substantial measure because Presidents always have running room in the international arena. At home, however, the dilemmas facing Kennedy, and his power to resolve them, were tough enough to make Vietnam and China look like walks in the park.

ROBERT KENNEDY HAD COME to the Presidency accompanied by a mass of contradictions. He was born into wealth and power, raised by a father who employed both with remorseless focus. He had spent three years at the right hand of Presidential power. Yet his life as the undersized outsider—the "misfit," as his oldest friend Dave Hackett called him—had attuned him to the pain of power's victims even before the shots in Dallas had driven him into exile. He could absorb into himself the hunger of a child in Mississippi, the deprivation of a migrant worker in New York or California, the need for work of a jobless miner in Eastern Kentucky; but he accepted as his due the luxuries and privileges that exempted him from the routine burdens of ordinary men and women. ("I could do much more," his longtime colleague Ed Guthman once said waspishly, "if I had someone to buy my clothes, pay my bills, do the taxes, watch the children, mow my lawn.")

He spoke to and of the new currents flowing through the cultural life of America in the late 1960s. But while he quoted Bob Dylan, his tastes ran to Broadway show tunes. He listened to Allen Ginsberg chant the "Hare Krishna" in his Senate office, but he quoted Ralph Waldo Emerson and Alfred, Lord Tennyson. He wanted the levers of power in his hands, but in those years with John Kennedy, he had learned what other Presidents had to learn on the job: the limits of knowledge, the illusion of omniscience, the vast distance between intentions and execution, the primal instinct of subordinates to tell the President what he wanted to hear, to shield him from unpleasant realities.

His years in the Senate had given him a chance to think through the hard dilemmas of race and poverty and crime, and his stature had provided him with an army of veterans from his brother's Presidency, as well as another battalion of thinkers and planners who were eager to share their thoughts with the young man who might soon be running the country. But he had also become well acquainted with some of the darker forces in American life: organized crime, a military hungry for conflict, shadowy forces within the government but accountable to no one, all of them forces that powerfully resisted change. Indeed, his father had partnered with organized crime, used its power to help win the Presidency for his son, and Robert Kennedy's own zealous determination to bring down Fidel Castro had led his brother's administration into alliances with gangsters and secret armies—so much so that in the years after Dallas, he was never fully free of the nagging questions that those alliances had somehow led to his brother's assassination. If he could not defeat or at least contain those same forces, he would not be able to do much of what he wished to do.

Just as deep were the conflicts within his political impulses. In 1960, he had fused the disparate elements of the Democratic Party into a mechanism that had—barely—elected John Kennedy. Ivy League intellectuals, big-city liberals and blacks, and Southern segregationists had all been part of that coalition. This year, without the support of Richard Daley and the power brokers in a dozen different states, he never would have been nominated, much less elected. And now, as he assumed the Presidency, the sizable Democratic majorities in the House and Senate would be critical to his success. Yet his time in the Senate had kindled his deep impatience with the pace of politics: the endless talk, the kabuki theater of Congressional hearings, and the narrow focus of the players.

And even this tension did not touch the most serious issue posed by the competing impulses of Robert Kennedy. If his core outlook could be summarized in a single sentence, it would be this: "Get your foot off the other guy's neck." Oppression could come in the form of a right-wing dictatorship, or a Communist apparatchik. It could come from the overseer of a migrant worker, or the multimillionaire CEO whose company was polluting a river, or from a labor union boss who sold out his workers for a payoff or financed the money-laundering schemes of organized crime. It could come from a feral pack that roamed city streets, terrorizing a neighborhood. It could come not from any individual, but from an entrenched system that looked to sustain and enrich itself rather than those it was supposed to serve, whether it be a sclerotic public school system or a callous legal system. As he said to the students at Berkeley in 1966, paraphrasing Camus, "We know now that the color of the executioner's robe matters little."

He would listen to the head of the Office of Education testify about grants to schools, and he would ask, what is happening with the money we've spent? Why do the IQs of Negro children drop between the third and sixth grade? He would quote the Philadelphia head of the NAACP who said that welfare "was the worst thing that ever happened to the Negro," because—as conservatives had argued—it fostered dependency and effectively told the men of the ghetto "we have no useful work for you to do." When he spoke of the crisis of black unemployment, he would argue that "something more is needed" but would add, "let us make clear what 'something more' is not. It is not a massive extension of welfare services or a new profusion of guidance counselors and psychiatrists." But by 1968, welfare workers, guidance counselors, social workers were all part of a growing cadre of public employees who were becoming an increasingly important part of the Democratic Party's base.

In fact, for most of those Democrats who held power in Washington, the thinking was very different from his. Men like Lyndon Johnson and Hubert Humphrey profoundly believed that government was the tool to better the lives of the have-nots, and when a piece of legislation was passed, the battle was over. If you wanted the poor to live better, you passed a bill to spend money on public housing. If you wanted schools to be better, you provided for federal aid to education. If you wanted to offer a measure of security, you created Social Security, Medicare, food stamps. For more than thirty years, since the first days of the New Deal—indeed, from the birth of the modern Progressive movement at the turn of the twentieth century—the expansion of federal power had formed the core DNA of liberalism. The expansion of federal power had come to be seen almost as an end in itself. Moreover, there was a reverse side of this coin. In FDR's Inaugural denunciation of "the money-changers" who had "fled from their high seats at the temple," in Harry Truman's 1948 whistle-stop denunciation of "gluttons of privilege" and "Wall Street reactionaries," to the fights over public power and offshore oil drilling giveaways under Eisenhower, liberals had come to identify private enterprise as an adversary. When Robert Kennedy had first proposed tax incentives to encourage business to bring jobs and housing into the ghetto, a number of liberal senators had objected on principle. We want *public* housing, a *federal* jobs program, they said.

Robert Kennedy's apostasy was often labeled "a move to the right." Without question, Kennedy understood the political danger if the middle class came to view the Democrats as the party of a growing government whose focus was primarily on the poor. Disaffection with big government, however, was increasingly coming from young thinkers on the left, who had formed Students for a Democratic Society before it plunged into fanaticism; from liberal neighborhoods like New York's Greenwich Village, and from radical thinkers like Paul Goodman. In the fall of 1966, speaking to a community college audience in Worthington, Minnesota, he'd deplored the "growth of organization, particularly government, so large and powerful that individual effort and importance seem lost . . ." Robert Kennedy, then, was arguing for a government that took the premise of social justice, and the premise of individual power and responsibility, and fused the two together. It was an approach that could reshape the Democratic Party's coalition; or alienate some of its most loyal foot soldiers—or both.

On October 1, 1969, Robert Kennedy stood on a makeshift stage in Chicago's Union Park on the city's Near West Side. A few blocks away stood the Henry Horner Homes, a public housing project of seven sixteen-story high-rises defined by graffiti, garbage, broken elevators, and bullet holes, and where one in fifty women lived with a husband, where children had grown to adolescence without ever seeing a gainfully employed man, where authority was enforced not by police or citizens, but by the Blackstone Rangers. It was a neighborhood where those in power had long since ceased to measure the high school dropout rate, or the jobless rate, and where the emergency room of the nearby University of Illinois–Chicago Medical Center provided primary health care.

The Secret Service pushed back hard at Kennedy's intention to travel here, but the President had long since decided that it was here where he would present his administration's answer to the crisis of the city. It had taken months of planning, negotiating, angry words, bare-knuckle

bargaining, but for Kennedy, Chicago made sense because of what it represented—and because of who governed it. However odd it may have seemed
that Richard Daley, the symbol of the old order, would preside over a near
revolution in public policy, it made perfect political sense. If you needed
a figure who could persuade, cajole, threaten, push the disparate interest
groups to embark on radically different courses, Richard J. Daley was as
good as it got.

Besides, Robert Kennedy owed his nomination to Daley; and Kennedy
knew that redeeming a marker of this size was the most elemental rule of
political success.

So he came to Chicago to show what he meant when he said, "we must
grasp the web whole" in confronting the ills of the inner city. Here in Chicago, as in every other major city, crime, race, education, health, and jobs
were strands inextricably bound to each other. And here, in front of 15,000
people, a platform filled with wary public officials, a congenitally skeptical
press corps, Kennedy laid out his intentions, all of which stemmed from
one central premise: *Put resources in the hands of the people you are trying to
help, and give them the tools so they might earn those resources.*

He called it "the Police Corps," a concept designed by his legislative
assistant, Adam Walinsky, with a concept that blended the Peace Corps
with the ROTC programs. The federal government would provide full
funding for the college education of low-income high school graduates—
funding channeled through local police forces. In return, graduates would
spend four years working with those local police forces, with their pay—
pegged well below the salaries of regular cops—partially subsidized by
Washington. They could then choose to make a career out of police work
or go on to other fields.

At root, the Police Corps was aimed at a set of interconnected goals:

—It would permit tens of thousands of people without resources to
   go to college, and it would redefine local police authorities as a
   source not just of armed force, but of opportunity.
—It would swell the ranks of local police forces at a far lower cost
   than simply hiring more police; and in the long run, it would
   save even more money, since most of those who served as Corps

participants would leave the force, and not add to the growing burden of long-term health and pension benefits.

—It would diversify the ranks of the police; not just by color, but also by infusing its ranks with the college educated.

—It would, over time, leaven the population of urban neighborhoods with Police Corps veterans, who would have a deeper understanding of law enforcement, and who might lessen the mutual distrust between citizen and police.

For many in the press, Kennedy's ideas posed a challenge: How were they to be characterized? Putting money into jobs and housing and schools was "liberal"; putting greater police presence in the ghetto was "conservative." Housing for the poor was "liberal"; tax incentives for private industry was "conservative."

Confusion in the press, though, was not Kennedy's biggest problem. From the moment he and his team had begun to sketch out these ideas in the first weeks of Kennedy's Presidency, the White House had been taking incoming fire from every direction.

Norman Frank of New York's Patrolmen's Benevolent Association called the Police Corps idea "the opening wedge of an effort to substitute ill-trained amateurs for the full-time, dedicated career officers who are the citizen's only real protection against crime." (Those officers, not so incidentally, would be full-time, dues-paying career members of organizations like the PBA.) Nor were their members thrilled at the prospect of working side by side with college-educated eggheads, or recruits who might well have run with gangs and muggers a few years earlier.

Betty Friedan, president of the newly formed National Organization of Women, told David Susskind's TV audience that "it's not surprising that Bobby Kennedy's 'boys' club,' which has almost no women in decision-making positions, would propose a massive college scholarship program in return for serving in police forces, many of which are either formally or in reality barred to women."

The educational establishment recoiled at another Kennedy notion: permitting young men and women to leave school for required work to help earn money for their families and to nurture a work ethic in communities where jobs had all but vanished. To them, it was an affront to the bedrock principle of universal education. The National Education Association agreed, not least because they feared that if fewer students spent full-time in school, it might mean that cities would need fewer (dues-paying) teachers.

AFL-CIO President George Meany, whose roots were in the craft union movement, where members had handed jobs from fathers to sons for generations, attacked the student-worker idea as "a barely disguised attempt to employ low-wage, dangerously unskilled 'scab' labor in the construction trades. It is shocking that a Democratic President could even suggest so reactionary an idea."

Black nationalists attacked "Massa Kennedy's 'slave labor' program, where young black men are ordered into dead-end jobs at subsistence wages."

There was, however, another, very different reaction, from sources that seemed almost incomprehensible to analysts whose frame of reference was the New Deal–Fair Deal–Great Society tradition. Within the black community, twenty-eight-year-old Georgia State Senator Julian Bond and *Manchild in the Promised Land* author Claude Brown joined more familiar figures like Professor Kenneth Clark in praising Kennedy's vision. Freshman Congressman Allard Lowenstein, who had forged the McCarthy campaign that had stunned President Johnson in New Hampshire, celebrated "a President who actually understands what the last years of protest were about." A surprising number of Republicans gave encouragement; many of the liberal Republicans in the Senate whom he'd courted when he put Tom Kuchel on the Court; governors like Michigan's William Milliken and New Jersey's Tom Cahill, House members like Connecticut's Lowell Weicker, Illinois Congressman Donald Rumsfeld (who saluted Kennedy's willingness to "face the known unknowns and the unknown unknowns of urban policy"), and Houston's George Herbert Walker Bush.

In Louisiana, a young Tulane University graduate student named Newt Gingrich decided to write his master's thesis on "Robert Kennedy's New Paradigm."

What he desperately needed, Kennedy had concluded, was an arena to put his ideas into action. Months of negotiations, bargaining, and deal sweetening had tempered some of the original objections; but in Chicago, Robert Kennedy had a city whose leader—*boss,* as Daley was affectionately and not so affectionately called—could pull the teachers, the cops, the construction unions into line at least enough to give the President's programs a testing ground.

"If you have a taste for irony," *Washington Post* reporter David Broder wrote, "consider that Richard Daley's Chicago, where nineteenth-century political organization still rules, will be Ground Zero for programs that could represent the first real post–New Deal governing philosophy."

"I ALWAYS FELT," his closest friend Dave Hackett recalled much later, "that he'd never be reelected, because the things that had to be done to change the course of the country would be very unpopular."

By the spring of 1970, there was good reason for Robert Kennedy's admirers to share that pessimism and good reason for his opponents to doubt it.

The Gallup and Harris polls gave the President respectable job-approval ratings, but a majority in both polls agreed that his agenda was too ambitious, too likely to raise taxes on the middle class. For all of the White House's attempts to focus on white working-class Americans—making pensions more portable, raising more Social Security funds from the most affluent—the country was divided on whether Kennedy's administration was being too generous to minorities. "Part of that," said Domestic Policy Council head Peter Edelman, "was that when he saw a hungry black kid, or an Indian with no job prospects, his indignation level just leapt into the red zone, and that's what Americans saw on the evening news." The best news for Kennedy was that those who strongly opposed him were outnumbered by those who strongly supported him. That support, however, came disproportionately from the young, the poor, the black, and the brown—precisely those voters least likely to turn out for the impending 1970 midterm elections.

Some of the clouds hovering over the Kennedy Presidency were predictable; indeed, Kennedy himself had cautioned his team about them even before he was sworn in. In South Vietnam, the always-shaky coalition government was increasingly unstable, and Communist insurgents were staging scattered attacks on hamlets and villages, while Hanoi's government was unleashing ominous propaganda attacks on the Saigon government. Governor Reagan, Senator Goldwater, and other prominent Republicans were firing shots across Kennedy's bow, warning the President not to "let North Vietnamese Communist aggression be tempted by weakness from Washington."

At home, there was trouble in the heart of Kennedy's domestic program. While there were clear signs of progress in a number of cities—a new shopping mall in downtown Detroit, visible rehabilitation projects in Brooklyn's Bedford-Stuyvesant—there were also headlines that produced migraine headaches in the Oval Office. The Community Development Corporations were premised on local control at every phase—investment, planning, design, execution, administration—and, to the surprise of no one, black officials, community leaders, and small businessmen proved just as willing to bend or break the rules and the law in pursuit of money as their white forebears had been.

A *Chicago Sun-Times* investigation revealed that the city's Near West Side Renewal Corporation had been heavily infiltrated by the Blackstone Rangers, the gang that had long effectively ruled Chicago's ghettoes. Unsurprisingly, to the more knowledgeable students of the ghetto, some of the most skilled administrators had gained that experience in the gang's far-flung enterprises, and the press did not always distinguish between those who had left their past behind, and those who hadn't. The scrutiny deepened when it was learned that one Corporation spokesman had authored a collection of virulently anti-white, anti-Semitic poems. These revelations frayed the bonds between the White House and Mayor Daley, who regularly called Kennedy aides to assail the flow of money to "a bunch of crooks and subversives. When Bobby told me he'd always respect the Organization, I didn't think he was talking about the Mafia and the Kremlin."

For all of the controversies, the resistance, the setbacks, however, the one that threatened not just his ambitious agenda but his Presidency itself, provided striking proof of one of the oldest adages in politics: *I can protect myself from my enemies, but God save me from my friends.*

· · ·

HE SAT AT HIS DESK in his small, dingy office in downtown Washington on this mid-September night, waiting for the phone to ring. He wasn't waiting for a prospective client to call, because his phone was unlisted. Nor was his name on the frosted-glass door of his office in a building well removed from the Connecticut Avenue palaces that sheltered high-priced law firms and lobbying powerhouses. There were no photos on the wall of him smiling next to powerful politicians or celebrities, no paintings chosen by a decorator with an eye toward impressing visitors about the occupant's taste or wealth. In fact, there were no photos, no paintings, nothing on the wall at all, and the office featured nothing but a battered metal filing cabinet and a simple metal desk, barren but for the single phone and the ashtray overflowing with the butts of Pall Malls. The man who sat at the desk was five and a half feet tall, permanently pale, and he spoke in a voice that sounded as if he gargled every day with gravel. He wore a cheap charcoal black suit—no one had ever seen him wearing anything else—and his oversized black fedora rested on top of the filing cabinet. Nothing about the man, or his office, or his anonymity, was intended to impress a potential client, because he had only one client: the same client he had had for almost ten years.

The road that had brought Paul Corbin into Robert Kennedy's life was long, winding, and paved with dishonorable intentions. He was born Paul Corbrinsky in 1915, the child of Russian émigrés who lived in Manitoba. He entered the United States in 1935—illegally—and reentered it several times after authorities shipped him back to Canada for a raft of misbehavior ranging from con games to assault. He abandoned his first family in New York, moved to the Midwest, where he supported himself in part by threatening businesses with wildcat strikes unless they bought advertising in a union publication, which did not exist. He was an organizer for at least one union that had been expelled from the CIO for its left-wing ties. Corbin himself was—literally—a card-carrying member of the Communist Party, but it was a measure of Corbin's flexibility that by the early 1950s he was a business partner of sorts with the red-hunting Wisconsin Senator Joseph McCarthy. (Corbin would travel to towns where McCarthy was scheduled to speak, selling American flags for the faithful to wave; he and McCarthy would split the profits.)

By 1960, he was a fringe player in Wisconsin Democratic politics, when Pat Lucey, a rising star in the party, brought him into the Presidential primary campaign of John Kennedy. His first meeting with Robert Kennedy was a profanity-ridden exchange of insults; but by the primary's end, Kennedy had come to respect Corbin's political instincts, as well as his highly unconventional approach to organizing. He would bring seminarians to work for the campaign in Protestant towns, but insist they wear sport shirts to hide their Catholic ties. He would introduce the devoutly Catholic Helen Keyes to Protestant voters as "a Baptist lady from Boston." He would make sure that scurrilous anti-Catholic diatribes against Kennedy were seen by Catholic voters. In Stevens Point, he convinced the local priest to ring the church bells on Primary Day to help get out the vote. (When the priest protested that the bells were only rung on holy days, Corbin argued that the election of the first Catholic President would someday be recognized as a holy day; the bells were rung.) Robert Kennedy was sufficiently impressed by Corbin to dispatch him to West Virginia, where he distributed ten-dollar bills like candy, and to New York, where he helped insulate upstate voters from the despised influence of Tammany Hall. By Election Night, Corbin was part of the inner circle that gathered at Hyannis Port to watch the returns.

Paul Corbin wanted nothing more than a nice, cushy sinecure on the federal payroll, enough to insure him a pension; and Kennedy found him a place in the Interior Department. But when a Kennedy aide read the FBI report, it was blindingly clear that there was no way to put him on any government payroll. So he was given a job at the Democratic National Committee. No one could say exactly what he did, but it was clear whom he was doing it for; he even had one of the two keys to Kennedy's private elevator in the Justice Department. It was an unsettling arrangement for many of Kennedy's associates; his Justice Department aide and future Senate office head Joe Dolan called Corbin "the dark side of Bobby Kennedy." Helen Keyes, the faux Protestant, once said, "If you have a job to do, and you want to get it done, and you don't care how it's done, send Paul Corbin to do it." Kennedy's eldest daughter Kathleen (who, like all of Kennedy's children, called Corbin "Uncle Paul") said that while Corbin was "a rascal," her father "appreciated someone who would find out what's going on in the government or in politics, and would be forthright about telling him, so he could have eyes and ears in places that he wouldn't normally have them." His job, then, was to use his preternatural instincts to find out who might be in a position to embarrass the Kennedy administration before their conduct made headlines.

Corbin's devotion to Robert Kennedy was absolute; the Jewish atheist even converted to Catholicism in 1961. And the loyalty was returned, insulating Corbin from the all-but-unanimous distaste of Kennedy's circle, who were frequent targets of Corbin's venom. (One of the items on Robert Kennedy's plate the day his brother left for Dallas in November 1963 was Corbin's charge that White House aide Kenneth O'Donnell was selling postmaster jobs for cash.) It was also the source of the first venomous split between Bobby and Lyndon Johnson in the weeks after Dallas. Early in 1964, Corbin began organizing a write-in "Kennedy for Vice President" campaign in New Hampshire. A furious President Johnson ushered Kennedy into the Oval Office after a Cabinet meeting, and snapped, "Get him out of there. Do you understand? I want you to get rid of him."

"He was appointed by President Kennedy," Bobby said, not entirely accurately, "who thought he was good."

"Do it," said Johnson. "President Kennedy isn't President anymore. I am."

"I know you're President," Kennedy said, before storming out. "And don't you ever talk to me like that again."

When Corbin was ousted from his post a few months later, he was put on the payrolls of the Merchandise Mart, the Kennedy-owned retail giant, and the Joseph P. Kennedy Foundation. And he found his way to insinuate himself into Robert Kennedy's public life in very private ways. In 1964, when New York Democrats kept him out of the Senate campaign, he set up shop across the river in New Jersey, where he installed so many phone lines that the police raided his operation, assuming he must have opened a bookie joint. In 1968, he showed up in California bearing the name of a retired military officer, where he tried to persuade young Kennedy supporters to dress up in outlandish hippie gear and pretend to be Kennedy-hating McCarthy supporters. And when J. Edgar Hoover's long-anticipated bombshells about the Kennedy family failed to appear, more than a few saw the fine hand of Corbin in whatever had persuaded the Director to stay his hand.

When Robert Kennedy won the Presidency, there was no chance, none at all, that Corbin would find any role in the administration, or even in the catacombs of the Democratic National Committee. For one thing, his reputation as a political fixer was too well known. For another, he had burned more bridges than Sherman, spreading dark tales about Kennedy's advisors. However, he was still on the payroll of two Kennedy family enterprises; and more important, he still had the affection and the trust of the one man who mattered. So he rented an office, installed his longtime secretary and an unlisted phone number, and assigned himself the job of protecting the man he loved. He had not been in that kitchen pantry in Los Angeles to save Kennedy's life; that task had fallen to Steve Smith, whose role Corbin deeply envied. Now, with the crucial midterm elections approaching, Corbin was certain that he knew the nature and the source of a different kind of attack; and he was determined to protect Robert Kennedy from it, whatever it took.

IN THE WAKE OF Richard Nixon's loss, the Republican Party concluded that it needed a makeover.

"The face of Richard Nixon cannot be the face of our party," House Minority Leader Gerald Ford told a closed-door meeting of top party leaders in Palm Springs. The gathering quickly settled on a handsome forty-four-year-old congressman from Texas, George Herbert Walker Bush, with impressive credentials: a World War II hero, son of a respected U.S. senator, roots deep in the New England aristocracy, father of five. (There were vague hints that the eldest boy, George W., was something of a hell-raiser at Yale, but as one fund-raiser said, "What family doesn't have its problem child?") When the committee elected Bush as its chair, his speech struck the post-Nixon note that they were looking for.

"I want," he said, "a kinder, gentler Republican Party."

Paul Corbin wasn't buying it, not for a minute—not when Bush hired as the party's policy director a thirty-eight-year-old ex-Marine who had run Nixon's key issues committee, Charles "Chuck" Colson. Corbin's seismograph had kicked into high when he learned from a source inside the Nixon campaign—he always had at least one source in the enemy camp—that Colson was a devotee of political hardball, who was often heard to say, "When you've got 'em by the balls, their hearts and minds will follow." (That was Corbin's own political philosophy as well.) And his suspicions deepened when Colson, in turn, hired a just-retired CIA agent, E. Howard Hunt, who had quit in large measure because he had never forgiven the Kennedys for refusing to topple Castro at the Bay of Pigs.

I know what those bastards are up to, Corbin told himself. *You don't hire men like Colson and Hunt unless you're plunging head first into the dark side.* He didn't know what they were looking for, but it didn't take a man of Corbin's intense, fevered imagination to assemble a list of possibilities:

—Were they looking for the FBI files on President John Kennedy and his after-hours pursuits?
—Was Hunt bringing matters long buried in the CIA files—about whom the government had reached out to in its efforts to remove Castro from power?
—Were they looking for dirt buried deep in the pasts of the new, younger breed of people now being drawn into Robert Kennedy's government?

What he did know was that the only way to protect the President was to find out exactly what Robert Kennedy's enemies were up to. And that's why he was here in his office, on a very late September night, waiting for the call that would tell him he had succeeded.

At ten minutes past midnight, the phone rang. And as soon as he heard who was on the other end of the line, Paul Corbin realized that he was in very serious trouble.

IT WAS during the California primary that Kevin McKiernan first crossed paths with Paul Corbin. The twenty-three-year-old native of Sherman

Oaks had taken a leave from his graduate studies at Georgetown University to work on the Kennedy campaign, and found himself drawn into the orbit of the mysterious operative who seemed to have no clear campaign role. McKiernan was one of the young volunteers who were asked by Corbin to dress up as unwashed street freaks and declare their love of Gene McCarthy and their hatred of Robert Kennedy. McKiernan declined, but was intrigued enough by Corbin to spend late nights over drinks, listening to Corbin's tales of political machinations.

If McKiernan was surprised to hear from Corbin after the election, he was stunned to hear what Corbin was proposing. *I think you should volunteer at Republican headquarters,* Corbin said. *Be a trooper. Work mornings. Work late nights. Run the copying machine. Answer phones. Make yourself useful. Even indispensable.* With a doctored resume listing grunt-level work in Ronald Reagan's 1966 governor's race and Max Rafferty's 1968 Senate campaign, and references that were mail drops, McKiernan was welcomed, and for the next year and a half appeared several times a week at the town house on First Street, just across from the U.S. Capitol. McKiernan would meet with Corbin over dinner at the A and T, an ill-lit, low-priced Italian restaurant a few blocks from the Capitol, to offer whatever intelligence he could provide. It was mostly thin gruel—intra-party feuds, sexual entanglements—until one evening in late summer.

I've been asked to come in late tomorrow for copying and collating, McKiernan said. I don't know exactly what they're preparing, but it sounds like this may be their campaign briefing book for candidates and surrogates. Strictly limited distribution, numbered copies, that sort of thing.

Corbin nodded.

We need a copy.

But . . .

This comes right from the Oval Office. We need a copy.

To veterans of the Kennedy organization, such a comment would have been shrugged off: Corbin was famous for insisting that anything he was asking for came straight from Robert Kennedy. For McKiernan, it had the ring of truth; hadn't Corbin gotten him an autographed picture of Kennedy, with a personal inscription thanking him for his help in California?

At 9:30 on the night of Tuesday, September 15, the last staffer left the building, leaving McKiernan to finish copying and collating the document. He reached for the Minox B camera tucked inside the waistband of his chinos, and began to photograph the document, page by page. It would take him an hour or more, but McKiernan had spent enough nights at headquarters to know that no one would be returning this late at night . . . except that Jennifer Fitzgerald, who had served under Chairman Bush in a variety of positions, and who was now the Committee's Chief of Staff, had forgotten her house keys, and had swung by the office after a working dinner with Bush. Between the noise of the Xerox 914 copier, and his absorption in the work of photographing the document, McKiernan never heard them coming. Thirty minutes later, McKiernan was being grilled by two District of Columbia detectives as an angry George Bush waited in his office. When one of the detectives found a piece of paper in McKiernan's wallet with a local phone number, it took one phone call to a local telephone executive to disgorge the name attached to the number . . . which is why, when the man in the downtown office answered the phone, he was startled to hear the voice on the other end say, "Mr. Paul Corbin? This is Sergeant Paul Leeper of the District of Columbia Police. We'd like to talk with you."

IT WAS another slow night on the city desk of the *Washington Post,* and the twenty-seven-year-old wondered if this was really what he wanted to be doing with his life: monitoring police scanners, answering phone calls reporting flying saucer sightings, taking down details of an obituary notice. Maybe he'd just skip the rest of his two-week tryout. But then a report came in about an arrest at Republican National Committee headquarters, and, with two nightside reporters out with a flu bug, the editor told him to work the phones, maybe get something for the late city edition. A few minutes later, the reporter hung up the phone and looked up at his boss, a thirty-year veteran of Washington journalism.

"Do you know anybody by the name of . . . Paul Corbin?" Bob Woodward asked.

"Hold front!" yelled the editor.

. . .

AT TEN A.M. THE next day, the White House briefing room was thick with reporters, cigarette smoke, and tension. In just about every hand was the *Washington Post*'s front page, folded to the above-the-fold headline that read "A GOP Mole—And a White House Link?" Bob Woodward's story reported that a young volunteer, caught photographing "highly confidential political documents," was found to have in his wallet a phone number belonging to a "longtime ally of Robert Kennedy, whose work has been shrouded in mystery." Paul Corbin, the story said, had been "questioned and released, but D.C. police say there are many unanswered questions about Mr. Corbin's relationship to the young man, who was released on $1,500 bail."

The White House senior staff that had gathered three hours earlier knew what that story would trigger. They quickly assured each other that none of them had had any contact with Paul Corbin. All of the men in the room had heard Corbin declare that "Robert Kennedy wants . . ." "the Attorney General wants . . ." "the Senator wants . . ." And in one way or another, all of the men in the room had been victims of Corbin's accusations of theft, double-dealing, and assorted other betrayals of Robert Kennedy. Indeed, over the years, they and other friends and colleagues had made their doubts about Corbin clear to Kennedy. The problem was that, over the years, they had also received variations of the same answer columnist Rowland Evans had gotten when he urged Kennedy to distance himself from Corbin: "When I want your opinion, I'll ask for it." But if Kennedy's link to Corbin was a mystery, one thing now was clear: for the first time, the scent of political blood was in the air—and there was little doubt about who would be the lead bloodhound. Clark Mollenhoff, the forty-seven-year-old Pulitzer Prize winner, had prodded the young Robert Kennedy into probing union corruption back in 1956. In more recent years, their friendship had soured. It was Mollenhoff who had also investigated John Kennedy's affair with a suspected East German spy, and late in the 1968 campaign Mollenhoff had agreed to join the White House staff if Nixon had won.

When Frank Mankiewicz walked into the briefing room, Mollenhoff was on his feet even before the press secretary had read his statement deny-ing any White House connection to Corbin, and promising the adminis-tration's "full, complete cooperation."

Don't you find it curious that a twenty-five-year-old volunteer at Republi-can headquarters would have the unlisted number of one of the most notorious political operatives in America?

"I haven't yet measured my level of curiosity," Mankiewicz replied.

Within twenty-four hours, an enterprising entrepreneur, seizing on the controversy surrounding a sexually explicit Swedish film import called *I Am Curious (Yellow)*, had printed up buttons and T-shirts reading: "I Am Curious, Bobby." What kicked the story into overdrive, however, was not the merchandising but the stories of Corbin's past—"colorful" was the most neutral description—that began to fill the newspapers over the next two days. Between the veteran Mollenhoff's FBI contacts and Woodward's intelligence sources he'd met during his five years in the Navy, the story gained enough traction for Congress to get into the act. That afternoon, Senator John McClellan called his Government Operations Committee into an emergency closed-door session. The same Senator McClellan had presided over young Robert Kennedy's probe into union corruption thir-teen years earlier, but civil rights and Vietnam had driven the two far apart. McClellan was more than receptive to launching an investigation, as was fellow Southerner Sam Ervin of North Carolina who declared, "I'm just a humble country lawyer, but I know if you see a turtle on a fence post, it didn't get there by accident." That left the committee deadlocked—and then Senator Eugene McCarthy spoke up.

"I ran for President to resist overweening executive power from a Dem-ocratic President," he said, with a smile on his face. "A foolish consistency may be the hobgoblin of little minds, as Emerson said, but so is a foolish inconsistency. I vote aye."

ON THE MORNING OF Tuesday, September 22, an overflow crowd of journalists, Senate staffers, and tourists crowded into the hearing room of the Senate Judiciary Committee on the third floor of the Russell Office Building. There was no live TV coverage of the event, but a thicket of cameras ringed the walls of the room. That morning, the *Washington Post* front page featured a Woodward exclusive: a detailed look into the entire 2,000-page FBI report on Corbin, highlighting his immigration troubles, his links to the Communist Party, his bare-knuckled fund-raising practices, and his labors in the political vineyards. So after the morning session, when Kevin McKiernan described his surreptitious work, the stage was set for an afternoon face-off between the committee and Paul Corbin, in a setting that had provided high political drama for decades. The going assumption was that Corbin would either take the Fifth Amendment, or deny Mc-Kiernan's claims, setting up a "he-said-he-said" clash. What they got was something utterly different.

Corbin strode into the hearing room alone, took his seat at the witness table with no lawyer at his side, and read an opening statement that assailed the committee staff for breaking its own rules by leaking his FBI report to the press.

"I'd like to ask this committee how it can suggest it is looking into 'unethical or illegal behavior in the political process' when it can't control the character assassins in its own ranks. This is McCarthyism, pure and simple." ("I thought he *worked* for McCarthy," said the AP man.) And he volunteered to take a polygraph test to prove his assertion that he had had no contact with the President or any of his staff—an offer that might have been less impressive had the committee known of Kennedy's response years earlier when Defense Secretary McNamara had proposed one for Corbin. ("A *lie-detector*?" Kennedy had said. "He'd break the machine!")

For the next hour, Republicans on the committee demanded to know if Corbin countenanced "political spying."

"Where you draw the line between dirty tricks and hardball and pranks—I don't know," he said. "What about a baseball coach stealing the other team's signs? I *do* know, Senator, that I can *certainly* think of examples where there'd be no question about unethical, immoral, illegal behavior. I mean, imagine a candidate for President who tried to prevent a peace agreement, who wanted to keep a war going that was killing American boys, in order to gain a political advantage. Doesn't that sound like something pretty close to treason, Senator?"

There was a pregnant silence as Mundt looked to his fellow Republicans for a lifeline, as Democrats took up the theme. Perhaps, Senator Ribicoff suggested, the committee's focus might be expanded, to examine alleged unethical or illegal conduct by political operatives on *both* sides. Perhaps, chimed in Senator Fred Harris, the FBI might be asked if they had gathered any intelligence about such behavior, perhaps in the last Presidential campaign. Republican Charles Percy reminded his distinguished Democratic friends that in 1964, the Johnson campaign had planted a spy disguised as a reporter on Barry Goldwater's campaign train.

It was at this point that the counsel for the Republican minority, a thirty-two-year-old lawyer who had recently moved over from the House Judiciary Committee, entered the committee room and exchanged a few, obviously urgent words with an obviously startled Chairman McClellan and Senator Mundt. McClellan declared a temporary recess, and summoned committee members to a private office.

"Counsel for the minority tells me he's just learned some information he wants to bring to your attention. Tell the members what you've learned," the Chairman said. "Go ahead, John."

"Well," said John Dean, "it appears there may be another way of learning whether the White House is involved . . . it seems that there is a taping system inside the Oval Office."

THERE IS NO SUCH thing as political science, but there are tendencies so strong that they might as well be called laws of nature. One of them is that a Congress dominated by one party is highly disinclined to embarrass a President of the same party. So it is impossible to know how the "First Street Caper," as the headlines had it, would have played out had the House and Senate been controlled by Republicans—or, for that matter, had Robert Kennedy and the press had a long history of mutual contempt. Had Republicans held the reins of power in the Senate, they might have demanded a release of all tapes, a standoff between the two branches of government that rose to a Constitutional crisis. So while Chairman McClellan's disclosure made headlines the next day, his announcement was quickly followed by a parade of Democrats, noting that Presidents going back to FDR had engaged in similar practices, and issuing dire warnings about exposing highly classified conversations or endangering the free flow of conversation and advice that Presidents have historically relied on. The White House, secure in its Congressional support, moved to lower the temperature.

"Legally," counselor Fred Dutton said, "it is clear that there are serious questions of executive privilege involved. The President's goal, however, is to cooperate with the legitimate interests of the Congress—and the people— to clear the air and put to rest false rumors and baseless allegations."

So the White House invited two of the most respected members of the Senate, Democrat Phil Hart and Republican John Sherman Cooper, to come to the White House and review "any relevant records and documents." The review showed "no evidence of contact between Mr. Corbin and any White House officials."

("Of course they didn't communicate from the White House!" thundered Roger Ailes, now planning the Republican Party's midterm advertising campaign. "Nobody would be that stupid! Does anyone need any more proof that the networks are all in Bobby's pocket?")

For his part, Corbin pled no contest to a misdemeanor charge of aiding and abetting the unauthorized misappropriation of information. He received a six-month suspended jail sentence, then faded from sight. In later years, there were those who wondered how that reclusive figure with no visible means of support had managed to buy a fourteen-room house on Madison's Lake Mendota.

Bob Woodward stayed on the First Street Caper story, but left the *Washington Post* for law school after the story lost traction. In later years, he joked that he'd someday write a book about the affair called *One of the President's Men.*

HE WAS RESTLESS, energized on this mid-October morning as he flew north on Air Force One. He would spend this noon at a massive rally for the Democratic Senate candidate from New York. No one had thought the party had a chance against Senator John Lindsay, a potential Presidential rival in two years—until Kennedy's two years of importuning paid off: CBS anchorman Walter Cronkite announced he was stepping down as anchor of the evening news to run for the Senate.

His thoughts, however, were on a broader horizon. He had survived two near-deaths—one personal, one political—but the gap between what Kennedy wished to do and what he had the power to do seemed more like a chasm. Even eight years, should he win a second term, seemed like a very short time for the work that needed to be done.

But if things broke right, by the time his Presidency ended, maybe there would be more men and women at work in the broken neighborhoods of the cities, maybe there would be fewer broken families, maybe there would be work that would keep America's small towns from hollowing out. Maybe what happened in that kitchen pantry in a Los Angeles hotel two years ago would someday be seen as the start of something.

And that was the most he could promise.

Maybe . . .

Reality Reset

Steve Smith was not in front of Robert Kennedy when he entered the kitchen of the Ambassador Hotel; no one was. Kennedy died on June 6, 1968.

The Democratic nomination went to Hubert Humphrey in a Chicago where violent clashes between police and demonstrators almost overwhelmed the political story. Despite the deep divisions in the party, Humphrey staged a comeback that ended just short of victory. The election may well have turned on the refusal of the South Vietnamese government to agree to peace talks—a refusal encouraged by sub-rosa contacts between the Nixon campaign and the Saigon government.

There were significant movements on the international front—a Presidential visit to China in 1972, a peace agreement in Vietnam in early 1973, but by 1974, the clouds surrounding the 1972 Watergate break-in at Democratic National headquarters had become a firestorm that drove Nixon out of the Presidency. Gerald Ford, appointed as Vice President less than a year earlier, took over, but he faced not just a heavily Democratic Congress but a fight for renomination within his own party from California Governor Ronald Reagan. Ford barely beat back the challenge, and when the fall campaign began, he was seriously— but not hopelessly—behind.

PALACE OF FINE ARTS, SAN FRANCISCO, CALIFORNIA

— ★ ★ ★ —

OCTOBER 6, 1976, 7:00 P.M.

He stood at the podium, hands lightly gripping the sides; he wore a three-piece gray suit, a tie with a light red pattern, and a placid, calm, controlled, expression. At six feet, 190 pounds, he retained much of the athlete's grace of his younger years, and he was remembering now that same feeling he'd had four decades earlier when his team would begin to move up inexorably on the other guys, when their once-commanding lead began to shrink, when that feeling took hold that was visceral, elemental: *We're going to beat those bastards after all.*

Less than fifty days ago, he'd left the convention battered, bruised, barely surviving what would have been the first time a sitting President had been denied his party's nomination since Chester A. Arthur. He was facing a united Democratic Party already measuring the drapes at the White House. But now, Jimmy Carter's thirty-point lead had shrunk to single digits. Now, it was the Democrats grumbling about their candidate, his inability to connect with the core of his party, the homilies about goodness and honesty beginning to curdle with labor and the liberals, his smile beginning to wear on the undecideds. Now, as it had throughout his life, the same fortune that had taken him into hostile waters seemed to be guiding him to a friendly shore.

> —His mother had fled her abusive husband when he was sixteen days old, leaving Omaha for her parents' home in Grand Rapids, Michigan. Two and a half years later, she remarried, and the boy took his stepfather's name: Gerald Ford, Jr.

—His stepfather was a good man and a good provider, but when it was time for Ford to go to college the Depression was deep, and the father had other children to support. But a small scholarship provided by his high school got him to the University of Michigan, where he washed dishes and sold blood to pay his bills.

—He was a star on two national championship teams, good enough to be courted by the Lions and the Packers, but he chose Yale Law School instead of pro football, and that choice proved to be the key that opened the door to a public life.

—When he served as assistant navigator on the USS *Monterey* in the Philippines in 1943, a violent typhoon almost washed him overboard; his life was saved by a two-inch-high metal railing.

—When he came home to Grand Rapids after World War II ended, the Republicans were looking for a young, internationalist-minded veteran to challenge the hidebound isolationist incumbent. Ford won, and joined the House where others of his generation had just begun to serve, men like John Kennedy and Richard Nixon.

—In 1965, after the Goldwater debacle, the meager ranks of House Republicans were looking for a younger face as the party's voice. So Jerry said he'd run, and ousted Charlie Halleck as the GOP leader. He was now closer to his driving ambition: to be Speaker of the House of Representatives.

—Then in October 1973, Vice President Agnew fled the Vice Presidency, one step ahead of federal prosecutors and a bribery indictment. When President Nixon, with the Watergate waters already up to his waist, asked the Congress for replacement names, they gave him one: Jerry Ford. And he became the first Vice President ever chosen by the mechanism of the Twenty-fifth Amendment. When he was sworn in, the Democratic Speaker of the House, Tip O'Neill said, *Yes, it was an impressive ceremony and we won't see another one like it for . . . months.*

—O'Neill was right. On August 1, 1974, the White House Chief of Staff, Al Haig, came to Ford and said, there's a White House tape . . . it's the smoking gun . . . you need to be prepared. And Ford had come home to Betty, who was packing up for the move into the brand-new Vice Presidential home and said, *Betty, I don't think we're going to be living there after all*

It was such a warm welcome at first. "Our long national nightmare is over," he'd said, and that's how the country behaved. He was a friendly, accessible President, without the palace guard, without the brooding, haunted look of his predecessor. There he was, toasting his own English muffins in the morning! There he was, cleaning up after his dog! Then, a month later, he announced that he would not put the country through a protracted criminal trial of the former President of the United States; he would pardon Richard Nixon. Some day, he knew, his decision would be seen as wise, courageous; but the political cost was enormous. His press secretary quit, and in the Congress and the press, there were dark mutterings about a deal with the devil: *You get the Presidency, Jerry, if you get me off the hook.* There was nothing to it; he'd even gone up to the Hill, testified before committee—a sitting President, when was the last time that had happened, Jefferson?—but the bloom was off the rose.

Then came the nasty stuff, the ridicule. He was the most accomplished athlete to hold the office since Teddy Roosevelt, maybe ever; but every time he slipped on the slopes, or bumped his head, it was all over the news, the photo splashed across every front page. A new late-night comedy show made a star out of a young man—Chevy Chase—who played Ford as an addled idiot. And *New York* magazine produced a cover with a clown sitting in the Oval Office, with the title: "Ladies and Gentlemen, the President of the United States." What made it worse was that the country was going through a bad economic patch, inflation was eating away at savings and some PR genius had come up with the idea of a "Whip Inflation Now!" stunt, with "WIN!" buttons, for God's sake. Between the economy and the Watergate hangover, the Republicans took a pounding in the '74 midterms, leaving Ford facing a Congress almost 2-to-1 against him in the House, and not that much better in the Senate.

And that wasn't the worst of it. Late last year, Ronald Reagan, the former governor of California, had called to tell him, *No hard feelings, but I'm going to challenge you for the nomination next year.* He'd beaten Reagan like a drum early on, just about driven him out of the race, and then with the

help of that wing nut, Senator Jesse Helms, Reagan had won the North
Carolina primary, run up a string of victories and come to the convention
in a virtual tie. It had taken every ounce of Presidential power to hold on:
bringing delegates to White House dinners, showering their states with
federal grants, tossing his own Vice President, Rockefeller, over the side
to feed the conservatives. The nomination had come down to a three-vote
margin in a crucial Mississippi delegation vote, and after he'd won he'd had
to grit his teeth and invite Reagan to the podium to make his own speech.

And yet . . . something began to happen that night after he'd (barely)
won. In his acceptance speech, he'd gone after Carter hard, the way Truman had picked himself up off the floor in '48 and gone after the "do-
nothing 80th Congress," when everyone had pronounced him dead. Ford
declared himself the tribune of middle America: "You are the people who
pay the taxes and obey the laws. You are the people who make our system
work. You are the people who make America what it is. It is from your
ranks I come, and on your side I stand."

And then Ford did something no incumbent President had ever done:
He'd taken the advice of two young aides who worked for Chief of Staff
Dick Cheney and challenged his opponent to debate! And in that first
debate, in Philadelphia, he'd gone right after the soft underbelly of the
Carter campaign—his vagueness, his lack of definition—with a response
he was prepared to deliver no matter what Carter said.

"I don't think Governor Carter has been any more specific than he has
been in the past" were his very first words. Since then, the polls showed
that Carter's eighteen-point lead was down to eight, and for the first time,
he and his team had seen a path to victory.

Not that they'd had any doubt about what they had to do. Two weeks
before the Kansas City convention, his top strategist, Stu Spencer, had presented him with a 120-page battle plan, and begun with this assessment:
"Mr. President, as a campaigner, you're no fucking good!" People know
you're a nice guy, the memo said, they admire you for having calmed the
country down after Watergate, but they think you're indecisive. To win, it
said, we need to bore in on Carter, and the fact that most voters don't really
know what he stands for.

Nor was there any doubt about which group of voters would decide whether Jerry would pull off the biggest upset since Truman. At the convention, adman Malcolm MacDougall had asked Bob Teeter, "What about the Catholics? And the Jews? Doesn't the Baptist thing scare them?"

"We're still not sure," Bob had said. "Maybe. Of course, the Jews are Democrats. You've got to scare the hell out of them to get them to vote Republican. Carter's too smart to do that. But the Catholics are something else. They could be the key to the election. Carter knows it. We know it."

And that, as it turned out, was exactly, precisely right.

And it all turned on a single sentence.

THEY WERE a half hour into this second debate, which was focused on foreign policy, and it was going fine, no slips of the tongue, no egregious factual errors, no flop sweat or stuttering, which was pretty much the only damn thing the press ever cared about. He'd begun with the same out-of-the-chute response he'd given in the first debate, answering Carter's attack on his foreign policy by saying, "Governor Carter is again talking in broad generalities," then charging that Carter's ideas on cutting the defense budget would result in "a weaker defense and a poor negotiating position." He jabbed Carter hard, charging that Carter had said he'd "look with sympathy" on a Communist government in NATO (if Italy voted in a Red government)—it was a stretch, but his campaign knew full well that Italian-Americans, devoutly anti-Communist, had been one of the first Catholic voting blocs to defect from the New Deal coalition.

It was going fine, but he couldn't fully rid himself of the distractions that were buzzing inside his head like a fly at a picnic table. Just a few days ago, he'd had to can Earl Butz, his Agriculture secretary who was wildly popular with the farmers, after a magazine writer revealed that Butz had told an obscene, repellently racist joke (*And who was the magazine writer? John Dean! The guy who told the Watergate committee about "the cancer on the Presidency!" The guy must be planning to make a career out of taking down Republican Presidents!*) And then there was the fact that he was coming to genuinely dislike Carter, whose profession of Christian love could not conceal a mean, spiteful streak; how many times was Carter going to link Ford to Nixon's crimes and misdemeanors?

So maybe he wasn't fully focused when it was Max Frankel's turn to question him. Frankel, an associate editor of the *New York Times* and former Moscow correspondent, took one of Ronald Reagan's central themes from the primary and threw it right at the President:

"I'd like to explore a little more deeply our relationship with the Russians," he said. "They used to brag back in Khrushchev's day that because of their greater patience and because of our greed for business deals, that they would sooner or later get the better of us. Is it possible that despite some setbacks in the Middle East, they've proved their point? Our allies in France and Italy are now flirting with Communism. We've recognized the permanent Communist regime in East Germany. We've virtually signed, in Helsinki, an agreement that the Russians have dominance in Eastern Europe. We've bailed out Soviet agriculture with our huge grain sales. We've given them large loans, access to our best technology, and if the Senate hadn't interfered with the Jackson Amendment, maybe we—you—would've given them even larger loans. Is that what you call a two-way street of traffic in Europe?"

From the command post just offstage, the Ford team of advisors relaxed. He was ready for this one, ready to hit it out of the park. All through the primary, he'd had to push back against Reagan's charge that "Dr. Kissinger and Mr. Ford"—that bastard Reagan knew how much that sounded like "Dr. Jekyll and Mr. Hyde"—had given away the store to Moscow. He'd been drilled on just how to argue that the Helsinki Accords did not accept Soviet domination as a fact of life. It was the perfect question from which to pivot and raise the issue of Carter's utter lack of foreign or defense policy experience.

"If we turn to Helsinki—" Ford began, "I'm glad you raised it, Mr. Frankel. In the case of Helsinki, thirty-five nations signed an agreement, including the secretary of state for the Vatican—I can't under any circumstances believe that His Holiness, the Pope, would agree by signing that agreement that the thirty-five nations have turned over to the Warsaw Pact nations the domination of Eastern Europe. It just isn't true. And if Mr. Carter alleges that His Holiness by signing that has done it, he is totally inaccurate." (*Let's see the peanut farmer explain that to the Catholics!*)

"Now," Ford continued, "what has been accomplished by the Helsinki Agreement? Number one, we have an agreement where they notify us and we notify them of any military maneuvers that are to be undertaken. They have done it. In both cases where they've done so . . ."

And then he added a final flourish, one he meant as a shout-out to the millions of Poles, Czechs, and Hungarians with strong sentimental ties to the Old Country: "There is no Soviet domination of Eastern Europe and there never will be under a Ford administration."

No Soviet domination of Eastern Europe? Did he just say that?

> —In a room just offstage where the Ford high command was watching, Stu Spencer looked over at National Security Advisor Brent Scowcroft. Scowcroft, Spencer said later, "turned white."
> —In another room just offstage, where the Carter high command was watching, Carter's campaign foreign policy advisor Zbigniew Brzezinski whispered, "Thank you, God, thank you, God."
> —In his home in Northbrook, Illinois, Aloysius Mazewski, president of the Polish-American Congress, leapt to his feet. "Is he *insane?*" he bellowed.
> —From an editing bay in St. Louis, where he was working on TV commercials, Doug Bailey stared at the screen and thought to himself: "This is a bad dream—I did not hear what I just heard."
> —And from the pressroom inside the bowels of the Palace of Fine Arts, where dozens of reporters were seated at long tables, watching the debate on TV monitors, came an insistent hum, a murmur that grew in intensity, as a hundred bodies leaned forward, a hundred minds came to the same, sudden realization: *There is blood in the water!*

It was now Carter's turn to respond. But as moderator Pauline Frederick began to call on him, Max Frankel held up his hand.

"I'm sorry," he said, with an incredulous smile on his face. "I—could I just follow—did I understand you to say, sir, that the Russians are not using Eastern Europe as their own sphere of influence in occupying most of the countries there and making sure with their troops that it's a Communist zone, whereas on our side of the line the Italians and the French are still flirting with the possibility of Communism?"

The President began his answer cautiously, as a soldier might walk across a field likely to be infested with mines.

"I don't believe, uh—Mr. Frankel that uh—the Yugoslavians consider themselves dominated by the Soviet Union." (*Okay, safe enough—Tito had broken with Moscow back in 1948.*) "I don't believe that the Rumanians consider themselves dominated by the Soviet Union." (*Okay, Ceaușescu had been drifting steadily away from the Soviets.*) And then . . .

> *And then the light went on in his head. Hearts and minds and souls, they had gone over this a dozen times in the mock debates. Hearts and minds and souls. And he paused and looked at the panelist with a smile.*
>
> *"And, Mr. Frankel—I am the Commander in Chief of the armed forces of the United States. Of course I know that the Soviet Union exercises military control over Eastern Europe; they have four divisions in Poland alone. But that's precisely my point: Why are those troops there? They are there because Moscow knows that if the Poles, the Czechs, the Hungarians were free to choose their destiny, they would never choose the Communist path. They would never embrace a system that stifles dissent, that denies them the right to worship God as their faith decrees. In their hearts and minds and souls, they are not and never will be dominated by the Soviet Union—and while we seek to preserve the peace, a Ford administration will stand with them in their desire for liberty."*
>
> *In the room just offstage, the color came back into Brent Scowcroft's face.*
>
> *In another room just offstage, Zbigniew Brzezinski swore softly.*
>
> *In his home in Northbrook, Illinois, Aloysius Mazesk nodded approvingly.*
>
> *From an editing room in St. Louis, Missouri, Doug Bailey brought his fist down on a table and yelled, "He shoots, he scores!"*

And from the pressroom in the bowels of the Palace of Fine Arts, a
hundred reporters leaned back in their chairs. No harm, no foul.

NO HARM, NO FOUL. It was a passing moment in the debate, one that stirred little comment in the first moments after it concluded. Ford had not, after all, broken new ground by praising the courage and faith of Eastern Europeans who lived under Communism.

And that is exactly why it changed the course of the election.

"All you have to do," said Doug Bailey much later, "is to ask yourself what it would have cost us in momentum and time if Ford had stubbornly insisted on arguing that the Poles and Czechs and Hungarians didn't consider themselves under Soviet domination. Imagine a week of outrage from every Democratic congressman and mayor from Milwaukee and Cleveland and Pittsburgh. Imagine the backbiting from the Reagan camp, all those whispers to the columnists that Ford didn't know what the Soviets were doing, and that Kissinger didn't care. And then we'd have had Ford—whose big campaign argument was that Carter didn't know enough about the world—backing and filling and finally acknowledging, 'Yes, I misspoke.' Thank *God* that didn't happen."

What happened instead were the kinds of conversations, hundreds of thousands, maybe a few million of them, that voters—ordinary people, regular folks, citizens who have jobs and families, whose interest in politics is not a daily obsession—have with each other during every election season. They took place in Ohio, in the butcher shops in German neighborhoods in Cincinnati, in the grocery stores of Toledo, in the chats after Sunday mass in Akron's St. Mary's Church and in Cleveland's St. Stanislaus Church. Others took place in Milwaukee, Wisconsin, in the AJ Polish Deli on West Lincoln, in the beauty shops along National Avenue, in the Italian and Serb enclaves in Lincoln Village, where anti-Communism was an article of faith. A lot of them liked what Ford had said. They had had a moment there when they were ready to believe the President was as clueless as the comedians said, but, no, he knew the score. They weren't sure who they would vote for, but it was good to hear the President say what he'd said about the bastards who had overrun the Old Country.

It was just another ripple in the campaign, one of dozens, hundreds that would alter the flow of the campaign ever so slightly.

And it was exactly the kind of ripple Jimmy Carter's campaign didn't need . . . not at all.

IT HAD BEEN the triumphant night of his life—and it could stand as the symbol of the trouble.

Little more than three months ago, he had stood at the rostrum of Madison Square Garden as 20,000 Democrats, in the sure and certain knowledge of their party's political resurrection, cheered his nomination for President, shouted themselves into a frenzy as he proclaimed, as he had at every speech for almost two years, "My name is Jimmy Carter, and I'm running for President." The words had seemed ludicrous when he began his improbable campaign more than two years earlier. In no other year could a figure like Carter have seriously contemplated a Presidential run. Since the Civil War, no Southerner had ever been elected to the White House. Moreover, the one-term governor of Georgia was so unknown that when he went on the popular game show *What's My Line?* no one guessed his identity—and the panelists weren't blindfolded. When he'd announced his candidacy, the *Atlanta Journal-Constitution* had headlined: "Jimmy Who? Is Running for What?"

What he and his skeletal staff had realized, however, was that in this first post-Watergate election, all the rules of the game were out the window. No experience in Washington? Great—he hasn't been corrupted. No link to the unions, the Democratic Party machines? Yes! A breath of fresh air! He was from a plain, small town in Georgia—in fact, that was the name of his home: Plains. And he lived there, farmed peanuts, taught Sunday school. His whole campaign was built around the iconic American symbol of the lonely stranger, come to save the people. He was Shane, Paladin, the Deerslayer, Gary Cooper in *High Noon*. He would stay not in fancy hotels, but in the homes of supporters, where he'd cook breakfast, make his own bed, carry his own garment bag! In the revulsion over the imperial presidencies of Johnson and Nixon, these gestures—economic necessities—became powerful virtues, even as his Southern roots became in themselves an argument for his candidacy. He rallied liberals to help him dispatch George Wallace in the Florida primary, and his victory there took on enormous significance. The endorsement of Atlanta Mayor Andrew Young spoke volumes about reconciliation between white and black. His homilies—"I want to see us once again have a government as good and honest and decent and truthful and competent and compassionate and as filled with love as the American people" and "I will never lie to you"—were the perfect antidotes to the obscenity-speckled conspiratorial mutterings of the Watergate tapes.

So he had persevered over a weak Democratic field (no Ted Kennedy, not this close to Chappaquiddick; no Hubert Humphrey, who was very ill), and while a late entry by California Governor Jerry Brown had inflicted damage in the primaries, he had won the backing of Chicago Mayor Richard Daley, and the laying on of hands by the symbol of the Old Order clinched it for the Exemplar of the New.

And that was the trouble. Moments after he had told his party, and the nation, "we just want the truth again! . . . It is time for our governmental leaders to respect the laws no less than its humblest citizens," he was surrounded at the podium by the very symbols of the Democratic Party he had defeated: Hubert Humphrey, the New Deal liberal; New York Mayor Abe Beame, the septuagenarian symbol of big-city clubhouse politics; George Wallace, of "segregation forever!" fame; Robert Strauss, Democratic National Chair, the very embodiment of the Ultimate Washington Insider, the honey-voiced sloe-eyed Keeper of the Secrets. It was, at root, a picture fundamentally at odds with the central premise of the Carter campaign: the Lonely Crusader, untainted by the greasy business of wheeling and dealing, the back rooms and marble halls and cushy suites.

Jimmy Carter knew full well what was happening.

"That caused me horrible trouble," he said much later. "I had run a kind of lonely campaign up to the convention; that's my nature and it's part of my political strength. . . . To campaign with local and state candidates not only removed the lonely, independent candidate image depending on the voter only but it was also a reversal of what I had been during the primary season. It contributed to the claim that I was a person of mystery, and that I was fuzzy on things. . . . I never could resolve that question."

Beyond the inherent contradiction of his campaign was an enervating lack of passion among the core elements of the Democratic Party he now led. More than any candidate in memory, Jimmy Carter had run a character-driven campaign: *Vote for me because of who I am, where I come from.* It was, therefore, rootless, unmoored in any familiar ideological terrain. It was not driven by a demand for economic fairness, for an end to an unjust war, for enfranchising the voiceless. And because his campaign was so self-centered—literally—it was almost inevitable that sooner or later, voters began asking, with increasing skepticism, one question: Who is this guy? As columnist Richard Reeves wrote just before the election, "When nobody knows where you've come from, it's hard for people to be confident about where you want to go."

To one key traditional base of the party—the white working-class voters of the Northeast and Midwest—Carter was a stranger, invoking sentiments that rang, if not false, then odd. A "born-again" evangelical was a creature alien to the people of Buffalo, Chicago, Boston, Cleveland, Detroit, Milwaukee. It was not that long ago when others of Carter's region and faith had seen in the candidacy of John Kennedy the hand of the Pope of Rome, the Antichrist. And for all the wattage of his smile, there was in Carter something guarded, suspicious in his interactions with the older Democrats, almost as if he feared the contagion of corruption would infect him should he embrace them too enthusiastically.

And they knew it; they could smell it. In Buffalo, New York, Democratic leader Joe Crangle told reporters the contest in this Democratic stronghold was about even. "We've got our work cut out for us," he said. In Boston, Mayor Kevin White gossiped with reporters about the bad vibes.

"It's not that he's a Southerner," White said. "It's him: he's a very strange guy, and people out there seem to sense it, too."

They were sensing it, too, at Ford headquarters, hints that the same traditional Democratic base that had fled from George McGovern in 1972 over crime, welfare, race, and patriotism might be targets of opportunity again. "Peripheral Urban Ethnics," the Nixon campaign had called them, but everyone knew what that really meant: white Catholics who worked with their hands. These voters had turned hard against the Republicans over Watergate and a lousy economy in the '74 midterms, but now the polling, and the intuition of the insiders, suggested that these Democrats might be giving Ford a second look—enough of them, anyway, to give him a shot. Their response to Ford's wholehearted embrace of Eastern Europe's hunger for freedom convinced the campaign to double down on its message. In mid-October, they added a day to Ford's Ohio schedule; he motorcaded through Akron, Toledo, Cleveland's Sloane Village, recounting the depredations the Soviets had inflicted on Warsaw, Prague, Budapest, and citing the "courageous fight of a Gdansk shipyard worker, Lech Walesa"—he pronounced the name "Letch Walooska," but the audience cheered anyway—"who lost his job for standing up for the rights of workers." On October 21, the day before the third and last debate, Ford flew to MacArthur Airport on New York's Long Island, and drove across the Long Island Expressway to Hempstead in Nassau County, home to hundreds of thousands who had fled the increasingly unlivable city, home to Joe Margiotta's muscular Republican machine. He then journeyed to the city itself, where, a year earlier, after he'd rebuffed a near-bankrupt New York's plea for aid, a *Daily News* headline bannered: "Ford to City: Drop Dead." That night, he went to the Al Smith dinner at the Waldorf, a white-tie-and-tails banquet showcasing the political clout of New York's archdiocese. After the obligatory self-effacing jokes—"If I offer a confession, I know His Eminence will pardon me"—the President concluded with an emotional paean to religious freedom, and recalled the struggle of Hungary's József Cardinal Mindszenty, who had lived for fifteen years in the U.S. Embassy in Budapest after the Soviets had crushed the 1956 uprising.

"He was forced to live fifteen years without breathing fresh air, or walking under blue skies," Ford said. "But one day, with God's help, his descendants will be breathing the fresh air and living under the blue skies of a free Hungary." (A few nitpickers noted that, given the Church's celibacy rules, the Cardinal was unlikely to have produced any descendants.)

"FORD'S ADDING days and money in New York?" a bewildered Hamilton Jordan said at a pre-debate prep the next morning. "This is a diversion, right?"

Pollster Pat Caddell shook his head, and showed Jordan the latest survey from the *New York Daily News* poll: Carter's lead in New York was dwindling, down to mid-single digits. Moreover, under the financial rules of this first post-Watergate campaign, the only way to deal with a threat to a campaign's political base was . . . triage. Each campaign was fueled by $21.8 million worth of public funds. That was it. Period. The lawyers and strategists who lived on campaign mechanics had not yet begun to fashion the loopholes, more like the size of the Lincoln Tunnel, that would permit millions, then hundreds of millions, of dollars to flood the political landscape. If Carter's campaign was in trouble in New York, if resources had to be found for more ads or get-out-the-vote operations, they would have to come from somewhere else. So a total of $50,000 was shifted out of Texas, Pennsylvania, Michigan, and Ohio, and the Carter campaign hoped the relatively small sums diverted from those states would not prove to be critical.

THE EARTH didn't move on Election Day; there were no violent tremors burying a candidate under an avalanche of votes, no stampede of voters leaving the habits of a lifetime to form a new coalition. New York held for Carter, though his two-point win demonstrated that the campaign's decision to move resources into that once-certain state had been a matter of urgent necessity. Wisconsin wound up a virtual dead heat; while a number of Democrats with ties to Eastern Europe had defected, Carter still pulled off a 15,000-vote victory. He swept virtually all of the South, where his appeal to the evangelical community bore fruit; he lost white evangelicals by three million votes, a far better showing than the seven-million-vote loss suffered by Humphrey in the region, and the twelve-million-vote gap that helped bury George McGovern.

What movement there was, in fact, was so slight that no political seismograph could have measured it. It was a series of minor, undetectable shifts that, in most cases, wouldn't have mattered at all . . . but they did this time.

In Ohio, more than four million voters went to the polls. Perhaps three in a thousand voters felt deeply enough about what the Russians were doing to their homelands to have cast their votes for President Ford because he had not stumbled on that issue. Or maybe if that Carter ad buy hadn't been trimmed, those missing ads would have changed that handful of votes. You couldn't even measure so slight a movement . . . except that it was enough to give Ohio to Ford by 12,000 votes and, by that whisper of a margin, 25 electoral votes fell into Ford's column. In Mississippi, 769,000 votes were cast. Maybe 10,000 of them would have gone with Carter instead of Ford had they watched the President spend a week trying to untangle himself from a rhetorical thicket. No such survey could have measured so insignificant a movement . . . except that those 10,000 voters were enough to push Mississippi's seven electoral votes over to Ford.

And with those statistically insignificant shifts in Ohio and Mississippi— 22,000 out of more than eighty million voters—Gerald Ford wound up with 272 electoral votes. Jimmy Carter, who had won the popular vote by one and a half million votes, had 266.

Incredibly, impossibly, Gerald Ford had won.

IN A SUITE on the twentieth floor of Boston's Copley Plaza Hotel, as he waited to celebrate his landslide reelection to the Senate, Edward Moore Kennedy nodded, smiled, and mouthed to an old ally across the room, *Off and running* . . .

In the living room of his ranch in the Santa Ynez Mountains, thirty miles north of Santa Barbara, California, former governor Ronald Wilson Reagan shook his head, and, ensuring that there were no women within range, muttered: *Shit* . . .

And in an office in the catacombs of the Capitol, a freshman senator saw the bulletin, and the first faint wisps of a ludicrous idea drifted into his mind . . .

THE FIRST MEDIA CONSENSUS notes were sounded as soon as Ohio fell into the Ford column, and the networks, one by one, trumpeted the news.

"Not since Harry Truman . . ."

"In the most astounding comeback since Harry Truman . . ."

"Twenty-eight years after an unelected Midwestern President, given up for dead, pulled off the most surprising upset in American history, another unelected Midwestern . . ."

It was a perfectly understandable comparison. But after the first flush of Trumania, a few unsettling facts began to emerge.

In 1948, Truman had won a clear popular-vote plurality, defeating Dewey by more than two million votes. Ford had lost the popular vote, becoming the first President-elect since Benjamin Harrison in 1888 to achieve such a dubious distinction. Within twenty-four hours, the media had begun to throw cold water on Ford's victory.

"Ford Stumbles Again—Back to the White House," read a *Washington Post* headline. More than a few Democrats argued that Ford had no moral right to the Presidency, suggesting that Ford electors be persuaded to vote for Carter, "the real winner." A newly elected twenty-eight-year-old congressman from Tennessee, Al Gore, Jr., announced that his first act would be to introduce a Constitutional amendment to award the Presidency to the popular-vote winner.

"It is indefensible," Gore said, "that a candidate who received the most votes would be denied the Presidency by an archaic, outmoded mechanism, and we must ensure that no future candidate will ever suffer this outrageous injustice."

In 1948, Truman had brought with him solid Democratic majorities in both houses of Congress. Ford, by contrast, would face a heavily Democratic Congress virtually identical to the one that had so frustrated him during the past two and a half years. Without an ability to claim any mandate—*a million more voters wanted the other guy!*—he had neither arithmetic nor political clout, and the Democrats, seething over losing an all-but-certain victory, would be in no mood for amicable, bipartisan cooperation.

Finally, none of the post-election analysis bothered to point out what had happened to Truman in the years following his astonishing comeback. However elevated his stature became in the decades after his Presidency, the four years of Truman's elected term were brutal: an unpopular war, postwar inflation and industrial strife, and an ugly political climate in which the President and his allies found not just their judgment but their loyalty questioned, all conspired to drive his popularity down to historically low levels.

On Election Night, Stu Spencer, one of the architects of Ford's comeback strategy, was standing against a wall in the White House, watching
the jubilation.

"You don't seem all that happy," a celebrant said to him. "This is as good
as it gets!"

"That," Spencer said, "is exactly what I'm afraid of."

AT NOON ON WEDNESDAY, Ford assembled his White House team in
the Cabinet Room, and formally requested that every one of them remain.
It was designed to draw a sharp contrast with Richard Nixon, who on the
day after his 1972 historic landslide, had asked for the written resignations of his entire team. Defense Secretary Donald Rumsfeld and Treasury
Secretary William Simon readily agreed. Secretary of State Kissinger, who
in the preceding two and a half years had threatened to resign somewhere
between twenty-seven and forty-two times, asked for time to consider the
offer; he agreed a few days later, after Ford politely but firmly informed
Kissinger that he would not agree to appointing him as both Secretary
of State and Secretary of Defense. With Brent Scowcroft staying on as
National Security Advisor, the Ford foreign- and defense-policy team represented a dramatic contrast in ideology and instincts from the one President Carter would have brought into the White House. Nowhere was that
more evident than in their response to what happened in one of the most
dangerous regions of the world.

FOR MOHAMMAD REZA Shah Pahlavi, His Imperial Majesty, Shahan-
shah, King of Kings, Light of the Aryans, Head of the Warriors, the surprise victory of President Ford was a blessing . . . and a curse. It meant
that the American President would be surrounded by officials and advisors
who saw in the Shah an invaluable ally, presiding over an Iran that shipped
oceans of oil to an energy-hungry United States, and that protected the
sea-lanes in and around the Persian Gulf from potential threats from the
Soviet Union and anti-American regimes in the region. It also meant that
the American President would be pressed by other high-ranking officials

who saw in the Shah's hunger for higher oil revenues a mortal threat to the economic fortunes of the West, even though that income from oil was crucial to the Shah's fragile hold on an increasingly unstable Iran. It was, the Shah understood, just another chapter in a permanent story of friendship and hostility.

It was the West that had put Reza Pahlavi in power at the start of World War II, and it was the Central Intelligence Agency that had restored him to power in a coup in 1953. U.S. Presidents from FDR to Nixon had embraced him, but under Nixon and Ford the embrace turned almost conjugal. Nixon called the Shah "our best friend." Ford's Vice President, Nelson Rockefeller, whose familial and financial ties with the Shah went back decades, said of him that "he'd soon teach us how to govern America." Secretary of State Henry Kissinger, a close Shah confidant, had said "how much he wished President Ford could emulate his example." This flattery flowed from strategic necessity. The Shah's forces guarded the Straits of Hormuz; his diplomacy made Iran Israel's only ally in the region. (Indeed, Israel's feared intelligence arm, Mossad, helped create the Shah's own secret police force, Savak.)

There was, however, another side to the Shah: a hunger for the huge sums of cash he would need to push, to drag, his country into the twentieth century. He thought his nation hopelessly backward, mired in religious and cultural mores that kept it from its destiny as a great nation. But modernization in Iran had fierce enemies. When, in 1963, the Shah had proclaimed the "White Revolution," promising land reform, votes for women, political rights for non-Muslims, and a literacy campaign in the nation's schools, a sixty-one-year-old cleric named Ayatollah Khomeini had led huge uprisings against the reforms. While the insurrection had been crushed and Khomeini driven into exile in Iraq, the discontent was never far below the surface.

Ironically, one of the Shah's efforts to deal with the discontents only made matters worse. In 1973, when the OPEC cartel launched an embargo against the West because of its support for Israel, the Shah, while refusing to join the embargo, enthusiastically quadrupled oil prices, and poured the money into massive construction projects and an immense arms buildup.

The unintended consequences—a huge population shift to the cities, an influx of foreign workers, the weakening of traditional family life in rural Iran, crushing inflation—combined with growing tension between a more visible Western culture and traditional Iranian customs, meant that by the end of 1976, Iran was on the boil . . . and for the Shah, the most urgent need in order to lance this boil was . . . more money from oil. That determination, in turn, opened up a civil war within the Ford administration.

For more than two years, Treasury Secretary Bill Simon and Defense Secretary Donald Rumsfeld had been at odds with Kissinger over dealings with Iran. For Simon, the huge oil price jump had been the key to the inflation and recession that had helped doom Nixon and that had been one of the biggest obstacles to Ford's reelection. For Rumsfeld, Iran was simply not to be trusted; its military procurement was infested with corruption and was also fueling Iran's dangerous inflation. Kissinger, as he so often did, waged an intense turf war for the heart and mind of President Ford, warning him on August 3, 1976, that "Treasury and Defense are going after the Shah . . . [they] are on a vicious campaign. . . . If we get rid of the Shah, we will have a radical regime on our hands." In this case, however, Kissinger was unsuccessful. The growing tensions between Ford and the Shah over oil prices reached a peak of sorts when the Shah wrote a confidential letter to the President on November 1. It was written with the expectation that Ford would lose to Jimmy Carter; in fact, the Iranian Ambassador was instructed not to deliver the letter until it was clear that Ford had lost.

The Shah's letter, in no uncertain terms, warned that the longstanding bilateral alliance could be ended at a moment's notice.

"If there is opposition in the Congress and in other circles to see Iran prosperous and militarily strong," he wrote, "there are many sources of supply to which we can turn, for our life is not in their hands. . . . Nothing could prove more reaction from us than this threatening tone from certain circles and their paternalistic image."

With Ford's upset win, this highly unsubtle threat to turn elsewhere—perhaps to Moscow?—was never delivered to the President. It did, however, wind up in the hands of the one individual most determined, and most able, to use it to shape the future of the nation . . . and the region.

.   .   .

IT WAS NEW YEAR'S EVE, but Henry Kissinger was in no mood to celebrate. Yes, he would continue as Secretary of State, but it was clear that Defense Secretary Rumsfeld would be a formidable adversary for the ear of the
President. Beyond the battle for turf—always one of Kissinger's obsessions—
was the perilous situation into which Iran was about to be plunged. Two
weeks earlier, in Doha, Saudi Arabia's Sheik Yamani had shocked the delegates to the OPEC meeting by announcing a three-million-barrel-a-day
increase in oil production, a jump that undermined OPEC's plan for big
price increases. It was clear who the Saudi's real target was.

"Yamani went into the OPEC meting intending to stick it to Iran," said
one U.S. observer. "We'll show the Shah who is boss of OPEC." Yamani
made the motive even more clear when he said, "We expect the West, especially the United States, to appreciate what we did."

Officially Kissinger celebrated the Saudi move, but he worried about
what the Saudi gambit would do to Iran's economy and to the prospects
of unrest. The Shah had often shown clear signs of uncertainty in how to
deal with such unrest: cracking down on dissidents with imprisonment and
torture, then loosening restrictions on assemblies and demonstrations. It
was essential to stiffen the backbone of the Shah, to offer clear indications
that, whatever the disputes about oil, the United States simply would not
permit the Shah to fall.

Sometime in the early evening, as the Secretary of State was struggling
into his tuxedo for a night of parties, a State Department messenger came
to his door, and handed him an envelope that had come through a series
of cutouts from a source deep inside the Shah's Niavaran Palace. Kissinger
read it with a growing sense of satisfaction: Whatever troubles the Shah
would encounter in the coming year or two, there was no chance at all that
this administration—the Kissinger–Ford administration—would preside
over the downfall of so crucial a friend.

IT DID NOT TAKE long for Kissinger's fears to become reality. Unrest had
been a more or less permanent part of the Shah's regime, from both the

left and the right. Now, without the flood of oil money that price increases would have bought, Iran's economy suffered a series of hammer blows through the first half of 1977. Cutbacks in arms purchases, suspension of construction projects, the cutting of subsidies to interest groups such as the influential mullahs, all made the fears of experts like political scientist James Bill more and more of an impending realty: "Time is not on the side of the Shah of Iran."

No one, of course, can say what would have happened in Iran had Jimmy Carter won the 1976 election. With no experience whatsoever in foreign policy, Carter would likely have relied on a mix of the Democratic Party's experienced diplomats and academic experts with a wide mix of hawkish and dovish views. Nor can anyone say for sure how Carter's emphasis on human rights would have shaped his policy toward Iran.

With the Ford victory, however, there was no ambiguity.

"Carter had Vietnam angst," Brent Scowcroft said much later. "He thought we had been wrong; he thought America would have to pay a price. I think with Carter, the U.S. would have been on the defense. Ford didn't have any of that. So when we saw what was happening in Iran, all of us thought as soon as the demonstrations broke out, that they had to be nipped in the bud."

If anything, that resolution was strengthened in early January, when Kissinger revealed the contents of the Shah's unsent letter to Ford. For the Shah, Kissinger said, survival of the dynasty overrode anything else. He was telling them in no uncertain terms that he was fully prepared to turn "elsewhere" for support—and if that meant a deal with Moscow, he would do it. The U.S. *had to* convey to the Shah its unconditional support, and give him all the help he needed to restore order.

So in September 1977, when 5,000 protesters gathered at a Muslim shrine in the holy city of Qom to protest a government-sponsored newspaper attack on the exiled Khomeini, and the Shah's troops fired on the crowd, killing twenty, the U.S. government expressed only "regret at the loss of life" and its "firm support for the government of His Imperial Majesty." That unwavering support was repeated when, forty days later, in accord with Muslim tradition, Shiites gathered in several cities to mourn the deaths at Qom, and once again the Shah's troops responded with deadly force, killing more than a hundred. Whatever doubts the Shah may have had about America's support, they were resolved by the strong messages of support—which may be why Reza Pahlavi was finally able to face head-on the most closely guarded secret of his life.

He was dying.

He had known it for years. In 1974, Dr. Jean Bernward, a prominent Paris-based hematologist, received an urgent request from a trainee of his to come to Tehran as soon as possible to examine a patient whose identity he would not reveal but who turned out to be Shah Mohammad Reza Pahlavi, who was bothered by an enlarged spleen. What was really ailing him, a bone marrow test revealed, was chronic lymphocytic leukemia. The Shah refused any more testing, out of fear others would learn of his illness; nor did he follow the doctors' advice to start taking an anti-cancer drug. By 1977, the Shah's physical condition was deteriorating, but a combination of tightly controlled public appearances and a heavily censored press managed to keep that fact largely hidden.

Indeed, the Shah made headlines around the world at the close of 1977 with a lavish New Year's Eve party at the Niavaran Palace, where President Ford, Secretary of State Kissinger, and former Vice President Nelson Rockefeller celebrated the Pahlavi Dynasty. The festivities, however splendid, could not hide the fact of mortality: Sooner, rather than later, he would be gone. And here is where the unremitting support of the Ford administration permitted the Shah to think about an Iran without him.

"There was no way he would have planned for his departure if he thought his most important ally was wavering in its support, or secretly working with his enemies," one high-ranking Ford official said. "I can't imagine what would have happened if Jimmy Carter had been elected, and had begun pushing the Shah on human rights and democracy. It was because Ford was so clearly on his side that the Shah began to really think about succession."

What that official did not know, what only a handful of people knew, was that there was one other element central to the Shah's willingness to turn over power: the elimination of his most tenacious, dangerous enemy— by any means necessary.

.   .   .

FOR ALMOST FIFTEEN YEARS, Grand Ayatollah Imam Sayyed Ruhollah Mousavi Khomeini had been calling for the downfall of the Shah from his home in exile in Najif, Iraq. It was Khomeini who had triggered the first mass uprisings against the Shah in 1963, and even from exile the seventy-six-year-old Khomeini was still an influential figure in Iran and a potential threat to the U.S. strategy in the region. A hostile Iran would be a dagger at the throat of American economic and geopolitical interests.

"It was clear from the beginning," Brent Scowcroft said much later, "that Khomeini was very dangerous."

It was also clear to three closely linked intelligence agencies: Iran's Savak, Israel's Mossad, and America's Central Intelligence Agency, headed by former Texas congressman George H. W. Bush, who had eagerly agreed to stay on after Ford's election. Because of Congressional hearings into CIA practices back in 1975, the Agency was under strict Congressional legislation about how it could deal with adversaries. This did not prevent increasingly urgent communications among Langley, Jerusalem, and Tehran about what Khomeini was saying and doing.

Perhaps it was simply a coincidence that in May of 1978, Khomeini was ordered to leave Iraq at the insistence of an increasingly important official, Vice President Saddam Hussein. It was perfectly plausible to believe the decision flowed from clear Iraqi self-interest: the government was in the hands of Sunni Muslims, despite the fact that Shiites formed a large majority of the population, and the fear of Khomeini stirring up Shiites within Iraq was surely reasonable. Nor was Iraq interested in a diplomatic confrontation with its well-armed neighbor to the East. So there was little reason to ask if there were any other motives behind Iran's insistence that Iraq expel the Ayatollah. It was less clear why French President Valéry Giscard d'Estaing would allow Khomeini to relocate to a comfortable suburban home in the Paris suburb of Neauphle-le-Château, a far more convenient location for journalists from around the world to seek out the cleric. Giscard, after all, had been concerned enough with access to Iran's oil to have made the Shah the guest at his first state dinner after his election as

President in 1974. Perhaps it was Giscard's intention to offer a gesture to the growing population of Muslims now living in France. And perhaps it was that explanation that was offered to the Shah during a visit to Iran by Giscard's personal representative, longtime French politician Michael Poniatowski.

Perhaps these were dots that could have been connected. Perhaps not. What is certain is that on Friday, September 1, 1978, the Ayatollah and two aides were driving in a black Mercedes-Benz 450SEL, heading to the al-Sallam Mosque on the Left Bank. Just as they entered the Pont de l'Alma underpass, the driver lost control of the Mercedes, and it crashed head-on into a pillar supporting the roof. In the confusion just after the crash, wildly conflicting reports emerged: that an unidentified car approached them at great speed and overtook them; that the driver of the Mercedes may have been blinded by flashbulbs from cameras pointed directly at him from the other car; that a person or persons leapt from the other car, briefly approached the Mercedes, then fled. There was one indisputable fact: Ayatollah Khomeini was dead, apparently of a heart attack caused by the trauma of the crash.

Under other circumstances, the death of Khomeini might well have triggered a full-scale civil war in Iran, ending in the violent overthrow of the Shah, and the imposition of a regime that fully embraced a rigid version of Islam, one that sternly rejected any hint of democratic freedoms and a separation of mosque and state. As it happened, the fate of the nation was held in the hands of the man Khomeini had designated as his successor, a man whose lifelong immersion in Islamic scholarship was fused with an outlook utterly different from that of the Ayatollah.

At fifty-eight, the Grand Ayatollah Hussein-Ali Montazeri was almost as prominent and revered a figure among Iranian's Shiite community as Khomeini himself. He had studied under the Ayatollah at Qom, the center of Iranian Muslim scholarship, and more important, had joined in Khomeini's campaign to fight the Shah's 1963 "White Revolution." When Khomeini was exiled, Montazeri became the key figure in the clerical network that continued organized protests against the Shah. He had, in fact, only recently been released from a four-year prison term for his campaign against the Pahlavi Dynasty. His credibility among the disaffected Muslim community was unchallenged. His loyalty to Khomeini, however, did not extend to his vision of a post-Pahlavi Iran. Montazeri leaned toward "quietism," the idea that mere mortals could not establish a "true" Islamic government. He favored a democratic republic, with Islamic jurists proving spiritual and theological guidance; he was fully capable of negotiating with disparate elements of the opposition movement, excluding only the Communists. In spite of these tendencies, and in spite of the fact that he could not claim descent from Muhammad, he had the one asset that could not be trumped: Khomeini himself had designated him as his successor.

Montazeri's first act may have been the most consequential: He "demanded" that the Shah permit the Ayatollah's body to be returned to Iran for burial. That established him even more completely as the voice of religious-based opposition to the Shah (not until years later was it learned that this "demand" had been pre-sanctioned by the Shah's closest advisors). It was, then, seen as a matter of obeisance to theologically sound thinking when Montazeri decreed that Khomeini be buried in Qom, where Khomeini had lived and taught, and not in Beheshit-e-Zahra, a graveyard in the Southern suburbs of Tehran named after the Prophet's daughter.

One U.S. Embassy official, Gary Sick, said, "We all breathed a sigh of relief when we heard the news. A funeral march through the streets of Tehran would have meant millions of Iranians, unhinged by grief and anger; it could have led to anything from mass suicides to mass slaughter of anyone who looked like a Westerner." With the funeral held ninety miles south of the capital, the frenzied crowds that surrounded the body were confined to Qom; they did not spill over into an attack on the nation's power centers. A week later, Montazeri came to Tehran to announce the formation of a broad coalition, including merchants and business leaders, students, and democratic reformers, to demand an end to the dynastic rule of the Pahlavis. In what was a carefully orchestrated sequence, the Shah engaged in protracted negotiations with Montazeri and his new allies, and then announced that he would step down from the Peacock Throne.

Not everyone who had opposed the Shah welcomed this transfer of power. Some of Khomeini's most fervent supporters protested that

Montazeri had "betrayed the Imam" by agreeing to a less-rigid Islamic supervision of a new government. They charged that he had become a "stooge of the Americans and their Central Intelligence Agency." The charge carried some weight, given that the U.S. ambassador to Iran, Richard Helms, had in fact once headed the CIA. And they did more than rally. On September 24, four hundred students, calling themselves "The Muslim Student Followers of the Imam," broke through the gates of the U.S. Embassy and took sixty-five embassy officials hostage. For five days, the students paraded blindfolded Americans in front of the embassy's entrance, demanding the establishment of an "authentic Islamic Republic" under strict obedience to Sharia law. Just as the spotlight of international media was shifting to cover the crisis, Montazeri ordered local police into the embassy grounds to break the siege and free the hostages. Four students were killed in the action, including a twenty-two-year-old student at the Iran University of Science and Technology, Mahmoud Ahmadinejad. It was unclear whether Ahmadinejad was part of the operation or had gone to the embassy to urge that the students end the "un-Islamic action."

(The swift end to the embassy siege had an immediate impact at home. On the third day of the hostage crisis, ABC News President Roone Arledge ordered up a late-night special, called, somewhat portentously, *America Held Hostage,* anchored by one of the network's most accomplished reporters, Ted Koppel. Using satellite technology to conduct simultaneous conversations with Iranian and American officials in Tehran and Washington, the specials won widespread praise. But just as Koppel was concluding the sixth night's broadcast, news came that the hostages were being freed. The program disappeared. Four months later, Koppel left ABC for CNN, where he anchored an hour-long late-night public affairs show; the ABC Entertainment division soon took the 11:30 time slot away from ABC News and filled it with a low-key talk-show host from Cincinnati named Jerry Springer.)

No one pretended that the new Iranian government was a permanent answer for the nation. The tensions among Islamists, political reformers, entrepreneurs, and remnants of the old dynastic order were palpable. Those same tensions, however, helped ensure that no one faction would be strong enough to topple the unwieldy mechanism; which meant that as the 1970s ended, the Ford administration could count several assets that would have vanished had the Shah been toppled by a regime led by Ayatollah Khomeini:

—The new government would need the money from U.S. oil purchases to reach something approaching solvency, so Iran would not use its oil reserves as a diplomatic or strategic weapon.

—Iran and Israel would remain strategic partners; there was no appetite within the ruling Iran coalition for a break with a nation that supplied it with arms and intelligence.

—Nor was there any appetite to make common cause with the more radical forces in the Middle East, now popping up everywhere from Jordan to Lebanon to Syria to the West Bank. When a militant wing of a Lebanese-based political organization, "the Party of God," or "Hezbollah," reached out to the Islamists within the new coalition government, Ayatollah Montazeri and Prime Minister Mehdi Barzagan sternly rejected any notion of tactical or financial support. That rejection, in turn, brought expressions of gratitude from Jerusalem, where the Israeli government began to send signals that continued calm on the West Bank might well lead to "reciprocal gestures" in the form of sharply limiting the growth of settlements.

In this sense, then, those insignificant clusters of Ohio and Mississippi voters in 1976 had been the first link in a chain of events that reshaped the Middle East. Unhappily for President Ford, the escape from a dangerously hostile regime in Iran led to other consequences as well, consequences that would demonstrate the truth of a piece of political folk wisdom: "When you are up to your neck in alligators, it is hard to remember that your objective was to drain the swamp."

FOR EGYPTIAN PRESIDENT ANWAR SADAT, and Saudi Arabia's royal family, the close relationship between the United States and Iran was a source of unease. Washington may have looked at the Middle East as simply one region in the worldwide Cold War, but for Cairo and Riyadh, Iran's role as a populous, well-armed nation of Shiite Muslims was the central fact of life. The 1,300-year-old schism in Islam, rooted in a strug-gle over who could legitimately claim the legacy of the Prophet Muham-mad, along with Iran's potential to dominate the Middle East, ensured that Cairo and Riyadh would instinctively regard its Persian neighbor with wariness, especially since both Arab nations, in strikingly different ways, were pursuing paths that put them a far distance from Iran.

Egypt's Sadat was a modernizer with little use for the customs of Islam. His scorn had earned him the wrath of Islamists, ranging from the Muslim Brotherhood to the younger, more militant students and intellectuals who called themselves the Islamic Brigade. Their leaders, including a medical student named Ayman al-Zawahiri, despised everything about Sadat, and among them, one of the continuing debates was whether to organize an assas-sination attempt against Sadat, or attempt a coup to topple his government.

By contrast, Saudi Arabia was ruled by a family that had long since made its peace with the most rigid, unyielding brand of Islam, one that went under the name "Wahhabi," although the Saud family preferred the term "Salafist." Under an agreement that stretched back decades, the fam-ily had agreed that not only was Islam the only religion to be permitted in the Kingdom—no churches, certainly no synagogues—but that only the Salafist version of Islam would be sanctioned. The rulers even permitted the clerics to operate their own "morals police" to roam the streets of the Kingdom, arresting or beating couples who dared to sit together in public, or women whose dress did not conform to the rigid Wahhabi code.

Given the enmity between the competing versions of Islam, the Saudi rulers might have been pleased when Ayatollah Khomeini was conve-niently removed from the field and that Iran's spiritual life would be guided by the far less rigid Ayatollah Montazeri. That theological issue, however, was more than trumped by the Saudi fears of what a post-Shah Iran, in col-lusion with its American allies, might portend for the region. Reza Pahlavi had made no secret of his belief that he was destined to be the domi-nant force in the Near East. And there were disturbing signs that, with his abdication, the Americans were prepared to indulge the Persians' insatiable hunger for something close to hegemony.

Worse, the continued Iranian partnership with Israel was making it harder for the Saudi Kingdom to maintain its own close ties with Washington. "How," the clerics demanded of the royal family, "can you continue to do the bidding of the Jewish-dominated American government when it favors the Persians?" The key members of the family—King Fahd, Prince Abdullah, Sheik Yamani—had their own grievances. They had saved America from a crushing economic blow at the end of 1976, when they had turned on the oil spigot to undercut the Shah's attempt at a price rise. And this is how the Americans were repaying their kindness? By nurturing the growth of more powerful Iran, by encouraging Tehran's close association with Israel?

Both Egypt and the Saudis took significant steps in 1979 to make clear their displeasure with Washington's Iranian tilt. Sadat stepped back from shaping a full-scale peace treaty with Israel; and with Jerry Ford in the White House, there was no chance that the American President would step in and prod the two sides into an agreement.

"Maybe," Brent Scowcroft reflected, "Jimmy Carter would have been persistent enough, or stubborn enough, to sit down with Begin and Sadat day after day to comb through the details. Ford just wasn't that kind of personality."

So Egypt and Israel remained in limbo: no longer adversaries on the brink of war, but no closer to a partnership in peace. That limbo may well have saved a life. "If Sadat had signed a peace treaty with Israel," Zawahiri said later, "he would have signed his own death warrant. There were a hundred people who would have been happy to pull the trigger."

If Egypt's hesitancy was a moderate diplomatic disappointment, the Saudi action was more like a multi-megaton hit. On May 25, 1979, just as the U.S. travel season was hitting its peak, the Saudis signaled their discontent with American policy by announcing a 20 percent cutback in oil production. What that did to America in the summer of 1979 was captured in striking images of long gas lines, shuttered businesses, major highways jammed with convoys of protesting truck drivers. Beneath the image was a reality even more grim: The oil shock was one more piece of evidence that the ground under some of America's most fundamental assumptions about itself was no longer secure. And that, in turn, would shape the terrain, and the course, of the 1980 Presidential campaign.

.   .   .

JERRY FORD'S SECOND TERM was doomed before it began—literally.

In late December 1976, President Ford and his advisors gathered in the White House Cabinet Room to talk about the agenda for the coming year.

"What we need, Mr. President," said Chief of Staff Dick Cheney, "is to use your Inaugural, your State of the Union speech, and your budget message to present a unified, clear message about your vision for the next four years."

"Excellent," said the President. "So what do I say then?"

That went to the essence of who Gerald Ford was—and was not.

"Just before the '76 convention," Republican adman Doug Bailey recalled, "my partner John Deardourff and I sat down with Ford. One of the things John and I tried to do was to elect a sense of vision. 'If you could wave a magic wand, what would you do?' John and I interviewed the President on tape for hours . . . we tried to get at this question. He just did not think in these terms. He was a wonderful family man, with a great sense of calm, but he could not project where he was going because there was no vision . . . Gerald Ford knew exactly how to deal with Congress, but he had nothing to put in front of them. Maybe Rockefeller could have done that, if he'd stayed as Vice President, but Ford had to dump him to save his nomination . . . and both Ford and Dole were creatures of the Congress. 'What do the leaders want done?' they ask, not, 'What do I want done?'"

It was, as author John Hersey described after spending a week of almost continuous close-hand observation of the President, "almost as if he were letting decisions happen to him."

Yes, Ford was returning to office under the most politically difficult circumstances any President had ever faced. However, even if President Ford had been gifted with a Republican Congress eager to do his bidding . . . if he had been blessed with the vision to make clear what that bidding was . . . if he had won a clear plurality of the popular vote . . . it still would have made no more than a marginal difference. As Senator Sam Ervin of North Carolina noted, in one of those down-home folk-wisdom observations for which the Harvard Law School graduate was famous, "Jerry Ford was caught in the barn when thirty years of chickens came home to roost."

. . .

FOR A GENERATION, post–World War II Americans had been living under what seemed like laws of nature:

—Life grew steadily richer, or at least more comfortable, year by year. In the 1950s, the real income of the average American leapt by 37 percent. Through the 1960s, it grew by 34 percent; and those increased incomes enabled these Americans to enjoy the explosion of consumer wonders once the restraints of wartime ended: televisions, air conditioners, refrigerator-freezers, washer-dryers.

—This ever-increasing affluence was powered by the unbroken economic growth of what was the unchallenged dominant world economy. From the end of World War II through 1970, the U.S. economy grew by an average of 5 percent every year, and the U.S. economy, the only one not ravaged by World War II, was permanently preeminent. "Made in the USA" was a powerful selling point; "Made in Japan" was a joke.

—The value of what the average American saved was insured by a stable, gold-backed U.S. dollar, relatively untouched by the inflation that had ravaged countries from Germany to China. The federal budget, too, was a model of prudence, under Democrats and Republicans. The two decades of the 1950s and 1960s saw budget deficits that averaged barely $5 billion a year.

—The federal government was, if not a partner, then at least an ally in raising the comfort level and the upward mobility of Americans. The GI Bill of Rights had sent millions of veterans to college, making middle-class men and women out of working-class boys and girls. Subsidized mortgages had put this generation into suburban homes, and a massive interstate highway system had linked their work to their homes, enabling them to enjoy the fruits of their labor in comfort undreamed of by their younger selves during the Depression and the war. It was the kind of assistance that persuaded millions that the sentence: "I'm from

the government and I'm here to help" was not the most terrifying
sentence in the English language.

—And each of these certainties combined to form one overarching
certainty: If life had become better for us than it was for our parents, life for our children would be better than it had been for us.

By the late 1970s, every one of those certainties had been knocked into
a cocked hat.

No one could say for sure when it had started, or where it had come
from, for there was no one source; it was a series of assaults, from disparate
sources without and within.

Part of it was the series of shock waves that were not economic at root:
the assassinations, the war in Vietnam, the crimes that drove a sitting President and Vice President from office, the spread of racial and generational
violence, the cultural upheavals that upended a long-established sense of
how life was to be lived, how the young should behave, how safe our streets
were supposed to be.

Part of it was the hidden cost of the Vietnam War, not in lives but in
dollars. President Johnson had sought to win that war on the cheap, neither
divulging its real cost nor asking Americans to pay that cost with taxes. It
was, therefore, "paid" for with cheaper dollars, and the first real contagion
of inflation had begun.

The massive American aid to its defeated enemies, and its decimated allies,
had created a more prosperous world beyond America's borders, and those
nations had begun to compete for the natural resources—coal, oil, minerals,
foods—that were the stuff of affluence. With that competition, the price of
these essentials began to rise. Worse (for America at least), these nations began
to offer cheaper, better products that were once our exclusive domain. Radio
and televisions, appliances of all sorts, began to flood into our ports—even
automobiles, the ultimate symbol of American affluence and mobility, began
to sport odd names: Toyota, Honda, Volkswagen. And as these imports arrived,
good-paying jobs for the skilled and unskilled began to depart. There was more
bad news from abroad: The dollars that flowed into Paris, Bonn, Zurich, and
Tokyo turned into a flood that investors increasingly sought to turn into the
gold that they backed. So threatened was Washington by the potential run on

the dollar that in April 1971, President Nixon took the United States off the gold standard. Currencies were cut loose from their mooring, and the prices of foreign goods, from coffees to automobiles, soared. The only way to appeal to dollar-wary investors was with sharply higher interest rates, which meant that at home, auto loans, mortgages, and cheap credit began to disappear.

And when the international oil cartel struck at the United States for its pro-Israel policies by quadrupling the price of oil in late 1973, the blow was felt everywhere: not just in the massive inconvenience and lost hours waiting in gas lines but in the hundreds of billions of dollars added to the cost of everything from a gallon of gas to a tank of heating oil to the plastics and synthetics in homes and clothes. If modern America had, in effect, been built on a foundation of cheap, abundant petrochemicals, how secure was that foundation if cheap, abundant petrochemicals were a thing of the past?

All of these ills had afflicted America by 1976, and Gerald Ford's response in the two and a half years he spent filling Nixon's second term offered no indication that he grasped the dimensions of what was ailing the American economy. Still, Gerald Ford had managed to retain the Presidency, even if it was the most unconvincing win since Rutherford B. Hayes's "stolen election of 1876." It was a testament to his amiable, unthreatening personality, and testament as well to a nagging sense of doubt about the little-known Georgia ex-governor.

It was, further, testament to the tactical skill of Ford's reelection team, which had managed to convince just enough voters that they were, indeed, "feeling good about America." When Gerald Ford rose on January 20, 1977, and stood where no one expected him to be standing, he tried to reinforce that message.

"I will say frankly that the American people delivered a divided message last November," he said, with a smile. "But there is no doubt that this January, we are united in our confidence that the next hundred years will see a strong, prosperous, united America. Just as the divisions of war abroad, and a Constitutional crisis at home, are behind us, so will the partisan divisions of last year yield to a common effort on behalf of opportunity, security, and a better life for our children." Unfortunately, Ford's attempt at rhetorical flight, an enterprise always fraught with peril, was victimized by a passing exchange at an Inaugural celebration the night before with

Michigan Congressman Guy VanderJagt, who had a reputation as a riveting public speaker. VanderJagt offered Ford one of his most surefire lines,
which the President interpolated into his address without informing any
of his advisors.

"My fellow Americans," Ford's Inaugural concluded, "if there are any
among us who doubt this great nation's capacity to master whatever challenges it faces, let them remember this simple truth: American ends in . . .
I-CAN!"

("That is undoubtedly true," said ABC commentator George Will. "On
the other hand, 'Pelican' also ends in I-CAN.")

Ford tried again two weeks later in his State of the Union speech to a
joint session of Congress, with a dramatic gesture intended to symbolize
his appeal for bipartisanship.

"I am here, Mr. Speaker, with an open mind—and an outstretched
hand." And he turned to face the newly installed Speaker of the House,
Tip O'Neill; unfortunately, having turned to his left and instead of his
right, the President found himself extending his right hand to Vice President Bob Dole, whose right hand was permanently disabled by a World
War II injury.

What became clear within a few months was that even the most finely
honed rhetoric, the most masterful political stagecraft, could not save the
second Ford administration from disaster. The White House and Cabinet
were exercises in dissonance; Treasury Secretary Bill Simon and chief economic advisor Alan Greenspan urged draconian measures to curtail inflation, while Ford's political team warned of the dire consequences of major
budget cuts. The overwhelmingly Democratic Congress pushed to expand
Medicare, Medicaid, aid to education, and tried to ease the pain of inflation by building in automatic increases in Social Security and other entitlements (food stamps, which cost the Treasury $13 million in 1961, cost
more than $12 billion when Ford's term ended). And the world beyond
America's borders, increasingly affluent, with currencies increasingly valuable against the no-longer-invincible dollar, was driving up the cost of . . .
everything.

Tens of millions of Americans, who could remember the days when they would shake their heads at inflation-ravaged nations and take comfort in the dollar that was "good as gold," now began to feel the impact viscerally. With inflation hitting 10 percent or more, their savings would lose half their value in five years; the $400-a-year college education of earlier days had become a $7,000-a-year burden, without counting room and board. The 37-cent gallon of gasoline at the start of the 70s would hit $1.60 by decade's end.

True to his instincts, Jerry Ford tried once again to convince Americans to meet inflation by changing their behavior. In a speech from the Oval Office, Ford sat in front of a fireplace rather than behind his desk, and wore a cable-knit cardigan sweater as he talked of "fighting the oil cartel with your thermostat," and invoked the days when "Mom and Dad would put a few dollars a week into their Christmas Club account at the bank." What Americans were actually doing with their money was what people do when their money begins to lose value: They began to spend it faster.

"'Never buy what you can't afford' was the admonition of our parents," wrote Paine Webber economist Christopher Rupkey in the *New York Times*. "Today, the sentiment has been changed to: 'You can't afford not to buy it.'" And why not? Thanks to the booming business of credit cards, a consumer could buy the big-screen TV, the cutting-edge stereo, the nuclear-powered barbecue grill with a flick of the VISA card, and pay it off with cheaper dollars down the line. In 1975, Ford's first full year in office, American consumers had borrowed $167 billion; by 1979, they were borrowing $315 billion.

And when it came time to pay the money back . . . several million of them found that their jobs had disappeared. Astonishingly, the United States found itself with an economy where the price of everything was spiraling upward, while the economy itself was sputtering.

The automobile industry, which had powered and symbolized America's postwar industrial supremacy, was staggering under the accumulated weight of years of complacency. Years of declining quality, higher prices, and a preference for oversized gas-guzzlers had led to hard times in the early 1970s, when the Arab oil embargo had made the fuel-efficient Nissans and Toyotas attractive to the American buyer. All through the second half of the 1970s, the auto industry was still trying to recover the lost jobs, some 200,000 of them since the decade began. When Americans turned away from cars made here, it wasn't just autoworkers who were laid off; so were the men and women who made steel, tires, windshields, brake linings, upholstery, car radios. When the Saudi squeeze hit in 1979, the American economy was hit in its most vulnerable spot, just as the U.S. auto industry was recovering from the effects of the *first* embargo back in 1973. Americans had begun to turn away from the smaller, fuel-efficient imports, back to the oversized gas-guzzlers of earlier times. When Ford displayed its models for the 1980 year, an executive proclaimed: "Welcome to the year of the Whopper." Now the nightmare began all over again. California took the first hit in May; by June, Florida was running dry. By summer, the gas panic went national, sometimes with fatal results. In Brooklyn, a motorist died in a shoot-out when he tried to cut into a blocks-long line. On weekends that summer, anywhere from half to 90 percent of New York's gas stations were shut for the weekend.

By autumn, Ford was projecting losses of a billion dollars for the coming year; 250,000 cars were cut from its production schedule; seven plants were closed; and from River Rouge to Rawsonville, tens of thousands of workers, from the unskilled floor sweepers to the skilled diemakers and die casters to middle managers, were laid off. And once again, what afflicted the auto industry also afflicted steel, glass, rubber, electronics, travel, finance. With similar hard times coming to construction, apparel, and appliances, the economy of the richest nation on earth staggered; by decade's end, the government reported a 5.5 percent drop in median family income: the worst ever recorded.

(It wasn't just the statistics that revealed what was happening. In 1978, writer-producer Norman Lear ordered up a drastic change in the plot line of *The Jeffersons*. Successful entrepreneur George Jefferson lost his dry-cleaning business and was forced to move to the Chicago projects where James and Florida Evans lived, and the show was retitled *Hard Times*.)

By April 1979, pollster Pat Caddell, who'd worked for both McGovern and Carter, sent a memo to friends and colleagues that declared: "America is a nation deep in crisis . . . a crisis of confidence marked by a dwindling faith in the future. . . . It is the natural result of historical forces and events which have been in motion for twenty years. This crisis threatens the political and social fabric of the nation."

From the second term's first days, Ford was taking incoming political fire from all sides on the economy. In the first nine months of 1977, the Democratic Congress passed laws mandating emergency public works programs, wage and price controls, extended unemployment benefits; Ford vetoed all of them. The White House sent to the Hill legislation that trimmed Social Security and Medicare increases; Speaker O'Neill and Senate Majority Leader Robert Byrd held a press conference at which they unceremoniously dumped the White House Emergency Budget Message into a wastebasket. Organized labor, its members watching their paychecks and savings eroded by the cost of living, staged strikes in both the public and private sectors, and when the government did mange to reach agreement with the U.S. Postal Service union, AFL-CIO Chief George Meany successfully urged the rank and file to reject the contract.

If President Ford was looking for support from within the ranks of his party, he was looking in vain. For one thing, Republicans were hopelessly divided. Deficit hawks like Alan Greenspan urged deep cuts in spending—the same medicine he'd prescribed just before the 1976 election, when unemployment was running at 8 percent. ("The damn fool almost cost us the election!" Chief of Staff Dick Cheney thundered at a White House senior staff meeting. "Maybe next week he'll try to sell us on privatizing Social Security!") The Federal Reserve Board chair, Arthur Burns, was acutely aware of the political implications of interest rates: He'd obliged President Nixon with easy credit to help him win reelection in 1972, and he firmly believed any tightening of credit that would drive unemployment too high was politically unsustainable. So the Fed essentially did . . . nothing.

And within the ranks of the conservative movement, a new doctrine was emerging, courtesy of economist Art Laffer, who argued that deep cuts in marginal tax rates could spur economic growth and therefore increase government revenues. Congressman Jack Kemp, former star quarterback for the Buffalo Bills and San Diego Chargers, was a forceful advocate for tax cuts, an idea that horrified more traditional conservatives. ("Maybe," President Ford said, "it was Jack who played football once too often without a helmet.") The problem was, this "supply side" idea had found favor with the single most significant voice in the Republican Party; and that voice was growing increasingly critical, on just about every important dilemma the Ford administration was facing.

THE RIFT BETWEEN Gerald Ford and Ronald Reagan had never really healed after their battle for the nomination in 1976. Reagan had campaigned that fall, but he had pointedly endorsed the party and its platform, rarely if ever invoking the name of the President. He had assumed until the very last days that Ford would lose to Jimmy Carter, thus enabling him to campaign in 1980 against a Democratic incumbent. And the Reagan team, it turned out, had done its part to help ensure that outcome. At a dinner of his inner circle in their Pacific Palisades home just after the President's surprise election, Nancy asked how many of them had voted for Ford; only three hands went up. (When President Ford heard of this episode, he turned to Stu Spencer and said, "Let's tuck that one way in the 'payback' file.") Ford's full term brought no sign of improved relations.

"When did the trouble start?" Press Secretary Ron Nessen asked rhetorically. "I'd say about five minutes after the President left the Inaugural platform."

Ford put it this way to a biographer:

"Reagan was right behind me—knife in hand."

When the administration concluded treaty negotiations to turn the Panama Canal over to the Panamanians, Reagan repeated his objections from his 1976 primary fight: "We bought it; we built it; it's ours; and we should keep it." When Washington and Moscow signed the SALT II agreement, providing modest cutbacks in the nuclear arsenals of the two nations, Reagan condemned it as "a dangerous exercise in wishful thinking about the intentions of our sworn adversary." When Ford renewed his support for the floundering Equal Rights Amendment, Reagan warned of "opening the door to platoons of federal bureaucrats, burdening businesses with rules and regulations that will harm both men and women." The only reason Reagan turned his fire away from Washington in 1978 was to campaign for Proposition 13 in California, the provision that slammed a lid on property tax increases. Even then, when the measure passed by a 2–1 margin in the spring of 1978, Reagan told a victory party, "We made one mistake—we should have had Prop 13 apply nationwide!" "Run, Ronnie, Run!" the crowd chanted at him, and he nodded: "You just may get your wish in two years!"

Ronald Reagan's disaffection was the embodiment of a broader ill plaguing Ford: The Republican Party he had served for some thirty years was barely recognizable to him. The party that had been dominated by the Eastern financial and publishing interests, the party of the country clubs and Wall Street was more and more the party of the Sun Belt and the South, where social issues that had never been part of the national debate drove the passions of the rank and file. Abortion, guns, prayer kindled their energies. Ford was a man of the legislature, a man who with his first words as President had promised "communication, conciliation, compromise and cooperation" with the Congress he loved, where a splitting of the difference was the rule of the road. These foot soldiers of the New Right would have turned their anger on whoever was tacking toward the center, whatever party that trimmer belonged to; by the time of the 1978 midterms, the Republicans were as hopelessly split as the Democrats had been a decade earlier over Vietnam and race. When the internal party rifts were combined with a sour economy and the historical pattern of midterm losses for the White House party, the 1978 midterm Congressional elections promised nothing less than a full-scale disaster.

And this was one political promise that was kept.

The Republicans lost three Senate seats, and sixteen seats in the House, including such familiar figures as North Carolina's Jesse Helms, voted out when just enough white working-class voters turned to the populist message of State Insurance Commissioner John Ingram, who attacked Helms not as a neo-racist or an extremist, but as "the hand-picked tool of the fat cats and special interests." In his bitter concession speech, Helms said, "The man who beat me is not John Ingram. The man who beat me is sitting in a big White House on Pennsylvania Avenue." One of the Democrats who narrowly won reelection was Iowa Senator Richard Clark, whose campaign received invaluable help from many of the field organizers who had worked in George McGovern's 1972 campaign. These McGovern foot soldiers signed on to Clark with the encouragement of the man who had run McGovern's campaign . . . a man whose interest in Iowa was growing by the day.

HIS OFFICE was like the core of a reactor, bursts of energy radiating outward, onto a hopelessly overworked staff. He was a stand-up guy— literally—writing in longhand at a stand-up rolltop desk, working at a large table, big enough to hold the papers, the clipped-out newspaper and magazine stories. (Even back in the McGovern campaign, there were no chairs in the offices where he'd hold meetings; if everyone had to stand, the meetings were likely to move faster.) Every day he'd put down the paper, clip a note to the piece, scribble out a terse, pointed inquiry: *Why haven't we reached out to Yergin on energy? Let's see if we can get Reich down from Harvard, he's got some good stuff on pension portability, did you read this story on demographics and crime? I gotta see this guy.* There'd be a never-ending stream of people in and out of his office, over breakfast at the Senate dining room. Bill Cohen, the Republican senator from Maine, had a little break-fast group that brought in speakers, and so did Marty Frost, the Texan from the House, and he would be there, longish hair curled down to the neck, thick eyebrows, easy to find by the laugh—more like a bark, really—that would signal his ironic amusement at one of the absurdities so common to his life now. He no longer dressed in the manner memorably described by Teddy White in his 1972 campaign book ("skin-tight jeans over slim cowboy thighs"—*gay porn!* a colleague had said.). Now he wore ill-fitting suits, Lucchese boots ("expensive, but they last"), and a belt with a thick Western buckle. He was strikingly handsome, but more compelling than the crinkled eyes, angular face, lean body, and broad smile was the driven nature of his curiosity. Ideas, ideas, ideas. They were what had brought Gary Hart to here before his fortieth birthday, and it was ideas, he was sure, that just might take him to a place that, by any conventional measure, was far beyond his reach.

.   .   .

HE GREW UP as Gary Warren Hartpence, in Ottawa, Kansas, a town of some 10,000 people fifty miles southwest of Kansas City, Missouri. His dad, Carl, sold farm equipment; his mother, Nina, was the driving force of the family, the classic Mother of the Prince, the one with the smarts, the energy. As a boy, Gary was drawn to the transcontinental trains that powered through the small town; he could tell you about the engine weights, the wheelbases. His parents were members of the Nazarene Church, a tiny denomination that frowned on drinking, smoking, and mixed dancing, and so did the college he attended: Bethany Nazarene College in a tiny Oklahoma town. His classmates remembered him as brilliant but shy, a bit standoffish—but not so shy that he didn't wind up marrying the prettiest girl on campus, and the daughter of the college president to boot. He thought he was going into the ministry for a time, attended Yale Divinity School, but somewhere around 1960, maybe drawn to the magnetism of John Kennedy, he entered Yale Law. This was about the time he and his sister changed their last name to "Hart." Gary and his wife, Lee, settled in Colorado, where he threw himself into Robert Kennedy's 1968 Presidential campaign—he was devastated by Bobby's death—and he had settled into a comfortable law practice when Senator George McGovern met with him in a room at Stapleton International Airport in the spring of 1970 and offered him a job with McGovern's shoestring Presidential campaign. In a few months, he was in charge because, it turned out, nobody was running things in Washington . . . and nobody thought McGovern had a chance in hell of beating Senator Edmund Muskie, the 1968 Vice Presidential candidate who had the backing of everybody who counted for anything.

What Gary Hart did was to run a classic guerrilla campaign. No big shots for McGovern? Fine; go scout out the veterans from the Kennedy and McCarthy '68 campaigns, the ones who were trying to stop a war, who saw in McGovern one of their most consistent allies. Decentralize the campaign: no hierarchical pyramid, but concentric circles, with power radiating out to the different states. Put decision-making power in the hands of the field organizers who lived and worked in key states, so there was no clash between the locals and the bigfeet coming from outside to order the troops around. *I want them young. Mobile, single, people who can accept a spartan life because we have no money.* If the guy running the Midwest, Gene Pokorny, was thirty-four years old, fine, if he could do the job. "The characteristics of a good political organizer," he'd write later, "are universal—efficient, low-key, persistent, methodical, durable." And always remember the example of General Mikhail Kutuzov, the real-life hero of *War and Peace,* the genius whose guerrilla campaign defeated Napoleon's forces, who counseled "everything comes in time to him who knows how to wait . . . there is nothing stronger than these two: patience and time, they will do it all."

Even then he was impatient with the demands of political protocol. McGovern, Hart wrote, "suffered fools too gladly. He often listened to people who wasted his time by their own ignorance or by telling him something he already knew. He found it very difficult to shut people off . . . many people [committed] theft or murder of his time."

Nobody stole or murdered Gary Hart's time.

The campaign lived on fumes, signing up supporters through direct mail, "enrolling" them into McGovern for President clubs, where they'd promise to send ten dollars a month. They looked for a place to make early news and found it in Iowa, where the traditional precinct caucuses that no one had ever cared about had been moved to January, and they brought every supporter they could find, so that McGovern wound up with 27 percent of the vote, well behind Ed Muskie, but good enough to raise some political eyebrows. By then the volunteers were coming out in force, determined not to let a politician who'd supported the Vietnam War become the Democratic Party nominee. By the time McGovern had held Muskie under 50 percent in New Hampshire, and won Wisconsin, the front-runner had collapsed and by summer the darkest of dark horses had become the nominee.

That was the high point for Hart: The pros started showing up and throwing their weight around, demoralizing the true believers, and the guerrilla campaign hopelessly split the party between the old and new. When the McGovern forces threw Mayor Daley's delegation out of the convention, that was the kiss of death, even before McGovern chose a running mate with a history of mental breakdowns who had to be removed from the ticket. It was a historic, crushing loss—Richard Nixon won forty-nine states!—but when the Watergate scandal broke, the McGovern campaign gained some posthumous props: *We weren't the guys who stomped all over the Constitution.* When Hart ran for senator from Colorado in 1974, the revulsion against the Nixon tactics, and the lessons Hart had learned about organizing a campaign, gave him a landslide victory of his own and sent him to the Senate. And he took with him the lessons he had learned in 1972 and in the years after . . . not just about organizing a campaign but about the country.

He was a Democrat, but it was clear to him that the verities of the party faithful had long ago lost their persuasive force. He'd been drawn to Robert Kennedy precisely because Bobby was challenging these ideas at their roots: Top-down government is oppressive, soul deadening; spending money is not the key to making life better.

"We're not a bunch of little Hubert Humphreys," he'd said of his generation, and while it may not have been the most *politic* way to express the idea, it was what he believed. "Time had made change a threat," he said of the old-line Democrats, and he said more: that liberalism had come close to "intellectual bankruptcy."

And what the failures of ideas hadn't accomplished, what the war hadn't accomplished in the snuffing-out of public purpose, the Watergate conspirators had.

"These selfish, power-lusting little men," he wrote, "in their greedy struggle for self-preservation, ruined decades of effort to restore the stature of public service, to exalt the role of government, and to inspire in men and women the highest aspiration of political involvement."

There was, he was sure, a discontent across the board, one that Jerry Ford had not come close to grasping in the two years since his remarkable comeback. People were fed up with the orthodoxies of both parties, especially now that the thirty-year postwar run of prosperity had apparently come to a dead end. Discontent is a lot easier to take when income keeps rising, when the cars and homes are bigger, the TV sets righter, the promise of comfort is kept. Now with inflation eating away at the future of millions, with once-mighty industries back on their heels if not on their knees, was the country really going to have a choice between the gauzy pastoral fantasies of Ronald Reagan and the tinny liberal trumpetings of Ted Kennedy? Or was it . . . barely possible . . . that 1980 would be a year when an utterly improbable, utterly audacious challenge . . . just might work?

FOR ANOTHER CONTENDER, there was no doubt, no hesitancy. It was his time.

He had been preparing for the office for thirty years, although he did not know it when he began, at work that no one could imagine was a prelude to the Presidency. All through the 1950s, he had traveled the country for General Electric, sponsor of the television series he hosted, touting the glories of the free-enterprise system, warning of the perils of rapacious government, preaching the conservative gospel that had lured him from his roots as a Roosevelt–Truman Democrat. When he finished speaking, he would talk with the workers gathered in the cafeterias, and would answer their questions. Before he ever gave a campaign speech, he'd spoken to more than 250,000 GE employees at 139 plants, meaning that he'd probably had more extended conversations with more working Americans than any elected official.

Those travels, those interchanges, had honed his speaking skills. It wasn't just the techniques he'd learned in the years in front of Warner Bros. cameras—the bob of the head, the dramatic pause—but the way to take an idea and put it on its feet, choosing the concrete image. He would describe a $10 billion deficit as a stack of hundred-dollar bills stretching six and a half miles into the sky. By the fall of 1964, when he'd made that nationally televised speech for the doomed candidacy of Barry Goldwater, he'd become the most compelling conservative spokesman in America. The Speech—that's what it would be called by his coterie forever, "the Speech"—raised a raft of money for Goldwater, and, more important, convinced a roomful of some of California's richest Republicans that they had found their next candidate for governor.

In that 1966 campaign, one of Ronald Reagan's greatest political assets was unveiled: His prior career as an actor, and his sharply drawn conservative

philosophy in an era of liberal ascendancy, caused his opponents to relentlessly, consistently, underestimate him. When he first announced for governor, movie studio mogul Jack Warner was supposed to have said: "Ronald
Reagan for Governor? No! Jimmy Stewart for Governor; Ronald Reagan
for best friend!" When he won the GOP primary in a landslide against
former San Francisco mayor George Christopher, aides to Governor Pat
Brown broke out in cheers: *We beat Nixon, for heaven's sakes. Taking down
this has-been will be a walk in the park.*

"Remember," Brown told a group of schoolchildren, "it was an actor
who shot Lincoln." With anger over taxes and crime, with working-class
fury over the tumult at Berkeley and other California campuses, Reagan
beat Brown by almost a million votes.

Reagan was set to pivot immediately into a race for the White House
in 1968 when a scandal inside the governor's office—the emergence of a
"homosexual ring" among the staff—diverted his energy. By the time he'd
launched a last-minute effort at the convention, Richard Nixon had locked
up the nomination.

In 1976, he tried again, this time taking on the sitting (though unelected)
Republican President. He had stumbled out of the gate, fallen hopelessly
behind, then regained his footing and come agonizingly close, closer than
anyone ever had, to depriving a President of renomination. Any one of a
dozen different decisions would have made the difference: Had his New
Hampshire chairman not predicted a landslide, thus making his tie seem
like a defeat; had he not left New Hampshire in the days before the primary, and beaten Ford decisively; had he competed harder for delegates in
New York and Pennsylvania; had he won over three or four more Mississippi delegates, giving him full control of the slate. Change any of those
outcomes and he might well have taken the nomination and, he was sure,
handily beaten Carter in November.

Now, as he prepared for his third try, Reagan was bringing to the campaign formidable assets—and potentially serious liabilities. He was the
most imposing figure in his party, who fused a commanding presence on
the speaker's platform with credentials as solid as any: eight years as the
chief executive of the most populous state in the union, where he had

governed, in the words of one reporter, with "a string of successes and a record on which he could run for President." His rhetoric delighted the true believers—he said of anti-war protesters, "Their signs say 'Make Love, Not War,' but they look like they couldn't do either"—but his record was far more nuanced. He'd signed one of the most liberal abortion bills in the land (which he later disavowed), supported a vigorous campaign to save the redwoods and other jewels of the California environment, and learned to work well with the solidly Democratic legislature. He had remained in the public eye after his nomination loss, writing hundreds of newspaper columns and radio commentaries; in 1978, he'd crossed the country for Republicans, had given 300 speeches, held 200 news conferences. He was as much "Mr. Republican" as conservative hero Robert Taft had ever been, except that Taft looked as if he had just chewed on a sour persimmon and Reagan lit up the room.

But it wasn't so simple.

There was, first, the Age Question. Reagan would be sixty-nine in 1980, and no one of that age had ever won the Presidency. Reagan was still vigorous, broad-shouldered, his hair so lustrous that people assumed he was coloring it (it was in fact Brylcreem, that survivor of the greasy-hair era, that darkened his locks, although that didn't stop comedians from noting his "prematurely orange" hair). His appearance, however, could not stop the questions, especially when Reagan had a tendency to offer evidence in support of his positions that were often flatly, factually false. ("Once he reads something and it strikes a chord," advisor Mike Deaver conceded, "it stays there forever.") So he would choke up every time he told the story of a doomed World War II plane plunging to earth with a young radioman trapped inside, and the heroic pilot who instead of bailing out, said to the terrified young man, "Don't worry, son—we'll ride this down together." And people would ask: *Hey, wait—if the plane crashed and they both died . . . how did we learn about this?* (They learned because it was a scene from a movie.) Or he'd tell an audience about what it was like to liberate a concentration camp, and the nitpickers would say: *Hey, wait—you made training films in Hollywood during the war. You were never in Europe.* Or he'd cite facts and figures and incidents that seemed to come from . . . thin air. And there was a danger here, not that he got details wrong, but that he'd be seen as a foggy senior citizen, not in full command of his faculties, maybe not the man you'd want with his finger on the button.

Then there was the problem of the man who occupied the White House. Reagan was a political figure who painted in bold stripes, who drew sharp distinctions between himself and the ideas of his adversaries, whose strongest argument was a call for a wholesale break with the past. He'd run for governor against a quarter century of "liberal" state government that had begun under Republican Earl Warren in the early 1940s. His argument for the Presidency would be a frontal assault on a big-spending, expansionist federal government.

And here was the problem: In 1980, the government was being run not by Lyndon Johnson or Hubert Humphrey, or even Jimmy Carter, but by Gerald Ford, who, in the oversimplified world of politics, was a Republican who espoused conservative principles, even if he did not really govern by them. The ills that were afflicting the American economy by the end of 1979 had festered over decades, but they had happened on the watch of a Republican President whose administration was staffed by many ardent conservatives, like Bill Simon and Alan Greenspan. Reagan would have had a far, far easier case if he had an all-Democratic Washington to run against, so that he could draw the contrast between their failures and his ideas in sharp, clear terms. But Ford? He'd proposed cuts in spending; he'd proposed tax cuts for business and investment; he'd assailed big government. How was Reagan going to paint himself as a radical change from that President?

And change is what the country wanted, after twelve continuous years with the same party in the White House. There would have been an appetite for something new even if conditions were reasonably good. "Twelve years is a long, long time for a party to hold office," Brent Scowcroft noted when the campaign began. Moreover, as his second term hit the clubhouse turn, Ford was a deeply, deeply unpopular President, with approval ratings in the mid-20s—about where Richard Nixon was in his last days before resigning. Ford might be as lame a lame duck as can be imagined, but his presence in the Oval Office would make Reagan's argument that much more difficult. (When John Sears, Reagan's campaign manager, was asked at the end of 1979 what one condition he wished were different, he said,

"I'd like to jump into a time machine, go back to 1976, and recount those votes in Ohio and Mississippi.")

Yet, paradoxically, despite Ford's unpopularity, he posed one more direct threat: He was President of the United States and he cordially despised Ronald Reagan.

Part of it was intensely personal: Reagan's primary challenge had almost deprived him of the nomination in 1976, had cost him immeasurable time, money, and energy, and had barely lifted a finger for him in the fall. "His lack of campaigning," Ford said to reporter and friend Thomas DeFrank, "was one of the three or four reasons that I lost the popular vote to Carter and almost lost the election."

Part of it was envy; unlike Ford's troubled relationship with speech, Reagan could bring a crowd to tears, bring it to laughter, bring it to its feet. "He had a helluva flair," Ford told DeFrank.

And part of it was the simple fact that, in DeFrank's words, "he neither liked nor respected the former Hollywood actor. He considered Reagan a superficial, disengaged, intellectually lazy showman who didn't do his homework, and clung to a naïve, unrealistic, and essentially dangerous worldview."

Armed with the White House, a President, even one with Ford's standing (or lack of it) could put roadblocks in the path of a Presidential campaign, leaking documents to undermine Reagan's views on U.S.–Soviet relations or tax policy, painting a picture of Reagan as an elderly, out-of-touch candidate. Well, Reagan and his team reasoned, with Ford as unpopular as he is, we should be able to overcome his opposition. And anyway, once we get the nomination, party unity will be a snap. Nothing will bring Republicans together like the man Ronald Reagan will be running against.

And in their certainty about the identity of their opponent, the Reagan team was in full agreement with just about every player in the political universe.

FOR ALMOST EVERY INHABITANT of the political universe, the identity of the 1980 Democratic Presidential nominee was a given, and had been from the moment Jerry Ford had claimed victory on Election Night 1976. Senator Edward Moore Kennedy was the heart and soul of the party, heir to two martyred brothers, heir as well to the hopes that survived the loss and grief. More than fifteen years had passed since Dallas, and time had erased any shadow that might have dimmed the memory of Jack Kennedy. JFK was not the President who had misguided America into a senseless war or a man with a reckless, dangerous personal life. He was forever a dashing young leader, with a glamorous wife and engaging children, a dazzling smile, flashing wit. Moreover, in the harder times of the late 1970s, with inflation eroding a fifth of a family's savings every year, with a crippling industrial recession shuttering plants and factories across the Midwest, Jack Kennedy was a link to better times, before the war and the spread of crime and racial upheaval and generational revolt, before the growing sense that America's best days were behind us. And in Robert Kennedy, all of the yearnings for a different kind of country could be invested in a sense of lost possibility. Bobby had never held the reins of ultimate power, so imagination could grant him the power to resolve every dilemma of race, crime, hunger, war, generational divide.

Ted Kennedy carried all of this and more. He was the most natural politician of all of his brothers, genuinely embracing the backslapping and backroom camaraderie that Jack found bemusing and Bobby found agonizing. In more than fifteen years in the Senate, he had become skilled in the legislative arts; he was far more comfortable in the corridors of power and in the late-night negotiations over an amendment than his impatient siblings had been. He was a guiding force behind some of liberalism's most significant legislative achievements. For good or ill, these were the measures that transformed America: the first immigration reform act; the National Voting Rights Act and its extensions; the Freedom of Information Act; the Gun Control Act; the campaign financing reform law; the comprehensive Selective Service reform act; the eighteen-year-old vote law; the Occupational Safety and Health Act; the war on cancer bills; the recodification of federal criminal laws; the Bilingual Education Act; the Fair Housing Acts; the age discrimination act; the airline and trucking deregulation bills; the Job Training Partnership Act. One of his severest journalistic critics wrote of him: "He has been an ally of blacks, American Indians, the poor, the sick, the aged, the mentally ill, starving refugees worldwide and immigrants. He has been an outspoken liberal, unafraid to take the controversial positions—on issues such as busing, abortion, gun control, the Vietnam War (late but forcefully), and capital punishment—that other senators clearly avoided."

With these familial and senatorial legacies, the core blocs of the Democratic Party were in his corner: blacks and Hispanics, the barons of organized labor, the professional pols who still held power in the big cities of the Northeast and Midwest. Jack had won their reluctant allegiance in 1960; Bobby had threatened them in 1968. Ted was one of their own. Back in 1976, when it seemed Jimmy Carter would win the White House in a walk, Ted and his troops had reconciled themselves to waiting until 1984. Carter was hardly their cup of tea—that moralizing, those self-aggrandizing platitudes—but the idea of another Kennedy challenging a sitting President for renomination in 1980? Better to wait. Then, incredibly, Jerry Ford had won! Carter could give all the speeches he wanted about the injustice of losing a campaign when he'd gotten almost a million and a half more votes than Ford, but the Democratic Party was not about to turn back to the guy who'd blown a bigger lead than Tom Dewey. If Carter did run again, he might be a problem in the South, and California Governor Jerry Brown might well take a run; he'd won a fistful of primaries in '76 as the stalking horse for the "Anyone but Carter" movement. Still, there was no logical scenario for anyone but Ted Kennedy.

"I don't think he can be denied the nomination if he wants it," House Speaker Tip O'Neill had said just after the midterms, and at year's end, at an informal poll taken among the insiders who attended Ben Bradlee and Sally Quinn's Christmas party in Georgetown, more than 150 of the 175 guests picked Teddy as the nominee. That same month, a CBS News poll showed Kennedy with a 53–16 lead over Carter, and showed him ahead even in the South.

Of course, there were those cleared throats and awkward silences among the party pros when a reporter would ask about . . . you know . . . the incident . . . the tragedy. *Well, yes it was a terrible lapse, but that was more than a decade ago, and you can't judge a man's whole life by his worst moment.* Look at his record on child care, the Equal Rights Amendment, health care, Head Start. Look at that CBS–*New York Times* poll, for heaven's sakes: 80 percent were familiar with the Chappaquiddick "incident" and 55 percent still said Teddy was "good under pressure."

Among those without a strong personal or vocational interest in not offending the likely next President of the United States, the comments were far less prudent. *For God's sakes, he drove off a bridge in the middle of the night with a young woman, and she drowned! It took him hours to call anyone, and then he tried to cover it up!* No, you didn't hear that sort of comment in the more prestigious political circles, but it was there, not far under the surface. By the late 1970s, there were media voices that had not even existed when Jack and Bobby were running, voices not yet fully appreciated by the older political universe, voices that were willing, even eager, to put Teddy's conduct front and center with the bark off.

The *National Lampoon* was a humor magazine a universe away from the days when political humor was Bob Hope joking about Eisenhower's golf game or Mort Sahl's brainy quips about John Foster Dulles. The *Lampoon* went straight for the jugular and often hit. In 1979, it ran a full-page "ad" for Volkswagen, showing the car floating on top of the water. "If Ted Kennedy Had Driven a Volkswagen," the copy read, "He'd Be President Today." Another issue featured a mock cover of the classic EC comic, *Tales From the Crypt,* that showed Kennedy accepting the nomination as the decomposed corpse of a young woman strode down the aisle with a placard reading: "CHAPPAQUIDDICK." And *Saturday Night Live,* a late-night comedy show with a cutting edge and a huge audience among under-thirties, showed Ted Kennedy—played by Bill Murray—entering his Presidential announcement rally dripping wet and covered with seaweed. Kennedy partisans could shrug off the dark humor—"Most of those kids don't even vote," one Kennedy ally said—but they were early signs that the eleven-year-old incident had not exactly been consigned to the past.

Beyond those early hints of potential trouble were the shifts in the political terrain that had redefined what was public and what was private: most notably, the emergence of the women's movement at the start of the

1970s. Back in 1960, and throughout his Presidency, Jack Kennedy's compulsive, reckless philandering was regarded as none of the public's business. During Bobby's '68 campaign, a rookie speechwriter was bluntly instructed by a veteran reporter: "Just remember Rule 1—nothing that happens west of the Potomac is ever mentioned east of the Potomac."

By the time the 1980 campaign season began, these rules had changed drastically. Teddy himself had been part of that change; when someone died in a car driven by a United States senator, that was hardly private. When the chairman of the House tax-writing committee jumped into a fountain with a professional stripper, when another powerful House chairman put his bedroom playmate on the public payroll, that was the public's business.

And something else had changed, something that posed as big a threat to a Kennedy campaign as any. The women's movement was marching under a powerfully provocative banner: "The Personal IS Political." *Don't tell me about your voting record,* the argument went, *tell me if you help care for the kids, respect your partner, treat women as equals, not servants or concubines.* There were those who scorned this line of attack—Could FDR pass that test? Should JFK have been tidying up during the Cuban Missile Crisis?—but in Ted Kennedy, the movement had found a vulnerable target. It wasn't just Chappaquiddick but a life punctuated by chronic, alcohol-fueled philandering, with Kennedy behaving like a Lord of the Realm exercising his droit du seigneur. In the fall of 1979, writer Sussanah Lessard wrote a piece for the *New Republic* about Ted Kennedy's extracurricular activities. When it was turned down, she took it to the *Washington Monthly,* a contrarian publication with a very low circulation but significant readership among Washington's political class.

Titled "Kennedy's Woman Problem; Women's Kennedy Problem," the article detailed the pattern of Kennedy's assignations—sending a staff member to approach young women, the swift postcoital dismissals—and the assertion that Kennedy's pattern suggested a severe case of arrested development, a kind of narcissistic intemperance, a large, babyish ego that had to constantly be fed. "I don't believe men who really like women carry on in this way." That piece, in turn, led to a brief *Time* magazine note that at a dinner party in Washington, "fourteen talented and interesting men and women spent an hour and a half talking of nothing but the sexual exploits of Edward Kennedy."

The Kennedy camp would have been a lot more unsettled had *Time* reported on another dinner party, this one in New York, where former White House press secretary and PBS host Bill Moyers asked the women at the table, all cosmopolitan urbanites, all willing veterans of the sexual revolution, if they would vote for Kennedy for President. Not a single hand went up, not a single head nodded in affirmation.

And about those dazzling poll numbers? It was left to longtime Democratic pollster Peter Hart to note that "nobody has measured the issue correctly. To really understand the impact of Chappaquiddick, it is necessary to ask a series of questions that are much more oblique." Nor, he might have added, did the relentlessly, incurably credulous reporting of polls ever contemplate the possibility that people might change their minds when they learned more. Kennedy hadn't run for President in 1972 or 1976— now he was. And the press, out of its deep-seated instincts, was turning its guns squarely in his direction.

IT WAS A SIMPLE act of fate that made the difference for Gary . . . as simple as who was at the desk next to his on the floor of the Senate.

Dale Bumpers had come to the Senate a little less than half a century after he had entered the world with prospects as barren as the land on which he was raised. Charleston, Arkansas, was a town of 851, set in western Arkansas's Hill Country, a town so small, Bumpers would say later, that "after the town band was formed, there wasn't anybody left to watch the parade." It had one paved street, and the dust from passing cars would choke his lungs; there was no running water, no sewer system. He and his brothers and sisters went shoeless in the summer; his mother made his underwear from sacks of flour. He lost a four-year-old brother to dysentery because the town doctor was too ignorant to take the simple steps that would have saved him. What put a light in his life was the journey his father took him on to Booneville in 1938 to see President Roosevelt on a campaign swing. When Dale asked his dad why FDR was holding on to the arm of his son, his father said, "He can't walk. He had polio when he was thirty-nine years old and he wears steel braces on his legs that weigh twelve pounds. Now, you boys should let that be a lesson to you. If a man who can't even walk and carries twelve pounds of steel on his legs can be President, you boys have good minds and good bodies, and there isn't any reason you can't be President." His dad was the civic center of Charleston, president of the school board, head of the local Methodist church, served a spell in the state legislature.

The GI Bill got Dale to college and law school, but it was at Northwestern that he got a call in the middle of the night: his parents had been in an auto accident, a drunk driver had hit them head-on. Neither survived. Bumpers scratched out a living—barely—running an appliance store and practicing law out of a cubicle-sized office. But he'd followed his father's footsteps to civic leadership; he helped make Charleston the first town in the South to voluntarily integrate its schools after the Supreme Court's 1954 decision and got the Methodist church integrated as well.

Still, it was sheer madness for Bumpers to challenge the segregationist ex-governor of Arkansas, Orville Faubus, when Faubus decided to run for another term in 1970. Bumpers sold the small herd of cattle he'd assembled, begged funds from a reluctant family, and traveled the state, speaking to the state's pride, how tired he was of its low ranking on education and income and health, how tired they all must be of muttering, "Thank God for Mississippi." And despite all the attacks on him—why, he'd actually said one time he didn't necessarily believe that every word in the Bible was literally true!—he swamped Faubus in the primary runoff, and in November unseated Republican Governor Winthrop Rockefeller. Two years later, he won reelection with 75 percent of the vote. But the governorship bored him, and, besides, Dale was thinking of a much bigger office, and how the hell could you run for President as governor of Arkansas?

So he ran for the Senate, taking on the legendary J. William Fulbright, who'd been there for a quarter century, who'd traveled the world, created the scholarship named after him. What Bumpers understood was that Fulbright was distant, rarely came home, had an aloof quality completely at odds with Bumpers's down-home way with voters. And on Primary Day, Bumpers beat Fulbright by thirty points.

When Bumpers came to Washington in 1975, he found himself seated next to another freshman senator, Gary Hart. All he knew of Hart was that he'd run McGovern's campaign in '72, somehow turning the long-shot anti-war champion into the Democratic Presidential nominee. He soon discovered that Hart was whip smart, a glutton for books, magazine articles, essays, news features, with an ironic distance from the idiocies of politics that mirrored his own. Bumpers and Hart were gym rats as well, working out with weights and the machines, and soon Bumpers became Hart's best friend in the Senate. They were, in one sense, an odd couple. Hart recoiled at the demands of politics, hated the glad-handing, the purposeless chats with contributors and the party hacks, the photo opportunities and the treacle that passed for so much political speechmaking. He wanted votes because of his ideas, because of what he proposed to do about military waste, the environment, the demands of a global economy.

Bumpers, by contrast, fully embraced the gestures and pieties that warmed the political climate. He could debate the intricacies of tax policy and geopolitics as well as any senator; but, back home, he had a satchelful of stories about small-town lawyers and retrogrades that could render a courthouse square crowd weak with laughter.

("I heard two women talking in a grocery store," he'd say. "One asked: 'Who's the best lawyer in Charleston?'

"'Dale Bumpers when he's sober,' the other said."

"'Who's next best?'

"'Dale Bumpers when he's drunk.'"

Or he'd get a bit risqué and tell about the man who saw a sign at a gas station that advertised free sex if you were the twentieth customer that day. He was always either nineteenth or twenty-first, but never twentieth. So he came home, complained to his wife that the whole thing was a fraud.

"'No, it's not,' his wife said, 'I've won three times.'")

There was, however, one aspect of political life they both embraced.

Both wanted very much to be President.

Bumpers was looking at a horizon in the mid-distance: 1984, or maybe '88. He'd be up for reelection in 1980, and, anyway, Jimmy Carter's loss in '76 had put the mark of Cain on any Southerner, at least in the short run. So while he felt a tinge of envy when Hart first raised the subject ("What do you think, Dale, is it just plain nuts for me to even consider . . . ?"),

Bumpers was clear enough about his own intentions—or lack of them—to begin counseling Hart about his audacious gamble.

"When it comes to ideas," he said, "nobody can touch you. But politics is an intensely visceral, human enterprise. You know, I have never walked away from a voter without calling him by his first name. It told him I had been paying attention—plus, there's no sound as beautiful to a person as the sound of his name."

And when Hart said he couldn't do that, couldn't run for President as if he were trying to sell an insurance policy after a Rotary Club meeting, couldn't turn himself into an actor, couldn't compete with Reagan, Bumpers said: "If you do this, you won't be running for Prime Minister. The President's the head of state. People don't want to just know what you'll do about their taxes. They want to know who you are. You don't have to pander, not really. But our young governor back home, Clinton? Thank God he's too young to run or you'd really be in trouble. He likes to say, 'If voters have to choose between pandering and condescension, they'll choose pandering every time.'"

There was no one moment that turned Hart around on his campaign approach, no blinding flash of light. As one of his closest aides said later: "If this had been '84 or '88, Gary might not have listened—especially since Bumpers might have been running himself. But the whole idea of running in '80—a first-term senator against the most famous, most powerful name in Democratic politics—was so insane, Gary was persuadable."

And the proof of that was what he did about The Name.

HE HAD BEEN BORN Gary Warren Hartpence. Gary regarded the name as an affliction, especially when his buddies in high school began calling him "Gary Hotpants." That nickname certainly did not fit the shy high school student, but, given the rumors that had begun during the McGovern campaign, it would not have been helpful had he kept the name. Instead, he, his wife, and his sister all changed their last names to "Hart" back in 1961, when Gary was about to enter Yale Law School.

No one around Gary had given it much thought; some of them didn't even know about it. But in September of 1978, when the talk about The

Race had gotten serious, the innermost "concentric circle" had gathered in Hart's office in the Russell Office Building and talked about some of the minefields that might be embedded in the ground under Gary's feet. It was an awkward conversation—how do you ask a man if the rumors about him and women were true?—but Gary reassured them, no, there'd been problems, like any marriage might have, especially given the demands on a senator's time, the enforced absences, the travel, but he and Lee had worked it out, there'd be no separation, legal or otherwise.

And about the name, Gary?

Well, it had been an inconvenience forever, and actually, it may have been Nancy's idea, so . . .

"If I could . . ."

The man who held up a cautionary finger was one of the most recognizable people in the country, whose indecently good looks had made him a movie star before his first movie was released and whose insatiable appetite for women had him better known for his private life than his public work. But at thirty-five, Warren Beatty had long since proven to Hart that he was a remarkably skilled political player. In 1972, Beatty had organized Hollywood for George McGovern, had invented the idea of the rock concert as a fund-raising device, had persuaded Carole King and Barbra Streisand, Jack Nicholson, Julie Christie, to raise more than a million dollars for McGovern's shoestring campaign.

Beatty was also a shrewd advisor on matters of media and public opinion and how to frame an argument. He'd retreated from the celebrity-endorser role, preferring to offer private counsel, and by the time the campaign ended McGovern had said of Beatty: "He was one of the three or four most important people in the campaign."

Now, with Hart planning his own Presidential run, Beatty was a voice that Hart listened to, even as he stayed out of the public spotlight; his nickname in the campaign was "The Phantom." Beatty vigorously underscored Dale Bumpers's advice that Hart reveal more of his human side. "You're tap-dancing, Gary. And there's no reason in the world why you have to. I think you can lance this boil in five minutes."

And he explained what he thought Gary ought to do.

Three days later, Hart held a press conference in the Senate TV gallery.

"As you all know," Hart began, "America faces an unparalleled series of crises at home and abroad: a nuclear superpower as a rival, global economic competition, inflation and recession at home, and a looming threat to our well-being in the form of a vulnerable energy supply.

"So today," he continued, "I want to talk about—why I changed my name.

"I was born 'Gary Hartpence'—one of three or four different versions of a family name about which no two families in our extended clan could agree." He beckoned to a man standing against the wall to come to the microphone.

"This is my uncle Ralph," he said. "Ralph Hartpence. Ralph, will you explain?"

"Well," Ralph said, "the family name was originally Eberhartpence. Some changed it to Hart, some went by Pence, some by Eberhart and some by Hartpence. I guess Gary and his family just decided to go for the simplest one."

"Thank you, Ralph," Hart said. "I guess some of you might be asking yourselves, 'Did he change his name with an eye on politics?' And the only honest answer is: 'Maybe.' I was twenty-four years old, and I know one of my ambitions was to be a writer. And 'Hartpence' sounded to me like someone who wrote about British country houses and riding to hounds. But I'm pretty sure I thought that 'Hartpence' was just not a name to take into the public arena.

"One more thing," Hart said. "I don't know how many Americans change their name every year. But I have decided that, if I someday seek higher office, I plan to reach out for the support of every American who has done what I've done. The numbers say I will win in a landslide. Those of you with more questions might wish to ask Archie Leach—that's Cary Grant—Marion Morrison—that's John Wayne—and a list of some four hundred others we have for your examination."

The issue of Gary's name change was never mentioned again.

FOR GARY HART and his closest advisors, the "women's issue" had been resolved months earlier. Hart's good looks and a few offhand remarks had raised more than a few eyebrows when he ran the McGovern campaign in 1972. Any number of women back then were surprised, to put it mildly, to learn that he was married. Indeed, in an interview with the *Washington Post*'s Sally Quinn, who described Hart in romance-novel terms—"very handsome ... chiseled, movie-star profile, tousled, styled hair, full lips, crinkly eyes ..." Hart had said cryptically, "Let's just say I believe in 'reform marriage.'" (He added: "I never reveal myself or who I really am.") And it was no secret that Gary and Lee had been going through a rough patch. There was talk of a trial separation; Gary had even talked about sharing a place with the *Washington Post*'s Bob Woodward.

The possible prospect of a Hart Presidential run brought Gary and Lee to a different place. Yes, Ronald Reagan and his first wife had divorced, but that was decades ago; he and Nancy had been married for twenty-eight years and he was besotted by her; the idea of a sixty-nine-year-old man stepping out on the woman he called "Mommy" was unfathomable. Hart, by contrast, was young, "studly," with a reputation. A candidate going through a marital separation was not the way to run as "the women's candidate"—and among the Hart inner circle, that notion was proving increasingly attractive. (You could see how the argument would be framed: *Teddy? The "women's candidate"? You have got to be kidding. His whole campaign is a boys' club. Gary's press secretary, his polling director, his scheduler are all women.*) And as a bonus, a Gary Hart who was married with children was a potent contrast with bachelor Governor Jerry Brown, whose monastic living habits drew much press coverage. "Teddy saved us from the 'other women' thing," one aide said, "and Jerry saved us from the 'weirdo' thing." So there was no separation; pictures of Gary, Lee, and his photogenic children graced campaign posters and brochures. It was a strong signal that, if the personal was political, then Hart's campaign would work to ensure that "the personal" would be, in more ways than one, the soft underbelly of the Kennedy campaign.

It would not be the only one. And here, the fact that Jerry Ford, and not Jimmy Carter, had won in 1976 would prove to be one of the Hart campaign's most formidable assets. Because what Ford's shaky stewardship had demonstrated—for the third time in as many Presidents—was the failure of the insider.

—No one had a better grasp of the mechanism of the Congress than Lyndon Johnson, who had spent thirty years inside the Capitol.

—No one had a broader experience with international geopolitics than Richard Nixon.

—No one was held in more affection among Washington's legislators than Gerald Ford, who entered the White House with twenty-six years in the House.

And each of them had presided over one disaster after another. A Carter Presidency might have demonstrated that inexperience was no magic wand either, might have made the idea of an experienced insider like Ted Kennedy appealing. Thanks to a last-minute fumble recovery by Ford in that San Francisco debate, it was another insider who had made a hash of things.

There was one other arena where Ford's comeback victory over Carter strengthened Hart's case immeasurably, a realm in which Hart felt most comfortable, the place, he had believed from his first days in the McGovern campaign, where elections are won or lost: the realm of ideas. However centered Jimmy Carter's campaign was in his personal qualities, a Carter Presidency could well have been interpreted as a significant departure from the traditional liberalism that Roosevelt, Truman, Kennedy, and Johnson had represented. And had Carter failed on the domestic front as thoroughly as Ford had failed, the case for resurgent traditional liberalism embodied by Ted Kennedy might well have been too powerful to combat.

Since it was Ford who had won, voters saw in 1980 not just the failures of insiders, but the failure of a traditional Democrat (LBJ), followed by two traditionally more or less conservative Republicans (Nixon and Ford). Those failed Presidencies, in turn, strengthened the political appeal of a bold departure from the past. Clearly, there was one credible Republican candidate who would offer a radical departure from business as usual: Ronald Reagan. What was less obvious was that a new breed of Democrats had come to power in the decade of the 1970s, with very different premises from those of Ted Kennedy and the establishment center of the Democratic Party; Democrats like Delaware Senator Joe Biden, elected before his thirtieth birthday, who was electrifying audiences by telling them that an advocate for education need not be an advocate for the agenda of teachers' unions; or New York Governor Hugh Carey, who stunned his free-spending legislature by asserting, "The days of wine and roses are over"; or Massachusetts Senator Paul Tsongas, who asked, "Why do some in our party think it's somehow wrong to identify yourself as 'pro-growth'? Do they think the Department of Labor creates jobs?" Democrats like Atlanta Mayor Maynard Jackson and New York's Ed Koch and Portland's Al Uhlman, who were being forced by simple arithmetic to confront the civil-service unions demanding higher wages and benefits.

And it wasn't just politicians. A whole new generation of thinkers, technology whiz kids, entrepreneurs had come of age in the 1970s, grounded in the values of the 1960s, but fed up with the sclerotic pace and calcified thinking of conventional liberals. ("If I could get my hands on the Post Office," a thirtyish businessman named Fred Smith told Hart in a 1975 meeting, as he prepared to launch an overnight airborne delivery service, "I could triple its productivity in a month. But maybe I should be grateful. Their incompetence is going to make me rich.")

Kennedy, by contrast, was most comfortable talking to the base of the party.

"Kennedy is always invited to speak at the convention, always makes a speech in prime time," the veteran political writer Jack Germond wrote. "But when it comes to the general-election campaign, if you bring Kennedy to Texas, you send him down to Rio Grande Valley to speak to the Hispanics. If you bring him to Florida, you send him to Miami to talk to the blacks. He is always used exclusively to talk to special interests. And not all of that is related to Chappaquiddick; it's related to issues."

With so many Democrats doubting the party's orthodoxies, Hart thought, there was a chance that if he could demonstrate some political clout in an early contest, he might be able to tap into this newer breed of Democrats, and into some deep veins of political and financial support; and that would change the whole political equation. He'd seen it with the McGovern campaign, hell, he'd helped make it happen. All those early polls, all that shoestring financing, went right out the window as soon as McGovern had scored an impressive showing or two. He hadn't even won those early races, just done "better than expected," finished "surprisingly strong." All the vaunted "inevitability" of Ed Muskie had collapsed like a tower of Legos the minute Muskie had shown a hint of vulnerability.

Now, as Hart prepared to enter the 1980 Presidential race, his camp drew comfort from the virtually unanimous conviction of the political insiders that Ted Kennedy's grip on the Democratic nomination was unshakable.

It meant the damn fools were making exactly the same mistake they had made in '72; they had remembered nothing, which meant that once again they would be startled, amazed, shocked. They would treat even a glancing blow as a direct hit on the Kennedy ship. And it would begin, of course, in Iowa. Ted Kennedy was forty, fifty points ahead of Jimmy Carter in poll after poll; Jerry Brown trailed badly, and Hart? "Hart," as columnist Carl Leubsdorf wrote, "would have to surge to be granted an asterisk." "The heart of the Democratic Party in Iowa belongs to Ted Kennedy," said former state chair Tom Whitney. "It's his for the asking."

All of which made Iowa a perfect fit for Gary Hart. Because he didn't just know the state—he had invented it.

WHEN GARY HART ANNOUNCED that he would run for President in April of 1979, he did so not from the Senate Caucus Room, where Jack and Bobby had declared, and where Teddy would do so six months later, but from a mountaintop outside his Denver, Colorado, home. Some of his words sought to link him and his campaign to the sacred memory of FDR.

"As America was in the years of Franklin Roosevelt, facing economic collapse and the passing of an isolationist world," he said, "we must once more become a bold, adventurous, and pioneering nation. In the 1930s, the task was to break the grip of paralyzing ideas about a do-nothing government and a see-nothing foreign policy.

"Half a century later, in the 1980s, the task is to break the grip of narrow, negative agendas and special interest government in Washington. Today the center of national interest has been made a center of insensitivity, inaction and special favor."

He ended with a more personal note, one that did not come easy, but one that hinted that the importuning of Dale Bumpers and others had in fact resonated:

"As the son of Dust Bowl farm parents who never finished high school, but who always had the greatest love and the highest hopes for their children, I want to see the American dream live and flourish for my children and the next generation," he said. "I am a man from the plains, a man of the West. I am new enough to Washington to see what must be changed, and I have seen enough, I believe, to see how it can be changed. And if you wish to know the kind of President I will be, I ask you to watch and listen to the kind of candidate I will be."

The fact was, though, almost no one was watching or listening. A snippet of his announcement, taped by local Denver stations, ran for a few seconds on the network newscasts, and only one UPI wire-service reporter flew with him on the United flight from Denver to Chicago to Des Moines. It was that way through most of the summer and early autumn of 1979. Hart would drive with Kathy Bushkin or Kevin Sweeney or a volunteer from McGovern days to a town like Shenandoah, to the Deli Depot on Railroad Street, where a plaque outside marked the rock on which Teddy Roosevelt had spoken during a Presidential visit and where mementoes of the Everly Brothers lined the walls. There'd be five or six folks gathered around the table, eating $1.25 hamburgers, listening to Hart talk about outmoded weapons systems, the need for lighter, cheaper planes and ships. He'd sit in Moose McDuffy's Tavern, off Interstate 384 in Cedar Rapids, and talk with folks on their way home from a shift at the meatpacking plant about an oil-import fee, and ask why workers should be locked into their jobs for a lifetime in order to protect their health care and their pensions. He'd walk the main street of Trear, population 1,456, and pose on Main Street by the famous cast-iron Winding Stair that led up to what were the offices of the *Star-Clipper* newspaper. He'd visit the weekly cattle auction in Tama, and during a break in the buying and selling he'd stand in the pit, avoiding the droppings, and he'd talk a bit about his upbringing as the son of a farm-implements salesman in Ottawa, Kansas, 335 miles to the southwest, but he'd talk mostly about new ideas.

"We cannot meet the future with the tools of the past," he'd say. "The more we care about keeping our historic commitments and meeting our traditional goals, the more we must innovate, the more we must create." They'd look at him, these men who carried fifteen, twenty extra years, thirty, forty extra pounds, and some of them would think, *What planet is he from?* But two or three others would nod and take a brochure when they headed home.

He'd spend his nights in budget motels, hitting the nearby bar if a big-foot journalist happened to be checking up, schmoozing over a Jameson's with Germond or Witcover or Wilkie. Then he'd head to his room, carefully unpacking completely, putting away all his clothes, and sprinkling his room with photos, mementos, tchotchkes to remind him of home, settling in after a long campaign day with a work of Tolstoy or Dostoyevsky ("I know I can cut a deal with Russia," he'd say half jokingly. "I've read their books!").

He'd hit every college and university that would have him, speaking scornfully of nineteenth-century politics in the run-up to the twenty-first century.

"Time," he would say of the old political leaders, "has made change their enemy. But it is long past time to embrace the change we need."

He was, as a campaigner, a work in progress, still pushing back against the plea that he loosen up, reveal a little more of himself, share a light moment.

("You know what a 'mensch' is, Gary?" Warren Beatty said to him after viewing a tape of his appearance at Drake University outside of Des Moines, when Hart had walked onto the stage, flipped open a binder, and begun delivering his speech without so much as a "Good evening." "It's kind of like 'good old boy' or 'soul brother' or 'salt of the earth.' And it's what there's not a hint of in that Drake speech. You had all the warmth of a clerk at the Department of Motor Vehicles explaining why an application wasn't filled out right.")

He was reaching two, three, four at a time—but this was Iowa, this was a caucus, not a primary state, and Hart had learned eight years ago that this was the key to providing a shock to the system. In 1972, the first time anyone had ever bothered to count Presidential preferences in the Iowa caucuses, McGovern had won a quarter of the vote, well behind Ed Muskie and "uncommitted," but enough to get the conversation going about the long-shot anti-war campaign. Four years later, the "Who the hell is this guy?" Carter campaign had packed the Iowa Jefferson–Jackson Day dinner in the fall of 1975, giving them a surprise win in the straw poll and—more important—front-page attention from the *New York Times*. Carter's performance in the caucuses the next year (he'd finished ahead of everyone except "uncommitted") had sent him on the road to the nomination. As the 1980 campaign approached, everyone knew that Iowa would be the first significant test, but very few reporters or Washington-based campaign operatives understood *how* it worked, how polls couldn't really measure much, because what mattered was *intensity*, whether you could summon your supporters to invest not five minutes in a voting booth but five hours in a high school cafeteria or library or living room arguing for your candidate, swapping votes with others whose candidate didn't have enough support to be counted. What mattered was carefully, painstakingly gathering those tiny handfuls of Iowa Democrats who would undertake that arduous night's work and who, under the arcane coding of the process, could be counted on to be "1's" and "2's," those really, really likely to be caucusgoers. Few understood, for that matter, that you could bring hundreds of people to a caucus, but what counted wasn't raw numbers but a formula of delegate allocation that would tax the brain of a mathematics professor . . . so that supporters in small towns and rural communities packed a lot more weight than those in Iowa's bigger towns and cities.

"You could almost see it coming," Elaine Kamarck, one of the Democratic Party's premier experts in the mind-numbing field of party rules and processes, said much later. "Kennedy's campaign was treating Iowa as if it was November: turn out numbers, win it all. It was a classic front-runner mistake, one that's made over and over again. You know that song from *The Music Man*? 'You Gotta Know the Territory'? Teddy didn't."

You could understand it. Inside Teddy's inner circle were veterans of the campaigns of Jack and Bobby, campaigns that had taken place when the Iowa caucuses did not even exist as a factor in the nominating process. Indeed, in the dozen years since Bobby had run, the entire nominating process had changed down to the roots, erasing virtually every premise on which the Kennedy campaigns had been built: how many primaries there

were, how they were run, how they were financed, how delegates were allo-
cated. Gary Hart had around him people who understood the new rules
better than any other team, because they were the very people who had
written those rules.

That unfamiliarity would have been trouble in and of itself. As Kennedy prepared to announce his Presidential run, more trouble surfaced—
incoming fire from a source that some of his zealous adversaries would
have found almost unimaginable.

MEANWHILE, no one in the Republican Party was more determined to
deny the Republican nomination to Ronald Reagan in 1980 than President
Gerald Ford.

And no one in the Republican Party was more important in Ronald
Reagan's campaign for the nomination than President Gerald Ford.

It was certainly not by choice. Apart from the anger from the 1976
primary fight and from Reagan's reluctance to campaign in the fall, the
Ford White House was certain that a Reagan nomination would doom the
party to certain, crushing defeat. They saw the former California governor as little more than "Goldwater with a dye job." Shortly after the 1978
midterm elections, outgoing White House Chief of Staff Dick Cheney
gave a speech to a private gathering of major Republican contributors at
the Sheraton Resort in Bal Harbor, Florida—a speech made public by a
freelance writer for *Rolling Stone* magazine who had slipped into the dinner
with a borrowed busboy's uniform.

"Nothing is more tempting in these complex times," Cheney said, "than
the siren song of simplistic solutions, clung to by those who remember the
'good old days,' but whose vision of the here and now is myopic at best.
They cannot grasp the fact that life does not lend itself to Hollywood end-
ings; and in a time when Presidents must deal—literally—with matters of
life and death, putting the awesome power of the President in the hands of
the purveyors of the politics of platitudes is like putting a loaded gun in the
hands of a novice and inviting him to hunt: Someone is likely to get hurt."

Cheney's speech drew cheers from the usual circles. A *New York Times*
editorial said, "If the Republican Party wishes to stake a claim as the voice

of reason, then it would be wise to heed the words of Dick Cheney as he carries the flag of prudent moderation. We urge the GOP to find a key leadership role for Mr. Cheney in the years ahead."

Many Republicans in office shared this view: senators like Javits of New York, Schweiker of Pennsylvania, Packwood and Hatfield of Oregon, Matthias of Maryland; congressmen like Broomfield of Michigan, Butler of Maryland; governors like Thompson of Illinois, Milliken of Michigan. So did the centrist opinion makers of Washington, like columnist James Reston of the *New York Times* and Ben Bradlee of the *Washington Post*.

The Republican rank and file, however, did *not* share this view; indeed, it was a rank and file that many of these opinion makers, and many of those elected Republican officials, would not have recognized. They were men and women of the working and middle class who had come to the party by choice, not by genealogy. Some of them had gone into battle for Goldwater; others had been driven from the Democrats by taxes, flag burners, rioters. And they had no affection at all for the centrist, moderate brand of Republicanism practiced by two Republican Presidents who had produced the biggest scandal in political history and the worst economy since the Great Depression.

Moreover, as Americans moved out of the Northeast and Midwest to the South and West, the traditionally liberal power centers of the old Republican Party had been supplanted by the growing numbers of religious conservatives and Sunbelt libertarians, who were strongest in states with ever-increasing clout. (In 1960, New York, Pennsylvania, and Ohio had outvoted Florida, Texas, and California in the Electoral College by a 102–66 margin; in November 1980, the three Sunbelt states would outvote their Frostbelt rivals by an 88–83 margin. That disparity was even wider when it came to votes at the convention.)

There was also a more fundamental problem for the moderates, the most fundamental of all: *Who* would be their alternative to Reagan? President Ford was constitutionally ineligible, having served more than half of Richard Nixon's second term, and his record-low job approval ratings made him politically ineligible as well. Under other circumstances, Vice President Bob Dole might have been a contender, but his position in the Ford administration would have made his candidacy a hard sell even if he hadn't dispatched his nascent candidacy with a mortal, self-inflicted wound, courtesy of his acerbic wit.

In November 1979, just after Cardinal Carol Wojtyla had succeeded the one-month papacy of John Paul I, a reporter asked Dole during his weekly press gaggle why the new Pope had chosen the name John Paul II.

"Hey, he's Polish," Dole said. "'John Paul' is real easy to spell." It was the kind of wisecrack the Capitol Hill press corps understood was not for publication. Unfortunately for Dole, his office had invited a reporter from *Our Sunday Visitor* to join the other reporters, as a way of getting Dole attention from the Catholic community. The front-page story brought Dole plenty of attention, enough to end his campaign before it officially began.

Former Texas governor John Connally was a formidable candidate on paper, a six-foot-plus alpha male with a commanding visage, CEO-silver hair, custom-made pin-striped suits, and access to money—lots of it. But his bluff style and swagger reminded voters of the kind of wheeler-dealer tactics that were out of favor in these post-Watergate years. Connally was also wedded to part of his Democratic past; he was given to praising the Great Society of Lyndon Johnson, as well as the wage-price controls he had administered as Richard Nixon's Treasury Secretary. And there was the aura this supremely self-confident man gave off. As conservative columnist James J. Kilpatrick wrote, "He looked like the banker who told you he was calling in your loan as he headed out to the country club in his Cadillac for a round of golf."

There were two Illinois congressmen running, from opposite ideological poles. The highly conservative Phil Crane appeared to be running just in case Ronald Reagan faltered; liberal Republican John Anderson seemed to be searching for that elusive pro–gun control, anti–tax cut Republican voter, who had been spotted slightly less often than the Loch Ness monster.

There had been a time when moderates had put their hopes on Texas Congressman George Herbert Walker Bush, a genuine World War II hero with energy, good looks, and an eminently civilized demeanor. But Bush had lost two races for the U.S. Senate, and had found a home in appointive offices. He was now running the Central Intelligence Agency.

And that left . . . Howard Baker from Tennessee, the fifty-five-year-old Senate Republican leader. Calm of demeanor, placid of voice, Baker had become a national figure during the 1973 Senate Judiciary Committee hearings into the Watergate break-in when he asked over and over: "What did the President know and when did he know it?" He had loyally fought for the doomed legislative agenda of Jerry Ford, and had voted to ratify the treaties that ended U.S. sovereignty over the Panama Canal, part of a record that commended him to the right-thinking brunch-and-cocktails world of Washington, but not to the party's foot soldiers.

Worst of all, Baker was a practicing Washington politician at a time when the Washington wing of the party, exemplified by Jerry Ford, had fallen into widespread disrepute. *What had compromise and accommodation gotten us? A Supreme Court that bans prayer and protects abortions . . . a foreign policy that drinks a toast to Mao-tse-Tung . . . an economy that's killing the American dream.*

So Howard Baker launched his 1980 Presidential campaign into a stiff political wind, carrying the message that "Reagan Can't Win" to a party whose heart and soul Ronald Reagan now owned.

It was a contest that was over almost as soon as it began, a nomination battle that validated the strategy of the man who had been guiding Ronald Reagan toward the White House for more than four years. It was a strategy whose very success that winter and spring would lead to real trouble when the leaves began to fall.

JOHN SEARS CAME to the political big leagues as a twenty-six-year-old lawyer in a New York law firm, where he caught the attention of one of the firm's partners. Richard Nixon had watched Sears the way a grizzled baseball scout might have watched the warm-up pitches of an eighteen-year-old Nolan Ryan; without question, the kid had it. By mid-1968, Sears was playing a major role in the delegate hunt that led Nixon to the nomination. He might have been a major player in the Nixon White House were it not for the jealousy he aroused in Haldeman, Ehrlichman, and especially John Mitchell. They knew a rival for the king's ear when they saw one . . . and given what eventually happened to the men who *did* wind up closest to Nixon's throne, it may have been the biggest break of the young man's life.

He practiced law in Washington, but Sears's driving ambition was to elect a President of the United States, and he found his candidate in Ronald Reagan. The attraction wasn't ideological; Sears had few if any overarching political beliefs. Reagan was, in Sears's judgment, "a superb piece of political horseflesh," and in 1975, defying the conventional wisdom that a sitting President cannot be denied renomination, Sears convinced Reagan to mount a primary challenge, and after a string of early missteps, Reagan almost pulled off the impossible. And among the Gipper's most devoted followers, a low grade argument broke out: Was Sears the tactical genius, or had he fumbled away the nomination by mounting a front-loaded strategy, by ignoring the delegate-rich states in the Northeast, by not launching an all-out convention battle for a more conservative platform?

Ronald Reagan had put Sears in charge of his 1980 effort, and from the beginning there was grumbling in the ranks of the true believers. Sears was no conservative; indeed, he disdained ideology, and in his frequent late-night chats with the press over drinks, he almost seemed to disdain Reagan's core convictions, treating them as something between an inconvenience and an embarrassment. Even more troubling, Sears made it clear that Reagan would run as the nominee-in-waiting. He was, Sears argued, far too prestigious a figure to spend his days at Iowa corn boils and steak fries, shaking hands at factory gates and shopping malls. As for debates . . . it was Ronald Reagan himself who had long ago proclaimed the eleventh commandment, "Thou shalt not speak ill of any fellow Republican," and what was a primary debate but the forum to do just that? The men and women who had been with Reagan from his first days as a candidate for California governor would shake their heads and say *Reagan needs to be out there in the arena, it's his natural turf; he needs to be spelling out how he's different from the Republican President we have.* But Reagan, who hated internal conflicts, followed Sears's guidance, even as the campaign chief began systematically removing old Reagan allies from the campaign: Lyn Nofziger, Martin Anderson, Mike Deaver.

Under other circumstances, the above-the-fray stance of Reagan would have opened the door for another candidate to deliver an early, paralyzing blow to the front-runner. A Republican equivalent of Gary Hart, moving into Iowa early, organizing from the ground up, might well have been able to shock Reagan in the caucuses, shattering the aura of inevitability. It would have taken a candidate unencumbered by official responsibilities, able to devote weeks to on-the-ground campaigning. (From his office in Langley, Virginia, CIA chief George H. W. Bush found himself musing about what might have happened had he stepped down as Director right after Ford's reelection.)

That door never opened. John Connally discovered that Iowans did not respond well to candidates showing up at six-girl high school basketball games in thousand-dollar suits, or lecturing Kiwanis club grocery store owners about the intricacies of floating currencies. John Anderson and Phil Crane had no money, no organization, no presence. And Senator Howard Baker had heavy responsibilities back in Washington, as his party's leader. When he did manage to come to Iowa, he was peppered with complaints about the economy, and the inability of Washington to improve it. He and the other candidates aimed their fire at Reagan's refusal to engage in debates; their television commercials implicitly raised the issue of Reagan's age and mental acuity ("Ready on Day One," said Connally's commercials; "A President We Won't Have to Train," said Baker's).

All to no avail. Reagan barely touched down in Iowa, gliding through appearances before friendly audiences, like the increasingly powerful Iowa Evangelical Assembly, here he demonstrated his brand of humor when the public address system failed. Placing his hands over the podium, Reagan said with a big grin, "at the risk of offending anyone here from the American Civil Liberties Union, I am praying for this microphone."

On January 21, Reagan received 48 percent of the votes in the straw polls taken at the precinct caucuses; Baker was a distant second with 19 percent. No one else managed more than 10 percent.

And for some of Reagan's old hands, the victory was very bad news.

"A lot of us were convinced that what Reagan needed was a swift kick in the butt," Mike Deaver reflected later, "an early warning shot to get him onto the playing field, to shock him out of that cautious, hold-the-ball-and-don't-shoot campaign that Sears was running. But when Reagan won so big in Iowa, it seemed to prove that Sears was right. It meant that the campaign would stay in the hands of a man who did not believe what Reagan believed, and who did not hold his own candidate in high regard."

In the four weeks between Iowa and New Hampshire, the moderate wing of the Republican Party tried hard to turn Howard Baker into a credible alternative to Reagan. President Ford himself gave an interview to the *New York Times*, in which he said, "Everywhere I go, people tell me Ronald Reagan can't be elected President." More than three dozen prominent senators, governors, and other officials signed full page ads that ran in the *Manchester Union-Leader*, New Hampshire's biggest newspaper, urging the voters to choose a Presidential candidate "who has proven experience, judgment, and temperament. . . . Your life may depend on it." (The *Union-Leader*'s fiery publisher, William Loeb, ran front-page editorials denouncing the "Cabal of Cowards who lacked the brains, the guts, and the more manly body parts to back a genuine conservative.")

On February 26, Reagan won the New Hampshire primary in a landslide, capturing more than 55 percent of the vote, to Howard Baker's 24 percent. John Connally said he would put all his resources into South Carolina's contest on March 8 (where Reagan beat him by a 2–1 margin); Phil Crane dropped out completely. John Anderson stayed in through the Massachusetts and Vermont primaries, and then announced that he would leave the Republican race to ponder the possibility of an independent run. For all practical purposes, the contest was over, although Howard Baker and John Connally did compete in later primaries, in states where Reagan participated in three uncontentious debates devoted to denunciations of Ted Kennedy and the Democratic Congress.

Reagan had won without breaking a proverbial sweat. There had been no compelling reason for him to plunge into the campaign frenzy, or to debate his rivals in settings where there was real pressure. Nor was there any reason for him to change the command or the direction of the campaign as it prepared for the general election. If Reagan's nomination had come with a certain lack of energy or passion in the party . . . well, that would surely change when Reagan and the Republicans found themselves fighting for the White House against the man who symbolized everything they opposed.

After all, there was no doubt that Ronald Reagan would be running against Ted Kennedy . . . was there?

AMONG THOSE ON THE right, the idea of Ted Kennedy as the "liberal media darling" was no more questionable than the idea that water is wet.

The press had helped create "Camelot," running all those pictures of Jack and the adorable Caroline and John Jr., while studiously ignoring the President's behavior. It had turned Bobby into a saintly martyr. It had lionized Ted, as well, the last lion, carrying the torch, the flag. But the conservatives' indictment missed one key point. However left the press tilts, there is one bias that overrides any ideology: The press desperately wants to see itself as the tribune that holds the powerful to account, and there is no one who is seen as more powerful than a Presidential front-runner. Ted Kennedy was about to find that out in the days before his announcement: hit first by two quick jabs, then by a roundhouse right that staggered him.

On November 1, ABC's *20/20* newsmagazine show ran an interview with Kennedy that began with Tom Jarriel asking him:

"Senator, you cheated in college. You panicked at Chappaquiddick. Do you have what it takes to be President?"

Two days later, *Saturday Night Live* opened with that sketch showing the dripping wet Ted Kennedy arriving for his announcement.

The next night, in prime time, a one-hour *CBS Reports* was telecast, anchored by veteran correspondent Roger Mudd, a MacLean, Virginia, neighbor and longtime friend of Robert and Ethel Kennedy (it had, in fact, been Mudd who took Ethel's hand on the night of June 4, 1968, and guided her to Robert Kennedy's side in his last conscious moments). If the Kennedy camp assumed that these cordial relations with the family would yield friendly interviews, they were quickly disabused of that assumption.

In fact, said one Kennedy aide, "if we'd known how bad it would be, we would have sprung a surprise announcement three days earlier, and under the Equal Time Rule, the damn program would never have run."

There was dramatic nighttime footage that retraced Kennedy's 1969 Chappaquiddick accident, the footage making it almost impossible to believe the Senator's account that he had turned onto a dirt road leading to a rickety wooden bridge by accident. Kennedy's attempt to explain those circumstances was not helpful:

"... the circumstances at that—that particular eve—evening did not involve physical trauma, did involve an accident, did involve enormous sense of—of—of loss in terms of the—the life of an individual.... Now I have served in the United States Senate for sixteen years, I've taken positions,

I've spoken out on issues . . . and there have been other factors that have impacted on my life and people will have to make that judgment."

There was a seemingly innocent question about the private lives of public figures, and after Kennedy talked about "the natural inquisitiveness of people," Mudd asked flatly:

"What's the present state of your marriage, Senator?"

Kennedy, who had been living apart from Joan for some time, answered:

"Well, I think it's a—we've had some difficult times, but I think we've—have—we've been able to make some very good progress, and it's—I would say that it's—it's—it's—I'm delighted that we're able to share the time and the relationship that we do have."

Most devastating was the question any candidate would pay a reporter to ask:

"Senator, why do you want to be President?"

What was clear from his first words was that, in the process of seeking endorsements, consulting with Congressional colleagues, governors, and party leaders, reaching out to old family friends and retainers, and raising money, neither Kennedy nor his campaign had ever bothered to think through that question. So the answer came out . . . like this.

"Well, I'm—were I to—to make the—the announcement and—to run, the reasons that I would run is because I have a great belief in this country, that it is—has more natural resources than any nation in the world, has the greatest educated population in the world, and the greatest political system in the world. And yet, I see at the current time, after twelve years of Republican rule, that most of the industrial nations of the world are exceeding us in terms of productivity . . . And it just seems to me that this nation can cope and deal with its problems as it has in the past . . . And I would basically feel that—it's imperative for this country to either move forward, that it can't stand still, or otherwise it moves back."

"Well, we got one break," Kennedy aide Dun Gifford said, when the broadcast ended. "No one was watching."

In conventional TV terms, Gifford was right; only 17 percent of the TV audience tuned in; more than three times that number were watching the first network telecast of the blockbuster shark-bites-man movie *Jaws* on ABC. Among those "no ones," however, was every political journalist, every operative, every financial contributor, and every citizen-activist who had been drawn into politics over the last twenty years, from Manchester to Des Moines to Milwaukee to Westwood. And, like that far larger *Jaws* audience, what they saw was . . . blood in the water.

And it was *not* just that audience. Yes, in an age long before computers and streamed video found their way into millions of homes, "Teddy" was seen in its entirety only once. But the half-life of the broadcast was significant, not just in the clips that led the morning newscasts the next day, or the evening news later that night, but in hoots of derision that came from some of Kennedy's most ardent admirers in the press.

Mary McGrory, the *Washington Star* liberal who all but worshipped at the Kennedy shrine, wrote that the program "reveals that the Senator, even when invited to expand on the themes of his own choosing, is not articulate or even coherent." Jimmy Breslin wrote that "I found Kennedy annoying, wanting, disturbing . . . I think people will think [about Chappaquiddick] 'if this guy doesn't care about what happened to the girl, why is he going to care about me and my kids?'" The *New York Times*'s Anthony Lewis described Kennedy as "stumbling, inarticulate, unconvincing."

From his room in the Savery Hotel in Des Moines, Gary Hart and two of his aides watched the program with a mix of disbelief and delight. For Hart, who had believed from his first days in politics that ideas were the keys to victory, the idea that a major political figure like Kennedy could not explain what he wished to do with Presidential power was almost unfathomable. For his aides, who were thinking in less cerebral terms, the sight of a highly respected newsman like Roger Mudd asking about Chappaquiddick meant that they would not have to fuel the "character controversy," thus risking exposure by a press that would deplore such tactics, even as it soaked up every revelation and rumor.

For the record, Press Secretary Kathy Bushkin issued a statement to the two Des Moines–based wire service stringers and a *Des Moines Register* reporter-intern, the only ones following Hart on this visit.

"Senator Hart," it said, "is staking his campaign on the ideas and proposals he has set forth in the 177 pages of his book, *A New Democracy*." Off the record, she offered to bet $100 with any member of the press who thought Kennedy would participate in an Iowa debate.

Neither the CBS broadcast nor the harsh reviews kept Kennedy's announcement from dominating the political news of November. On the morning of November 10, the Senate Caucus Room was ablaze with lights from the network crews, every square foot of the cavernous chamber packed with longtime Kennedy supporters, curious Congressional staffers, and several platoons of journalists.

His speech, crafted by a committee that included Ted Sorensen, Carey Parker, Dave Burke, and Bob Shrum, was a compendium of liberal pieties, coupled with a pointed assault on "twelve long years of Republican misrule."

"The Nixon–Ford years," he said, "put people before profits, corporations before compassion, wealth before workers. Gerald Ford is a nice man, but he has stumbled into misadventure after mistake, and what has been lost is a sense of hope for the future. America needs a Presidency at the center of the action, fighting for the dream that must never die."

While the announcement was packed with proposals—universal day care, universal health insurance, a return to wage-and-price controls—it did not stop a series of hostile questions from the press, beginning with columnist Bob Novak asking, "How long did it take your staff and your speechwriters to figure out why you want to be President?" and ending with CBS's Leslie Stahl asking, "What would you say to millions of women who want to know if Chappaquiddick and the rumors about your conduct as a married man make you unfit for the White House?"

Later that day, Kennedy flew to Boston, where he repeated his announcement in the historic setting of Faneuil Hall, then flew to Manchester, New Hampshire, and Des Moines, Iowa. It was the premise of the Kennedy campaign that victories in those first two states would effectively end the nomination contest. More than a premise, it was an assumption rooted in the numbers in the polls, the instincts and inclinations of the pols, and the accumulated wisdom of the press.

Only a few outliers among these circles asked what was a hopelessly naïve, embarrassingly simplistic question: *Suppose it didn't exactly happen?*

GARY HART DIDN'T WIN the Iowa caucuses. He did much better than that.

When Ted Kennedy touched down in Des Moines that November evening in 1979, it looked like the Democrats would not even need to hold the caucuses. Fifteen thousand greeted him at a boisterous rally in the Convention Center, and just about every significant Democrat from Senator John Culver to Congressman Tom Harkin to ex-governor and Senator Harold Hughes was there for the laying on of hands. It was that very success that led to Kennedy's first trouble in Iowa. Late that night at the bar of the Savery Hotel—the all-but-official Ground Zero for information, rumors, speculation, and wisecracks—a Kennedy advance man, a familiar campaign figure going back twenty years, took a sip from his fourth Scotch and soda, and said to a table of reporters, "It's like that governor from Louisiana once said: The only way Teddy doesn't crack 60 percent here is if he's caught with a live man or a dead . . . uh . . . well . . ."

The reporters kept that unfortunate image to themselves, but not the number. Since it had come from the campaign itself, it replaced the quadrennial attempt by the press to figure out how to measure a win. Four years earlier in New Hampshire, Ronald Reagan's state chair had airily suggested his candidate would win two-thirds of the vote, thus making Reagan's tie against a sitting President look like a defeat. Now, thanks to the hapless Kennedy staffer (who found himself dispatched to Utah the next morning), a Kennedy landslide was the officially sanctioned benchmark. And no matter how dominant a figure Ted Kennedy was, racking up 60 percent in a multi-candidate field was a daunting proposition.

It was a field that included California Governor Jerry Brown, who was campaigning in Iowa solely for the right to be included in the *Des Moines Register* debate; South Carolina Senator Ernest "Fritz" Hollings, whose razor-sharp mind was disguised by a voice that sounded remarkably like the old radio character Senator Beauregard Claghorn (of South Carolina); ex–Pennsylvania governor and cable-TV millionaire Milton Shapp, making his second run at the job; and California Senator Alan Cranston, running as a peace candidate devoted to sharp decrease in all military spending— except for the B-1 bomber, responsible for thousands of California jobs.

It was a candidate who was *not* running, however, who proved to be as significant an obstacle to Ted Kennedy's Iowa fortunes as the mob of actual candidates.

Ever since his last-minute, "I still don't believe it" loss in 1976, Jimmy Carter had made no secret of his desire for another shot at the White House.

"I don't think it's unreasonable," he said over and over, "that a candidate who wins a million more votes than the next man has a legitimate claim on his party." In fact, Carter felt so strongly about his claim on the nomination that he felt no need to invest months of his time begging for votes in Iowa; he'd *done* that already, he'd *won* the popular vote by a greater margin than John Kennedy and Richard Nixon *combined*. He would wait, at least until Iowa and New Hampshire were done, and then let his natural base in the South propel him to the lead with a series of primary victories on "Southern Super Tuesday" later in the spring. That strategy required one crucial element: Ted Kennedy *had* to be stopped before he became inevitable.

That was not, of course, the explanation given by Jody Powell and Hamilton Jordan, the two young Carter aides who had engineered his '76 nomination, for their presence in Iowa in early January. They were, they explained, "visiting old friends, reliving good times," and providing commentary for ABC's TV and radio networks. What they did not explain was that they were meeting with Gary Hart's Iowa organizers, providing them with invaluable lists of caucus goers from 1976, and reaching out to those caucus goers with suggestions on "how to keep the nominating process open, how to give Democrats from around the nations the chance to be heard on who should lead the party to victory." Not that the Carter backers needed much guidance; many of them came from inside Iowa's thriving evangelical community, with strong views about the private behavior, or misbehavior, of public men, and the prospect of a Ted Kennedy Presidency . . . well, if a vote for Gary Hart could help prevent that disaster, fine.

Kennedy himself campaigned as front-runner, as though the successes of the McGovern and Carter campaigns had never happened. He stayed out of the four debates among Democrats, and his speech at the Jefferson–Jackson Day Dinner was aimed solely at "the crimes, misdemeanors, misadventures, and misbegotten failures of the Nixon–Ford administration." It was Gary Hart whose speech stirred the most reaction: In simple, blunt language, he told the assembled Democrats that "we must face hard facts: some of the programs and policies that have fostered our prosperity and progress for more than thirty years have ceased to work. We will not forge a better future if we cling to the past."

In the days just before the caucuses, Kennedy suffered another media blow, one that came not from a rival campaign, nor from a political reporter. *Reader's Digest*, the second-biggest-selling magazine in the U.S., best known for its evocations of a simpler, small-town America, published a lengthy investigative report on Chappaquiddick, using computer studies to prove that Kennedy had to have been driving at an excessive rate of speed. Worse for Kennedy was a nationally aired TV spot promoting the story, featuring a trench coat–clad "reporter" describing an event "which may have changed history. This is Chappaquiddick—and this—is the bridge." In the small towns and farm communities of Iowa, where back issues of *Reader's Digest* could be found in thousands of attics and basements, the article, and the commercials, carried heavy weight.

On Monday, January 21, on a dry, relatively mild night, more than 90,000 Democrats attended the Iowa caucuses. When the arguments and the horse trading and vote swapping were done, Ted Kennedy had won 38 percent of the precinct delegates . . . and Gary Hart had won 33 percent. For the broadcast networks that night, the story line was obvious.

"Ted Kennedy's 'Inevitability Express' may have jumped the tracks tonight," CBS's Dan Rather reported from Des Moines. When Kennedy appeared on the late-night network specials, the questions were virtually identical: "Is your campaign in trouble?" The next day's political headlines asserted "A Hart-Stopper for Ted," "The Front-Runner Stumbles," and, from the now-conservative *New York Post*: "Teddy Unsteady."

For his part, Hart expressed gratitude that Iowans "have given me the chance to take my campaign forward, and offer my ideas about how to meet the challenges of the future." And his campaign breathed a sigh of relief that he had finished second, *not* first.

"A win," his closest aide, Billy Shore, reflected, "would have over-whelmed us. We would simply not have had the resources to deal with the onslaught of the press, the demands on his time, the drain on the money. What we needed was a surprise that began to narrow the choices of the Democrats. And that's exactly what we got."

The Kennedy forces argued that "a win is a win is a win. We got more votes than anyone else. Period." ("That's what President Muskie said in New Hampshire," shot back the *Boston Globe*'s Curtis Wilkie.) Another Kennedy aide said, "Thank God for the primary calendar. We have a month until the next test—and it's in our own backyard."

He was right about the calendar and the geography. In a larger sense, he was dead wrong, on both counts.

The four weeks between Iowa and New Hampshire gave the Hart campaign the most precious of all gifts: time. The candidate whose press office had had to beg for a line or two was now besieged by requests for interviews, profiles, face time. Dozens of reporters, columnists, TV bigfeet and their camera crews were asking for—or demanding—access. Hart volunteers in states across America were calling, pleading for a day or two of the Senator's time: *They want to see him in Cleveland! . . . I've got three hundred contributors in Pacific Palisades—that's three hundred grand if he'll do a Q and A! . . . We can fill the Union Theater if he can come to Madison, and remember, Wisconsin was McGovern's first primary win!* The campaign was still running on financial fumes, with payless paydays for staff members, with money being wired into bank accounts to keep the phones and electricity in campaign offices from being turned off. And some of the more savvy veterans of past insurgent campaigns had begun to notice a potentially fatal problem: In some of the biggest states, like Pennsylvania, Ohio, and New York, the campaign had failed to file full slates of delegates. If those slates were not completed quickly, it didn't matter how well Hart might do in those later contests; he would have deprived himself of hundreds of potential convention votes.

Had the New Hampshire primary come a week or so after Iowa, the Hart campaign would have had no time to deal with any of this; the demands of the first-in-the-nation contest would have taken all of the resources, all of the energy. Instead, there was a month with nothing in between Iowa and New Hampshire. That calendar had been specifically pushed by supporters of both Jimmy Carter and Ted Kennedy to ensure that an unknown candidate would not be able to score a surprise in Iowa, and then catapult into New Hampshire a week later. Now, that calendar was giving Gary Hart breathing room.

Under the direction of Tim Kraft, who had been national field director of Carter's 1976 campaign, Hart supporters succeeded in filling out full delegate slates in virtually every state, as Hart stole a day every now and then from New Hampshire to campaign elsewhere, hitting college campuses wherever he went in search of volunteer troops. (At Occidental College, a gangly nineteen-year-old undergraduate from Hawaii shook hands with Hart while a friend snapped a picture. "I'm going to hold on to that," said Barry Obama. "Might come in handy someday.")

With painful memories of the divisions that had splintered the Democrats in 1968 and 1972, Hart's forces were instructed to broaden the slates beyond the reformers' obsession with blacks, women, and the young. *Find young union leaders, women bankers, black business folks, and for God's sake, don't tell us you can't find any Catholics in Ohio and Pennsylvania and Wisconsin who are for Gary!*

Equally important was the campaign's success in tapping new sources of campaign money. Back in 1972, a young entrepreneur named Morris Dees had created a highly successful direct-mail effort for McGovern, signing up supporters who agreed to contribute $10 a month or more. Using a similar device—with a $25-a-month pledge and coupon books to make the club seem more official—the "Hart for President" club began generating hundreds, then a few thousand, dollars a day. Hart's campaign also reached out to a whole new generation of businesspeople, whose work, and whose existence, was unknown to the more traditional insiders who dominated Ted Kennedy's campaign. In California's Silicon Valley, where technology geeks had become multimillionaires, Gary Hart's blend of social liberalism and pro-growth economics was striking a chord among the creators of Tandy, Commodore, Texas Instruments, and Atari, and among younger entrepreneurs like thirty-one-year-old Richard Dennis, who said, "I am trying to get a Democrat nominated who's not in the special interest generation." (Hart had even sent his official announcement to users of a commercial online information service called CompuServe. When one of Kennedy's campaign chiefs was told about it, he said: "'CompuServe'? What is that, a ball machine for tennis players?")

And Hart's appeal went beyond the computer world. A new financial player named Mike Milken, who specialized in raising venture capital for start-ups, was particularly helpful tapping into colleagues. And in

Hollywood, Warren Beatty was reviving the rock concerts that had raised the money to power George McGovern's 1972 campaign.

That four-week spread between Iowa and New Hampshire also enabled Hart's campaign to use one of its key resources—its deep familiarity with the Byzantine rules of the process—to use its funds in "creative" ways. In the post-Watergate world, before the lawyers began drilling loopholes and sinkholes in the campaign finance rules, there were strict limits on how much a campaign would spend in each state, based on population: In New Hampshire in 1980, the limit was $294,000. Some of the ways around this limit were obvious; campaigns would stay just across the border in Vermont or Maine and charge the costs to those states. They'd advertise on Boston radio and television and charge the costs to Massachusetts's primary, where the limit was much higher. For Hart, something else was needed, some way to enable them to use the money now flooding into headquarters to overcome Ted Kennedy's name, stature, and ties to the Democratic Party.

It was four days after the Iowa caucuses when a beaming Tim Kraft walked into a senior staff meeting at Hart headquarters in Denver and held up his hand.

"Has anyone ever heard of 'delegate committees'?" he asked. After a moment of silence, Kraft explained. In most primary states, voters chose not only Presidential candidates, but slates of delegates; and those delegate candidates were also allowed to raise and spend money on their behalf. In the first week of February, Kennedy's campaign began getting troublesome calls from New Hampshire: *I saw three ads this morning on the* Today *show for guys I never heard of, but they're running for delegates, and the ads are all about how great Gary Hart is.* By the time the primary was over, more than $135,000 worth of ads, brochures, and mailings had been spent on Hart's delegate committee. The Federal Communications Commission found violations of campaign spending limits, and sanctioned Hart's campaign— eighteen months later.

If Kennedy's campaign team misread the impact of the calendar, they made an even-bigger miscalculation in assuming that Teddy would benefit from New Hampshire's proximity. Familiarity may not always breed contempt, but in Kennedy's case, it meant that New Hampshire voters had been consistently exposed to Kennedy's career, and his political philosophy;

and that was definitely a two-edged sword. All through the 70s, Boston television had shown southern New Hampshire, the state's population center, the incendiary battles over school busing, with white working-class parents in South Boston—"Southie"—fighting to stop their children from being transported into the heavily black neighborhood of Roxbury. It was a policy Senator Kennedy had supported. For blue-collar voters in and around Manchester, who worked the mills and factories that had survived into 1980, the images of angry parents and frightened children struck with primal force. There was also the political reality that tens of thousands of Massachusetts residents had fled over the border to escape the burdens of "Taxachusetts"; in fact, New Hampshire was one of the only states in the Union that had neither an income nor a sales tax. For many of these refugees, "Massachusetts" was the symbol of the costs of government they no longer chose to bear. The "Live Free or Die" slogan on New Hampshire license plates could have come with a footnote: "Live Free of Taxes." The kind of liberalism championed by Kennedy, the kind that Massachusetts seemed to symbolize, was a hard sell once politicians crossed the border into Nashua, Manchester, and Concord, even to many Democrats.

And there was one other factor about the New Hampshire primary: It was *open.* Any voter, Democrat, Independent, or Republican, could choose to vote in either primary. For genuine independents, Gary Hart's "heresies" on economic growth, on military reform, on the perils of overgrown government, struck responsive chords. For Republicans, there was something even more appealing about crossing over to vote in the Democratic primary: They wouldn't have to wait until November to vote against Ted Kennedy. The walking, breathing embodiment of everything they were against was on the ballot *right now.*

The Kennedy campaign, for its part, stayed on a comfortable, familiar course, convinced that the close call in Iowa was an aberration. The state's AFL-CIO held rallies that packed the Notre Dame hockey arena in Berlin and the Civic Center in downtown Manchester; students jammed into the theater at St. Anselm's College and his television ads showcased Kennedy with his children, and with prominent Democrats who endorsed him. He still turned down all debates, leaving Hart and the other candidates to taunt him for his absence. Senator Hollings, quoting Eleanor Roosevelt's crack about Jack from 1960, suggested that "Teddy might want to show a little less profile and a little more courage." (Hollings also aimed one of his sharper darts at California Governor Jerry Brown. After listening to him explain that his campaign was "serve the people, save the earth, explore the universe," Hollings extended his right hand, separated his middle and ring fingers, and said, "Live long and prosper, Jerry.")

Hart's campaign in those last weeks was a blur of eighteen-hour days, guided by New Hampshire native Jeannie Shaheen and scheduler Sue Casey: He worked the town dumps on Saturday morning; bantered with Connie and Maria at the Merrimack Restaurant in downtown Manchester; shook hands at plant gates at five a.m.

And then there was the annual Woodsman Conclave in Berlin, where fate took an ax to Ted Kennedy's hopes for a landslide win.

Hart arrived clad in a checkered shirt, Levi's, and boots, familiar garb for the Coloradoan. Passing over the offer to compete in the log sawing and pole climbing, Hart instead reached for a full-length double-bit ax, and eyed the three-foot target just twenty yards away. His first throw bounced off the target, but the cameras of the press corps had been out of position, and the gaggle yelled at him to try again. And he threw . . . and the ax revolved once, and then again—and hit square in the bull's-eye—and stayed there.

The footage made every network weekend newscast, and became the image in every piece all that week in the run-up to the primary. It made the front page of every New Hampshire paper, including the *Manchester Union-Leader,* whose publisher, William Loeb, thought Ronald Reagan's conservative credentials were shaky. Its impact was clearly felt when New Hampshire's primary voters went to the polls on February 26.

Ted Kennedy once again got more votes than Gary Hart, winning 48,500 votes to Hart's 46,300, with the other Democrats trailing far behind. And once again, Kennedy suffered a serious political defeat. "They say most accidents happen close to home," CBS's Bill Plante reported from the Sheraton-Wayfarer in Manchester. "Well, tonight, Senator Kennedy suffered a near disaster right in his own backyard." The next day's New York *Daily News* showed a front-page picture of a clearly discomfited Kennedy under the banner headline: "Hearing Hart Beats, Ted?"

Within a matter of days, two more pieces of bad news hit the Kennedy camp. First, on the morning after the New Hampshire primary, the senior staff learned what no campaign ever wants to hear: it was broke.

The premise of the campaign, fully understandable given his clear front-runner status, was that victories in Iowa and New Hampshire would effectively end the race just as it was starting. There was no reason not to sign up the whole first tier of consultants, pollsters, strategists, advance men, and media producers months ahead of time. Twenty years earlier, they had been hungry young men, happy to spend months in no-star motels for subsistence wages. Now they were no longer young, and it was their families who were hungry. From countless onetime foot soldiers came the same message:

"I have a mortgage, I have two college tuitions, I have a weekend getaway. I love Ted, but I can't sign up for less than forty thousand dollars."

Then there was the plane, the chartered 727 that cost $12,000 a *day* when it was flying, and $5,000 a day when it was just sitting on the damn tarmac. And there were the hotel rooms, and the meals on the road, and the phone bills, and the postage for the mailings . . . and when New Hampshire was over, the campaign had raised $4.1 million and had spent all but $160,000 of it. What was worse, the rules were so damned *different* from the way the game had been played. There were plenty of allies who'd be happy to write a $50,000 check to Ted, but they couldn't—$1,000 a person was the maximum, and even if you got checks from husbands, wives, and children, that would take you only so far. And anyway, the friendliest supporters had already contributed, were, in the parlance of 1980, "maxed out." The family had money, of course, but there was something most people didn't know. Back in '68, when Bobby jumped into the race at the last moment, the family had put millions into the campaign, fully expecting that they could raise it when the campaign ended. Robert Kennedy would either be President or a powerful senator. But after he was killed, the appetite for contributing to that effort faded; that money was never recovered. And now, with two "victories" that looked more like defeats, some potential donors were beginning to develop a serious case of buyer's remorse.

Gary Hart's campaign, by contrast, had been a guerrilla operation from the beginning, with unpaid volunteers doing the bulk of the logistical work,

making the phone calls, advancing the candidate, leafleting the neighborhoods. Now that he was emerging as a contender, those next-generation
entrepreneurs and their friends were starting to open their checkbooks, and
the direct-mail solicitations of Morris Dees began to bear negotiable fruit.

And Warren Beatty was working the celebrity circuit again. While
much of the Old Guard Democrats were in Ted Kennedy's camp, the
younger generation—Nicholson, Gene Hackman, Diane Keaton, and
younger rock acts like the Talking Heads—helped bring large sums into
Hart's campaign.

'I don't believe this!" one of Hart's senior advisors said a week after New
Hampshire. "I think we're gonna have more money than Ted!" He was
cautioned, on pain of serious bodily injury, to keep that fact quiet until the
last possible moment.

The second piece of news was, if possible, more devastating to Kennedy.
On February 29, Jimmy Carter announced he would *not* be a candidate for
President. "If I were to run," he said from his front porch in Plains, Georgia, "I am confident I would win the nomination. But the other day, I was
talking with my daughter, Amy, and she convinced me that my work as an
international emissary of peace, spiritual leader, and symbol of goodwill is
too important to be diverted into political conflict."

The problem for Kennedy wasn't that Carter posed any kind of threat to
the liberal base that was the source of Kennedy's strength. The problem was
the damn *calendar*. When the Democratic National Committee designed
the rules for 1980 nomination, Jimmy Carter's supporters still held the whip
hand; they very much wanted to keep the South as a key player in the process, something the Southern states wanted as well. So three major Southern states—Georgia, Alabama, and Florida—set their primaries for March
11. With Carter out of the race, and with the nomination rapidly turning
into a two-person race, the voters in those three states found themselves
with a clear choice: Ted Kennedy . . . or the guy who *wasn't* Ted Kennedy.

In 1980, several million Southern whites, who had started pulling the
Republican lever for President years earlier, remained enrolled in the party
of their ancestors. For them, the Kennedys were the symbol of Northern
intrusion into their customs and mores. It wasn't that they wanted to go

back to segregationist days—hell, look at some of those football players
wearing the uniforms of the Crimson Tide and the Gators and the Bull-
dogs now that integration was a fact of life!—but old wounds of pride still
remained. And it was more than race; Teddy had lined up with the anti-war
crowd, the longhairs, the flag burners, and, besides, did anyone believe we
really knew the story of what had happened with him and that young girl?

By conventional measures, it would have seemed impossible for Gary
Hart to exploit Kennedy's weakness in the South. It was John and Robert
Kennedy who had drawn him into politics in the first place; he had run
the campaign of the most anti-war, "radical" Presidential nominee since
William Jennings Bryan. His age, his dress, his whole affect spoke of a
candidate utterly at odds with a Southern sensibility, one that included a
deep reverence for the U.S. military and its traditions.

Except . . . one of Hart's abiding passions as a senator had been military reform, a movement that argued, in Hart's words "we are spending
ourselves weak" by throwing billions at gold-plated weapons systems fated
to break down in combat, to leave the U.S. forces weighed down, bereft
of the mobility that won modern wars. This was by no means a movement from the ideological Left. The "Military Reform Caucus" that Hart
helped found included Republicans like Representatives Charles Grassley,
Newt Gingrich, Senator William Cohen. And he had become a very close
friend of the forty-four-year-old Naval pilot who had become the Navy's
liaison to the U.S. Senate in 1977 and whose father and grandfather were
both senior admirals. Hart had traveled abroad with the liaison, even been
a groomsman at the ex-pilot's wedding, and had shared many conversations about defense policy . . . and about a potential political career for the
ex-pilot.

Two weeks before the trio of Southern primaries, the pilot resigned his
commission. A week later, TV ads began running throughout the region.

"I'm retired naval aviator John McCain. My seven years in a North
Vietnamese prison gave me plenty of time to think about how America
must defend itself from its enemies. The stale arguments about 'more' or
'less' are meaningless. What we need is 'better'—ships and planes that can
fight the conflicts of the late twentieth century. I've watched Senator Gary

Hart for three years. As a member of the Armed Services Committee, he's fought those who would weaken our defenses, *and* those who would waste taxpayer dollars. Wouldn't it be great if our fighting men had a President who had their back? A President like Gary Hart."

On March 11, Gary Hart beat Kennedy in Alabama and Georgia, and held him to a virtual tie in Florida (in each state, 10 to 15 percent of voters voted for Jimmy Carter, unable to stomach either of the major contenders). Hart also won 120 of the 205 delegates at stake, putting him ahead of Kennedy. The calendar, however, now turned ominous for Hart. The coming tests in March and April were all in the heart of Kennedy's strength: Illinois, where Chicago Mayor Jane Byrne and the remnants of the Daley machine were solidly for Ted; New York, where the old Democratic alliance of labor, blacks, and Jews were all but bound by blood; Pennsylvania, where the Philadelphia machine of Billy Green had helped put Jack Kennedy in the White House. The mood was understandably somber at Hart's Denver headquarters, as pollster Dottie Lynch combed through the numbers.

"Here's the paradox," she said. "When voters are reminded about Chappaquiddick, Ted's support falls right through the floor among women, even self-described 'Kennedy Democrats.' But the same voters *also* say they'd punish anyone engaging in 'negative' campaigning by voting against them."

"In other words," said Billy Shore, "we have to remind them about Chappaquiddick without . . . reminding them of Chappaquiddick."

At that moment, the phone in the conference room rang.

And Ray Strother, Gary Hart's media producer, looked at the phone, leapt to his feet, and ran out of the room.

The ad that began running in Illinois, New York, Wisconsin, and Pennsylvania was stark, with nothing on camera but a telephone, the only color in the ad a bulb on the phone blinking red, as an announcer, his voice pitched low, began to speak:

"The most awesome responsibility in the world lies in the hand that picks up this phone. It must be a steady hand, who can face a crisis calmly, firmly, resolutely. Because when that phone rings, panic or paralysis will put our freedom, our survival at stake. When you come right down to it . . . is there anything more important in a President? Gary Hart: a steady hand for troubled times."

The message helped keep Kennedy's margins down in the big industrial states, but Kennedy's strengths among traditional Democratic blocs were simply too strong. From New York's Garment Center to Chicago's Grant Park to Philadelphia's shipyards, Kennedy spoke of "a battle for the soul of the Democratic Party," the threat to the progressive tradition posed by "those who march under the flag of justice, but neither understand nor respect nor support it." With the strong backing of labor and blacks, he won by clear margins in Illinois, Pennsylvania, and New York; only in Wisconsin did Hart's "new politics" message prevail. Yet once again the rules and the calendar combined to make Kennedy's victories pyrrhic.

By 1980, Democrats had disposed of virtually every vestige of the "winner take all" approach to the primaries; more than nine of every ten delegates were chosen by "proportional representation." You could win by a landslide in a Congressional district, and still get only one more delegate than the opponent you'd crushed. You could lose a state by fifteen points and still wind up with almost as many delegates as the winner. Hart's showing in Pennsylvania's small towns and in New York's suburbs and upstate communities kept Kennedy from piling up the kinds of margins Ronald Reagan was racking up on the Republican side, where "winner take all" was alive and well.

("It's a basic difference in philosophy," explained a CBS analyst. "Republicans treat Presidential politics like a poker game: You win the pot, you win the money. For Democrats, it's like a children's birthday party, where everyone gets the same size piece of cake as everyone else.")

And now, with the end of March, spring became the season of Ted Kennedy's discontent. The battlegrounds shifted to the Midwest, the South, the Mountain West, where the Kennedy brand lacked the power, and where "New Democrats" like Hart were prevalent. These were also states where the Hart volunteers had been at work for months, culling lists of likely voters, drilling foot soldiers in the art of turning out caucus goers and primary voters.

"If you remember nothing less about this process, remember this," Tim Kraft had instructed his lieutenants. "*This is not November. This is not the Electoral College.* The big states may actually be less valuable, because you get more delegates winning big in small states than you do winning closely in big states."

All through April and May, Hart's tactics, his "not from the East" persona, and his now-significant financial advantage, yielded wins in Indiana, North Carolina, Nebraska, Oregon, Arkansas, Kentucky, Nevada. The big Southern prize, Texas, went for Hart by a fifteen-point margin. ("From the Great Beyond, LBJ Wins Last Fight With the Kennedys," headlined a *Dallas Morning News* postmortem.) Now only the last contests lay ahead, on June 8, with California, Ohio, and New Jersey the major prizes. The inevitable sports metaphors flew: "Kennedy, Behind in the Last Round, Seeks a Knockout"; "It's Fourth and Long and the Clock's Running Out"; "Five Lengths Behind Down the Stretch."

A buoyant Gary Hart teased some of the biggest of the journalistic bigfeet when they met for an off-the-record breakfast in Washington six days before the Super Tuesday contests.

"Can't you guys come up with some fresh clichés?" a buoyant Gary Hart asked. "You know, 'Ted's Down a Pawn and a Knight' or 'Out of Trumps on a Six-Heart Bid'?"

"Maybe you can use that line when you see Ted," breakfast host Godfrey Sperling said, as he looked at a piece of AP wire copy. "Or haven't you heard? Kennedy just challenged you to debate before Super Tuesday."

Hart paused for a moment, then retreated to familiar ground.

"I've been calling for debates for six months," Hart said. "The fact that I have more delegates now doesn't change anything."

There was considerably more skepticism among Hart's senior staff when they met that night over dinner in a private room of Washington's Hay-Adams Hotel. There was no misreading the strategic shrewdness of Kennedy's debate challenge. Hart was 100 delegates ahead, but there were more than 600 delegates at stake the following Tuesday. Kennedy needed to win by big margins to overcome Hart's lead, and the debate challenge would essentially freeze the "Ted Is Dead" narrative that was driving media coverage. Nor was there any doubt what Kennedy's line of attack would be. *Gary Hart's not a real Democrat; he's no friend of labor; he opposed domestic content laws, he's against auto import quotas; he's for tax breaks for business. He wants to take an ax to Social Security and Medicare and other entitlements.*

"The problem," Kathy Bushkin said to her colleagues, "is that Gary thinks his ideas are good enough to get you to vote for him. He's got more positions than the Kama Sutra—I'm talking *policy* here, guys—and when the press asks him to put them in a sentence, he snaps: 'You mean, what's my bumper sticker?' We have *got* to keep him out of sounding like a Brookings Institute Fellow with ice water in his veins."

The campaigns agreed to a one-hour debate on the Saturday evening before the primaries, moderated by ABC's Frank Reynolds. The Hart campaign cleared Friday evening and Saturday morning and early afternoon for debate prep. The first session did not go well at all: A young political journalist named Michael Kinsley had come to Los Angeles and played Ted Kennedy in a mock debate; his jabs and talking points clearly discomfited Hart. Worse, Hart found himself unable to articulate his idea in the sixty- and ninety-second time limits. When he abruptly cut the prep short—"I wonder if Lincoln *rehearsed* before he debated Douglas," he snapped—the aides sat silently for a few minutes, then adjourned for the night. They could only assume that Hart was retreating into himself, and was relying on his own instincts . . . or else was indulging in private relaxation. ("I wasn't interested in exploring just how private," one staffer told a friend.)

None of them knew what happened in the hours after that session until after the debate. None of them knew that Warren Beatty had come down from his penthouse suite in the Beverly Wilshire, had visited Hart until well after midnight, bringing with him a sheaf of papers that had been collected for them by a onetime senior staffer in the late Senator Robert Kennedy's Senate and campaign offices. What was clear was that when Hart emerged from the lobby of the Biltmore Hotel for the drive to ABC's studios, Billy Shore thought he seemed remarkably at ease, "almost mellow—not a word you think of when you think of Gary."

Hart won the coin toss and chose to let Kennedy go first with his opening statement. It began with a brief indictment of the Ford administration, but turned quickly to an unsubtle assault on Hart as a Democrat marching under false flags.

"When you attack the federal government, that's the government that created Social Security, the GI Bill, Medicare, food stamps, Head Start, aid to education, the safety net for the least among us, that doesn't sound like a Democrat—that sounds like Ronald Reagan.

"When you aim your fire at the public school system that has given millions of our citizens a chance for a better life, or the social safety net that keeps our poorest Americans from hunger and homelessness, that doesn't sound like a Democrat—that sounds like Ronald Reagan.

"When you talk about tax breaks for big corporations to bribe them into bringing jobs into the ghetto they should have been providing decades earlier, that doesn't sound like a Democrat—that sounds like Ronald Reagan.

"We've already got one Ronald Reagan who'll be running for President, and he's where he belongs: on the far right wing of the Republican Party. We don't need a Ronald Reagan as the nominee of the Democratic Party."

"Senator Hart, your opening statement," moderator Frank Reynolds said.

From his seat in a holding room one floor above the studio, Billy Shore watched the monitor as Hart began his response with a small smile on his face. Shore thought: *Never seen that before.*

"I'm running for President," Hart said, "because America cannot build a better future if it is chained to ideas of the past." Then he turned away from the camera, something his media advisors repeatedly instructed him *not* to do, and talked directly to Kennedy.

"Senator, I do believe that one of our goals must be 'to halt and reverse the growing accumulation of power and authority in the central government in Washington, and to return that power of decision to the American people in their own local communities.' Does that really sound like Ronald Reagan to you? I'm surprised . . . because the man who spoke those *precise words* was Robert Kennedy in 1966, and again in his Presidential campaign.

"Do tax credits for businesses that bring jobs and housing into poor neighborhoods sound like Ronald Reagan to you? I'm surprised . . . because that is at the heart of Robert Kennedy's Community Development Corporation proposal, one he put into action in Brooklyn's Bedford-Stuyvesant neighborhood.

"Does a plan to reform the public school system really sound like Ronald Reagan to you? I'm surprised . . . because it was Robert Kennedy who said, 'When I go into the ghetto, the two things people hate most are the public welfare system and the public school system.'

"For millions of Americans, Robert Kennedy's legacy is not some sentimental fantasy. It's the moral and political courage he demonstrated in challenging us—whatever our party—to face conditions *as they are,* and not to evade hard decisions with soft thinking about hard choices. That is what the great leaders of our party, from Roosevelt to Truman to John and Robert Kennedy have always done. I think that's what Democrats must do if we are to protect this country from the tender mercies of Ronald Reagan."

The next fifty-five minutes of the debate might as well have been canceled. The exchanges over Afghanistan, the Middle East, inflation, recession were consigned to the last few sentences of the network news reports, and to inside pages of the next day's newspapers. What filled the screens and the front pages was a confrontation played almost like a gunfight from an old Western movie: the challenger, facing his rival, the look of surprise on Kennedy's face when Hart revealed he had been quoting Kennedy's brother, the sheer *audacity* of claiming as his own the legacy of his rival's brother.

(Hart never revealed the identity of that mysterious political operative; as Hart and his team were celebrating what one journalist called "the likely defining moment of the primary campaign," one of his aides asked him what had convinced him to challenge Ted Kennedy directly. Said Hart: "You remember in '68 those protesters with the signs that said 'Bobby Ain't Jack'? Let's just say there are a few folks with ties to the Kennedy family who think that 'Teddy Ain't Bobby.'")

On June 3, Hart won primaries in New Jersey, South Dakota, New Mexico, Montana—and California, where Kennedy's strength in black and Hispanic neighborhoods could not overcome Hart's appeal in the suburbs and in the more conservative inland neighborhoods. He held Kennedy to a two-point win in Ohio. Only in Rhode Island (a Massachusetts neighbor) and West Virginia did Kennedy win convincingly. Hart captured more than 350 of the 600 delegates at stake, giving him an overall edge of more than 200 delegates.

In another time, with different rules, it might have been possible for Kennedy to turn his attention to the convention, and to appeal to the Democratic Party's old bulls for their support. The 1980 rules made that impossible; delegates were bound to their candidates for the first two ballots. In fact, many of the most significant figures in the party might not even *be* delegates. There was no provision for automatically seating senators, governors, members of the House. Indeed, many of those officials, who had run as Kennedy delegates when it was certain he would be the nominee, found themselves shut out, until the Hart campaign, wanting no rerun of the 1972 regular–reformer split, found room for them as substitutes.

After two days of deliberations, Steve Smith came to Ted Kennedy's home in MacLean, Virginia, and delivered the verdict: There was no plausible path to the nomination. On Tuesday, June 10, Ted Kennedy walked into the same Senate Caucus Room where he and his brothers had announced their candidacies . . . and suspended his campaign.

For the third time in as many contests, a long-shot, insurgent Democrat had captured the Presidential nomination of his party. There was celebration in the Hart camp, of course, but it was tempered by two daunting facts. First, while Democrats had held the Congress for decades, the fracturing of the old New Deal coalition had made winning the White House an uphill slog. Since Roosevelt's fourth term victory in 1944, only one Democratic candidate—Lyndon Johnson—had won more than 50 percent of the popular vote (Jimmy Carter hadn't been able to win an electoral majority even while winning the popular vote). Second, Ronald Reagan was a far more formidable candidate than either Richard Nixon or Jerry Ford had been. Of course, Ronald Reagan *was* a Republican. And in the climate of 1980, with President Ford serving out his term with record-low job-approval ratings, running as a Republican was the equivalent of running a footrace with a fifty-pound pack on your back.

NOTHING BETTER CAPTURED the fortunes of the Republican Party in 1980 than its choice of the site of its thirty-sixth national convention. When President Ford's first full term began in January 1977, there was strong sentiment to hold its next convention in Detroit. For Ford, it would mean a valedictory in his home state. For Ronald Reagan, it would symbolize his appeal to working-class Democrats, who had helped propel him into two terms as California's governor. "When you play on the other guy's turf," Reagan often said, "you're likely to win." When it came time in early 1978 for the Republican National Committee to choose a host city, it was already clear that the battered auto industry, and the urban nightmare that was Detroit, would be exactly the wrong backdrop for the party's national convention.

"Detroit would have been the perfect setting for an indictment of the liberal welfare state," said National Chairman Bill Brock. "Unfortunately, it would have been hard to convince America that the country had been run for the last twelve years by two flaming liberals named Richard Nixon and Gerald Ford." So the Republicans turned instead to the South. While Carter had carried almost every state in the Old Confederacy, the region had long ceased to fit the old "Solid South" category. The combination of backlash against the civil rights revolution, a resurgent patriotism in the face of the Democrats' influential peace wing, and the emergence of politically engaged religious conservatism made the region a clear target of opportunity. So the Republican National Committee chose Dallas, Texas, as its convention site, despite some hesitancy over lingering memories of the Kennedy assassination. For all the optimism about its prospects in the South, the mood when the Republicans gathered for the August 11 opening was decidedly muted.

They had watched a cautiously upbeat Democratic Party nominate Gary Hart a month earlier in the very city they had shunned; Detroit would stand as the embodiment of what the party's convention call dubbed "twelve long years of a Republican-led assault on the hopes and dreams of working Americans." They had watched a feisty Senator Joe Biden deliver a keynote address that invoked the Magna Carta, Patrick Henry's "Give Me Liberty or Give Me Death" speech, his father's folk wisdom, Franklin Roosevelt's Inaugural, John Kennedy's Inaugural, Pope John XXIII's encyclicals, Martin Luther King's "I Have a Dream" oration, Shylock's "Hath Not a Jew" soliloquy, Satchel Paige, and a litany of the moderate Republican attacks on nominee-to-be Ronald Reagan ("Jerry Ford was right—and Ronald Reagan is wrong! Dick Cheney is right—and Ronald Reagan is wrong!"). It was after Biden's one-hour forty-minute speech that CBS and NBC independently decided to end the tradition of live gavel-to-gavel convention coverage.

They saw the delegates give a prolonged standing ovation to Senator Ted Kennedy's embrace of the party platform, and heard NBC's Tom Brokaw observe drily, "nobody writes a better concession speech than a

Democratic speechwriter. After all, they've had a lot of practice." They watched Hart's name placed in nomination by ex-representative Barbara Jordan, whose rich-timbered voice echoed her classic keynote speech from 1976.

"This November," Jordan said, "two men of the West will compete for the most powerful office in the world. One clings to the past, to old, weary ideas that time has passed by; one young man beckons us to a future with energy and vision, and fresh ideas. Is there any doubt which path this vibrant, still-young nation will choose?"

And they watched with some unease as Gary Hart chose his running mate. In three consecutive elections, Presidential nominees had chosen a Vice Presidential candidate who'd proved a serious weight on the ticket. In 1968, Spiro Agnew had become so much a laughingstock that the Humphrey campaign cut a TV ad that simply showed the words "President Agnew?" as hysterical laughter played in the background. In 1972, George McGovern's campaign imploded after he learned that Senator Tom Eagleton had been repeatedly hospitalized for emotional ills and so had to be dumped from the ticket. In 1976, Senator Robert Dole's invocation of "Democrat Wars" had scarred the Ford campaign, foreshadowing his essay into Papal humor that had ruled him out as a Presidential contender. Hart's June primary triumphs had spared him a convention battle for the nomination and given him a month to weigh his choice. He'd toyed with the prospect of a woman on the ticket, but there were none with real Presidential credentials (Connecticut Governor Ella Grasso would have worked, but she was ill with cancer). He looked hard for a Catholic, as a gesture to the Kennedy wing of the party; there were plenty to choose from, including Kennedy himself, New York Governor Hugh Carey, even Representative Lindy Boggs of Louisiana, whose faith and gender made her a genuine twofer.

On the Saturday before the convention opened, Hart made his choice by picking up the telephone.

"Since you're the one who got me into this," he said, "it's time for payback."

"Well," said the voice on the other end, "I'm thinking of Lincoln's story about the man who was ridden out of town on a rail, and said, 'If it weren't for the honor, I'd just as soon walk.'"

"You're riding with me," Hart said.

"Well, then, I'll take one for the team," said Dale Bumpers. "But let me check with our illustrious governor, and make sure Bill can get the legislature to let me run for senator as well . . . just in case. *You* may be crazy enough to risk a Senate seat, but I'll be damned if I'm going to spend the rest of my life trying fender-benders in Franklin County."

The Bumpers choice told Republicans that Hart had learned a lesson many Democrats had come to ignore since the upheaval of 1968: *Values trump programs.* You could talk all you want about your eight-point health care plan, and your fifteen-point jobs-and-education plans, but voters possessed an extraordinarily well-calibrated bullshit detector. If they thought you had no respect for their region, their beliefs, their accents, they would not give you the time of day. Few understood that better than Dale Bumpers.

And Republicans heard Gary Hart give an acceptance speech that encapsulated his campaign's theme. While never mentioning Ronald Reagan's age, it relentlessly hammered the idea by indirection.

"John Kennedy reminded us that 'change is the law of life. Those who live only for the past or the present are certain to miss the future.' We are the only nation on earth whose very creation was born out of the faith that free men and women could shape that future. We dare not abandon that faith in these troubled times."

He spent little time on the compulsory denunciation of the Ford administration, because, he said, "The record is clear beyond measure: inflation that steals a family's life savings and shadows a trip to the supermarket with anxiety; an industrial depression that shatters the dreams of families from Pittsburgh to Akron to Macomb; interest rates that make the bedrock goals of a middle-class life—a home, a college education, a small business— beyond the reach of all but the most favored. But much as we would wish to put the blame on the Republicans, and much as they must be held accountable for their failures, these afflictions stem from fundamental changes in the economy of America and the world—and America *must* choose leadership that understands these challenges, and can master them."

With the Democratic convention as prologue, there was no false illusion among the Republicans as they filed into Dallas's brand-new Reunion

Arena. They were trying for a fourth consecutive Presidential victory (something only FDR had managed to achieve, and that was in the middle of a World War); their incumbent President was hugely unpopular; the economy was in dire straits; and the Democrats were unified. As former National Chair Rogers Morton acknowledged to ABC, "We are sailing into the wind this year." And the opening of the convention was shadowed by another development: John Anderson had decided to abandon his Independent campaign for the White House. In a race with Ted Kennedy and Ronald Reagan, he told a press conference, "I could have occupied the sensible center. But Senator Hart's nomination has given the Democrats a candidate who is making a sharp break with the past, offering many of the same proposals I would have brought to the campaign." Anderson denied he was endorsing Hart, but the impact of his withdrawal was clear: Anderson would have taken far more votes from Hart than from Reagan.

Still, they were about to nominate a formidable campaigner in Ronald Reagan, and one who could persuasively argue that he had very different ideas from those that had governed Washington under both Republicans and Democrats. He had made that clear throughout his campaign.

And there was something else about Reagan: His instinct for the bold gesture was as sharp as his instinct for the right turn of phrase. He knew that in the political climate of 1980, he had to make the convention a stage for something unprecedented, wholly unexpected, that would make it impossible for voters to see him as a candidate of the past.

And by Wednesday, when he would be formally nominated, he had decided exactly what that would be . . .

WHEN THE MAJOR TELEVISION networks came on the air Wednesday evening, committed to live coverage of a suspense-free Presidential nomination, the only topic of conversation was the likely identity of Ronald Reagan's running mate. With the help of carefully constructed misdirection from the Reagan campaign, many of the best-known, highest-paid anchors, correspondents, and analysts exchanged the same nuggets of misinformation, all rooted in the certainty that Reagan would "move to the center" in an effort to shape a ticket that would appeal to moderates as well as conservatives. This is what winning nominees had always done, whether it was FDR picking Southern conservative John Nance Garner in '32, or liberal Republican Tom Dewey picking isolationist Ohio Senator John Bricker in '44, or Ike picking Nixon in '52 or JFK turning to LBJ in '60. Reagan himself had followed the pattern four years earlier—in a last-ditch effort to seize the nomination from President Ford, he had announced that he would pick liberal Pennsylvania Senator Richard Schweiker as his running mate (it had been a ploy designed to force Ford to declare his own running mate, thus alienating whatever wing of the party he rejected. The failure of the convention to adopt such a mandatory declaration ended Reagan's hopes for victory).

Surely, the speculation went, Reagan would do the same, most likely turning to his vanquished primary opponent Howard Baker of Tennessee, the Republican Senate leader.

"The parallel with John Kennedy and Lyndon Johnson is as striking as it is appealing," wrote the *New York Times*'s James Reston, who had touted Baker as "far more reasonable, far more seasoned, far more electable than the movie star turned political star. It would reassure those thoughtful Republicans troubled by the often myopic world view of the ex-governor that perhaps he agrees the world is round after all."

And maybe Reagan would have done just that had he been running against an incumbent Democrat as unpopular as Ford had become. Under those circumstances, a sense of reassurance was all the electorate might have needed to turn to a challenger. Four years of Gerald Ford, however, had radically changed the equation. There was nothing "reassuring" about a Washington Republican who had spent four years carrying water for a President who had lost the confidence of the people. Fairly or not, they were seen as the folks who had driven America straight into the ditch. No, Baker would signal "business as usual" when the country was hungry for a sharp, clean break with "business as usual." A choice that in other years might have seemed ideal could well be seen this year as a confession of resignation.

Reagan, unlike so many more conventional politicians, was secure enough in his own beliefs, comfortable enough in his own skin, to recognize his potential liabilities. His age, his invocations of traditional American values and heroes, made him vulnerable to the charge that he was out of touch, that he did not understand the newer currents in American life ("Reagan spent years," one wisecrack had it, "working in Hollywood, for Eighteenth Century Fox"). More than anything else, Reagan was looking to signal with his Vice Presidential choice that he was making a bold choice that embraced the America of 1980, not 1880. And so he asked his aides to cast the widest possible net.

"If you think of someone who seems too radical, too offbeat, make sure that name goes on the list," he said.

So when Reagan, Sears, Meese, and the others in the inner circle met in Reagan's suite on the sixteenth floor of the Loew's Anatole Hotel on the Tuesday night of the convention, the "safe" choices quickly fell out of the running. They turned to the wild cards beginning with . . . Democrats. Henry "Scoop" Jackson, from Washington State, was an ardent hawk on defense spending, and was far closer to Reagan than to Hart on the use of American might abroad. But on domestic issues, he was an equally ardent liberal, a favorite of the AFL-CIO, and would likely cause insurrection on the convention floor. Georgia Senator Sam Nunn, a recognized expert on defense, had battled for years against the peace wing of his own party; back in '72, he'd openly backed Nixon's reelection, and might well be unhappy now that McGovern's campaign manager was the Democratic Presidential nominee. Nunn, however, had Presidential aspirations of his own down the line, and would almost certainly turn the offer down. "We'll keep him in mind for Defense Secretary, though," Meese said.

And then he said, "Governor? If you're really serious about someone from left field . . . and you want someone who shows that you're serious about bringing power back to the states . . . and you want someone who came up the hard way, even to overcome discrimination, served in every branch of state government . . ."

"Sounds like a possibility," Reagan said. "Who is he?"

"Well," Meese said, with a broad smile, "that's the other thing . . ."

IT WAS RICHARD WIRTHLIN, Reagan's longtime pollster, who'd said it weeks ago.

"If only we could get a woman."

"Never thought I'd hear that from a devout Mormon," said Reagan. "Still waters run deep."

But they all knew what Wirthlin was pointing to. In every poll, Reagan ran well behind Gary Hart among women, while men slightly preferred Reagan to Hart. "The gender gap," the press was starting to call it. Never before in American politics had the genders split so dramatically; evidence that Reagan's firmness, or truculence, on foreign policy was troubling women, and evidence as well that the Republican Party's retreat from supporting the Equal Rights Amendment was costing it.

There was, Wirthlin argued, a deeper dimension to the idea of a woman on the ticket. It was a gesture that, in a single stroke, would dispel any lingering sense that Reagan was a man wedded to the old ways, unwilling to strike out in a bold, new direction. The question, of course, was which woman.

There was one only woman Republican in the U.S. Senate, Nancy Kassebaum from Kansas, but she had long ago told the Reagan campaign that she would reject the offer, feeling she lacked the qualifications to be President. There was Anne Armstrong, former Ambassador to France, former co-chair of the Republican National Committee. Four years earlier, she'd been on Ford's short list for the Vice Presidential spot before he'd chosen Dole. There was Carla Hills, Ford's Secretary of Housing and Urban Development, but there was no love lost between Carla and Rod Hills and the Reagans. Now Ed Meese was suggesting someone none of them had ever heard of to stand a sixty-nine-year-old heartbeat away from the Oval Office.

After Meese put the biographical details of his choice on the table, the resistance was instant and heated: *We're talking nuclear weapons, Ed. Armageddon, mushroom clouds. No question she sounds like prime goods, but . . .*

"I think we should remember Ed's point," Reagan said. "Washington experience hasn't exactly paid off in the last . . . oh, thirty, forty years, and particularly not recently. And I have to tell you, when I think about the folks who got to the White House who didn't come from Washington—like Lincoln, Franklin Roosevelt—I could have some fun with that in a debate . . ."

"There's something else to think about," Meese said. "Think about what it would do to the Democrats. Their convention adopted a formal rule that no campaign help will go to any Democratic candidate who doesn't support the Equal Rights Amendment. It's the *only* issue where a candidate'll lose support if you don't toe the line. You can be for an end to Social Security, abolition of the minimum wage—but not the ERA. The women were pushing Hart very hard to name a woman running mate, even threatened a floor fight, which they did not, unfortunately for us, get. A woman nominee would certainly put them in a box . . . damn if I'm not starting to like the idea. But, Governor, this is going to be a genuine shock to the system. If you announce this on Thursday at noon, the delegates will only have a few hours to absorb it before they file into the arena."

"You're right, Ed," Reagan said. "I've been trying to think of a way to break with tradition—you know, Roosevelt flying to Chicago for his acceptance speech, Kennedy giving his outdoors. So here's what I think . . ."

IT WAS CBS'S LESLEY STAHL who broke the story, twenty seconds ahead of NBC's Chris Wallace.

"Walter!" she said, simultaneously talking to the network anchor and her source at the other end of a telephone. "We've just learned that Governor Reagan has left his suite and . . . am I getting this right, Jim? . . . yes? . . . Walter, Governor Reagan *is* on his way to the Reunion Arena here to speak to the convention, and will apparently announce his choice for Vice President in just a few moments! We're being told that this is the first time *ever* that a Presidential nominee has declared his choice this way." Minutes later, Reagan, resplendent in a blue suit, red-striped tie, white handkerchief in his breast pocket, bounded onto the stage, waving and smiling through a five-minute ovation.

"I'm sorry to be interrupting your party, which I've been enjoying back in my hotel, but I've never forgotten that it isn't the candidates who are in charge of a convention, it's you, the duly elected delegates [prolonged cheers], and I wanted to be sure that when I made my choice for Vice President, before the news was leaked to the good ladies and gentlemen of the press, *you* would be the first to know [sustained applause and cheers].

"As you may imagine, I've gotten a lot of advice over the last several weeks, including a letter from an eight-year-old boy in Perkinsville, Ohio, named Bobby Warren, who suggested that I pick someone 'who would scare the bad guys into behaving themselves.' I hate to tell you this, Bobby, if you're up this late, but Clint Eastwood turned me down [laughter and applause]!

"But there's one piece of advice I did *not* take—and that was to follow the old, familiar path of choosing someone from inside the corridors of power of Washington, D.C. [prolonged ovation]. There are many fine public servants in the Capitol [mild booing]. No, please, there are. But I have long believed that there's something about that town—maybe it's in the air or water—that keeps people's minds locked into the same narrow limits. Besides, if the voters want the same old Washington ways, why, they can just look to our Democratic friends, who've picked *both* of their candidates from Washington, D.C.

"The choice I will recommend to you has taken a very different path to distinction and achievement"—and now the huge hall began to still—"and in doing so has overcome barriers that would have defeated someone of lesser strength and conviction.

"Born and educated in Texas, raised on a cattle farm, my nominee attained academic distinction at one of the finest universities in the land, Stanford University and Stanford Law School. . . . But because of the prejudices of the times, was denied the chance to work. But perseverance, and dedication to public service, earned my choice high positions as an assistant attorney general . . . and then the highest leadership post the state legislature can provide . . . and then a significant role in the judiciary . . . serving, in other words, in *every* branch of state government."

(From his perch in the anchor booth high above the arena, NBC co-anchor David Brinkley turned a pair of binoculars toward the floor and said, "Chet, I don't know exactly what this means, but the Arizona delegation is going nuts!")

"At the risk of immodesty," Reagan said, "I am prepared to say that my choice has demonstrated a blend of background, experience, and judgment that can stand with any Vice Presidential nominee of either major party. Oh," he added, and the camera caught the twinkle in his eye and the smile that was almost playful. "One more thing I almost forgot to mention: After listening to the other party *talk* about how much they cared about opening the doors of opportunity, I thought it was about time that someone actually *did* it. Fellow Republicans, fellow Americans, I proudly offer you my choice as our candidate for Vice President of the United States—the Honorable Sandra Day O'Connor."

ON THE MORNING of Sunday, October 19, tens of thousands of Americans, tethered to the Democratic Party by ties of family, ideological preference, economic interest, or campaign wager, awoke with a common question: *Is it really possible we're going to lose another Presidential election?*

The Republican recovery had begun nine weeks earlier, in the first moments after Ronald Reagan stunned the delegates, the press, and the country with his choice of Sandra Day O'Connor.

"As obscure a choice as any Presidential nominee has made in the modern history of the Republic," campaign chronicler Teddy White had pronounced on NBC.

Nor were movement conservatives exactly thrilled.

"In my youth," columnist/author/TV host William F. Buckley, Jr., said on ABC, "I once noted that I would rather be governed by the first two thousand names in the Boston telephone directory than by the faculty of Harvard. It appears that Governor Reagan has thrust his hand into the Phoenix, Arizona, telephone book and plucked out a nominee by random choice." A clutch of longtime stalwarts of the right, led by Phyllis Schlafly, threatened a floor fight when they learned that O'Connor's anti-abortion credentials were suspect.

The mood changed dramatically when Sandra Day O'Connor, a handsome fifty-year-old blonde, strode onto the Reunion Arena stage, her simple light blue dress playing off the deep blue half-circle stage flanked by red and white carnations, and delivered what John Chancellor called "a knockout of an acceptance speech."

"I've heard it said that we Republicans are making history tonight," she began, "and there is no denying a sense of pride in this hall that the party of the Emancipation Proclamation and the guarantees of liberty and equal protection enshrined in our Constitution is now the party that has opened the door to real political power for half the population of the United States. And that will be the first legacy of our next President, Ronald Reagan.

"But I have to confess to you that after listening to some of the comments from the media, I had a moment or two of real doubt. Maybe those of us who have worked closer to the people just aren't prepared to live and work in the world of Washington.

"After all, in the world where Ronald Reagan and I come from . . . if you don't *have* the money . . . you can't *spend* the money.

"In the world Ronald Reagan and I come from . . . if someone threatens your safety, or your family, or your well-being . . . you make damn sure you are strong enough to protect yourself—and you don't apologize for it.

"So maybe Ronald Reagan and I don't belong in Washington. Or maybe"—she let the laughter and applause build—"maybe it's time for people like *you* to send people like *us* to remind people like Gary Hart and Ted Kennedy and George McGovern what it means to be a public *servant.*"

Then it was Ronald Reagan's turn; and after a brief joking reference to his earlier career ("If you keep cheering, you're going to push me out of prime time!"), he used fresh words to strike familiar themes of biography and optimism.

"I've seen America," he said, "from the stadium press box as a sportscaster, as an actor, officer of my labor union, soldier, officeholder, and as both Democrat and Republican. I've lived in an America where those who often had too little to eat outnumbered those who had enough. There have been four wars in my lifetime and I've seen our country face financial ruin in Depression. I have also seen the great strength of this nation as it pulled itself up from that ruin to become the dominant force in the world.

"There are those in our land today, however, who would have us believe that the United States, like other great civilizations of the past, has reached the zenith of its power; that we are weak and fearful, reduced to bickering with each other and no longer possessed of the will to cope with our problems.

"Much of this talk has come from would-be leaders who claim that our problems are too difficult to handle. We are supposed to meekly accept their failures as the most which humanly can be done. They tell us we must learn to live with less, and teach our children that their lives will be less full and prosperous than ours have been; that the America of the coming years will be a place where—because of our past excesses—it will be impossible to dream and make those dreams come true.

"I don't believe that. And, I don't believe you do, either."

He mentioned President Ford only once, to argue that "even those with good intentions, like Jerry Ford, have found their efforts to curb the size and scope of the federal government frustrated by a Congress which, like an infant, has an unlimited appetite at one end and no control over the other.

"That is why, once and for all, we must put an end to the arrogance of a federal establishment which accepts no blame for our condition, cannot be relied upon to give us a fair estimate of our situation and utterly refuses to live within its means. I will not accept the supposed 'wisdom' which has it that the federal bureaucracy has become so powerful that it can no longer be changed or controlled by any administration. As President, I would use every power at my command to make the federal establishment respond to the will and the collective wishes of the people."

And he ended by invoking two of his favorite themes:

"A troubled and afflicted mankind looks to us, pleading for us to keep our rendezvous with destiny; that we will uphold the principles of self-reliance, self-discipline, morality, and—above all—responsible liberty for every individual that we will become that shining city on a hill.

"I believe that you and I together can keep this rendezvous with destiny."

In a sense, the speech of Ronald Reagan—and his pick of Sandra Day O'Connor—defined how the Republican ticket managed to stay competitive with Gary Hart and Dale Bumpers. Every public opinion survey showed the country was overwhelmingly in favor of change; but the public was almost evenly divided about whether Hart or Reagan represented "the change America needs." As Reagan campaign chief John Sears put it: "Politics are always played against a cultural perspective. From FDR on, the cultural perspective has always been with Democrats. That is no longer the case."

Sears was talking about matters beyond the economic. For millions, the tectonic shifts in the cultural landscape were at least as unsettling as the weakening of the dollar or the erosion of America's manufacturing base. The upheavals of the late 1960s may have taken place a decade earlier, but the aftershocks were still rippling through the terrain of 1980. Visions of long hair, burning flags, tribes of the naked young ingesting illegal drugs, the banning of prayer in school, struck at the deepest convictions of millions. For these voters, Gary Hart's "new ideas" campaign carried with it an implicit rejection of *their* ideas, *their* convictions. And no one better affirmed the vitality of those convictions better than Ronald Reagan.

There was a geographic dimension to all this: In 1976, Jimmy Carter's victories in all but two Southern states had brought him within two electoral votes of the Presidency. His strength in the Old Confederacy came in part from his Georgia roots, and in part from his open proclamation of his born-again faith, which had won him the implicit backing of such influential figures as Pat Robertson. Now it was Ronald Reagan who was winning their hearts and minds, telling a gathering of religious broadcasters, "I know you can't endorse me, but I can endorse *you.*" And while Reagan pledged to enforce the Civil Rights and Voting Rights Acts—"at the point of a bayonet if need be"—his longtime embrace of states' rights and his former opposition to those civil rights laws was bringing conservative Democrats firmly into his camp. Hart's campaign could take solace from its prospects among longtime moderate and liberal Republicans in New England and the Northeast, but as Mississippi-born *Boston Globe* columnist Curtis Wilkie wrote, "You do not need a degree from MIT to figure out that swapping 100 electoral votes from the land of grits and fatback for twenty or so votes from the land of beans and chowder does not make for a happy Democratic Party on Election Day."

And yet . . . the same strengths that Reagan brought to the campaign illustrated why Gary Hart may well have been the Democrats' best choice for 1980. If traditional liberalism as represented by Ted Kennedy was in disrepute, Hart had spent his six years in the Senate separating himself from that tradition, embracing a far more entrepreneurial, far less bureaucratic version of progressive politics. If older, socially conservative Democrats were drawn to Reagan, then younger, socially liberal Republicans and independents found in Hart a candidate who seemed much like themselves.

There was a geographic dimension to Hart's appeal as well. One of the least-attended facts of Presidential politics by 1980 was that the West had become a wasteland for Democrats. With the exception of Lyndon Johnson's 1964 landslide, Democrats had been all but shut out of the Mountain West (Kennedy had—barely—won Nevada and New Mexico in 1960). Those eight states added up to thirty-one electoral votes, more than any state save New York and California; and Gary Hart, out of Colorado, with his Lucchese boots and snap-button shirts and lean, cowboy looks, with his disaffection with Washington's ways, had a connection to the West no other Democrat—certainly not Jimmy Carter or Ted Kennedy—could match. Hart's nomination also put the fifteen electoral votes of Oregon and Washington in play, and some optimists around Hart also argued that he might even force Reagan to devote time and resources to his home state of California, a state that had gone Republican in every election but one for the last thirty years.

Yet as the *New York Times*'s Johnny Apple noted, "For all of the potential altering of Presidential geography—a Republican strong in the South, a Democrat with appeal in the West—this election will almost surely be decided in the familiar battleground of the industrial heartland: Pennsylvania, Michigan, Ohio, Illinois, Wisconsin. But here, too, the candidates will be seeking votes in regions that have traditionally voted with the other party."

In early September, Ronald Reagan returned to Milwaukee's Serb Hall, a thirty-year-old community center off West Oklahoma Avenue that was a magnet not just for Serbs, but for Czechs, Poles, Hungarians, whose ties to the Democratic Party of Roosevelt, Truman, and John Kennedy had been frayed by the decades-long tensions over war, race, crime, welfare. He had drawn thousands of onetime Democrats into the Republican primary in the spring, and he was reaching out to them now with familiar lines.

"For those of you who may feel uncomfortable about voting for me . . . well, I used to be a Democrat myself. I didn't leave the party, the party left me." He pledged a foreign policy that would permit "no more Vietnams— never again will we ask American boys to fight and die in a war we're not prepared to win, never again will we permit a small nation to be driven into a godless Communist tyranny by our weakness and indecision."

As Reagan was seeking traditionally Democratic votes, Gary Hart was speaking to a large crowd at Royal Oak High School, an upper-middle-income suburb of Detroit. The audience was well dressed, well heeled, well bred, the kind of college-educated citizens who could be found at the Town Hall lecture series, on the board of the United Fund, in the ranks of the League of Women Voters. They were "DNA Republicans," more or less genetically inclined to the party, but they had voted for Howard Baker in the primary, and they were both unsettled by much of Reagan's agenda, and drawn to a new kind of Democrat who seemed very different from the New Deal–Great Society model.

And Hart was playing on those impulses.

"What kind of 'conservative,'" he asked, "would turn our land and water over to the despoilers, squandering the most precious legacy we can leave to our children?

"What kind of a 'conservative' would bring the criminal powers of the federal government to bear on a pregnant sixteen-year-old girl, forcing her to bear her rapist's child?

"What kind of 'conservative' would risk another nuclear confrontation by threatening an illegal blockade against Cuba as a diplomatic tool?

"What kind of 'conservative' wants to spend tens of billions of dollars on gold-plated weaponry that may well break down in actual combat, putting our men in fatal danger, leaving us *less* able to fight and win the conflicts of the future?

"And what kind of 'conservative' would attack America's fiscal integrity by exploding our deficit by enriching the most comfortable among us, and leaving the least among us unschooled, unfed, unhoused?"

Without question, Reagan's choice of Sandra Day O'Connor was giving him protective cover from the charge that he was too old, too mired in the past. *Look at who he put on the ticket; there's never been a bolder choice.* And O'Connor's low-key, thoughtful demeanor, on display in a series of interviews with network anchors Cronkite, Chancellor, and Reynolds, helped ease the doubts of voters worried over so unknown a choice. As Reagan aide Lyn Nofziger said, "It's not as if she's stuck for an answer when you ask her what she reads." The choice also helped heal, or at least paper over, some very hard feelings in the Ford White House. The President had announced the day after the Republican Convention that "as a loyal Republican, I am of course supporting the ticket, and Betty and I are delighted that we will have the opportunity to elect the first woman Vice President." ("Why didn't Ford mention Reagan's name?" Lesley Stahl asked press secretary Ron Nessen. "Because he chokes on it," Nessen said.) Secretary of State Kissinger had ceased sharing his contemptuous views of Ronald Reagan's knowledge and wisdom in late-night phone calls with reporters and columnists, perhaps because he was sending clear signals to the Reagan campaign that he would be willing to continue on as Secretary of State.

In a larger sense, it was the White House that was indeed the heaviest weight on the Reagan campaign. A Republican was campaigning to succeed a Republican when the economic fortunes of America were as bleak as they had been in half a century. For all that Ronald Reagan was arguing for a "sharp break with the failed policies of *both* parties," the impulse of voters when confronted with hard times was to toss out the people who'd been in charge and turn to the other guys. If the mid-October polls were right, the voters were inclined to follow this practice; Hart's lead in the Gallup, Harris, CBS, and NBC polls was somewhere between three and seven points.

So why, on this morning of October 19, were so many Democrats so nervous? Because at 9:30 p.m., Reagan and Hart would meet onstage in Cleveland's Music Hall for the first and only Presidential debate. And no one, but *no one*, was a more effective political debater than Ronald Reagan.

He had reluctantly followed the advice of John Sears and stayed out of the primary debates until his nomination was assured, but in those three encounters he'd presented an amiable, gracious, often humorous personality. When asked about age and price controls just before the Ohio primary, Reagan had noted that they had failed when Emperor Diocletian had imposed them 1,700 years ago.

"And I'm the only one here old enough to remember that," he'd said.

"People tuned into these debates having read or heard that Reagan was some kind of right-wing zealot, ready to throw women and children into the street and start lobbing nukes at the Kremlin," Wirthlin said to reporters at a breakfast a day before the first October debate. "What they saw was an assured, unpretentious man comfortable in his own skin, fully engaged in the give-and-take of ideas. As for Hart? He's obviously smart, but there's something grim, something . . . *intense* about the guy, almost as if he can't wait to prove he's the smartest guy in the room and tell you how complicated and difficult everything is."

That was precisely the specter that was haunting more than a few in the inner circle of the Hart campaign.

"Gary *loves* intellectual thrust-and-parry," one of them said. "He drills down into the subsurface of ideas. But in a debate format, do you really win by talking about accelerated depreciation schedules versus a tax-based incomes policy? And then there's the atmospherics; if anyone tries to remind Gary to smile during a debate, he'll go ballistic. But if we get a stone-faced Hart spewing statistics up against genial Uncle Ron . . ." He gave a brief shudder.

At eleven a.m., the Hart campaign team assembled in the living room of the candidate's suite in the sixty-two-year-old Cleveland Hotel. Hart's debate preparation consisted of absorbing reams of information and strategy memos, then batting around questions thrown at him by his researchers and strategists. (Reagan, by contrast, had prepped with full-blown rehearsals conducted in the garage of his Wexford, Virginia, campaign retreat, complete with a mock stage and a stand-in Hart, played by Congressman David Stockman.) The living room was cluttered with coffee cups, half-eaten muffins, congealing strips of bacon, and two dozen staff members who were convinced that the Presidency hung on their presence in the inner circle. When Hart walked in, he looked for the one face he did not see.

"Where's Warren?" he asked.

"Said he was flying in this morning," Billy Shore said. "Said he was bringing a surprise."

There was a collective groan. While Warren Beatty was no stereotypical Hollywood celebrity, while he was well grounded in substance and tactics, the same obsessive impulses that could lead to seventy-five takes for a simple reaction shot, or to the relentless bedding of every conscious female in a three-mile radius, could also bog a strategy session down for hours in haggling over a singe phrase, a single *word*. So when Beatty said he'd bring a "surprise" to the debate prep, no one could imagine what that might be.

Certainly no one imagined that it would turn out to be a five-foot eight-inch fireplug of a man, who stalked into the room with a scowl on his face, took a thin, malodorous cigar out of is mouth, jabbed it at Hart, and said, "Hi, Senator—you ready to stop fucking around and win this goddamn campaign?"

AT FIFTY, DAVID GARTH was too old be called "the *enfant terrible* of politics," but he was surely one of the most accomplished, and most feared, of political players—feared as much by those on *his* side of the political wars as his opponent's. Over the last decade, he had become one of the most successful, and best paid, of the political consultants whose radio and television spots had come to dominate American politics. And in many significant ways, he was unlike his competitors. His graduate degree was not in media or public relations but in mass psychology. He had spent a chunk of his youth in bed with rheumatic fever, listening to news reports and the speeches of politicians. He had gotten his first foothold in the TV production business with a ruse, telling a local New York TV station he had the broadcast rights to high school football games while simultaneously telling the high schools he had a contract with a local TV station.

And in his approach to media, Garth was an outlier. He believed deeply that you *cannot* sell candidates like soap, that political communication was radically different from the selling of a product whose attributes could be more or less invented.

"Candidates speak," he'd say. "They think. They take positions, make decisions."

And above all, Garth preached, "If there's an elephant in the fucking room, tell the fucking people you *see* the fucking elephant."

So when New York Mayor John Lindsay ran for reelection in 1969 with a trouble-plagued first term to explain, Garth was one of those who insisted the aristocratic, "too good-looking to be good" mayor look at the camera and admit to making a mistake or two (it took a lot of takes to get Lindsay to deliver that line). When Tom Bradley tried to become the first Los Angeles black mayor in 1973 after a losing campaign four years earlier, Garth shot Bradley talking about why he lost, acknowledging that "maybe some of you thought I'd favor one group over another." *Jesus, a black guy talking about racial voting! And then pointing out there weren't enough blacks in the city to get him elected!*

The Bradley ad was a classic demonstration of one of Garth's key concepts: political judo, where a presumed weakness of a candidate is turned into a strength. When Congressman Ed Koch, a balding, singularly unprepossessing figure, ran for mayor in 1977, this was Garth's slogan: "After Eight Years of Charisma, and Four Years of the Clubhouse—Why Not Try Competence?" Garth was also famous—or notorious—for stuffing his ads with information, lots of facts and figures, on the assumption that a viewer would likely see an ad many times and would take new information from it each time. His slogans were impossibly long: "This Year, Before They Tell You What They Want to Do—Make Them Show You What They've Done." Or "Isn't It About Time We Had a Mayor Who Wanted to Be Mayor? Vote for Tom Bradley—He'll Work As Hard for His Paycheck As You Do for Yours." And more often than not, "Fight" would show up in the slogan—an unsurprising preference for a campaign consultant who combined the single-mindedness of Vince Lombardi with the subtlety of a pile driver.

And now here he was, in Gary Hart's hotel suite, brought by one of the Senator's most trusted friends, staring balefully around the room, as Beatty explained to Hart that he thought it would be a good idea to have a brief chat, just a few minutes, with just the Senator, Warren, and Garth. And when the other aides reluctantly fled out, Beatty explained to Hart that he'd known Garth for years, that he had a thought or two to share.

"When Warren called me to tell me he was worried about tonight," Garth began, "I had a tape put together of every Reagan debate my guys could find—the one with Bobby in '67, right through to the primaries. He's never lost one, *never*. And you know why? Because everybody makes the same fucking mistake every fucking time. They try to scare the voters; they try to paint him as a nut case from Whackoville. They try to show his numbers don't add up. Let me ask you: When some reporter proved there weren't twenty-three thousand people at GM filling out government forms like Reagan had said, only five thousand—you know what people thought: 'That's five thousand too many!'

"And one other thing," Garth said. "He's always the most comfortable guy in the room. Everyone else looks like the camera's going to attack them . . . he couldn't be happier to be there. Ask him a toughie? He smiles, he nods, he explains it all away. You know what Reagan knows that nobody in politics seems to understand? The number one rule: 'In politics, Bugs Bunny always beats Daffy Duck.'"

Hart started at Garth as if he had arrived from another planet.

"What the hell does that—?"

But Warren Beatty was chuckling.

"You need to broaden your movie watching, Gary," he said. "Daffy's always going berserk, jumping up and down, fuming, yelling. Bugs is . . . well, a bit like Cary Grant. His eyes are lidded, he's got that sly, small smile, like he always knows what's up, like nothing can ruffle him."

"Here's the thing," said Garth. "When you whipped out those Bobby Kennedy quotes in that debate with 'Splash,' you threw him completely off his stride."

"'Splash'?"

"That's Dave's nickname for Teddy," Beatty said. "Look," he added quickly, seeing Hart's grimace. "Everyone who waves Reagan off as an actor misses the point; but there *is* something about acting that's deep in his gut: He knows his lines, he's comfortable with them, he'll reach back for them the same way a comic reaches back for the killer joke, to get into his comfort zone. You take that comfort zone away from him, you win. You don't, you lose."

"So," Hart said, "the fate of America hangs on whether you can turn me into a talking rabbit? I guess I missed that part of the Federalist Papers."

RONALD REAGAN NEVER KNEW what hit him.

He was the picture of confidence when he walked onto the stage at Music Hall a few minutes before 9:30, clad in his traditional blue suit, red-patterned tie, and white handkerchief folded into his breast pocket. He looked across the stage . . . and Gary Hart wasn't there. Both candidates had been cued by stage managers to walk onstage at exactly the same time, but Hart had taken what Garth called "a standing eight count" before walking onstage to greet Reagan with an extended right hand—and then proffered a picture frame with his left.

"I thought we agreed on no props," Reagan said.

"I just thought you'd like a copy of one of the earlier versions of your defense policies," Hart said—and handed Reagan a framed newspaper ad for *Secret Service of the Air,* a 1938 film starring Reagan as Lieutenant "Bass" Bancroft. Reagan had the presence of mind to smile broadly, but the sub-text of Hart's gesture was clear: *I'm comfortable, I'm at ease out here in front of the bright lights.*

That subtext became overt when Hart, who had won the coin toss, chose to go first with his opening statement:

"Let me first extend my deep thanks to Governor Reagan, for his mag-nanimous refusal to use the 'age' issue in this campaign, now that we've firmly established just what my age is."

And then Hart delivered an opening statement sharply different from the traditional "I run for President because . . ." recitations.

"In fact, one of the significant differences between the Governor and myself is that I believe the way out of our current troubles is to reach back to our founding principles to shape the new ideas we need. Mr. Reagan is fond of saying that 'we have it in our power to begin the world over again.' I happen to think the Founding Fathers who won our independence and wrote your Constitution had it right—that the way to really build that 'city on the hill' Governor Reagan speaks of is to understand what those prin-ciples are, and how we have strayed from them.

"It was unchecked executive power from a Democratic President that led us into Vietnam; that led a Republican President to the Watergate, and then to claim 'if a President does it, that means it's legal.' You can almost hear Jefferson and Madison and Hamilton rolling in their graves. And, Governor, I'm frankly puzzled about why excess power doesn't seem to bother you at all when it's found in the boardrooms of our corporate giants that put unsafe automobiles on the street, or spew cancer-causing waste into the air and water . . . or when an unelected Federal Reserve Board drives interest rates so high it makes it impossible for our elected representatives

to shape a plan for economic recovery. Theodore Roosevelt, a great Republican, understood that. Franklin Roosevelt, a great Democrat, understood
that. I don't understand why you can't see or hear what they did.

"Oh—and as Columbo used to say . . . 'just one more thing.' Over the
next ninety minutes, tens of millions of Americans will have the chance to
judge for themselves which of us has the record, and the ideas, to lead this
country. It seems to me that both of us should have enough confidence in
our ideas and our record to withstand the tough questions—not just from
this distinguished panel, but from each other. Now, I know the rules of this
debate don't specifically permit that—but there's nothing to prevent each
of us from posing a "rhetorical question" which we can choose to answer—
or not. So in that spirit, Governor: In 1965, you were part of a nationwide
campaign by the American Medical Association to stop Medicare. You
called it, and I quote, 'socialized medicine.' Do you still believe that, and if
not, why did you change your mind?"

It was not the substance of what Hart said that seemed to throw Reagan
off his stride; it was the wholly unexpected framework of it. In the rehearsals back in Virginia, David Stockman had channeled Gary Hart brilliantly,
but it was the Gary Hart whose platform style was earnest, intense, focused,
the Gary Hart who still found it difficult to remember to smile. And here
was Hart speaking the very words—"begin the world over again," "a city
on a hill"—that had been the pillars of Ronald Reagan's oratory for years.
And why was Hart asking him a question? Didn't the rules specifically
forbid that? He knew what he was going to do if Hart challenged him on
Medicare; it had happened during a rehearsal, and Reagan had snapped
at Stockman, "Damn it, there you go again!" Everyone had laughed, and
Reagan had said, "I think I'll use that." But this question was . . . out of
sequence, a hit from the blind side.

And Reagan's opening statement showed that he'd been knocked a bit
off his game. The lines were there—the rejection of the pessimism among
"Washington voices who tell us that our best days are behind us," the assertion that "we don't have inflation because the people have been living too
well—we have inflation because the *government* has been living too well";
the pledge "to turn Americans loose to do the great things you have always
done."

But Reagan seemed compelled by Hart's unorthodox opening to retake the language he had claimed as his own for so long, saying, "Yes, we *do* have it in our power to begin the world over again, but not by following Senator Hart and the Congressional Democrats off the cliff, by spending billions we do not have, and fueling the inflation that has robbed millions of their savings. Now," he added, furrowing his brow and setting his jaw in that familiar expression of indignation, "with regard to Medicare, Senator Hart knows full well that I have always supported health care for our senior citizens. I was speaking on behalf of a *different*—"

"Governor," said moderator Howard K. Smith, "I'm sorry but time's up."

Inside the Reagan holding room just offstage, Reagan advertising chief Peter Dailey shook his head. Reagan *never* let himself be cut off by the clock; he'd learned the art of pacing back in his days rebroadcasting Chicago Cubs games on WHO in Des Moines. *That bastard Hart is gaming him.*

And it didn't stop when panelist Marvin Stone asked the first question, on who could better keep the peace. Reagan went right after Hart and the Congressional Democrats for "tempting aggression" by blocking increases in the defense budget, cutting sixty ships out of the Navy, blocking the B-1, delaying the cruise missile, the Minuteman missiles, the Tridents. "It was John Kennedy who said of our adversaries: 'We dare not tempt them with weakness. For only when our arms are sufficient beyond doubt can we be certain beyond doubt that they will never be employed.' That is still the way to ensure that our adversaries will not be tempted into a nuclear war which cannot be won, and must never be fought."

"Senator Hart?" moderator Smith said. And Hart looked over at Reagan—and he *smiled*.

"Let's just note for the record that Governor Reagan never got to explain if he still thinks Medicare is 'socialized medicine' . . . or maybe thinks he was saved by the bell. But as Joe Louis said, Governor: 'You can run, but you can't hide.' There'll be plenty of time for Mr. Reagan to explain—if he cares to do so.

"But the question is about war and peace—the most solemn responsibility any President can bear. I've spent the last four years on the Senate Armed Services Committee. I've listened to literally hundreds of experts—active duty and retired military officers, defense and intelligence analysts, many of whom we heard in top secret testimony behind closed doors. Their testimony, taken together, is one reason why I joined with colleagues from both sides of the aisle to form the Military Reform Caucus. It comes down to one simple idea: If we spend tens of billions of dollars on weapons that may well not work in actual combat, we end up risking the safety, the lives, of our soldiers and sailors and airmen; and we literally will spend ourselves weak, finding ourselves without the funds to buy the weaponry that *will* work in the conflicts we are likely to face.

"But there's something about your approach to the military, Governor, that you didn't share with us—and I thought it would be helpful to use some of *my* time to do so. Back in April in . . . Grand Island, Nebraska, I'm pretty sure . . . you charged that the GI Bill did not cover educational benefits for Vietnam veterans. Now, to your credit, you admitted you'd gotten that wrong—maybe we'll revisit some of your other remarkably inaccurate misstatements later—but then you explained *why* you'd made that mistake. You said a couple of four-star generals had misinformed you and, you said, 'Having only gotten to two bars myself, when four-stars told me something, I figured it was right,'

"Governor, you cannot be serious! The reason why the Constitution makes the President the Commander in Chief is to ask the tough questions—even of the top military officers. If ex-lieutenant John Kennedy in the Cuban Missile Crisis had listened to the commanders who argued for a military strike—who did not know that there were tactical nuclear weapons in Cuba—we might not be here today. If Kennedy and Johnson had asked harder questions about Vietnam, we might have saved fifty-five thousand American lives and hundreds of billions of dollars. A President who is too weak to ask the hard questions, too weak to demand a dollar's worth of defense, is a President who is going to leave our country weaker, not stronger."

(It was no accident that Hart repeatedly used the word "weak." A one-time Reagan confidant who had turned sharply against the candidate had told David Garth earlier that "the two things that really anger Reagan is an attack on his manhood and his intelligence." Now Hart was doing both with the same word.)

It was, however, in the final moments of the debate that Hart delivered his most memorable words, the words that, in retrospect, summed up the burden that Reagan was carrying. The inspiration came not from Garth, or Warren Beatty, but from an old acquaintance of McGovern campaign days, who had kept the typewritten draft of a speech that McGovern had autographed for her, and who had passed a paragraph of the speech on to Hart.

And now, in his closing statement, after Reagan had once again invoked the city on the hill and the world begun over again, Hart borrowed the words of the men he had once worked for:

"You have a choice to make a few weeks from now. And I'd like to suggest a couple of questions you might ask yourself when you go to vote.

"How many of you can really say that your life has improved in the last twelve years? How many of you can say that your city streets are safer, your tax burdens fairer, your grocery bills lower, or your sense of security and well-being stronger? Is our position in the world stronger, are we more respected? Have we moved even one step away from the shadow of nuclear war? Do you really want four more years of leadership from the party that has held power for the last twelve? That's the decision you will make on Election Day. We are the first nation on earth to entrust this decision to the people; and whatever your decision, I have to believe that if the Founders could know that two hundred years after their work, a salesman's son from Illinois and a salesman's son from Kansas would be competing for the highest office in the land, they would know their faith had been justified."

It was, one of Reagan's aides said much later, "exactly the kind of closing statement Reagan would have made, had he been running against a Democrat. He was the candidate of 'change' from the moment he stepped onto the public stage, and the truth is, he was *still* a candidate of change. But with Ford in the White House, and Gary Hart so different from the traditional Democrats, we could never fully capture that high ground."

In a normal political year, Reagan would have had another chance before a national audience. Four years earlier, Ford and Carter had met in three debates, and there had been a Vice Presidential debate as well. Here again, the shadow of that earlier race altered the terrain of the 1980 contest. Because Ford was so unpopular, the normal clout of an incumbent

President over his party's choice of successor had shrunk to near invisibil-
ity, and with it, the strength of the moderate-liberal wing of the Republican Party. With Reagan's victories in Iowa and New Hampshire, and
his glide path to the nomination, the hyper-cautious, risk-averse strategy
of campaign chief John Sears was never seriously challenged, despite the
conviction of Reagan's longtime allies that it was at odds with the fundamental political character of their man. And because John Sears profoundly doubted Reagan's intellectual skills and endurance, his continued
control of the campaign ensured that the candidate would be wrapped in
protective political padding. Reagan had refused debates in Iowa and New
Hampshire, had engaged his rivals only when his nomination was a fore-
gone conclusion, thus depriving him of a political "spring training" debate
season. In his negotiations with the Hart team, Sears had raised so many
conditions and objections—about location, length, format—that in the
end, the two camps could agree on only one debate.

And now that Gary Hart had shocked the old media master (and some
of his followers as well) with an impressive debate performance, and with
the instant post-debate network polls showing a decisive victory for Hart,
there was no platform for a recovery, no second round. Backstage at the
Music Hall, a furious Nancy Reagan had confronted Sears.

"I wish we'd have lost in Iowa. Then Ronnie would have fired you in
New Hampshire. You don't *trust* him, you don't *respect* him!"

"What makes you think he would have done any better in a second
debate?" Sears asked.

It was the last time he would see either Reagan face-to-face.

With no direct confrontation in the two-week run-up to Election Day,
the campaign armies clashed by night—and day—with television commercials. There was one in particular that stood out.

When the debate had ended, Warren Beatty turned to David Garth
in the candidate's hotel suite, where they had watched the debate, each of
them having chosen to avoid the media chaos of the debate venue.

"It's not over yet, you know," Beatty said. "The guys around Gary think
they can close the deal if they can paint Reagan as Dr. Strangelove."

"Is that what America saw tonight?" Garth said, narrowly missing Beatty's $50 million face with the cigar he was brandishing. "Gary didn't make

him look dangerous; he made him look shaky. That's what your commercials need to do."

"Got any ideas?" Beatty asked.

"Give me forty-eight hours," Garth said.

On Wednesday, October 22, at 7:26 p.m., just after Cronkite, Chancellor, and Reynolds were signing off on the network newscasts, viewers on all three networks saw a black-and-white photo of Hart and Reagan facing each other in Cleveland. As the announcer began to speak, Hart slowly disappeared, to be replaced by a reverse image of Reagan, so that he appeared to be facing . . . himself.

"Ronald Reagan only wanted one debate," the announcer said. "And if you saw it, you know why. So, here's the next debate Governor Reagan might want to have:

"In 1967 and 1969, Governor Reagan signed two of the biggest tax increases in the history of California. Now he says he wants to cut taxes, even for multimillionaires.

"In 1968, Governor Reagan signed the most liberal abortion law in the nation. Now he runs on a platform that would force a teenage girl to bear her rapist's child—even if it would threaten her life.

"In 1965, Ronald Reagan said Medicare was 'socialized medicine' and toured the country to block it. Now he says he was always for health care for the elderly—just not the one that now protects twenty-five million senior citizens.

"How can one politician have so many profound disagreements with . . . himself. Doesn't he remember what he once said? Or is it . . . that he's hoping you'll forget."

"So . . . if you want a candidate of real change—instead of a candidate who just . . . changes . . . vote for Gary Hart for President."

IT WASN'T A LANDSLIDE.

But it wasn't that close, either.

On November 4, ninety-one million Americans went to the polls. Some forty-seven million of them—52 percent—voted for Hart and Bumpers. Forty-six percent chose Reagan and O'Connor, with minor parties picking up the balance. Reagan won the South except for Dale Bumpers's Arkansas and Florida, where older Democrats in and around Miami and Palm Beach, and newer, younger arrivals along the I-4 corridor from Tampa to Orlando to Daytona Beach, narrowly outvoted the Cuban-Americans of Miami, and the older Republicans along Florida's West Coast, and the conservatives up in the Panhandle.

Hart took all of New England except for New Hampshire, and all of the Mid Atlantic states: New York, New Jersey, Pennsylvania, Delaware, Maryland. In the West he took Colorado, New Mexico, Oregon, and Washington, while holding Reagan to a relatively narrow 250,000-vote plurality in California, pressing Reagan hard enough to force him to spend time and money in a state his campaign had earlier thought safe.

And in the end, for all the arguments over war and peace, nuclear weapons and Soviet aggression, family values and social upheaval, the election came down to the conclusion of several million voters in the industrial heartland that twelve years of Republican Presidents had left them more insecure, more vulnerable, more threatened than they had felt little more than a decade earlier. In effect, enough of the working-class Democrats in Michigan, Ohio, Illinois, and Wisconsin who had drifted toward Nixon in '68, flocked to him in '72, and divided between Jimmy Carter and Jerry Ford in '76, moved back to the Democrats in 1980 to give Hart their electoral votes, and with them the Presidency. Democrats did lose three seats in the Senate, and fourteen seats in the House, most of them in the South, where Reagan's margins were substantial, but the party remained firmly in control of both houses of Congress.

—In New York City's Biltmore Hotel, where the city's Democrats had gathered, Senator Daniel Patrick Moynihan was explaining the election to a gaggle of reporters. "Voters paint with a very broad brush," he said. "They knew who was in charge. They didn't like what was happening. So they threw them out. If we'd been in charge, they would have thrown us out."

"So," *New York* magazine's Michael Kramer asked, "If you had to explain the campaign in one word?"

Moynihan smiled at Kramer.

"It was . . . the economy, stupid."

—In the Blue Room of the White House, where Gerald and Betty Ford were hosting a small Election Night party of their closest friends, a tentative smattering of applause broke out when Walter Cronkite announced that "CBS News can now declare that Gary Warren Hart has been elected the fortieth President of the United States!"

"Allow me to propose a toast," Betty Ford said, "to the judgment, wisdom, and common sense of the American people."

—And in Denver's historic Brown Palace Hotel, where Gary Hart and a dozen of his intimates were gathered in the Boettcher Board Room, the just-declared President-elect saw Warren Beatty motioning him inside the adjoining bedroom for a private chat. When Hart entered, he saw that Beatty was holding the hand of a tall, brown-haired, bronze-skinned young woman whose commitment to a rigorous fitness regime was clear.

"Gary—sorry, Mr. President," Beatty said, "I want you to meet a very good friend of mine, Serena . . . what is your last name, dear?"

"Brown," the young woman said, extending her hand. "Serena Brown. And congratulations, Mr. President."

"Serena is going for her Ph.D. in political science at UCLA," Beatty explained. "She's one of the most creative thinkers I've met in years. I think she would bring incredible energy and creativity to your White House."

"I'm sure we can find a place for her," Hart said.

AT 6:45 on a brisk morning in late March, the Deputy Chief of Staff turned off Pennsylvania Avenue, walked through a gate that led to a guardhouse, flashed the White House pass, and walked down the walkway into the West Wing of the White House. The promise of spring was in the air, the cherry blossoms had made their Washington debut a week ahead of schedule, and the political portents were bright as well.

Some of the good fortune was happenstance: In late November, a lightning coup in Baghdad had overthrown the eighteen-month-old presidency of Saddam Hussein and installed a military-civilian regime dominated by Shiites. The Iranian government of Hussein-Ali Montazeri, which had been bracing itself for a war with Saddam's massive army, recognized the new government within minutes (in fact, there were whispers that a joint effort between Iran's now-reformed intelligence arm, and the Central Intelligence Agency, may have had something to do with Saddam's sudden removal, but, then, there were always rumors of that sort circulating in the region). By year's end, the two nations were negotiating a mutual defense agreement, one that clearly, if unofficially, included Israel. With Iraq no longer a potential aggressor, Israel felt secure enough to signal its interest in a comprehensive peace accord by moving to stop the spread of settlements in the West Bank.

As for the Soviet Union, its invasion of Afghanistan was rapidly turning into a nightmare—"our Vietnam," as Soviet Ambassador Dobrynin admitted at a private dinner party for half a dozen senators. With neighboring Iran opening its borders to thousands of anti-Soviet fighters from the Muslim world, the Soviet military was suffering a terrible loss of men and materiel. Worse, from Moscow's point of view, the close ties between Iran and the United States were beginning to win America a measure of affection among some of the militant followers of Islam. There was, in fact, a serious doctrinal debate emerging between those who insisted that the United States was indeed the Great Satan, and those who thought that infidels who supported Muslims in their fight against atheistic Communism might not necessarily be worthy of death. Hadn't the United States distanced itself from the criminally corrupt regime of Saudi Arabia? Hadn't the Americans forsworn any intent to set foot in the holy lands of Mecca and Medina? This development, Ford administration officials suggested to their successors, might well throw the Soviets onto the defensive in regions across half the globe, making Moscow amenable to the kind of sweeping agreement on nuclear weapons that was at the center of Hart's foreign policy.

(It was profoundly reassuring to the Deputy Chief of Staff, indeed, to the mainstream moderate-to-liberal center of America's political community, that America's next President was prepared to come to a long-term modus vivendi with the Soviet Union.

"Imagine," said outgoing Secretary of State Kissinger at a dinner he hosted for President-elect Hart's incoming foreign policy team, "if we had elected a President who believed that someday the Soviet Union would simply . . . disappear. That kind of simplistic thinking would have been a disaster.")

It wasn't just a matter of good luck. The President had surrounded himself with men and women that reflected his refusal to be defined by any ideological label. Any Democrat would have put former Deputy Defense Secretary and Vietnam negotiator Cy Vance at the top of his list for Secretary of State. And it was not exactly daring to ask Republican Senator William Cohen to serve as Secretary of Defense. No one, however, could have imagined that Hart would ask seventy-four-year-old former Defense Secretary Clark Clifford to leave his law practice and return to government service in the role of National Security Advisor . . . or that Clifford would accept the offer.

"Clark Clifford has demonstrated the kind of thinking that a President desperately needs and rarely receives," Hart said, when he announced Clifford's appointment. "At the height of the Vietnam War, he had the courage to tell the President that he had changed his mind, that the facts did not support the policy he had embraced. And while others were keeping silent for fear of losing their place at the table, Clark Clifford had the courage to tell the President what he did not want to hear. I do not exactly look forward to receiving that kind of candid advice, but without it, a President is all but ensuring that he will fail."

There was also clear political calculation at work. For the first time in the Republic's history, someone other than a white man was chosen to fill one of the "Big Four" Cabinet jobs. With Vance at State, Cohen at Defense, and Senator Lloyd Bentsen at Treasury, Hart named as Attorney General the Chief Justice of the California Supreme Court, Rose Bird.

("Don't throw out our 'short list' for that job," White House counsel Walter Dellinger told an assistant. "She's only going to be there until one of the Justices leaves, and Gary can name the first woman to the Supreme Court.")

And there was a clear recognition of the rough political road ahead when Hart designated Vice President Bumpers as his point man with the

Congress. Sure, it was in Democratic hands, but those were hardly guaranteed to be helping hands. Senate Majority Leader Robert Byrd and House Speaker Tip O'Neill were classically old-school. Ask them to help stem the rising cost of Social Security and Medicare and you were likely to get an indignant refusal to "balance the budget on the backs of the elderly." Push the auto industry to raise fuel efficiency, and the Democrats from Michigan and Ohio would argue that you were going to throw more UAW members out of work. Unlike many of the younger, Ivy League–educated wine-and-cheese members of the White House team, Bumpers had the kind of engaging, regular-folks personality that could help sway a reluctant politician. If he could just get these troglodytes to understand that if Detroit pushed its fuel efficiency up by two to three miles per gallon, then in five years America wouldn't need to import *one drop* of Middle Eastern oil! We could break the back of inflation without the killer interest rates that choked off economic growth.

That was a lot to put on the back of the Vice President. But the Deputy Chief of Staff had a good deal of faith in Dale Bumpers . . . not to mention that there was a more personal connection. It was Bumpers who'd suggested that Gary Hart look beyond the traditional Beltway candidates to staff his White House, someone like a highly skilled lawyer with demonstrated political skills, who (not so incidentally) would win him points on the diversity front. Hart's offer came at a propitious moment for the Deputy Chief of Staff: There was trouble on the domestic front, so a move away from home (maybe temporary, maybe not) would provide some breathing room, a chance to think things over.

And besides, it was a job that came with real clout, the kind of clout every player in Washington understood. The Deputy's office was in the West Wing, just down the hall from Chief of Staff Billy Shore. And it was one of only six White House staff positions that came with "walk in" privileges: no appointment necessary, just come to the Oval Office, check with his assistant, and knock. In fact, much of the time the President could be found in a small study tucked away in the West Wing, where he retreated for quiet time, a chance to read through the intelligence estimates, or dip into a Russian novel for diversion, or . . .

. . .

IT NEVER WOULD HAVE happened if Secret Service Agent Michael
Stoddard hadn't had that third cup of coffee after wolfing down a burrito
for lunch. It had been a late night with a colicky nine-month-old; his shift
with the bottle had turned into a four-hour marathon, as his exhausted
wife caught up on some desperately needed rest. By noon, Stoddard could
barely keep his eyes open, and a stiff dose of caffeine seemed required. But
shortly after returning to his post outside the President's private study, his
insides began sending urgent signals that his lunch was pursuing a rapid
exit strategy. There was a bathroom just fifty feet down the hall, and it
would be a matter of a minute or two. Technically it was a violation of
protocol, but Hart had been in that study for forty-five minutes, and there
were no scheduled visitors on any list . . .

It never would have happened if the Chief of Staff hadn't taken a late
lunch out of the White House to dine with his daughter, who was home
from college for the first time since the Christmas holidays. Had the Chief
been in his office, the call would have gone to him, and he might well have
sought guidance before seeking out the President. The Deputy Chief, a
relative newcomer to the inner circle, was less familiar with Hart's work
habits; moreover, the President had said just the day before that a threatened strike by the nation's air traffic controllers was fraught with serious
consequences for the economy, the national safety, and his political stature.
This will be, he said, *the first real test of how this White House will act in a
crisis—we have got to get it right.*

So when the Deputy Chief picked up the phone there was no question
about it—this was a crisis, pure and simple.

"Rejected?" the Deputy Chief said incredulously. "I thought the settlement was a done deal."

"So did we," the Labor Department's chief mediator said. "Fifteen percent raise, immediate upgrade of the workplace, mandatory limit on maximum hours . . . but there's a real fight for the union leadership, and Evans
apparently felt he had to posture. Of course a 75 percent raise is insane.
And yes, he knows what the law says about a strike. But he's fighting for

his job . . . and frankly, I think he thinks there's no way a President can fire all his members, much less Democratic ones."

"When are they threatening to walk?"

"Twenty-four hours."

"I've got to let the President know," said the Deputy Chief.

It never would have happened if the President had locked the door to the private study, but the Secret Service had told him his first day in office not to do that: What if he had a heart attack, what if he choked on a peanut, what if he were suddenly tackled by a visitor gone berserk? Besides, it wasn't as if anything had been *planned,* exactly. In the Senate and on the campaign trail, he'd made a practice of reaching out to young men and women, checking in on them to find out what they and their friends were thinking, what they were reading and listening to, what ideas were gaining traction. There was nothing untoward about the President engaging one of the young interns in an earnest conversation about national service, then continuing the conversation over lunch in his study, then . . .

The Deputy Chief of Staff half walked, half ran down the hall that led to the President's study, knocked once, and then opened the door an instant before Secret Service Agent Stoddard returned from his urgent mission and called out a desperate "wait," started to say "Mr. President, the air-traffic controllers . . ."

. . . and looked down toward the floor, into the face of President Hart . . .

. . . and looked down toward the floor, into the face of White House intern Serena Brown . . .

. . . and realized *why* she was able to look into both of their faces at the same time . . .

. . . and bolted from the room, ran down the hallway into her office, grabbed for the phone, and punched the speed dial.

"Bill! You're never going to believe what just happened!" yelled Deputy Chief of Staff Hillary Rodham.

"Try me," said Governor Bill Clinton.

HOW REALITY SHAPES SPECULATION

The alternate histories in this book represent events that might have happened. They all begin with events that almost did happen, but in other hands, these triggering episodes could well have led to drastically different results. Maybe Richard Pavlick's jerry-rigged bomb would have failed to detonate, or maybe Soviet Premier Khrushchev would have been sufficiently wary of Lyndon Johnson's approach to foreign policy to have abandoned any idea of placing nuclear weapons in Cuba. Perhaps Steve Smith would not have saved Robert Kennedy that night in June; perhaps either Hubert Humphrey or Richard Nixon would have bested him in their contests. Maybe Gerald Ford would have lost to Jimmy Carter even if he had given a sharper answer on the question of Soviet domination in Eastern Europe. Maybe Gary Hart's impulse toward self-immolation, on display when he actually did run in 1984 and—famously—in 1988, would have undermined a 1980 campaign.

My goal here has been plausibility. Many of the words, thoughts, and deeds described here are taken from the real-life record. Many of the words spoken by the principals were actually spoken by them, in different settings, of course. The political terrain on which these stories played tracks as closely as possible to reality; and where I have turned an "almost happened" event into reality, I've tried to shape an altered political atmosphere based on history. For instance, if we want to imagine the political impact of Robert Kennedy surviving an attempt on his life, we don't need to rely on our imagination alone; we can see what happened after Ronald Reagan narrowly survived the attempt on his life in March of 1981.

What follows is in no sense a "bibliography," since the books that track the last half century of American politics number in the tens of thousands. It's simply my effort at saying that if you think what I've written is too weird for you to suspend disbelief, take a look at where these speculations came from.

You may be surprised. I know I was.

Palm Beach, Florida, December 11, 1960, 9:45 a.m.

PAVLICK'S ATTACK: Richard Pavlick's attempt on the life of John Kennedy is one of the most forgotten events of our time. The estimable historian Richard Dallek, who wrote a book on JFK titled *An Unfinished Life*, had no knowledge of the event until a newspaper reporter called him about it back in 2003.

That reporter, Robin Erb of the *Toledo Blade*, provided the most complete account of the incident in a November 21, 2003, article. It is described in a brief account by U. E. Baughman in his memoir *Secret Service Chief*.

"The closeness of the call was appalling," Mr. Baughman wrote. "Hardly anybody realized just how near we came one bright December morning to losing our President-elect to a madman."

It is also mentioned in passing in Arthur Schlesinger, Jr.'s *A Thousand Days*.

LYNDON JOHNSON'S 1960 MOOD: In his oral history on file at the LBJ Library, Johnson's former press secretary George Reedy says of LBJ in 1960: "He'd reached the stage where he wanted to go into some sort of a skidding reverse. He at times talked about it. He talked about it quite often, really . . . dumping politics altogether, usually in very short monosyllabic Anglo-Saxon words. I think that he was more or less dissatisfied with his whole life. Very frankly, that's where he began expressing dissatisfaction with his family, with his friends, with almost everything. He was on the verge of a second childhood syndrome." Reedy is only one of the many Johnson aides who have described his behavior on the Vice Presidential campaign trial, complete with drinking bouts and abuse of the staff.

All of the words spoken by Johnson, and the incidents described in this first section, come from biographies, including Randall Woods's *LBJ: Architect of American Ambition.* Robert Caro's three volumes only take us up to his work as Majority Leader, but in a coda Caro describes the rebuff suffered by Johnson when he sought to retain control of the Democratic caucus.

His comment on Clare Boothe Luce—"I'm a gamblin' man . . ."—was actually spoken to Luce, on the night of the 1961 Inaugural, according to Randall Woods's book.

THE AFTERMATH: Speaker Rayburn, Lyndon Johnson, and other Congressional leaders regularly met in Rayburn's "Board of Education," the room described in many books and articles about Rayburn, including *Sam Rayburn—A Biography* by Alfred Steinberg. The design and look of the room—H-128—comes from a monograph prepared by the architect of the Capitol. And Johnson did keep a bottle of Cutty Sark in the hideaway.

Senator Everett Dirksen of Illinois, along with Republican national chair Thruston Morton, senator from Kentucky, were among those most convinced that Richard Daley's Chicago machine had stolen the electoral votes of Illinois, as well as the votes from Texas. Earl Mazo, the *New York Herald Tribune*'s national political correspondent, came away from his reporting convinced that fraud determined the outcome in both states. Richard Nixon publicly accepted the outcome of the 1960 election, and waved off efforts by Republicans to challenge the outcome. In the wake of the trauma of a Kennedy assassination, the impulse toward national unity and the avoidance of a Constitutional crisis would have been immensely greater.

. . .

**THE HUMPHREY CHOICE, THE ELECTORAL FIX, AND JOHNSON'S
EARLY STEPS:** Johnson's relationship with Humphrey is described in
detail in Caro and Woods, and other biographies of LBJ, and the events in
this alternate history closely follow reality. Johnson was well aware of the
suspicion in which he was held by liberals—they had staged a near revolt
at the convention when JFK chose him—and Humphrey would have been
the likeliest candidate to ease their fears. When President Johnson was
weighing his choice for a running mate in 1964, Senator Richard Russell,
whom Johnson described as a "father" figure, advised him that "you couldn't
make a better move" than Humphrey, according to a telephone conversation between the two men, found in Johnson's White House tapes.

Because the Electoral College was scheduled to convene on December 16, 1960, Kennedy was not yet the "President-elect" on December 11.
I have dealt at book length with the dilemma of a winning Presidential
candidate dying before the Electoral College meets (*The People's Choice*,
1995), and, in this case, I am working on the (reasonable) assumption that
in the less polarized world of 1960, there would be a rapid acceptance of a
resolution.

Johnson's outreach—to liberals, Jews, and fellow Southerners—
closely follows the steps he did in fact take after Kennedy's assassination in November 1963, with a fair amount of the dialogue taken from
transcripts of recorded telephone calls. In his call to Martin Luther King,
Jr., the words he reminds King of are from a speech given by the civil
rights leader at an early March on Washington in 1959. The line written by Ted Sorensen—"Though I cannot fill his shoes, I must occupy
his desk"—comes from a draft Sorensen offered for Johnson's speech to
the joint session of Congress on November 25, 1963. LBJ did not use the
line.

The line that Dick Goodwin uses from T. E. Lawrence achieved wide
circulation among young aides who worked on Capitol Hill in 1967—
of whom I was one—and who found themselves working in one way or
another for a peace candidate in 1968.

. . .

THE MELANCHOLY: Camelot opened on Broadway on December 3, 1960. Elvis Presley's "Are You Lonesome Tonight?" and Ferlin Husky's "On the Wings of a Dove" were both among the top songs receiving radio airplay at that time. The Kingston' Trio's "New Frontier" was released in the spring of 1961.

Johnny, We Hardly Knew Ye, a well-known Irish lament of the horrors inflicted on a soldier, was the title of a memoir of JFK by Kenneth O'Donnell and Dave Powers, published in 1972.

The James Bond boom was triggered by an interview President Kennedy gave to *Life* magazine, published on March 17, 1961, in which JFK revealed that *From Russia with Love* was one of his five favorite books. In the alternate history, there would have been no such interview (it's also an open question whether Kennedy's enthusiasm for James Bond inspired his enthusiasm for the Green Berets and Special Forces, and whether that approach to unconventional warfare would have been embraced by a President Johnson in 1961).

FULBRIGHT TO STATE: In an oral history interview, and in an interview with me, Harry McPherson notes Johnson's close friendship with Fulbright, and his strong recommendation to Kennedy that he choose the Arkansas Democrat as his Secretary of State. It was Fulbright's civil rights record that stayed JFK's hand, and it would have been in keeping with Johnson's political instincts to pair Fulbright's nomination with the designation of the first black member of the Cabinet.

RFK TAKES JACK'S SENATE SEAT: The antipathy between Robert Kennedy and Lyndon Johnson was by all accounts chemical, beginning when RFK served in the Senate as counsel to Senator Joseph McCarthy, then as counsel to the Democratic minority on the government operations committee, then as chief counsel to the Rackets Committee that investigated corruption in the Teamsters Union. It was fed by LBJ's patronizing of Robert at his ranch on the Pedernales River, and flourished into full-fledged mutual contempt at the Democratic Convention in 1960, when LBJ was convinced Bobby had tried to get him off the ticket. The most complete account of this long-term mutual contempt is found in Jeff Shesol's book titled—appropriately enough—*Mutual Contempt*. Even without much antipathy, the Kennedy family's sense of filial responsibility would almost surely have put Robert in Jack's Senate seat—in 1960, Ted Kennedy would have been twenty-eight, and thus constitutionally ineligible.

JOHNSON'S SELF-APPRAISAL: According to those who worked with him, both in the Senate and the White House, Johnson was acutely aware of his weakness when it came to direct communication with the electorate. He was both fearful of the press and clueless about how to deal with it (according to Doris Kearns Goodwin's *Lyndon Johnson and the American Dream*, he offended some in the White House press corps in the first days as President when he said to them: "I'll make big men out of you if you play ball"). Goodwin also recounts that, whether in the White House or even as he was writing his memoirs, he felt the press and the better educated—the "Harvards," as he called them—would scorn him if he showed his character and personality "for real." In his efforts to seem more "Presidential," she concludes, he came off as pompous, stiff, insincere. Goodwin assisted him in the preparation of his memoirs, but, she reports, he would refuse to let her include any revealing, candid stories about his past, fearing they would appear undignified. The result, *The Vantage Point*, is a thoroughly unreadable, eye-glazing book.

In this imagined TV interview, all of the words Johnson speaks are words he actually uttered at one point or another in his career, or in conversations recalled by aides and confidants.

JOHNSON'S CIVIL RIGHTS STRATEGY: The words he spoke to Hubert Humphrey about the centrality of the right to vote come from Woods's *LBJ: Architect of American Ambition*. His request to Whitney Young to "come to Washington and start 'civil righting'" were spoken to NAACP

Executive Secretary Roy Wilkins on January 6, 1964, in a phone call whose transcript can be found in *Taking Charge: The Johnson White House Tapes, 1963–1964*, edited by Michael Beschloss. (In this regard, Johnson was following the path of his hero, FDR, who would often encourage his allies to start criticizing him, so that he could be seen to be moving in response to political pressure.) His understanding of the roots of Southern bigotry is a major theme of every Johnson biography. CBS's Frank Stanton was in fact a confidant of LBJ during his White House years.

The conversations with senators are a blend of my imagination and of conversations as recorded on White House tapes—for instance, his promise to "run right over" Senator Richard Russell, and Russell's warning that it will cost him the South and the election (in fact, his civil rights stand cost him five Southern states in 1964, and helped turn the South Republican in Presidential elections from 1964 on, with the single exception of Jimmy Carter's 1976 campaign—the first time a Southerner was directly elected to the White House).

His persistent flattery of Republican leader Dirksen is taken virtually verbatim from White House tapes, and is covered extensively in Woods's book. He also told Robert Kennedy, still serving as Attorney General, that he saw the 1964 civil rights act as a memorial to JFK.

The bombing of the Sixteenth Street Baptist Church in Birmingham actually took place on September 15, 1963, during John Kennedy's Presidency. LBJ's speech to the Congress is imagined; the speech he did give to Congress, on March 15, 1965, drafted by Richard Goodwin, the "We Shall Overcome" speech, remains the most eloquent and powerful Presidential address of the twentieth century.

JOHNSON'S FOREIGN POLICY: The judgments of Reedy and McPherson are taken directly from their own words, as are Johnson's comments on the nature of Soviet aggression, and his conviction that the President ought to be given wide latitude in the conduct of foreign policy. Kennedy's ingrained skepticism about the military, born in his days in the Pacific, is embedded in the letters he wrote home; and the campaign speech about America's lack of omniscience or omnipotence is quoted verbatim. The account here of Johnson's reluctance to intervene for France in Indochina in 1954 closely tracks reality.

CUBA: The plans by the Central Intelligence Agency to depose Fidel Castro have been public matters for decades—see, for example, David Talbot's book *Brothers*. While there is no direct reporting of Lyndon Johnson talking with Richard Bissell while seated on the toilet, he was in the habit of conducting such conversations with, among others, National Security Advisor McGeorge Bundy, according to a source who worked in the White House at that time.

For a detailed accounting of how the Bay of Pigs turned into a disaster, see—among countless sources—*Bay of Pigs Declassified: The Secret CIA Report on the Invasion of Cuba*, edited by Peter Kornbluth. The success of the CIA's 1954 overthrow of Guatemalan leftist Jacob Arbenz gave the Agency unwarranted confidence that it could replicate this success in Cuba.

The stormy meeting on the night of the White House Congressional reception took place on April 18, 1961, with President Kennedy confronting a frustrated group of the highest-ranking military officials.

Had Robert Kennedy taken over JFK's Massachusetts Senate seat, he would have done so as a relatively conventional Cold War thinker, whose anti-Communism was deeply rooted (see, for example, Evan Thomas's account in his biography, *Robert Kennedy*, of his refusal to be treated by a "Communist" doctor when he fell ill on a trip to the Soviet Union with Justice William Douglas). The distance between Robert Kennedy's outlook in 1961 and his outlook when he became a senator in 1965 is best measured in light-years.

As for how a President Johnson would have regarded the Bay of Pigs failure, Norm Ornstein, who has been observing Washington for decades, said in an interview, "Clearly, he trusted generals and top military people way more than JFK did."

THE VIENNA SUMMIT: The setting, logistics, and substance of the Vienna Summit is drawn from Michael Beschloss's book *The Crisis Years: Kennedy and Khrushchev, 1960–1963*. The advice given to LBJ from "Tommy"

Thompson and Averell Harriman is the same advice the two gave to JFK before he sat down with Khrushchev in Vienna, as described by Beschloss.

Johnson's pungent advice to Khrushchev—"never shit a shitter"—was never said by LBJ to Khrushchev, since the two never met. That sentiment *was* uttered by Senator Joe Biden to a surprised Soviet official during a Congressional visit to Moscow, according to a fellow U.S. senator who was in the meeting.

The Soviet Union's greatest fear in the early 1960s was that the United States would seek to use its clear superiority in the nuclear weapons arena to launch a preemptive strike on the Soviet Union. When President Kennedy described the forces of the two superpowers as being "more or less in balance," Khrushchev was pleased, because, Beschloss says, he knew that in fact the United States held clear superiority.

On September 13, 1961, U.S. officials learned from a briefing by Lyman Lemnitzer, Chairman of the Joint Chiefs of Staff, that the Soviet Union's nuclear force was something of a Potemkin village, that it had only ten to twenty-five missiles on launchers capable of hitting the United States. And on October 21, the U.S. in effect made that fact public knowledge, in a speech to the Business Council in Hot Springs, Virginia, by Deputy Secretary of Defense Roswell Gilpatric, in which he said that the United States "has a nuclear retaliatory force of such lethal power that an enemy move which brought it into play would be an act of self-destruction on his part" and possessed "a second strike capability which is at least as extensive as what the Soviets can deliver by striking first." The speech was widely— and correctly—interpreted as a declaration of superiority by the U.S. in the nuclear weapons arena, although its purpose appears to have been an effort to damp down war fears in the U.S.—fears fed by John Kennedy's charge in his Presidential campaign that America suffered from a "missile gap."

KHRUSHCHEV AND THE CUBAN MISSILE CRISIS: Beschloss's book has an extensive account of the Soviet leader's decision to put offensive nuclear weapons in Cuba. Khrushchev described his plans for Cuba by saying "it is time to put a hedgehog in Uncle Sam's pants." Because President Kennedy used a taping system during many of the most critical meetings of "ExComm," the words and thoughts of many of the participants can be seen in a 1997 book by Philip D. Zelikow with Ernest R. May, *The Kennedy Tapes: Inside the White House During the Cuban Missile Crisis.* However, since President Kennedy did not tape every meeting or every White House conversation, this cannot be seen as a complete picture of the deliberations.

In October 2002, on the fortieth anniversary of the crisis, a three-day conference in Havana brought together officials and scholars from the U.S., the former Soviet Union, and Cuba. Highlights of that conference were published in November 2002 in *Arms Control Today*, a publication of the Arms Control Association, and is available online at armscontrol.org/act/2002_11/cuban missile. It features a speech by former Defense Secretary Robert McNamara, revealing what U.S. officials did and did not know about the presence of Soviet tactical nuclear weapons in Cuba, and conversations among McNamara, Georgy M. Kornienko, former first deputy foreign minister of the USSR, and Nikolai S. Leonov, who was chief of the KGB's Department of Cuban Affairs for thirty years. (The question of just how much authority Premier Khrushchev gave to Soviet commanders in Cuba to use those nukes continues to be a matter of debate.)

The words spoken by Tommy Thompson, Curtis LeMay, Maxwell Taylor, and others come from the transcripts of the White House tapes. Dean Acheson's advice to Kennedy, including his judgments about the likely response from Moscow, can be found in books such as Douglas Brinkley's *Dean Acheson: The Cold War Years, 1953–71.* Acheson continued to argue that the peaceful resolution of the crisis was a case of "plain dumb luck."

Lyndon Johnson's history of suffering physical ailments during moments of crisis is told in the biographies by Dallek and Woods.

For other versions of how the Cuban Missile Crisis might have played out—with John Kennedy in the White House—see the essay by historian Robert L. O'Connell, "The Cuban Missile Crisis—The Second Holocaust," in which a series of misunderstandings leads to a tactical nuclear strike by Soviet commanders, which triggers a massive retaliation that wipes out the Soviet Union. In *Resurrection Day*, novelist Brendan DuBois imagines a 1970s United States decimated by a limited nuclear war, for which John Kennedy is blamed.

Ambassador Hotel, Los Angeles, California, June 4, 1968, 11:45 p.m.

AMBASSADOR HOTEL SUITE: The scene in Robert Kennedy's hotel suite on the night of June 4, 1968, is described in many books, including Jack Newfield's *Robert Kennedy: A Memoir*, Evan Thomas's *Robert Kennedy,* and Thurston Clarke's *The Last Campaign of Robert Kennedy.* I have also relied on my own memories of that night. The exchange between Roger Mudd of CBS and Kennedy took place as chronicled.

Steve Smith's interview for the RFK Oral History Project describes his work that night culling primary results, working in his stocking feet.

I was the Kennedy aide who went with Jack Newfield to McCarthy's hotel to talk with McCarthy supporters about joining forces after the primary.

"DALEY'S THE BALL GAME": Clarke's book details the meetings between Richard Wade and Daley; Wade says Daley seemed to be sending a signal that if Kennedy won the California primary, he'd win the support of the Chicago mayor.

SIRHAN SIRHAN: The movements of Sirhan on the night of June 4, as well as his childhood, upbringing, and growing anger at Robert Kennedy, are drawn from Robert Sam Anson's book *RFK Must Die!*

STEVE SMITH'S MOVEMENTS: In reading Smith's oral history at the JFK library, I found these words that—as far as I can tell—have never been published before: "If I had been with Senator Kennedy in that ballroom in the Ambassador Hotel, he might not have been shot . . . Curiously enough, for some reason I can't explain, during the course of the campaign, whenever I was with the Senator, I made it a point to place myself in front of him and sort of move as if I were clearing a way . . . I think it helped expedite his getting from one place to another . . . Had I been part of that group, I probably would have been walking in front of the Senator as he left the stage and went back to the kitchen, [so Sirhan] would have had to come by me to do it."

KENNEDY IS DIRECTED THROUGH THE KITCHEN: This decision was by all accounts a last-minute, on-the-fly call, to save the exhausted Kennedy from making another appearance in another ballroom before another group of supporters. By exiting the ballroom and walking through the kitchen, Kennedy would have been able to go directly to a press conference. The decision left his security agent, former FBI man Bill Barry, as well as Roosevelt Grier and others in his entourage, at a distance from Kennedy. He was shot as they were moving to catch up with him.

ROBERT KENNEDY'S POLITICAL SITUATION: The belief among most political watchers was that Kennedy was well behind Vice President Humphrey as of June 4. The on-air commentators, including ABC's William Laurence, all offered variations of the theme that the "winner" of the primaries was the man who hadn't competed in any of them, Hubert Humphrey, and that with no more primaries after New York on June 18, there were few levers available for RFK to use in order to change minds.

A chart prepared by Kennedy's chief delegate hunter, David Hackett, to be analyzed at a June 5 meeting in Steve Smith's Ambassador Hotel cottage, gave this "educated estimate" of the delegate breakdown:

Humphrey: 994
Kennedy: 524½
McCarthy: 204
Undecided: 872
Needed for nomination: 1.312

The "objective" was to get Kennedy to 1,432½ votes, with Kennedy gaining virtually all of the Illinois votes (the Daley factor), and majorities in the key non-primary states of Michigan, New Jersey, Ohio, and an effective split in Pennsylvania. The objective also assumed that Kennedy would get no more than 45 of the 600+ delegates up for grabs in the South and Southwest.

The chart was published in the back of the book *On His Own* by Kennedy aides William vanden Heuvel and Milt Gwirtzman.

THE MCCARTHY MELTDOWN: Sam Brown, the twenty-five-year-old who organized the "Clean for Gene" brigades in New Hampshire, told me that he and several other senior McCarthy campaign officials were preparing to announce their support for Robert Kennedy if he won the California primary, and were going to make that announcement within forty-eight hours of Kennedy's victory.

THE NEW YORK TIMES editorial praising McCarthy for his wit was published during the Oregon primary; it can be found in Clarke's *The Last Campaign,* which also describes McCarthy's "joke" in Oregon about the Kennedy campaign leaking a story that someone took a shot at him. In the wake of Kennedy's death, and McCarthy's suspension of his own campaign, the remark never received any public attention. Whether the then-liberal *New York Post* would have switched its endorsement from McCarthy to Kennedy is, of course, a matter of speculation.

LBJ AND KENNEDY: The "nightmares" envisioned by Johnson—Robert Kennedy denouncing him as a coward and a weakling—were described by Johnson to Doris Kearns Goodwin, according to her book *Lyndon Johnson and the American Dream.* The background of the tensions between Johnson and Robert Kennedy, as noted above, are described in detail in Jeff Shesol's *Mutual Contempt,* which includes Johnson's comment that "I believe that Bobby is having his governors jump on me, and he's having his mayors jump on me, and he's having his nigras and he's having his Catholics. And he's having them just systematically, one after the other, each day, go after me."

In his memoir *Remembering America,* Richard Goodwin—who worked in JFK and LBJ's White House—writes that he and White House Press Secretary Bill Moyers independently came to the conclusion that Johnson was demonstrating paranoid tendencies in the White House. He and Moyers, without knowing what the other was doing, consulted psychiatrists to try to gain insight into paranoia.

Evan Thomas's *Robert Kennedy* leaves little doubt that the Johnson White House was the source for Drew Pearson's column charging—accurately—that Kennedy authorized taps on Martin Luther King, Jr.'s telephone.

DALEY'S ENDORSEMENT: Daley's quotes about the Vietnam War are authentic, as is the story of the "golden boy," Joseph McKeon, a native of Daley's Bridgeport neighborhood and a Harvard graduate, killed just weeks after his arrival in Vietnam.

THE WHISTLE-STOPS: John Barlow Martin, the Indiana native, deserves credit for prodding Robert Kennedy into the whistle-stop train trips through Indiana, Nebraska, and California. The words Kennedy speaks in this section, including the jokes and lighthearted mocking of the conventions of campaign speech, are almost all words he uttered during those primary campaigns. The special car he used in those train trips is as described.

The Fourth of July speech, including the critique of the "growing power and authority . . . of the central government in Washington," is composed almost entirely of words delivered by Kennedy during his Senate career and during his Presidential campaign. They can be found in *Collected Speeches of RFK*, edited by Edwin Guthman and C. Richard Allen.

THE CREDENTIALS AND DELEGATE CHALLENGES: Milt Gwirtzman, a more or less permanent Kennedy family retainer, says in his oral history that a credentials challenge was to be part of the post-primary nomination strategy. At the Democratic Convention in Chicago, the Humphrey forces supported the successful challenge to the virtually all-white Mississippi delegation, replacing it with an integrated "loyalist" delegation, and helped design a compromise over the Georgia delegation, splitting it in two. In both cases, the insurgents gave most of their votes to Eugene McCarthy or George McGovern, running in 1968 as a stand-in for the murdered Robert Kennedy. The convention also voted to abolish the unit rule. More conservative Democrats, very much including Texas Governor John Connally, were furious at Humphrey's campaign for these decisions.

POST-PRIMARY TACTICS: Gwirtzman and others raised the possibility of a "mock" primary in Pennsylvania to pressure the pro-Humphrey mayors of Philadelphia and Pittsburgh. A "lightning trip" abroad was also up for discussion, but these and other tactics were on the agenda for a June 5th meeting to be held in Steve Smith's bungalow at the Ambassador.

NIXON CHOOSES LINDSAY: William Safire, who was a speechwriter for Nixon in his 1968 campaign and at the White House, writes in his book *Before the Fall*, that Nixon told him: "I gave a lot of thought to Lindsay— surprised?—but what the hell, he'd cut you up. Big gains up North, but Lindsay would lose us Florida, Texas, Kentucky, the Carolinas, Tennessee." Republicans in the House of Representatives backed Lindsay as Vice President by an overwhelming majority. The possibility of a Robert Kennedy on the Democratic ticket—either as President or Vice President—suggests that Nixon would have taken a much closer look at the New York mayor. As for conservative outrage, the lessons of the 1960 Democratic Convention—when John Kennedy chose Lyndon Johnson in the face of liberal fury and very likely won election by that choice—would have provided an instructive example for Nixon as he pondered how to deal with RFK in the fall.

THE CHICAGO CONVENTION SETTING: The conditions in Chicago— the war-zone security, the work stoppages and strikes, the logistical nightmare confronting the armies of the media—are described in rich detail by Theodore H. White in *The Making of the President 1968*.

William Kunstler's comment that RFK's survival was "the worst thing to happen to the movement years" is a reworking of a comment Kunstler made in my presence to an interviewer in the green room at WNET, New York's Channel 13, shortly before a taping of a talk show called *We Interrupt This Week,* in 1979, on which we were both panelists. What Kunstler did say was that the deaths of John and Robert Kennedy were the best things that happened to the radical movement, because it removed from the scene two men who might have diverted energy from the cause of revolution.

LYNDON JOHNSON'S HOPES FOR RENOMINATION: Johnson expressed his dissatisfaction with Hubert Humphrey as a candidate on many occasions to many people. The comments in this section are all taken from comments recorded in Dallek's *Flawed Giant,* Woods's *LBJ: Architect of American Ambition,* and White's *The Making of the President 1968.*

Astonishing as it may sound, Johnson *did* plan to fly to Moscow for a flash summit with Soviet Premier Kosygin, announce a groundbreaking agreement on arms control, then fly to the Democratic Convention to address the delegates. Teddy White recounts the plan in a footnote in *The Making of the President 1968.* He was talked out of this dramatic move by Defense Secretary Clark Clifford, according to Clifford's memoir *Counselor to the President.* But the White House was set to announce plans for a U.S.–Soviet summit to take place in October; the announcement *was* set for Tuesday, August 20, less than a week before the start of the Democratic Convention. That evening (as described in the chapter in this book), Soviet Ambassador Dobrynin asked for an urgent meeting, and informed them of the Soviet invasion of Czechoslovakia. The announcement—and the summit—were scrapped.

As for Johnson's hopes for renomination, he had a full team of operatives at the convention, including Postmaster General Marvin Watson and the convention's executive director, John Criswell, who was in fact reporting back to him under the code name "Bert." The speech quoted in this book—"as long as I have breath in my body I shall use it to encourage my country . . ."—was in fact a speech that was drafted for him for delivery at the convention.

The story is told in detail in an article by Justin Nelson titled: "Drafting

Lyndon Johnson: The President's Secret Role in the 1968 Democratic Convention," published by *Presidential Studies Quarterly* in 2004.

RFK CONFRONTS THE RADICALS: Robert Kennedy's willingness—even eagerness—to engage in face-to-face arguments with radical critics is almost a pattern in his public life. All the confrontations described in this chapter happened. (See, for example, Evan Thomas's biography *Robert Kennedy,* Richard Goodwin's *Remembering America,* and Clarke's *The Last Campaign of Robert Kennedy.*) Kennedy's more civil engagements with college students, in which he expressed his opposition to student deferments, is an integral element of every story on his 1968 campaign—including a fortieth-anniversary retrospective piece I did for *CBS Sunday Morning* in June 2008. His remark that a black man like John Lewis might someday be President was made frequently during his campaign and often drew hoots of incredulity.

Hubert Humphrey's anger at the media coverage parallels his reaction to the coverage of the disorder around the convention; he did in fact say, according to Teddy White, that he would be appointing the FCC Chairman, and that an investigation of the coverage might be in order.

HUMPHREY BREAKS WITH JOHNSON: The reality here is very different from my speculation. At the 1968 convention, an agreement was reached between Humphrey's forces and the anti-war campaigns of Eugene McCarthy and George McGovern for a compromise peace plank. But President Johnson's representative, Marvin Watson, told Humphrey that the President would not accept it, and threatened to deny Humphrey the delegates he needed for nomination if he went along with the compromise. In his memoir *The Education of a Public Man,* Humphrey expressed regret at his failure to confront Johnson.

"Now I know, in retrospect, that I should have stood my ground," he wrote. "I told our people I was still for the plank, but I didn't put up a real fight. That was a mistake . . . I should not have yielded. Having said that, I feel it is highly questionable whether I could have succeeded. President

Johnson, enraged, would have become a formidable foe, causing troubles that I could probably not have overcome."

THE CONNALLY–RIBICOFF FACE-OFF: All right, I am playing here. At the 1968 convention when Senator Abe Ribicoff of Connecticut rose to nominate George McGovern, he said, "With George McGovern as President, we wouldn't have to have Gestapo tactics in the streets of Chicago." From his front-row seat, Mayor Daley yelled at Ribicoff what many amateur lip readers took to be an ethnic insult fused with a popular obscenity. Daley's friends insisted he was using one of his favorite terms of scorn: "You Faker!" rather than "Jew F—er!"

THE NOMINATION: I make no pretense here of engaging in anything other than educated guesswork. Any successful credentials challenge to Southern delegations would have meant *some* increase in Robert Kennedy's delegate strength; and (see above) the projections by Kennedy's campaign as of June 4 assumed he would have almost *no* delegates from the region. Pennsylvania would have been the toughest of the big non-primary states for a breakthrough, while Ohio and Michigan seemed more promising at the time of Kennedy's death.

Humphrey and Kennedy had genuine affection for each other, so the prospect of a unity gesture—the loser introducing the winner to the convention—is well within the realm of possibility. Shortly before the California primary, I asked Fred Dutton whether RFK would accept the Vice Presidency with Humphrey, and Dutton said (as he does in the book) that he was certain Kennedy would say yes.

Similarly, I have no special insight into whom Kennedy would have chosen as a running mate. The choice of Terry Sanford as a running mate fits the "plausibility" standard: He was from the South; he had a progressive record on civil rights; he was a governor; and as the head of Humphrey's Citizens' Committee, he was a symbol of unity.

Virtually all of Robert Kennedy's acceptance speech was taken from speeches he delivered at one time or another in the last four years of his life.

. . .

Nixon's strategy: Nixon's plans to run against Johnson (and then Humphrey) as the candidate of change is spelled out in memos (including the one quoted here) included in Safire's *Before the Fall*. With RFK as his opponent, another strategy would have been required.

Hoover and Bobby: A shelf of books describes the growing gulf between FBI Director Hoover and Robert Kennedy; Evan Thomas's *Robert Kennedy* is one excellent guide to the story.

As to Hoover's relationship with Clyde Tolson, some things are matters of fact. They did lunch every day at Harvey's Restaurant (and later the dining room of the Mayflower Hotel). They did vacation together. Tolson was Hoover's sole heir. He did move into Hoover's home after the Director's death. And FBI agents did refer to them as: "J. Edna and Mother Tolson." When a *Time* magazine writer implied there might be something curious about the relationship, the reporter was subject to a full-field FBI investigation.

On the other hand, the widely circulated story that Hoover dressed as a woman stems from one thoroughly *un*confirmed rumor. Some who knew Hoover well suggest that the relationship between the two was simply a very close friendship, with no sexual overtones.

Billy Graham: The visit by Reverend Billy Graham to President Johnson on September 15, and the message he conveyed to the President from Nixon, occurred just as described (see Woods's *LBJ—Architect of American Power* and Dallek's *Flawed Giant*).

New York City school strike: Not one but a series of school strikes shut down the New York City public schools in the fall of 1968. For a detailed account of the strikes, in a book essentially highly critical of John Lindsay, see Vincent Cannato's *The Ungovernable City*.

. . .

THE FALL TELEVISION CAMPAIGN: Some of the ads described in this section were aired during the primaries, but were for obvious reasons never seen nationally. A few of them are available on YouTube, including the ads broadcast during the Nebraska primary, in which Kennedy (and, on occasion, his mother) spoke to an audience of Midwestern clubwomen. Richard Nixon's TV campaign, orchestrated by Roger Ailes, was the subject of *The Selling of the President 1968* by Joe McGinniss, which became a number one best seller. The ads described in this book hew closely to the style of the ads used by the Nixon campaign.

CLARK CLIFFORD: In his memoir, *Counsel to the President,* Clifford describes with great candor his steadily growing conviction that the war in Vietnam had to be ended rapidly and thoroughly, and his growing conviction that Lyndon Johnson preferred Richard Nixon to Hubert Humphrey, and cites LBJ saying that on Vietnam, "Nixon is closer to me than Hubert." Clifford notes that Charley Murphy, the liaison to the Humphrey campaign, told him that "if Humphrey did not stand firm on Vietnam a Nixon victory would be better for the country." With Robert Kennedy as the nominee, that sentiment would have been multiplied geometrically. On a visit to Washington for a funeral, Averell Harriman, the chief U.S. negotiator at the Paris peace talks, told Clifford that if he concluded Johnson was trying to assist Nixon's election chances, he would resign.

In late October, President Johnson held a conference call with the three major Presidential candidates—Humphrey, Nixon, and George Wallace—to reveal plans for a total halt to the bombing of North Vietnam.

Clifford also writes about the discovery that the Nixon campaign, through Anna Chennault, was covertly encouraging the South Vietnamese government to reject the Johnson administration's proposals to enable the National Liberation front (the Vietcong) and the South Vietnamese government to join the Paris peace talks. He discusses this as well in his oral history, available online from the LBJ Presidential Library in Austin, Texas. There are several explanations for the failure to make this information public: it was obtained through surreptitious wiretaps on Anna Chenault; it would have created a crisis on the eve of a Presidential election. For his part, Clifford argued at the time, and in his memoirs, that the information should have been made public.

THE ELECTION: In the 1968 election, Richard Nixon won the popular vote over Hubert Humphrey by a margin of one half of 1 percent. While Nixon won 301 electoral votes to Humphrey's 191—with Wallace winning the remaining 46—the electoral vote contest was far closer than the totals suggest. Nixon won Illinois by a margin of less than 3 percent. He won New Jersey by 2.3 percent. He won Ohio by 2.28 percent. He won California by a shade over 3 percent. Humphrey's closest big state margin was in Texas, which he won with a 2.27 percent margin.

Given these actual results, it is hardly a major leap of faith to imagine how Robert Kennedy could have beaten Richard Nixon in November. Assume that New Jersey remained in Nixon's column, and assume that the hostility of Johnson, Connally, and company would have cost Kennedy Texas. If we also assume that Kennedy would have had a greater appeal to Wallace voters than Humphrey, that appeal by itself would have made a major difference in major states. For example, if Kennedy had managed to win one in five Wallace voters in Ohio, that would have been enough for him to win the state, even if he did not win a single additional vote. It is reasonable to believe that in states like Ohio, Illinois, and especially California, minority turnout would have been significantly higher, with almost all of those additional votes winding up in Kennedy's column.

THE WAR ENDS: In his campaign, Kennedy had sent clear signals that he was not prepared simply to walk away from Vietnam; as he said in his San Francisco debate with McCarthy, "We can't just run up the white flag." It is pure conjecture to imagine a back channel from Kennedy to Hanoi through Soviet Ambassador Dobrynin. On the other hand, Robert Kennedy was very much given to establishing back channels to Moscow; he had done it while Attorney General, most notably with Georgi Bolshakov, and during the Cuban Missile Crisis as well. Thomas's biography *Robert Kennedy* has full details on these dealings.

Daniel Ellsberg was in frequent contact with members of Robert Kennedy's Senate staff. And in breaking with President Johnson on the Vietnam War, Kennedy was careful to point a finger of responsibility at himself, and did so throughout his Presidential campaign. For instance, just after announcing his candidacy, he said at Kansas State University:

"I was involved in many of the early decisions on Vietnam, decisions which helped set us on our present path . . . I am willing to bear my share of the responsibility, before history and before my fellow citizens. But past error is no excuse for its own perpetuation. Tragedy is a tool for the living to gain wisdom, not a guide by which to live."

Ieng Sary was one of the highest-ranking leaders of the Khmer Rouge, whose leaders declared 1975 "Year Zero" when they took power and commenced a campaign to eliminate every trace of "bourgeois" influence—a campaign that may have taken as many as two million lives.

Robert Altman's *M*A*S*H* was released in 1970, as the Vietnam War was in its sixth year of full-fledged combat, and went on to earn more than $80 million at the box office. The TV spin-off, starring Alan Alda, ran on CBS for more than a decade; its finale, broadcast in February 1983, was watched by more than a hundred million people.

Robert Kennedy's comment about his "influence over the federal prison system" was made to me, in a conversation in his Senate office.

CHAPPAQUIDDICK: Secret Service protection extended to the families of Presidents, and the members of the Kennedy clan were in frequent attendance at the Edgartown Yacht Club regatta.

CHINA: Ted Sorenson relates David Ben-Gurion's comments about a possible Robert Kennedy visit to China in his book *The Kennedy Legacy*. Richard Nixon's essay "Asia After Vietnam" was published in *Foreign Affairs* magazine in October 1967, providing what in retrospect appeared to be a hint that he intended to reach out to the Communist nation he had spent a political lifetime opposing.

ROBERT KENNEDY'S CONTRADICTIONS: The public policy positions described in this section can be found in detail in his speeches and statements, particularly those from his years in the Senate, when his legislative assistants, Adam Walinsky and Peter Edelman, helped turn RFK's instincts into specific programs, such as the Community Development Corporation and the Police Corps. Kennedy once described Che Guevara as "a revolutionary hero," according to Arthur Schlesinger, Jr., in *Robert Kennedy and His Times.* And, according to Evan Thomas's biography, he told guests at a Georgetown dinner party that if he had it to do over again, he'd be "a paratrooper."

PAUL CORBIN: The relationship between Corbin and Robert Kennedy, which puzzled (and disturbed) many in Kennedy's circle, is sketched out in Evan Thomas's *Robert Kennedy.* It is described most fully in Craig Shirley's book on Ronald Reagan's 1980 campaign, *Rendezvous with Destiny.* In an oral history at the JFK Library, Corbin tells the story of his participation in John Kennedy's Wisconsin primary campaign in 1960, where he met Robert Kennedy. It was Corbin's (apparently) self-propelled efforts to get Kennedy nominated for Vice President in 1964 that triggered the blowup between Kennedy and President Johnson described in many books. Evan Thomas recounts his plan to disguise Kennedy supporters as freakishly dressed backers of Eugene McCarthy during the 1968 campaign.

Corbin's last appearance on the public stage—and the reason why he appears at such length in a book about Reagan's 1980 campaign—was in 1983, when a book by journalist Laurence Barrett, *Gambling with History,* disclosed that a briefing book prepared for use by President Carter in his debate with Reagan somehow found its way into the hands of the Reagan campaign. A Congressional investigation chaired by Michigan's Donald Albosta laid out an intriguing, though not conclusive, trail that linked Corbin, former Wisconsin governor Pat Lucey (who wound up in 1980 as independent candidate John Anderson's running mate), and a onetime Lucey aide who was working in the scheduling department of President Carter's White House. Investigations revealed that Corbin had visited Reagan headquarters on several occasions in 1980, had met with top campaign aides William Casey and James Baker, and had received a check for $1,500.

In his book, Shirley writes: "At the height of the Albosta investigation, Baker received a call from Congressman Dick Cheney (R-Wyo.). Cheney told Baker that a member of his staff who had long known Corbin, Tim Wyngaard, confided that Corbin had privately acknowledged orchestrating the theft of the Carter briefing books and giving them to Casey. Wyngaard, the executive director of the House Republican Policy Committee, confirmed to Albosta committee investigators and to the *New York Times* that Corbin had claimed credit for lifting the briefing books."

Baker himself, who had been handed the briefing book by Bill Casey, was cleared of any wrongdoing by the investigation. However, in his 2006 memoir, *Work Hard, Study . . . and Keep Out of Politics!*, he notes: "I wasn't responsible for obtaining the briefing book, and I told the truth. But should I have asked Casey where he got the book? Should I have refused to pass the material on to those preparing Reagan? These are legitimate questions. In hindsight, my answer to both questions is yes."

The character Kevin McKiernan is fictional.

For a radically different, far more ambitious view of what would have happened had Robert Kennedy lived, see *A Disturbance of Fate*, a nearly seven-hundred-page book by Mitchell Freedman published in 2003 by Seven Locks Press. It deals with every Cabinet post, every White House staff position, every domestic and foreign issue, and twenty-plus years of alternate American history following Robert Kennedy's election in 1968.

Palace of Fine Arts, San Francisco, California, October 6, 1976, 7:00 p.m.

THE POLITICAL TERRAIN: The events in this section that lead up to the second debate are given a full account in Jules Witcover's *Marathon: The Pursuit of the Presidency 1972–1976*, and a more interpretive account in

Theodore H. White's valedictory *America in Search of Itself: The Making of the President, 1956–1980*.

The exchange between Malcolm MacDougall and Bob Teeter about the importance of the Catholic vote—to Ford and Carter—is discussed in MacDougall's book on the campaign, *We Almost Made It*.

"No Soviet domination . . .": According to Witcover's *Marathon*, Ford "was convinced he'd get questions on the Helsinki Agreement and its relationship to Eastern Europe and Soviet domination . . ." It was one of those issues Reagan had used throughout the primary campaign to criticize "Dr. Kissinger and Mr. Ford." Stu Spencer told Witcover that, after hearing Ford's first answer on Soviet domination, National Security Advisor Brent Scowcroft "turned white." In the wake of the debate, President Ford called Aloysisus Mazeski, President of the Polish-American Federation, to apologize.

Doug Bailey's observation about what a failure to correct Ford's answer *might* have done is a reworking of his view of what that failure *did in fact* do: that it cost the campaign a week of lost momentum just at the point when the gap between Ford and Carter had been closing rapidly. Ford pollster Bob Teeter told Witcover: "His surveys showed the loss was not in any segment of the electorate so much as in momentum and time. The controversy used up valuable campaign days when there were all too few left, and the campaign leveled off when a steady climb had to be sustained."

Jimmy Carter's troubles: Jimmy Carter described the political cost of campaigning with traditional Democrats, and the damage it inflicted on his image, in a post-election interview with Jules Witcover for *Marathon*. The critical comments by more traditional Democrats are also found there.

The election results: It's a recurring theme in American political analysis that once a Presidential election ends, the results are often seen as part of a sweeping historical pattern, rather than as a result that, in many cases, could just as easily have had a different outcome. The 1976 election is a classic example.

The Carter–Mondale ticket won a popular plurality of slightly less than 1.7 million votes out of about 81.5 million votes cast and beat the Ford–Dole ticket by a 50–48 percent margin. In the Electoral College, Carter won 297 electoral votes to Ford's 240. But a look at the key competitive states shows that Carter's real margin was almost infinitesimal.

In Ohio, Carter won by 11,100 votes out of more than *four* million cast—a margin of less than *three-tenths of 1 percent*. Put another way, if 6,000 Ohio voters had decided to switch from Ford to Carter because of Ford's clumsy "Soviet domination" answer, that by itself would have switched Ohio's 25 electoral votes.

The same story is true in several other states. Mississippi went for Carter by a margin of 15,000 votes, a spread of less than 2 percent. Wisconsin, with its considerable population of Poles and other Eastern Europeans, broke for Carter by a 1.7 percent margin. Hawaii wound up in Carter's column with a 7,000-vote plurality. Less than three percentage points separated Carter from Ford in Pennsylvania. Even New York State gave Carter a relatively narrow four-point victory.

Given the closeness of this race, it is hardly a reach to suggest that the impact of Ford's "walkabout" on the Soviet domination question—the weeklong confusion, the loss of momentum, the self-inflicted wound in an area where an incumbent President is presumed to be strong—was more than enough to cost Gerald Ford the White House.

FORD'S SECOND TERM: For the record, Henry Kissinger did not seek to hold two Cabinet positions simultaneously while serving Presidents Nixon and Ford. He did serve both as Secretary of State and as National Security Advisor until Ford put Scowcroft in the latter position. Volumes (literally) have been written by and about Kissinger. For an overall view of Kissinger's behavior, character, competence, and turf protection, drawn almost exclusively from the public record, see Richard Reeves's book *President Nixon*.

THE SHAH, THE FORD ADMINISTRATION, AND THE MIDDLE EAST: For a shorthand look at the background to the Shah, Iran in the late 1970s, and his complicated relationship with the United States, see (to mention a few from a library full of references) a *Washington Post* obituary when the Shah died, published on July 28, 1980, and another *Post* piece, this one by Scott Armstrong, published on October 26, 1980. For a critical look at how the Carter administration handled the upheaval, see Don Oberdorfer's *Post* piece of September 7, 1980, and Betty Glad's book-length look at Carter's foreign policy, *An Outsider in the White House.*

For a detailed examination of how Saudi Arabia undercut the Shah's efforts to keep oil prices high at the end of the Ford administration, see Andrew Scott Cooper's "Showdown at Doha—The Secret Oil Deal That Helped Sink the Shah of Iran," published in *Middle East Journal,* August 2008. It includes an account of the rifts within the Ford administration between Kissinger, on the one hand, and Rumsfeld and Simon on the other.

Brent Scowcroft's observation that "Carter had Vietnam angst," and that a Ford administration would have worked to help nip the Iran insurgency in the bud, comes from an interview I conducted with him in Washington on March 24, 2010.

The rise of Islamic fundamentalism is the subject of Lawrence Wright's book *The Looming Tower: Al-Qaeda and the Road to 9/11.* One of its major subjects is Ayman al-Zawahiri, who became the operational head of al-Qaeda under Osama bin Laden. He was arrested in the wake of the 1981 assassination of Egyptian President Sadat, and spent three years in prison, undergoing treatment that, Wright's book suggests, turned him into even more of a militant. While it's beyond the scope of this book, it's fascinating to speculate whether the lack of a deal between Egypt and Israel would have prevented the assassination of Sadat. Without the years of torture he underwent, would al-Zawahiri's radicalism have turned quite so remorseless and violent?

FORD'S "DOOMED" SECOND TERM: Doug Bailey's observations about Ford's lack of "vision" come from an interview I conducted with him in Washington on June 29, 2010.

John Hersey spent a week with President Ford in 1975 for the *New York*

Times Magazine. His essay is included in his book *Aspects of the Presidency,* published in 1980.

The growth of inflation as the dominant economic fact of American life in the late 1970s is recounted in chapter five of Theodore H. White's book *America in Search of Itself.* For another account, see *The Seventies* by Bruce J. Schulman.

The line in Ford's imagined 1977 Inaugural ("'American' ends in I CAN") was delivered by Michigan Congressman Guy VanderJagt during his keynote address at the 1980 Republican Convention.

The details of the American automobile industry's afflictions in the late 70s come from David Halberstam's 1986 book *The Reckoning.*

The Principal Players in 1980

GARY HART: The description of Senator Hart's office and work habits was provided by two of his senior aides: former press secretary Kathy Bushkin Calvin and former chief of staff Billy Shore. Many biographical details and observations were based on the work of Richard Ben Cramer, whose 1992 book, *What It Takes,* is the best single volume ever written about Presidential campaigning. Hart's own 1973 book, *Right from the Start,* covers his role as the chief of George McGovern's campaign for the 1972 Presidential nomination and sets down the organizing precepts quoted here.

RONALD REAGAN: The best one-volume account of Reagan's career I know of is Lou Cannon's *The Role of a Lifetime.* For a close look at Reagan's 1976 challenge to President Ford, see Craig Shirley's *Reagan's Revolution.* Shirley also wrote *Rendezvous with Destiny,* which covers the 1980 campaign in depth.

Gerald Ford's dyspeptic view of Reagan can be found in Thomas DeFrank's book *Write It When I'm Gone,* in which Ford says Reagan's lack of campaigning in 1976 was "one of the three or four reasons that I lost . . ." (I have altered the quote to reflect the alternate history in which Ford almost lost.)

.   .   .

TED KENNEDY: I have "borrowed" from my 1982 book *The Real Campaign* to describe the political position of Kennedy in 1979, when the political universe was more or less convinced that he could take the nomination from President Carter without breaking a sweat. The barbs coming from disparate media sources such as the *National Lampoon, Saturday Night Live,* and the *Washington Monthly* are described as they happened. The same is true of pollster Peter Hart's warning about the danger of misreading Kennedy's poll numbers.

HART, BUMPERS, AND BEATTY: Dale Bumpers has told the story of his life in his uncommonly candid and compelling memoir, *Best Lawyer in a One-Lawyer Town,* which includes the stories and jokes in this section. According to Kathy Bushkin Calvin and Billy Shore, Bumpers and Hart were seated next to each other on the Senate floor and became best friends and fellow gym rats.

Warren Beatty met Gary Hart during the 1972 McGovern campaign, in which Beatty acted less as a "celebrity" and more as a behind-the-scenes advisor. He organized major fund-raising events, including one of the first rock concerts ever held to raise political money. The details can be found in Peter Biskind's 2010 biography of Warren Beatty, *Star.*

Gary Hart's Uncle Ralph provided the history of the Hart family's many name changes during Hart's 1984 campaign, when the name change—along with changes in his birth date and handwriting—raised the "weirdness" question. Jack Germond and Jules Witcover's book on the campaign, *Wake Us When It's Over,* has all the details.

Hart's announcement speech is composed of words he spoke and wrote, the latter in his book *A New Democracy,* which came out shortly before he announced his intention to run for President in 1984. I fashioned the account of Hart's travels in Iowa in 1980 from my own travels through the state in covering six caucuses and from the recollections of Hart aides about his habits while campaigning.

In this section, and in the later stories about Hart's campaign for the nomination, the most indispensable guide was Elaine Kamarck's book *Primary Politics,* about which more later. As Hillary Clinton's campaign discovered in 2008, a campaign will fail in Iowa, no matter how well known the candidate, no matter how much "insider" support it has, if it does not understand the peculiar political terrain of those caucuses, and more generally, the rules of how delegates are chosen in the Democratic Party.

REAGAN'S ROMP TO THE NOMINATION: When Reagan ran for President in 1980, he followed the advice of his campaign chief, John Sears, and stayed above the fray, refusing to debate and refusing to campaign in Iowa. With George H. W. Bush all but living in Iowa, Bush narrowly defeated Reagan in the caucuses, leading pundits to prepare his political obituary. As NBC's Tom Pettit said the morning after the caucuses, "I would like to suggest that Ronald Reagan is politically dead." That defeat prodded Reagan into overruling Sears and throwing himself fully into the New Hampshire primary, including the famous debate in Keene, New Hampshire, in which Reagan, in the midst of a heated argument with the debate moderator, bellowed, "I am paying for this microphone!" His unhappiness with Sears, fueled by the campaign chief's repeated sacking of Reagan's political team, resulted in Reagan's firing of Sears and two of his key allies on the day of the New Hampshire primary. Craig Shirley's *Rendezvous with Destiny* has the most thorough account of these events.

It is plausible to think that without a real battle for the nomination, Reagan would have fired Sears anyway and become a bolder candidate. But, as Shirley recounts, Reagan shied away from conflict in his own campaign; and without a primary setback, the case for changing course would have been harder to make.

THE KENNEDY-HART BATTLE: The harsh coverage of Ted Kennedy from the mainstream media is described as it happened.

In the nomination scenario, Elaine Kamarck's *Primary Politics* became my guiding star—especially as it related to the primary calendar.

To understand why, this point is essential: In 1980, four weeks separated

Iowa from New Hampshire. In 1984, when Hart in fact ran, eight days separated the two events.

When Gary Hart ran in 1984, he finished far behind former Vice President Walter Mondale in Iowa, with 16 percent of the vote to Mondale's 49 percent. The *New York Times*, on the day of the New Hampshire primary, reported that Mondale had the biggest lead of any candidate in primary history. The surge of "Anybody but Mondale" sentiment, and Hart's winning ways with an ax throw, won him a solid victory in New Hampshire—one that his campaign was completely unequipped to deal with. The sudden mass of attention, the demand for press interviews, the instant tug on his time from every corner of the nation, completely overwhelmed the campaign. Had Gary Hart had a month to deal with a "better than expected showing," he would have had time to do everything from fund-raise to travel around the country. And he would have been spared the "Who is this guy?" response from an electorate that had never heard of him until he became an instant giant-killer.

The primary calendar also made a huge difference to Ronald Reagan. When Bush beat him in Iowa in 1980, Reagan had a month to respond, to begin campaigning vigorously in New Hampshire, and to debate. Had the 1984 calendar been in effect, Bush's momentum might well have carried him to victory in New Hampshire eight days after Iowa; and that might very well have proven fatal to Reagan's chances.

The use of "delegate committees" to skirt campaign spending limits was actually used in 1984—not by Gary Hart, but by Walter Mondale's campaign, as extensively covered in Germond and Witcover's book. That book also recounts Hart's success in hitting a bull's eye with an ax at the Woodsman Conclave in Berlin.

Ted Kennedy's 1980 campaign was effectively out of money by the end of the New Hampshire primary. If readers see a parallel between the hypothetical Hart-Kennedy battle of 1980, and the Obama-Clinton struggle of 2008—congratulations!

John McCain, who served as the Navy's liaison to the Senate, worked across the hall from Hart, who served on the Armed Services Committee. They became close enough so that Hart served as a groomsman when McCain married Cindy Hensley in May of 1980.

The "red phone" ad was used by the Mondale campaign in the 1984 primary to suggest that Gary Hart was an "unsure, unsteady, untested hand . . ."

The abolition of "winner take all" primaries in the Democratic Party continues to be a defining difference between the parties. In 2008, for example, Hillary Clinton's victories in the Ohio and Pennsylvania primaries netted her fewer delegates than Obama got by winning the Idaho and Kansas caucuses! Had the Democrats had the Republican Party rules—with "winner-take-all" primaries in states such as New York and New Jersey—Hillary Clinton would almost surely have beaten Obama for the nomination. At the risk of repeating myself, if you want to understand how important these rules are, read Kamarck's *Primary Politics*.

THE REPUBLICAN CONVENTION—AND REAGAN'S RUNNING MATE: In 1980, Republicans met in Detroit, Michigan—a perfect venue for highlighting the failure of the Carter administration and the Congressional Democrats to deal with the collapse of the auto industry and the decline of urban America. With a Republican in the White House, it would have been exactly the *wrong* signal, but exactly the *right* signal for Democrats. And without an incumbent President Carter running, the South would have been the Republicans' best target of opportunity (the 1984 Republican Convention was held in Dallas).

Reagan and his campaign manager, John Sears, had shown a willingness to play high-stakes poker with a Vice Presidential choice back in 1976. Coming into the convention a few dozen delegates behind President Ford, Reagan broke with tradition by announcing he would choose as his running mate Pennsylvania Senator Richard Schweiker. In part, the choice of a liberal Republican was designed to show that Reagan was no zealot. The tactical intention was to force Ford to announce *his* choice, thus alienating partisans of other contenders (the ploy failed).

In 1980, much attention was focused on the "gender gap." Democrats ran better among women than among men. Had Reagan been running to succeed an unpopular Republican incumbent, with Gary Hart staking a plausible claim to be the "change" candidate, choosing a woman running mate would have made real political sense. In his campaign, Reagan promised to put a woman on the Supreme Court, which he did at his first opportunity in 1981, when he named Sandra Day O'Connor. Further, John McCain's choice of Governor Sarah Palin as his running mate in 2008 was seen—at first—as a political ten-strike after she delivered a masterful acceptance speech at the convention. Only later, especially in her interviews with CBS anchor Katie Couric, did her limitations emerge.

Reagan's acceptance speech is composed largely of speeches he delivered during the 1980 campaign.

THE REAGAN-HART DEBATE, AND DAVID GARTH: Reagan prepared for his debates with full-blown rehearsals on a mock stage in Wexford, Virginia, as described in many accounts of the 1980 campaign, including Craig Shirley's *Rendezvous with Destiny*. Gary Hart's method of debate preparation was described to me by Kathy Bushkin Calvin. Warren Beatty worked with Hart as a behind-the-scenes advisor in George McGovern's 1972 campaign and in Hart's own 1984 run for the Presidential nomination (see Peter Biskind's *Star*).

My knowledge of David Garth, whose career as a prominent political-media strategist spanned three decades, comes firsthand: I worked for him from 1970 to 1976 helping to shape campaign themes, draft speeches, create political commercials, and work on debate preparation. The best neutral appraisal of Garth I've seen was written by Robert Sam Anson for *New Times* magazine in 1978, "The World According to Garth." The ad he and I did for Tom Bradley in his 1973 race for Los Angeles mayor—where he talked bluntly about racial fears—remains in my mind as the best work he and I ever did.

Garth's rule that "Bugs Bunny always beats Daffy Duck" comes from a piece I did for *Slate* magazine in the 2008 campaign.

The substance of Hart's opening remarks can be found in his 1983 book *A New Democracy,* where he presents the themes he would use during his Presidential run the following year. Ronald Reagan's misstatement about the GI Bill of Rights is cited in my book *The Real Campaign.* None of his primary opponents challenged him about it—at least, not in any debate—and it had been forgotten by the time Carter and Reagan debated in 1980.

For David Garth, who employed first-rate researchers to comb the records of both his clients and his adversaries, it was the kind of mistake that would never have gone unremembered—or unused.

Reagan's closing statement in his debate with Jimmy Carter—"Are you better off than you were four years ago?"—has rightly gone down in political history as a classically effective summation of his case. I was astounded to discover that George McGovern had used not just that same argument, but almost those same words, to encapsulate his case against Richard Nixon in 1972.

Nancy Reagan's dissatisfaction with John Sears is recounted in Shirley's book. In the 1980 campaign as it unfolded, old Reagan hands that John Sears had forced out of the campaign kept up backchannel communications with Nancy Reagan, which helped lead to Sears's ouster on the day of the New Hampshire primary.

IN CONCLUSION: The idea of a sitting President of the United States engaging in intimate physical contact with a woman half his age within the very walls of the White House is, of course, unthinkable. I apologize for permitting my fevered imagination to run away with my better judgment.

ACKNOWLEDGMENTS

My first debt is to my publisher, Putnam, and my long-suffering editor, Neil Nyren—for what may appear to be an unlikely reason: They threatened me.

For years, I drifted between evasion and struggle in an attempt to produce the novel for which Putnam had delivered a significant amount of money (significant to me, if not Stephen King). And for years, I suggested, then implored them, to employ the one method of inspiration sure to invigorate my sclerotic creative impulses: Give us a book or give us back the money.

Finally, they made me that offer I could not refuse.

Thanks to the efforts of my longtime literary agent, Sterling Lord, the agreement we reached proved . . . agreeable.

More significant was the encouragement I received from Neil—and from many others at Putnam, including president Ivan Held, and publicity director Marilyn Ducksworth—after they saw the first section of this book. Their enthusiasm was the best source of energy an author can have.

My second debt is to one of my best friends in the world, Pat Mitchell, who runs the Paley Center for Media. As it happened, I was on a panel at the Center just after Putnam made its demand, to discuss a film about Robert Kennedy's memorable speech the night Martin Luther King, Jr., was killed. I was asked (as I have been innumerable times), "What would have happened had he lived?" I started to answer, as I always have, "Who knows?," and then found myself talking about the strong possibility that Chicago Mayor Daley would have backed RFK and how that would have changed the whole dynamic at the Chicago convention, and . . .

. . . And that was the germination of this book.

Along the way, I was helped by the generosity of friends, colleagues, and players in these events, over breakfasts, lunches, dinners, interviews, and e-mail exchanges that form much of the spine of these stories.

Harry McPherson, who worked closely with Lyndon Johnson in his Senate and White House years, provided shrewd insight into how LBJ might have governed had he been thrust into the White House, not in 1963 but before John Kennedy had ever been inaugurated.

Richard Goodwin, whose experience spanned JFK's 1960 campaign and his White House years, LBJ's Presidency, and RFK's doomed 1968 campaign, spent an evening with me, along with Doris Kearns Goodwin, who was Johnson's closest confidante in his post–White House years, and whose sense of the interplay between personality and history was invaluable to me. Dick was also one of Robert Kennedy's best friends, and his take on Kennedy's character and impulses was of enormous help in shaping the history of that 1968 campaign that never was.

Doug Bailey, the legendary Republican media master, guided me through the strategy, tactics, and ultimate frustration of the campaign that almost pulled off a 1976 upset worthy of Harry Truman's 1948 victory.

Brent Scowcroft, Ford's National Security Advisor, cheerfully took up the challenge of assessing the response of a Ford Presidency to upheaval in Iran, and helped sketch for me what a very different Middle East might look like.

For the imagined 1980 campaign of Gary Hart, I received guidance from two of Hart's closest Senate and campaign colleagues: press secretary Kathy Bushkin (now Kathy Bushkin Calvin) and top staff aide Billy Shore.

I also had the great good fortune to have the best possible guide through the 1980 political terrain: Elaine Kamarck, a veteran of Democratic Party wars, whose knowledge reaches from the most serious of public policy disputes to the Byzantine rule disputes that have driven generations of Democratic Party operatives to drink and drugs.

Throughout my work on this book, I found myself turning for help to one of Washington's most insightful thinkers: Norman Ornstein, resident scholar at the American Enterprise Institute. Norm has for decades been one of the most quoted figures on everything from elections to Congressional-Presidential relations to Constitutional matters. It turns out that there's a reason: In contrast to much of what passes for "analysis" on cable news and talk radio, Norm actually is deeply grounded in what he is talking about.

For well over twenty years, one of the greatest pleasures during campaign season has been the companionship of journalist-author Joe Klein; we have broken bread from one end of the country to the other, and on several occasions have gathered a gaggle of colleagues for lengthy lunches and dinners. Beyond that, Joe is a good friend and a one-man generator of ideas. He was especially helpful in guiding me through the construction of an "alternate" Middle East.

When it comes to dedication to the coverage of politics, no one can top Walter Shapiro, who is even now (I suspect) staking out the opening rounds of the 2012, and 2016, and 2020 Presidential campaigns. He is also a man on whom fortune has smiled; he gets to be married to another first-rate journalist, Meryl Gordon. Had I incorporated all of their worthy notions about alternative political histories, the book would have been twice as long.

For nearly thirty years, I have been part of a standing Wednesday lunch group, with exclusive membership standards (no diphtheria allowed). Each of these miscreants, in their own way, were of inestimable—make that estimable—assistance.

Michael Kramer, who's spent decades committing first-rate political journalism for *New York, Time,* the New York *Daily News,* and other publications, was terrific about the domestic politics of the times covered in this book, and about the dynamics of the Middle East—thus confirming the suspicions of his fellow lunch companions that he must have been a contract employee of the Central Intelligence Agency.

Andrew Bergman, the writer-director who has given us *Blazing Saddles, The In-Laws, The Freshman, Honeymoon in Vegas,* as well as the Jack LeVine detective novels, inspired some of the twists and turns in the world of popular culture seen here.

For help in conjuring up advertising campaigns, who better than Jerry Della Femina, whose stature as a Madison Avenue icon is (subtly) celebrated in many of the most talked-about episodes of *Mad Men,* as well as in his classic memoir, *From Those Wonderful Folks Who Gave You Pearl Harbor.*

Dr. Gerald Imber, one of New York's most prominent plastic surgeons, was of particular, if not exactly traditional, help. His relentless insistence that I "would never finish that —-ing book!" was a reliable source of inspiration.

One of our group, the film critic Joel Siegel, died in 2007. I miss him every day, and know that, had he been around, he would have argued strongly for changing the book's plot so that all of the principal players would have discovered their Jewish ancestry.

In my effort to learn the thinking of those close to Robert Kennedy about the fight for the Presidential nomination that never happened, I read through a sheaf of oral histories on file at the John F. Kennedy Presidential Museum and Library. My thanks to its Director, Thomas J. Putnam, and to Research Archivist Stephen Plotkin.

At CBS News, I found a powerful ally in the person of Cryder Bankes, the Manager of Library Services at the CBS News Reference Library. He was able to find for me shelves full of long-out-of-print books, as well as obscure monographs and research papers, with astonishing speed.

For more than a decade, Beth Goodman-Plante has worked with me: as an assistant at CNN and CBS News, as a researcher, as a coordinator of logistics. Let me not overstate the case: There is no one in the world I would want at my side, in any work that I do, more than Beth Goodman-Plante. Period. End of story.

Finally: On February 12, 1997, through a series of coincidences worthy of a Nora Ephron movie, I met Dena Sklar. I fell in love with her that night; and, thanks to some karmic good deed I must have performed in an earlier life, she fell in love with me. We have been together since, now as husband and wife. If it is true that one of the keys to happiness is a sense of gratitude, then I am among the happiest of men. The twist of fate that brought us together that night is one for which I am immeasurably grateful every day.

CHAOS

Patricia Cornwell is recognized as one of the world's top bestselling crime authors with novels translated into thirty-six languages in more than 120 countries. Her novels have won numerous prestigious awards including the Edgar, the Creasey, the Anthony, the Macavity, and the Prix du Roman d'Aventure. Beyond the Scarpetta series, Cornwell has written a definitive book about Jack the Ripper, a biography, and two more fiction series among others. Cornwell, a licensed helicopter pilot and scuba diver, actively researches the cutting-edge forensic technologies that inform her work. She was born in Miami, grew up in Montreat, NC, and now lives and works in Boston.

www.PatriciaCornwell.com

@1pcornwell

Facebook.com/Patricia.Cornwell

1pcornwell

ALSO BY PATRICIA CORNWELL

SCARPETTA SERIES
Depraved Heart
Flesh and Blood
Dust
The Bone Bed
Red Mist
Port Mortuary
The Scarpetta Factor
Scarpetta
Book of the Dead
Predator
Trace
Blow Fly
The Last Precinct
Black Notice
Point of Origin
Unnatural Exposure
Cause of Death
From Potter's Field
The Body Farm
Cruel and Unusual
All That Remains
Body of Evidence
Postmortem

NONFICTION
*Portrait of a Killer: Jack the
    Ripper—Case Closed*

ANDY BRAZIL SERIES
Isle of Dogs
Southern Cross
Hornet's Nest

WIN GARANO SERIES
The Front
At Risk

BIOGRAPHY
*Ruth, a Portrait: The Story of
    Ruth Bell Graham*

OTHER WORKS
*Food to Die For: Secrets from Kay
    Scarpetta's Kitchen*
Life's Little Fable
Scarpetta's Winter Table

Patricia
Cornwell
CHAOS

HarperCollins*Publishers*

HarperCollins*Publishers*
1 London Bridge Street
London SE1 9GF

www.harpercollins.co.uk

First published in Great Britain by HarperCollins*Publishers* 2016

2

First published in the United States by William Morrow,
an imprint of HarperCollins*Publishers* 2016

A catalogue record for this book is
available from the British Library

ISBN: 9780008150631

Printed and bound in Great Britain by
Clays Ltd St Ives plc

MIX
Paper from
responsible sources

FSC
www.fsc.org   FSC™ C007454

Find out more about HarperCollins and the environment at
www.harpercollins.co.uk/green